Oh I Say!

D0674739

For Con, Jay, Robin, Chris and Kay

Oh, I Say!

DAN MASKELL
with
JOHN BARRETT

FONTANA/Collins

First published by Willow Books,
William Collins Sons & Co. Ltd, 1988
First issued in Fontana Paperbacks 1989

Originally published under the title *From Where I Sit*

Copyright © Dan Maskell 1988

Printed and bound in Great Britain by
William Collins Sons & Co. Ltd, Glasgow

CONTENTS

ACKNOWLEDGEMENTS

This book could never have been completed without a great deal of help from many people. It would never have been started at all if John Barrett had not undertaken to collaborate with me in the writing of it, for there was no one else with whom I wanted to undertake the task. John has been a close friend for the past forty years and, happily, he was prepared to set aside the time from his own crowded schedule to record our many hours of conversation and reassemble the material in a logical sequence. To him and to his lovely wife, Angela, who at times must have thought she had acquired a new lodger, I owe an enormous debt of gratitude.

That Leonard Cheshire should have contributed the foreword to this volume I take as a great compliment. As the world knows, his contribution to the alleviation of human suffering has been immense. There are few men in life who have shown such dedication to a worthwhile cause and I am proud to be among his friends.

My own family has been marvellously understanding during the book's gestation period. The past eighteen months have been a difficult time for my wife, Kay, who eventually got used to being woken in the middle of the night as I suddenly remembered some elusive fact and committed it to paper. My daughter, Robin, and her husband Chris, my sister, Jean, and husband Frank and my brother, John, have been of immense help in piecing together the hazy memories of family history.

After a long and richly varied life, how do I set about the

7

task of acknowledging the debt I owe to the many friends and acquaintances who have helped to shape it? To include them all individually would be quite impossible. However, I do want to pay a collective tribute to the friends and colleagues in the five major areas of my life whose help and guidance have had an immense influence upon me. At Queen's Club, where I served my apprenticeship; at the All England Club, where I spent most of my active teaching life; in the RAF, where I was proud to help in the rehabilitation of wounded aircrew; at the LTA, where I helped to guide the next generation; and with the BBC, where under a succession of imaginative Heads of Sport, and talented producers, directors and their personal assistants, I learned the craft of communication – in all these areas I have been influenced and assisted by some truly wonderful people. Within these pages the names of most of them will appear but I am equally indebted to those unsung people whose lives have touched mine only fleetingly yet nevertheless enriched it. To them all, my thanks.

On a more personal level there are others whose friendship I value beyond price. Our neighbours during the days when Con and I lived at Steeproof, Peg and Len Morgan and Maggie and Gerry Greig, have always been towers of strength in times of need while Betty Monroe was a saint in looking after Con's parents when the old couple were on their own at Wimbledon Park. At crucial moments in my life these good friends were there to help me and I thank them all.

The Days of my youth, Frank and Barbara, have been firm friends ever since those wonderful times together at Winchelsea before they were married. Barbara's family home, The Manor at Icklesham, was open house and the Merricks seemed able to cope with a limitless number of young guests. After their marriage, Blue House Farm at Marden in Kent, which lies deep in the beautiful hop and orchard countryside

8

with its superb hard tennis court, became another delightful refuge from the hurly-burly of London life.

Two other couples have played a special part in my life. Emlyn and Inez Jones were always marvellous hosts during their days at Crystal Palace but they were especially understanding during those difficult months following Con's death. Bill and Jill Moss have been equally close and our golf holidays with them in Scotland (where Bill was the National Coach and Jill, a talented musician at the King's Theatre, Glasgow, became probably the first woman in the British theatre to be appointed as Musical Director), have always helped us to recharge run-down batteries.

There have been two other places in my life where I have been able to relax from the pressures of the daily round. Among the mountains in Switzerland I learned to love the great outdoors, thanks to the kindness of Mary Hess who has been a good friend for over fifty years. On the golf course I became fascinated by the challenge of learning a new discipline – a marvellous experience for a teacher – and have made a host of new friends. For twenty-two years I served on the committee of the Wimbledon Common Golf Club. I first swung a club there when I was seventeen and living nearby with brother Bill and his wife. Perhaps this is the moment to thank all those long-suffering partners and opponents at the club who have waited patiently while I readjusted my swing and have been prepared to listen to my hard-luck stories.

The brunt of the punishment has been borne by Len Wallis, Reg Curtis and Tommy Mahon. Len was one of England's great amateur footballers just after the war and, like me, served with the RAF. He and his wife, Joy, have been friends for some forty years. Reg, too, was a fine soccer player who was a member of post-war Wimbledon sides. His father had been a professional footballer so I suppose the game was in Reg's blood, a fact that his wife, Babs, learned to live with. I have known Tommy and his wife, Bridie, for

9

just as long and listened in awe to his tales of the attack on Nijmegen when he had been seriously wounded. Tommy, like Len and Reg, had been a great amateur sportsman, a rider of class and a fine boxer. Tommy's Irish charm never failed to keep us all relaxed on the many golfing holidays we have all enjoyed together in Ireland, Spain and many testing courses in Britain. Chief among the latter must be Saunton in North Devon, where I have spent dozens of memorable days with so many friends who are members of that superb West Country links with its two challenging courses.

The credit for suggesting the title for the hardback edition of this book must go to our close and delightful friends, Peter and Pam Scott. The vast chore of typing both the original conversations which have been the raw material for this book, and the second half of the manuscript, has fallen on the willing shoulders of Judy Williams, John Barrett's industrious secretary. A cheerful New Zealander, Judy has worked long into the night at the critical moments to meet our ever-shrinking deadlines. To her I wish to record a special word of thanks. For my publishers, William Collins, Louise Haines has been an understanding task-mistress who has always been ready with a helpful suggestion to overcome the inevitable problems that arose along the way. Kirsty Ennever, too, has been a most judicious editor whose judgement on balance and style I came to trust implicitly.

I can hardly believe that the gigantic task of assembling the material of a lifetime is at last complete. Having resisted the blandishments of several publishers in recent years who asked me to tell my story, I am delighted that it was to Collins that I finally succumbed. It was a natural choice for there has long been a close association between the Collins family and lawn tennis. Ian Collins was a stalwart member of British Davis Cup teams in the late 1920s and his brother, W. A. R. Collins, was a member of the committee at the All England Club for some years. I would like to thank Alan Smith and his team for their unfailing enthusiasm and hope that together we have produced something worthwhile. After a careful and exhaustive check of the thousands of facts that appear within these pages I am satisfied that the major errors have been eliminated. I must take full responsibility for any that remain.

DM

PHOTOGRAPHIC ACKNOWLEDGEMENTS

For permission to use photographs reproduced in this book, the author and publishers would like to thank: London Borough of Hammersmith and Fulham Libraries Service; Queen's Club; *Radio Times* Hulton Picture Library; and Thames Television.

FOREWORD

By Group Captain Leonard Cheshire, VC OM DSO DSC

Whoever is in any way attracted to tennis will most surely welcome this book and in reading it will find much to entertain, much to enlighten, indeed much to edify. It is the story of a man whose life has spanned three generations and embraced three separate roles, that of player, coach and commentator, in each of which he has held his own with the best in the world. It is, however, far more than just another book on tennis. Its pages have a message for everyone who is searching for the secret of how to live one's life to the full.

Perhaps the strongest chapter of all is the one on the war, when Dan Maskell, with the rank of Squadron Leader, was made the RAF's first Rehabilitation Officer and given the task of helping injured aircrew back to duty. Here, in what for him was an entirely new world, Dan demonstrated his flair for picking the right personnel, building them into an outstanding team, and for inspiring those under his care with the feeling that they would succeed in overcoming the handicap of their injuries, no matter how severe these might be. Here, too, the caring side of Dan's nature – the fact that he has so deep an interest in people and values relationships more than anything else – comes to the fore. This, combined with his extraordinary zest for life, a zest that the passing of eighty years has in no way diminished, is in my view the driving force which has turned him into the institution he has become. All of us can benefit from his example.

Leonard Cheshire
April 1988

INTRODUCTION

There are those in life upon whom fortune smiles. I am just such a lucky man. Despite two great personal tragedies, the pain of which I will share with you as my story unfolds, I still consider myself to have been unequally favoured for I have been blessed with three of the greatest gifts a man can enjoy – good health, a loving family and loyal friends.

To have enjoyed life so much for a full decade already beyond my allotted span of three score years and ten (and still in reasonable control of all my faculties, so those friends assure me), is in itself a bonus. Each new experience has brought fresh challenges: I have met people from every walk of life, and been stimulated by the company of all of them; I have travelled widely, refreshed by each changing scene; I have consumed every new morsel of experience associated with my life's work, the game of lawn tennis, with enormous pleasure. For that I shall be eternally grateful; earning one's living in an occupation that is also one's first love is a privilege given to few men to enjoy. Now, in my later years, I sit content with glass in hand and savour the memories. Yes, I am indeed a lucky man.

Each of us arrives upon this planet with certain traits of character that are hereditary, while others are fashioned and developed as our lives unfold. The personal quality for which I shall always be most grateful – whether inherited or acquired I do not know – is adaptability. Having lived through two world wars I have witnessed profound changes, in the fabric of society, in attitudes towards family and towards authority of all kinds, in the changing status of nations and individuals. Throughout all this change I have adapted to new situations with the minimum of fuss. Indeed I am still adapting even now – and enjoying every moment of it, too!

As you will discover, my life began unexceptionally. A simple working-class boy, I grew up in London – not quite a Cockney, for the bells of Bow were too far distant from Fulham to be heard at all – and was attracted to lawn tennis as if to a magnet. From the age of thirteen I knew where my destiny lay. Those were the formative years when that young sport was still the pursuit of amateurs and gentlemen. It seemed to me, as first I glimpsed them through the main gate of Queen's Club in West Kensington, that the beautifully dressed devotees of this glorious game, who swept to and from their courtly pursuits in highly polished limousines, were superior beings. To the boy Maskell, wide-eyed with wonder, they seemed to inhabit a world of influence and affluence that was far different from my own.

Gradually I came to understand that, for all their outward appearances, these men were mortal like myself, subject to the same stresses, with the same hopes, the same fears as the rest of us. At Queen's Club, and later at the All England Club, Wimbledon, many of the members became personal friends. During the heady days of British tennis success in the 1930s my horizons expanded significantly, and the game became a passport to international travel and modest fame.

Marriage added a new meaning and a new dimension to my life. Sharing brought the unexpected discovery that one plus one could equal more than two. Three idyllic years, during which we explored the joys of skiing together, came to an abrupt end with the outbreak of war. It was during the grim realities of that desperate time that I finally matured. Life was put into proper perspective by the bravery and sacrifice of some magnificent young men whose battered bodies I had the privilege of helping to heal. Their unquench-able spirit and the sense of dedicated purpose they inspired in our rehabilitation teams at Torquay and Loughborough had a profound impact upon my attitudes. Things I had once deemed important now seemed trivial. The basic things in life, love and human relationships, assumed a greater significance.

The joyous arrival of our first child after fifteen months of war reinforced those attitudes and the safe delivery of our second within a year of its end further strengthened them. Now the pleasure and pain of bringing up two lively young-sters in the immediate post-war years introduced new prob-lems that all parents must face. For me, time was the greatest problem. Absorbed by what I was doing to help rebuild the post-war game and constantly in demand at meetings and conferences, I saw all too little of my children while they were growing up. With the wisdom of hindsight this is the one thing about my life that I would change, given a second chance. Yet how could I have known what tragedies lay round the corner? Increasingly television began to eat away at my time. The precious years passed all too swiftly, and were gone forever. So, too, within the space of a few cruel years, were two of my loved ones, gone beyond recall.

It was now, in the time of greatest stress, that luck was with me once more. I came into contact with an old friend whose own life had been tinged with sadness. Our sub-sequent marriage, unexpected and unsought, transformed my life. Instead of facing an uncertain future, I was now expanding my interests and widening my circle of friends with new family responsibilities. I can truly say that the last few years have been among the happiest of my life.

So here I am remembering the past and revelling in the present, an old man I suppose by conventional standards but one who certainly does not feel his age and is fortunate to enjoy good health. Inevitably there are things about today's scene that I deplore – especially within my own sport. But when I become upset by what I see some of the players do today on a tennis court I try to remember that sport merely mirrors the society of which it is a part. Whether we like it or not, society is more violent today than it was when I grew up. Sadly, respect for authority is diminished. Yet even so I still believe that we have brought many of these problems upon ourselves by abdicating our responsibilities – as parents, as teachers, as leaders. I still believe that if only we had applied the rules that existed at Wimbledon in 1981 against John McEnroe, when he was indulging in some of his worst excesses in a first-round match against Tom Gullikson on court number one, we might have saved ourselves a lot of future strife. By encouraging John to impose a little self-discipline we might also have helped him to develop his wonderful skills still further.

Once you condone bad behaviour you have opened the door to further abuse. The same is true in a wider context. The general deterioration in behaviour and moral standards is the result of a lack of proper control by parents, an undermining of the authority of our school-teachers, a bewildering reluctance in our courts to mete out punishments that fit the crime and a regrettable lack of leadership by the church.

Among professional sportsmen the blame for deteriorating standards must be laid at the door of our administrators. Instead of leading by example and imposing proper discipline they have condoned actions that have brought several sports into disrepute. Principles have been sacrificed on the altar of expediency. Moral courage has been in short supply.

The accelerating decline in interest in sport at our schools is another feature of modern life that disturbs me. Once again those in authority seem to have abrogated their responsibilities. Here, surely, is the proper place to instil some of the old-fashioned principles about teamwork and fair play. I know that I learned some of my most valuable lessons on the sports field as a lad. Yet even as long ago as the mid-fifties I found, as I toured our schools, a distinct lack of pride in sporting achievement. In my day, to represent the school at anything was the height of ambition. Next one hoped to be chosen for a club team, then to play for the county and ultimately to represent one's country. There was a disappointing absence of that sort of ambition on my visits to schools.

In today's pop culture world it seems that rock stars have replaced sportsmen as the heroes of the young. When I was a schoolboy the latest exploits of Jack Hobbs and David Jack, Gene Tunney and Sir Malcolm Campbell were on everyone's lips. This was the time when the new Wembley Stadium became the showcase of international football. The first Cup Final there in 1923 is still etched upon my memory, even though I was not present. David Jack's opening goal for Bolton within two minutes of the start and the policeman on the white horse who controlled the crowds that had flooded on to the pitch are the stuff of legend. My own particular heroes were those wonderful golfers, Harry Vardon and J. H. Taylor, the Oxford and Cambridge athletes D. G. A. Lowe and Harold Abrahams, and, of course, Suzanne Lenglen and Bill Tilden. Their achievements expanded our universe and set us off on youthful dreams of what one day we might become. These were the days of Corinthians like B. Howard-Baker, who was an international footballer, an Olympic high-jumper and also a fine tennis player. Somehow the world seemed a much more wholesome place then.

These may sound like the idealized memories of a man out of touch with the times, but I make no apology. I simply happen to believe that the quality of life when I grew up, poor as we were, was better than it is today. I feel rather sorry for today's young people who, individually, are every bit as good as we were. But they are subjected to frightening pressures now that we never had to face. In this over-commercialized and permissive world where racial tensions,

19

drug abuse and violence are the signposts of the times, the wonder is that so few of them go off the rails.

Like Maurice Chevalier, I'm glad that I am not young any more. But if I were a young man starting out again I think I would aim to become a GP in a small country town – preferably via a spell at Cambridge University, a place that has always cast a spell on my emotions. It may surprise you that inside the tennis teacher and television communicator there has always been a medical man struggling to get out. At first sight there is no obvious connection. However, as I lead you along the highways and byways of my life, the paradox might be resolved, for I shall be amazed if you cannot mark the moment when I felt myself to be most completely fulfilled.

It is time, then, to invite you to take the first steps on that eighty-year journey.

ONE

Origins

I can hear my mother's voice now. Across the years it echoes in my head against the boom of distant guns, the familiar warm tones carrying an unmistakable air of gravity. Clutching her shopping basket, she stopped walking, took my hand firmly in hers and looked down at me with an intensity I had never seen before. With tears of joy already moistening the corners of her eyes, she said: 'Always remember this moment, Dan. We have just ended the war to end all wars, thank God.'

Even to a ten-year-old, enjoying a day off school on 11 November 1918, the news did indeed make a lasting impression. Every year, when I hear the sombre boom of the maroons at 11.00 am on Armistice Day, that childhood memory comes flooding back.

Throughout the later stages of the war, when food was rationed, shopping was an important and taxing daily ritual, for we were a large family. We lived in Fulham, first at number 15 Everington Street and then, from the end of 1917, at The Pear Tree pub, a few streets away in Margravine Road. Many were the times when, as an eight- or nine-year-old newly arrived home from school, I would suddenly be despatched to Peark's the grocer, round the corner in Greyhound Road, to queue for butter as the word flashed round the bush telegraph that they had just had a delivery. Or it might be news of fresh bread at Mellor's, the baker on the corner of Greyhound Road, or the arrival of a fresh supply of meat at Downing's, the butcher, or perhaps a delivery of

21

paraffin oil at Stafford's, the general store at the end of Everington Street, that would precipitate a sudden rush in their direction. Such were the day-to-day realities of wartime life.

I was born on 11 April 1908, the seventh of eight children and the fourth boy. Looking back it is hard to understand how our parents managed to provide for us all in those difficult pre-war days when work was none too plentiful and the average wage for those lucky enough to have a job was a mere £2 10 shillings (£2.50) per week. My father had been christened Henry George but everyone called him Harry. He was an engineer whose work often took him north to Darlington where, he told us, the cold winter winds were so strong that they very nearly blew him out of bed. To a man who was conscious of even the merest suspicion of a draught at home, this must have been a most uncomfortable experience.

My father had been born in 1873 in London and never wanted to live anywhere else. He had met my mother, Emma Pearce, when her family had moved down to London from Burton-on-Trent where Emma had been born in 1875. She was eighteen years old when they decided to get married. Harry Maskell was a tall, angular man with the slim build of a natural games player. He was keen on cycling, a relatively new pastime which had become popular in the 1890s at the nearby Queen's Club, especially among the lady members and the many visitors. In view of my own close association with Queen's in later years, it is curious to think that my father may have been a regular visitor there. Although my frequent enquiries among members could never establish the fact, he must have been among the many enthusiasts who cycled on the old ice-skating rink (where the four new covered courts now stand) when that area was turned over to the new craze in 1890.

According to Queen's Club historian Roy McKelvie, the

ice-rink had melted several times, flooding homes in Greyhound Road, so it was decided to close it. Now the three thousand square yards of smooth asphalt swarmed with bicycles of all shapes and sizes. Another popular area for cyclists was the open space of the cinder running track, on which the young men of Oxford and Cambridge competed annually in the Varsity athletics match. Machines could be hired by members and visitors at sixpence an hour for ladies, and one-and-six for gentlemen. For an extra shilling you could also obtain an instructor. This is probably what my father was doing, earning a few extra shillings to feed his growing family.

Even in my earliest memories of him he has grey hair. Like most of my contemporaries, I showed my father the greatest respect. He was always strict with his children and expected all the younger members of the family to call him 'sir': and we did. At meal times, especially, he demanded discipline. No one ever thought of resting their elbows on the table or speaking out of turn. Looking back, I suppose I was subconsciously learning the basis of the self-discipline which I was to need in later life, both as a teacher and as a rehabilitation officer in the Royal Air Force during World War Two.

I vividly remember one evening when I was nursing a painful hand which had been injured during our supervised boxing lesson at school. I must have been about nine at the time. For some reason, 'Snuffy' Moore, the master who organized all sport at Everington Street School just down the road from our house, had given me a pair of light, thinly-padded gloves for my bout against Albert Lancaster, one of my class-mates. As I swung a right, Albert ducked so that my punch was delivered to the top of his head. A searing pain shot up my arm and I could feel my hand and the area round the knuckle of my index finger swelling painfully inside the glove. The fact that Albert was suffering from a nasty headache was little consolation. Snuffy immediately removed the glove and sent me off to bathe the hand in cold water to minimize swelling, telling me it would soon be all right. I can still see the concern on his face. He was a popular and hard-working master with a great sense of humour and the bandy legs of many natural games players – like the great South American tennis player, Pancho Segura, who in later years I came to know and admire as one of the game's great tacticians. During Snuffy's maths lesson we would be set some work to keep us occupied and then he would disappear behind the blackboard on its large easel, holding the small embossed box that he kept hidden inside his desk. When he reappeared, you could see the tell-tale brown stains beneath his nostrils that revealed the reason for his nickname.

Clearly, though, Snuffy was not much of an amateur doctor. That night at family supper I tried to hide the damaged hand from my father's gaze. However, it was impossible to eat properly with just my left hand and suddenly he asked me what had happened to my other one.

'Nothing, sir,' I replied.

'Then please show it to me,' he demanded.

When he had seen the damage and heard the story, he immediately sent me off on my own to the West London Hospital at Hammersmith with two pennies for the tram fare there and back. Looking back, it is amazing to think that it was considered safe to send a nine-year-old off to hospital by himself on a dark winter's evening. Such an act would be unthinkable today – a sad commentary, perhaps, on increasing dangers of city life. I cannot remember now whether my hand was put in plaster or merely strapped, but I do recall that it was some weeks before I regained full use of it. Even today on very cold days there is a feeling of discomfort in the knuckle joint – rheumatism, I suppose.

As I was growing up there were already six older children to look after so my father could not spare me too much individual attention. A rare treat was to be taken to Craven Cottage, the home of Fulham Football Club, to watch a

Saturday league match. From home we would go down Everington Street, across Lillie Road, through Fulham recreation ground (which was later to become the scene of many happy childhood hours spent kicking a football about with my school pals), across Fulham Palace Road and down one of the many side roads that led to the Thames-side ground. Besides being a keen sportsman my father was also a great walker and my young legs had the greatest difficulty in keeping up with his – I always seemed to be running. I was most relieved if he met one of the neighbours and stopped for a short chat, as he often did. The conversation was usually about the war – swapping news about sons at the front and wondering when it would all end. I cannot ever remember hearing bad news on one of these outings although I do recall standing in silence when the whole school was assembled to hear that an Old Everingtonian had lost his life in battle. Masters and pupils stood with bowed heads, united in grief and respect, as the headmaster, John Holloway, read the sad details and led us in a simple prayer. It was at moments like this that the war suddenly became real. I would screw my eyes tightly closed and ask God to look after my brothers, Bill and Bert, who had been among the earliest to join the fighting.

Bill was nineteen when the war broke out. He had gone straight off to France with the British Expeditionary Force because he had already become a soldier the year before. He had always loved horses and was thrilled when he was accepted early in 1914 at the cavalry school at Tidworth. He was even more excited when he learned that he was being posted to the 9th Lancers. I remember being immensely impressed when Bill came home on a weekend leave after passing out, resplendent in his colourful dress uniform. Because he was always away I never really got to know him at that stage of our lives, although after the war I grew closer to Bill than to any other member of the family.

We all still laugh about the piece of family history in which

Bill disgraced himself. Like all us boys in our turn, Bill was a keen and moderately talented young footballer. It seems we had all inherited an instinctive games sense from our father. One day when he was about fourteen Bill was entrusted with the task of taking me, a baby of one, in my pram for a walk in Fulham recreation ground. Inevitably, Bill became involved in a game of football with some of the local lads and parked the pram under the shade of a tree. Eventually, when the excitement of the game had subsided, Bill made his way homeward, tired but happy and relishing the thought of the tea that would be waiting for him. When my mother saw that he was alone she panicked and said, 'Bill, whatever has happened to the baby?' With horror he realized what he had done. 'Oh, my goodness – I've left him in the park,' he replied, and dashed out of the house to find me. Happily I was still there, gurgling contentedly and amusing a group of bystanders, apparently unaware that anything was amiss.

Shortly before the outbreak of war Bill had become batman to a Captain Phipps-Hornby who, like so many of the cavalry officers, was a keen polo player. One weekend they had matches at Hurlingham and Roehampton, the two great West London clubs that eventually I would come to know so well. Accordingly Bill was able to live at home. That is the last time I really remember him before he went off to the front. Bill had a good war – if any participant in that wasteful slaughter can be said to have had a good time. It was in France that they engaged the Uhlans, the crack German cavalry regiment. According to Bill, the Lancers met them in an old-style cavalry charge, almost like one of those legendary battles in the Middle Ages with the two armies lined up facing one another and, on the bugle call, charging at each other with lances pointed and swords waving. Whenever I heard Bill telling this story in later years I used to wonder whether he was romancing a little.

However, there is no doubt about the terrible casualties in the battle. Some of the wounded fell, so each regiment regrouped and charged again. When it was all over the Lancers picked up their casualties and retired two miles behind the lines. Bill said that they were just tethering their horses for the night near the tents when suddenly the German artillery opened fire on them and virtually wiped them out. Never was the futility of matching outmoded methods against modern weaponry more graphically illustrated. Fortunately Bill escaped, but the battalion was decimated.

From France Bill was sent to the Curragh, in Ireland, where the regiment was being remounted and brought up to strength. This was in 1916 when the Sinn Fein troubles erupted. Later the regiment became part of the Surrey Yeomanry who were despatched to Mesopotamia and Gallipoli so we didn't see Bill again until the war was over. At home we were all very proud of him, though, especially when he was twice mentioned in despatches. Of course my mother was filled with anxiety, like so many other mothers, but she tried not to show it. Many families we knew did lose their sons so that we were all dimly aware that many lives were being lost. This gruesome fact was forcibly brought home to us right at the end of the war when my father actually received his call-up papers, at the age of forty-five. Fortunately hostilities ceased before he had to present himself for enlistment.

Senior amongst us was Dorothy, who was twenty-four when the war ended and really more like a second mother to me than a sister. 'Dod', as she was known to all of us, used to go out to work during the day. She was seeing a lot of Walter Faulknall at this time, a young man who must have been extremely fit and energetic. Once during the school holidays, after a dawn start, Walter cycled all the way to Windsor and back with me behind him on the pillion seat – a journey of some forty-five miles! The expedition took us the whole day. It was an exciting time for me because I hardly ever left the comfortable and friendly environment of our local community, except for the annual Sunday School outing. One Sunday in summer we would be taken to places like Park Royal, Eastcote or Pinner, to the north-west of London in Middlesex, areas which in those days were open meadowland. Already, though, the developers were moving in and it would not be long before these beautiful unspoilt areas would become part of the commuter belt.

Windsor made a great impression on me. I found it difficult to believe that anyone actually lived in that huge castle. Certainly I would have laughed if anyone had suggested that one day I would meet the Queen there, and later receive a decoration from her at Buckingham Palace. We ate our sandwich lunch beside the castle from the supplies that Walter had brought in his rucksack. Its bulk had made my outward journey rather uncomfortable, bulging into my face whenever Walter sat upright as we free-wheeled on the downhill sections. Now that it was almost empty it was less of a problem as we returned wearily homeward in the long summer twilight.

Bert I hardly remember at all. He was eleven years older than me but, even so, was still too young to enlist in 1914. However, like Bill, he wanted to play his part and, like so many other eager young patriots, he talked his way past the officials at the enlistment office. He joined the 7th City of London Regiment and spent the entire war in France without ever coming back on leave. None of us at home had any idea just how desperate their situation was at times. Only afterwards (and Bert, like Bill, was fortunate enough to survive the conflict) did we hear just how terrible things had been. When he had been demobbed Bert joined the Metropolitan Police and earned something of a reputation as a bowler in police cricket. He had also been a good footballer who played occasionally for Fulham in the days when Andy Ducat was the manager. Bert remained in the service until he retired at the age of sixty-five and went with his wife to live in Somerset.

The brother I related to best as a boy was John, even though there was an eight-year gap between us. We were all keen on our sport but John was the best footballer of the family and eventually was to play centre-half for Wimbledon in the old Isthmian League. After finishing his schooling he had decided to join the Royal Air Force for three years and was posted to Quetta in India. While he was there he sent me a used football home for Christmas, a much-prized present that was to see plenty of action in the local park. Later John played in the Amateur Cup Final of 1931, as the right full-back for Hayes. The match was played on the Arsenal ground at Highbury against Wycombe Wanderers, who won by a single goal. It appears that we were all good all-rounders, for John also played club cricket with distinction for West Drayton.

Many years later when I had become the professional at the All England Club I met a director of Brighton and Hove Albion Football Club, a Mr Brazier. He was the father of one of my pupils, Pat Brazier, who was to win the Junior Championship of Great Britain in 1930. Mr Brazier asked me if the John Maskell who played for Wimbledon was any relation, and I told him that he was my brother.

'Do you think he'd ever consider turning professional?' he asked.

I said I doubted it very much indeed and explained that when he had left the RAF John, like Bert, had joined the police. He was committed to his new career and only had time for amateur sport.

'Then would he come down and play as a guest in our Combination side, on Thursday?' enquired Mr Brazier.

I promised to pass on the enquiry. John did go down once or twice after that to play for them but he was never tempted to turn professional.

After John came Lilian (always Lal to us) and Elsie, then myself and Jean, the last member of the family, who was eight years younger than me. Even with three sisters in the house I still had to do my full share of the household chores. In those days, before the arrival of today's mechanical aids, there was plenty for all of us to do. I was never allowed to get away with anything. There had to be a degree of co-operation amongst the entire family if the household was to operate at all efficiently. It was an early introduction to the concept of team spirit which was to play such a major part in my professional life with British Davis Cup and Wightman Cup teams.

My memories of life in Everington Street are entirely happy ones. There were always many people about in those wartime days, probably because my mother was so popular with the neighbours. A group of them would congregate at our house during air-raids. The wardens would come cycling by, wearing their tin helmets and blowing their whistles, with warning placards hanging front and back displaying the message 'Take cover, take cover'. There was a black-out at night and I used to be sent off to bed early. Downstairs my mother would keep everyone's spirits up, smiling and joking.

My mother was a large, big-boned, cheerful woman with dark brown hair and a warm, friendly manner. She seemed always to be on the go either cooking, washing, shopping or mending our clothes. Her mother, Granny Pearce, was living with us in those days. She was a marvellous old lady who eventually died in 1935 at the age of ninety-four. She had actually gone off to live by herself again in 1922, when my mother had died in childbirth at the age of forty-seven. Proudly independent, Granny Pearce somehow epitomized the spirit of the age.

It was always Granny Pearce's job on a Monday to prepare the hot lunch which, in common with all our contemporaries, we used to call 'dinner'. I would come home down the road from school for Monday dinner, nursing the happy thought that we would soon be enjoying one of those delicious suet puddings, securely wrapped in muslin as it boiled cheerfully away on the kitchen stove, full of succulent meat and gravy

– assuming, of course, that Downing's had had a delivery of meat. Then it would be 'spotted dick' for afters (another helping of suet) with its sparse sprinkling of currants and awash with custard. I used to love Monday dinner – especially after my early start. For Monday was washday, and every week at 6.30am I had to light the fire for the copper which stood in a corner of the scullery, next to the kitchen. To start the blaze I would use screwed-up pages of old newspapers and a bundle of sticks purchased from Stafford's. There was always a large stack of these bundles neatly piled in front of the counter. The Staffords were a quiet, dignified couple who had no children and were always nervous that the local youngsters would disturb their well-ordered empire. Mr Stafford, a short, spare man, would bob up from beneath the counter and say: 'Take care, now. One little jog and you'll have the whole lot over . . . and then you'll have to build them up again.' It always seemed to me that the Staffords were out of place running a general store. Such a cultured couple should surely have been running a bookshop or the local library.

We had a large kitchen at Everington Street with one of those big, white-wood farmhouse tables in the centre and a tall, wooden dresser in the corner under which Caesar, our black Labrador, used to sleep. I would sometimes take Caesar for his daily romp in the park and throw sticks for him to chase. He was a favourite with everyone in the neighbourhood, a big, gentle, cuddly creature with whom occasionally I used to hide under the dresser at bedtime, hoping not to be discovered. Of course I always was and never could successfully avoid that final moment when there was no escape from bath and bed. Sometimes I would tie my bootlaces together so that I could answer my mother's shouts from upstairs with 'I won't be long . . . I'm just trying to get my bootlaces undone.' She soon became wise to that one.

Regularly on a Saturday morning Granny Pearce would scrub the kitchen table-top with strong soap until the wooden surface was covered in a white lather. I used to watch her at work and marvel at her energy. Before she was married Granny Pearce used to be Miss Griggs but I have no clear recollection where the Griggs family came from, though it was probably the West Midlands, somewhere near Burton-on-Trent where my mother had been born. Nor do I remember anything about my grandfather. First the war and then my mother's death split us all up so that I never seemed to spend any time with relatives hearing about the family history, even on those happy occasions at Christmas when the depleted family would all crowd into the front room and gather round the piano for a singsong, always singing one especially for Bill and Bert away at the front. Not that we were a particularly musical family, but in our parlour we did have the piano and the aspidistra, on its special stand near the window, in the approved manner of the time. Granny Pearce used to love those gatherings, joining in the fun and smiling round proudly at the grandchildren. She was one of those dependable fixtures who, it seemed, would always be there. She must still have been with us at the end of 1917 when we moved.

For many years my father had been very friendly with Harry Barker who owned The Pear Tree, the popular and attractive 'local' in Margravine Road. In 1917 the Guv'nor, as Harry was universally known, lost his manager and suggested to my father that he give up his engineering job to manage the pub for him. My father took little persuading, for he had been suffering from a chest condition that made the occasional journeys that he had to make an arduous undertaking. Happily, though, his condidition did not prevent him from spending many happy hours in the garden tending his prize sunflowers and dahlias. He even specialized in these two varieties when he later retired to the south coast.

Curiously enough I remember very little about our life at The Pear Tree although I can clearly remember much earlier incidents from the years at Everington Street. Perhaps the shock of losing my mother two and a half years after we had moved, when I was just fourteen, had the effect of erasing from my memory that period of my life which, perhaps, had been an unhappy one.

I have relied upon the much clearer recollections of my younger sister, Jean, to fill in these details. She had been a babe-in-arms at the time of the move but went on living at The Pear Tree long after I had gone to live with Tom Jeffery's family to become a fully-employed ballboy at Queen's Club at the age of fifteen. We had a housekeeper, Mrs Brickell, who came to look after my father and us younger children at the pub from 1920 onwards, whom I never really knew because in 1923 I had gone to my new life at Queen's Club.

My days at Everington Street School were very happy ones although I might never have remained there if my father could have afforded to send me to Childerley Street School. In fact I had done well enough in the scholarship exam to have gone straight to Upper Latymer, the grammar school that still exists in King Street, Hammersmith. However, it seemed that before going to Latymer one had to spend a year at Childerley Street where they used to have their own school caps and blazers. I was desperately keen to go there and pleaded with my father to be allowed to attend. However, he was adamant. 'If you go to Childerley Street you will be committed to going on to Latymer and that means you will stay there until you are seventeen. We simply cannot afford it.'

I soon got over my disappointment and became thoroughly involved in all the activities at Everington Street where the headmaster, John Holloway, made a great impression on me. He was a tall, striking man who used to walk up and down during our playtime for exercise. His very presence demanded respect but some of the other masters were less successful at keeping order.

Mr Gregory was a new master who taught us history, a stern and officious sort of man who was greatly disliked by the boys. One day some of them decided to test his patience. I was the form prefect at the time and unaware that any mischief had been planned. Accordingly when we returned to our classroom after the dinner break I was suprised to see Mr Gregory recoil as he opened his desk to reach for the form register. He must have been even more surprised, for he had been greeted by the cold stare of a grinning cod's head. As you can imagine, all hell broke loose. Neither questions nor threats could reveal the culprit so eventually Mr Gregory announced: 'Very well, unless someone owns up I'll send for the headmaster.'

Nobody did. The dignified Mr Holloway was duly summoned. He treated the matter with cold logic. 'It seems the only solution is to punish the whole class. There will be no more football in the dinner hour for any of you until someone owns up.'

Left to ourselves, we soon discovered that the culprit was a boy who was about to leave the school. He had scrounged the fish head from Ennefer's, the fish shop in Greyhound Road. Secretly we all admired his nerve but were relieved that he was at last prepared to take his punishment so that we could return to our dinner-time football.

Most of the teaching staff took our misdemeanours in their stride. Mr Bratherton, who taught us history and geography in my early years there, was typical of them. A dignified, quiet man who dressed smartly, he had earned our respect by his firm air of authority, and thus never had a moment's trouble. In fact we were all sorry to see him leave – an occasion when the headmaster said a few appropriate words before presenting the departing master with a handsome writing set to which both masters and boys had contributed. Nor did we ever cause problems for Snuffy Moore, apart from attaching the nickname that revealed his secret habit.

Little Mr Woodman, who taught us geography, was a very

natty dresser and wore false shirt-cuffs made of celluloid which he would remove during the day and place in his cupboard. This fastidiousness was by no means unusual in those days and it never occurred to us to make fun of Mr Woodman. He also wore spats and a bowler hat and he always seemed to have with him an elegant blue overcoat, whether it was winter or summer.

On the other hand our new Irish Music teacher, a Miss Murphy, would be driven to distraction by our merciless disregard for the proper words of the songs she would try to teach us.

'Just a moment,' she would say, breaking off in the middle of a phrase, 'I'm not sure you are singing the right words, are you?'

'Yes we are, miss,' we would chorus.

Only half-convinced, she would play the introduction again and off we would go. The first chorus would be fine – '*Rifol, rifol, fol de riddle rido, rifol, rifol fol de riddle dee*' – and Miss Murphy would be smiling happily at our robust rendering. Then we were into the second chorus, '*Rifol, rifol . . .*' With one accord the words were changed to the rude version, and Miss Murphy, getting angry now, would lift her fingers from the keyboard and her eyes towards the heavens as if seeking some divine inspiration to deal with our inexcusable bad manners.

Being a keen games player I contributed in full measure to the school's activities on the sports field and in the playground. I should explain that there were two playgrounds, one for the boys and another, slightly larger, for the girls and infants. Although we were a mixed school in the sense that boys and girls were taught under the same roof, we never saw the girls during school hours and might just as well have been miles apart. We entered the building by separate entrances and had separate classrooms. I really believe that this system is preferable to the present preoccupation with mixed classes. We had fewer distractions than today's young-sters and those who did want to work could get on with it.

Only once a year, on Empire Day, did we join forces, when we would assemble in the girls' playground. There the Union Jack would be flying proudly on its flagpole alongside the twin sets of steps which rose either side of the school entrance at first-floor level, to form a natural platform on which were placed six chairs for the senior staff and visiting dignitaries. After singing some patriotic songs and listening to the Empire Day address we would all raise our voices for the National Anthem in a manner that left Miss Murphy in no doubt of our true vocal abilities, before setting off for our half-holiday. Little did any of us realize at the time that, even while we were singing, the country was engaged in a mortal struggle in Europe that would ultimately lead to the break-up of that once mighty empire whose glories we had just been celebrating.

Our daily sport at school was highly organized – cricket in the summer and football in the winter. The twenty-minute break each day from 10.30 to 10.50 was the the occasion for each of the four senior forms – X7, 7, 6 and 5 – to engage in single-wicket cricket played with an old tennis ball. Each form had its own territory. Our bowler in X7 delivered the ball from a conveniently-placed drain alongside the school shed towards the batsman who stood with his back to the school wall that divided us from Lillie Road. At the start of each week the form's cricket monitor would collect from each boy the halfpenny that entitled him to participate and would duly add his name to the list that was pinned to the back of our free-standing 'wicket'. If you could not pay, you could not play. No one objected if they were forced to watch that week's games. It just meant that you would go off and persuade someone to let you earn a few pence by carrying out some essential task, like delivering the papers or cleaning the windows of one of the local shops.

Then at dinner-time the precious forty minutes between

12.00 and 12.40pm were filled with inter-class matches. These used the entire area of the playground with two free-standing wickets placed in the centre and a full complement of fielders spread around the open spaces. Feelings ran high during these matches, upon which a great deal of local prestige rested. If necessary a match would continue after school at 4.15pm, until it had been decided.

One of the best cricketers was a boy named Ted Surrey who lived just down the road from us, almost opposite the school gates. He was a year or two older than me and everyone predicted a great future for him as a batsman. When we used to play our games of street cricket across Avril Street, with a wicket chalked on a wall and the bowler and batsman operating on opposite pavements, there had to be a special rule for Ted. As soon as he had been batting for ten minutes or had scored ten runs his innings was automatically over. It was the only way to ensure that the rest of us would have a chance to bat; no one ever bowled him out. It came as a terrible shock to all of us, therefore, when Ted became a victim of the nationwide 'flu epidemic in 1918 and died at the age of twelve. I remember the numb, empty feeling that terrible morning when five or six of us who had been close friends formed a guard of honour and followed the horse-drawn hearse on its mournful way from his house, down Everington Street, along Lillie Road, left into Fulham Palace Road and in at the cemetery gates just beyond the recreation ground.

There were some two hundred and fifty boys at the school in those days and on icy winter mornings after a light snowfall many of us would arrive early to prepare a slide across the smooth surface of the playground. It was an exhilarating feeling charging towards the glassy strip and then launching oneself on a frictionless, silent glide towards the piled-up snow. We always knew that Mr Day, the caretaker, would have salted the slides before morning break so we had to make the most of it before the bell went at 8.45am to summon us to assembly in the playground. There we would line up in forms and file in to our classrooms where the form master would call the register before conducting morning prayers.

There were some dark, foggy days when it was impossible to play any games at all. In today's relatively clean London air it is hard to believe that the old 'pea-soupers' really did bring the city to a complete halt. Not only was it extremely uncomfortable to inhale lungfuls of dense, yellow fog but it was also impossible to see more than a few feet in front of you so no one went out unless they had to. I would grope my way to school along Everington Street but sometimes coming home early on a prematurely dark evening I would find myself completely disorientated, even along familiar pavements. I am convinced that these unpleasant fogs contributed to the death of my father whose lungs were always a cause of concern in later life.

We played our winter football in the playground only at dinner-time. The classes were organized into leagues on a handicap basis with the older boys giving the younger ones one or two goals start. We used to have a daily half-hour match playing into home-made free-standing goal posts that had a piece of wide tape stretched between the uprights as a crossbar. Unless the 'pitch' was under snow or running with water the matches were certain to go ahead. Those who had not been selected to play used to line up behind the goals and cheer their form-mates to victory. We must have made an awful lot of noise.

Equally noisy was the climax of the season, the end-of-term play-off between the two forms at the top of the league. Members of the staff used to take part in this hour-long encounter so that there was a constant stream of encouragement and abuse from the packed throng of onlookers.

On Saturday mornings we used to play matches on a proper grass pitch in Bishop's Park, the open space on the Fulham side of Putney Bridge that had once been part of the

Bishop of London's Fulham Palace estate. The pitches are still in use today. We played against the seven or eight other schools in the locality: Lillie Road School, Star Road School, Fulham Palace Road School and Queensmill Road School were among them. It amazes me now, in these days of large comprehensives, that there were so many individual schools in our neighbourhood then. Often present at these matches were the talent scouts from Fulham, Chelsea and occasionally some of the other London clubs. In fact one or two of my contemporaries did become professional footballers. There was a boy called Sid Booker who was our centre-forward. He joined the playing staff of one of the London clubs when he left school. John Pryke was another who, I think, went to Fulham. Besides being a good footballer he was a bright lad and eventually became the editor of one of the leading local newspapers.

Another close pal was Len Oliver, a future international footballer. He was a year or two older than me and easily the best player among us. It was no surprise when the local talent scouts persuaded him to join Fulham where eventually he would become a distinguished club captain. Len's uncle had a farm near Hampton Court and on several occasions the two of us would go there for the day on a Sunday. His uncle or another member of the family used to meet us off the train at Hampton Court station with his pony and trap and I always enjoyed the ride back to the farm as we clattered along the country lanes at a smart trot. Returning on the train one evening from such a visit the lights suddenly went out as an air raid alert sounded. It was the night when one of the German zeppelins was brought down at Potter's Bar, though we were not fortunate enough to witness the event.

In my last year I was the captain of our football team and played centre-half. The Saturday morning matches in Bishop's Park were sometimes a bit of a problem for me because there was often some queueing to be done at Read's if they had had a delivery of vegetables. It really was as bad as that during the war. Furthermore, my father was never keen for me to escape these family obligations but usually my mother would intercede so that I could play. Several of the other boys had Saturday morning jobs, delivering the papers or helping with the milk round, so they, too, had to find someone else to do those tasks if they wanted to play.

One Saturday we were playing Queensmill Road School in the final of the annual competition for local schools. By half-time we had not scored but mid-way through the second half we were awarded a penalty. There were no nets on the goal posts in Bishop's Park and we were shooting towards the end that backed on to the Thames. I decided to take the penalty myself and swung the ball fast and low towards the left-hand post. 'Goal!' shouted our team as the ball flashed beyond the reach of the diving goalkeeper. But the master who was refereeing could not decide which side of the post the ball had passed, even after he had consulted his linesmen. We could have told him but he did not want to know. Accordingly I had to take the shot again and this time I ballooned the ball over the top. Inevitably we lost 0–1. Life is like that. There are times when things go against you and you can do nothing about it. It was a wonderful lesson.

There was another occasion when for some reason our Saturday morning match in Bishop's Park could not be played. However, someone had got permission for us to play next door on the Fulham Football Club's pitch. All we had to do was to walk a hundred and fifty yards and there we were, starring at Craven Cottage! It was a memorable experience for twenty-two excited schoolboys and I always thought how far-sighted it was of the club to let us play. At one stroke they had created twenty-two lifelong Fulham fans. Curiously I do not remember anything about the match: I cannot even tell you who won!

There is an amusing sequel to this story. In 1985 I was telephoned by Dennis Turner, who publishes the weekly programme for Fulham Football club. He explained that

40

nowadays the club invited a celebrity to attend each home match and wondered if I could join them for the game against Carlisle United.

'I'd be delighted,' I replied. 'It will revive some very happy memories of the time I once played there and it will also be a tribute to my brother Bert who played under Andy Ducat.'

'You mean two Maskells have actually played at Craven Cottage?' he asked, with some surprise.

Needless to say he was thoroughly amused by the story of my schoolboy experience and used it in the programme. Unhappily the game itself was a goalless draw, not at all like the exciting matches I remember so vividly from those visits long ago with my father.

Out of school hours and in the holidays there always seemed to be plenty to occupy our time. Apart from cricket or football in the park we used to visit the local cinema, explore the district, swim in the Thames, cycle round the neighbourhood or generally muck about as young boys will. There was no radio or television, of course. The British Broadcasting Company Limited was not established until 1922 and did not become a public corporation until 1927. However, various entrepreneurs devised ingenious ways of disseminating information and promoting their events. In 1921, when I was thirteen, there was a European Championship fight in London between Joe Beckett, the British champion, and the great French boxer, Georges Carpentier. I had read in our daily newspaper that the result would be indicated by the colour of a light on the wing tip of a small aeroplane that would fly over London after the fight had been decided; a red light would indicate a victory for Carpentier and a green one for Beckett. Everyone seemed to know about it and not surprisngly there was an excited crowd of people in the street at the appointed hour. Fortunately it was a clear evening with good visibility. We heard the plane first and then there was an expectant hush as it

41

came into view . . . followed by a groan as the red light became clearly visible.

These were the days of the silent cinema and, like every district in every town and city throughout the country, our local picture-house was a magnet that drew people of all ages to see what new marvel had been created on celluloid. I spent many happy hours with my friends at the Penny Cinema in Munster Road, a centre of romantic make-believe that was irresistible. The cinema stood opposite the rear entrance of the cemetery and was one of the oldest in the country, typical of the period. We used to live for those exciting Saturday mornings when we would all crowd into the rows of tiered bench seats, enjoying that delightful tingle of expectation as we waited for the lights to go down.

The format of the programme was always the same. It would start with a short comedy film, often one of those Mack Sennett one-reel or two-reel classics that were produced by his Keystone Company from 1912 onwards, containing perhaps a fast, daredevil car chase which was a masterpiece of trick photography. Like so many of my generation I grew to love the amiable clowns in those knockabout stories which were often improvised on the spot in Los Angeles to take advantage of any local happening like a fire or a parade. Artistes like Marie Dressler and Gloria Swanson, Charlie Chaplin, W. C. Fields and Harold Lloyd were the new Sennett stars who set the standard of humour for a whole generation.

The comedy would be followed by a short animal feature or, perhaps, a lively circus film. Then would come the main attraction, the latest instalment of the weekly *Perils of Pauline* serial which had been left agonizingly the previous Saturday with the heroine, Pearl White, abducted by the villain and left down a snake-pit one week or strapped to a bed post inside a blazing building the next with, apparently, no possible means of escape. We would watch the re-run of those closing scenes with delicious anticipation, wondering

42

what miracle would occur this week to rescue her. Then, as the violent storm erupted drenching the house and putting out the flames, some of the older lads would jeer at the utter improbability of it all. But so real did it all seem to me that my innocent young heart simply overflowed with relief at the sight of the handsome hero arriving among the smouldering ruins in the nick of time to cut Pearl free. Today's James Bond adventures may be more sophisticated but, I can assure you, the threats he has faced from the evil lieutenants of SMERSH are no more alarming than were the predicaments of our schoolboy heroes and heroines.

In order to be able to visit the cinema each week I used to earn extra pennies at home doing those jobs which my father thought were good for my understanding of family solidarity. On a Friday night my task was to clean the cutlery. We had one of those knife-boards on which you had to sprinkle the cleaning powder before rubbing the knives vigorously up and down to make them shine. Then it was a matter of pure elbow-grease on the forks and spoons. Granny Pearce would often watch these domestic proceedings and sometimes, if she knew I was particularly hard up, she would carelessly mention that she was feeling rather tired and would I mind helping by scrubbing the table for her tonight to save her the trouble in the morning. We both knew why she was asking but we also knew that my father would have disapproved most strongly if I had been given any money without earning it.

Other pocket money would be earned helping the local tradesmen on their early delivery rounds before school. There was great excitement when Mellor's bought a motor van to deliver the bread, the first in the district. Before the roundsman had pulled the light bread cart himself, leaning forward between the shafts to get it going again after each stop. The first time I went on the van to help deliver the bread I felt a helluva chap!

It took Davies's rather longer to mechanize. The milk

roundsmen in the shop at the end of Everington Street, on the other side from our house, used to leave the hand-pushed milk barrows overnight in the large yard at the side of the shop. Early in the morning the men would load two large, heavy churns on to each barrow and many small pint-size cans, each with a lid and the name of the customer written on the side. To have your own named can was a mark of social disinction. Ordinary customers would emerge from their houses with one or two jugs that would be filled from the taps on the churns. At the end of each day the men would empty the unsold milk into the large main tank and then scrub out the churns with boiling water in readiness for the next day's deliveries. In due course Davies's, too, acquired a motor van to deliver the milk as the new world began to overtake the old.

Not all the extra pennies earned were spent at the Munster Road cinema. Regularly outside the school at closing time would gather the street vendors whose wares ranged from chestnuts to sarsaparilla and ice-cream. They were always a great temptation to us. I used to love the distinctive sweet but sharp fruity taste of the sarsaparilla which was sold from a long, low, horse-drawn van, rather like a gypsy's caravan, beautifully painted in a variety of bright colours. For a halfpenny you could have a glassful, the cold mauve-coloured liquid jetting out of the tap and bubbling up the glass – a wonderful sight on a hot summer's day. Equally popular was the Mancini ice-cream man who pushed his barrow all over the district. There were cornets and wafers in two mouth-watering flavours – vanilla or strawberry – which were dispensed from two small churns that sat inside the barrow, packed round with pieces of chipped ice. Every few hours a new, large block of ice would be delivered by van from the ice-maker's premises in Chancellor's Road.

In the winter it was the man selling hot chestnuts and baked potatoes from his hand-pushed cart who did all the trade. The chestnuts were served in brown paper bags while the potatoes would be wrapped in a piece of cut-up news-paper, a supply of which hung on a piece of string from a hook on the side of the cart. It must have been exhausting and uncomfortable work pushing that heavy barrow, complete with iron stove and hot coals, around the streets on a cold winter's day but, if it was, the cheerful, ruddy-cheeked vendor with his cloth cap, bright yellow scarf and heavy army overcoat, its wide collar turned up against the biting wind, never showed it.

Nor had mechanization yet been embraced by all the public services. One day in Fulham Palace Road I saw the horse-drawn fire engine galloping headlong past The Grey-hound pub towards some emergency in the direction of Putney Bridge with the fire bell clanging an urgent warning. It was a brave sight indeed with two firemen in bright red uniforms and shining brass helmets sitting in front, one driving the pair of horses for all he was worth, the other ringing the bell above his head to clear the road ahead. There were two more firemen clinging to the sides, with the huge bulk of the water tank towering above them.

Much to my dismay, no fire engine had arrived in Everington Street the day a motor-bike mysteriously caught fire in the road right outside our house. It happened at dusk and drew an excited crowd of onlookers as the flames leapt upwards amid the dense black smoke. Lying on its side in the middle of the road, the bike continued to smoulder in the growing darkness for some time. Unable to restrain my curiosity I crept out of bed and stole into the front bedroom to see from the window what was happening – until my mother discovered me and sent me back to my own room.

Such excitement was rare. Most days passed in a busy round of activity, even in the school holidays. Overriding everything else was a sense of urgency about the routine matters of everyday life. Wartime life created an unmistakable feeling of tension. Not that this prevented us youngsters from getting away to enjoy the usual schoolboy pursuits.

Everington Street was roughly midway between Hammersmith Bridge and Putney Bridge and with the Thames so close it was inevitable that the river figured in many of our activities.

One day in 1920 we were given a half-day off from school to watch the great oarsman, Ernest Barry, racing for his ninth World Professional Sculls title which he duly won. The Barrys were a famous rowing family. Ernest's brother, W. A. Barry, had won the Doggett's Coat and Badge in 1891 and his two sons, Ernest's nephews, carried on the tradition. Bert became the World Professional Champion in 1927 and retained the title for five years, while Louis, who died in April 1987 at the age of eighty-one, was the British champion in 1936 and became the fourth member of the Barry family to win the Doggett's when he was successful in 1927.

We watched Ernest's race from the bank between the two bridges and saw the two slim boats glide by in rhythmical bursts as each man swung forward in his sliding seat, chest to bent knees, and then dug the blades into the water as the muscles of legs and arms tautened to drive forward and propel the craft onwards through the rippling waters. It all looked so well-controlled and so powerful yet seemed completely effortless. This, I later learned, was the secret of all physical activity in sport.

There was a short cut to Hammersmith Bridge – along Fulham Palace Road, left down Chancellor's Road then along Crisp Street and into Queen Caroline Street – which brought you right to the water's edge beneath the towering steel structure of the suspension bridge. In front of the waterside pub there was a little beach at low tide where the locals would come for a picnic and it was from here that occasionally on sunny summer days we would swim. One day, three of us decided to try to swim right across to the Surrey side and back. We had seen some older boys attempt it and watched them land about two hundred and fifty yards downstream towards Harrods' Repository as they had been

46

swept along by the outgoing tide. Accordingly, to allow for drift, we decided to head off at an angle in the direction of the bridge and agreed that as soon as our feet touched bottom at the other side we would set off for the return journey. All went well on the crossing but, working against the current, the journey felt much further than it looked. As I headed back I began to tire and thought for a moment I wasn't going to make it. However, after spending a few moments swimming on my back to recover my strength I eventually touched down, exhausted, almost as far downstream as the other boys had been, despite my intention to allow for the tide. Accordingly, feeling somewhat embarrassed, I had to make my way back through the clinging mud to join the others on the beach.

Cycling was another favourite pastime. I had learned to ride on Bertie Bray's machine. The Brays were our next-door neighbours, a quiet, serious couple who would sometimes ask me to join them for tea. Bertie, an only child, was equally serious and a year older than me. He was not much concerned with sport but nevertheless we were pretty good friends. When they went away to Devonshire for their summer holidays Bertie used to lend me his bike.

During term-time, of course, I couldn't borrow it, so on a Saturday three or four of us would walk the other way down Fulham Palace Road towards Putney Bridge, making for the Surrey side of the river where bicycles could be hired. Occasionally, if we all had a spare penny, we would take the ferry across. The pick-up point on the Middlesex side was the flight of steps just beside the football club ground so it was a shorter journey for us to walk down through Bishop's Park towards the ferry than to go over the bridge. The only drawback was the ferry's infrequency. The boat, which held eight people, was operated from the boathouses opposite and you had to stand on the steps and wave a handkerchief until you were spotted by the boatman. Even then he was most reluctant to set off until he had collected two or three customers who wanted to cross in our direction – as he always did on football days when the steady flow of customers kept the ferry in a state of perpetual motion. Accordingly, if we did not get a quick response, we would abandon the idea of the ferry and walk along the riverside promenade and through the gate that led on to the bridge just beyond the point where the trams turned round and alongside the Shilling Theatre where, many years later, I would see an amusing comedy called *Rookery Nook*.

Once across Putney Bridge we would turn right into Lower Richmond Road. Just before you reached Putney Hospital there was a shop where you could hire bicycles for sixpence an hour. One day I had to take a ladies' machine with no cross-bar because all the men's bikes were out. We had been enjoying some speed runs down the steep slope from the top of the bridge in Queen's Ride. It was my turn again. As I gathered speed towards the level ground the bike suddenly collapsed beneath me. The frame had severed at the point just behind the pedals, and I fell headlong into the road. Fortunately in those days there was very little traffic so I was not in danger of being run over but it is a wonder that I escaped with only a few grazes and bruises. The fall shook me and I was mightily relieved that the man in the cycle shop seemed genuinely concerned about my injuries and did not try to charge me for the damage when I delivered the broken machine to him in two sorry pieces.

Another route would take us along the embankment beside the river and across the footbridge over Beverley Brook which led to the towpath past the large reservoirs and the Waterworks and on to Hammersmith Bridge. Then it was up the steep slope on to the road, down Castlenau and Rocks Lane, across the edge of Barnes Common, left into Mill Hill Road and back once more to the Lower Richmond Road and the shop. It was the first part of this route we chose on boat race day in March, though it was not always possible to cycle past the huge crowds which used to line the river bank. More usually we would go on foot to the start at the Star and Garter Hotel and then run along the road past the boathouses – Phelps, Aylings and the rest – along beside the river and on under Hammersmith Bridge, past another small reservoir and the playing fields that are now part of the new site of St Paul's School and on to Barnes Railway Bridge, just short of the finish at Mortlake.

I was always a Cambridge man and it was a very sad day for me if Oxford were in the lead at this point because no crew ever seemed capable of making a comeback so late in the race. Many times I have watched the race from the Middlesex side, either from the garden of The Crabtree pub near the Fulham Football Ground or from Craven Cottage itself in the days before they built that large grandstand which blocks out a view of the river.

Many years later I watched part of the preparations for the boat race from a launch. When I had become the coach to the All England Club I used to make a point of visiting the river during the last days before the race to see how the coach prepared them for the ordeal ahead. As a teacher myself I was always interested to see how another instructor in a different sport would tackle the job of imparting knowledge and instilling confidence in his charges. The practice starts were always worth watching. You could stand with your binoculars outside the Phelps boathouse and see and hear all that was going on.

In 1952 I had Jay, my seven-year-old son, with me. We were watching the crews at work when I was greeted by Hylton Cleaver, the distinguished rowing correspondent, whom I knew quite well.

'Hello Dan,' he said. 'What are you doing here?' I explained that I always came down to watch the crews at this time.

'Then why don't you join us on the press launch?' he asked.

'Well, I've got Jay with me – you won't want us getting in

49

the way while you are busy making notes and consulting your stop watches,' I replied.

'Nonsense – you won't be in the way at all, there's plenty of room,' he insisted. 'What is more, Cambridge will be doing more than just starts today. They plan to do a fast piece of work to Hammersmith Bridge, then some more starts.'

We duly clambered aboard the Phelps launch and felt a surge of excitement as the engine fired into life and the craft started to pull away from the mooring. We waited in midstream as the Cambridge crew moved to their stake boat. Then, as the flag dropped and the cox's urgent voice rose above the noise of the engine, the flashing blades were suddenly digging rhythmically into the water to propel the sleek boat forward in controlled surges with ever-increasing velocity. We started to follow but after moving about a hundred yards there was a spluttering noise from the engine which finally coughed and fell silent. As the crew disappeared into the distance we were left stranded, rolling gently as we drifted along on the strong tide. Eventually we were towed back to the boatyard to learn that our breakdown had been caused by sand in the petrol tank. Apparently this was not the first time that the boat had been sabotaged while it had stood moored at night. The local pranksters probably had no idea just how much damage they were doing to the engine.

Later still, the boat race became a thoroughly civilized occasion when my wife, Con, and I were invited to join Pete and Mary Halford at their annual party in their riverside home in Barnes. We used to watch the preliminaries and the start on television in the living-room of their house just off Lonsdale Road and would then rush out, champagne glasses in hand, across the strip of grass to the towpath in time to see the crews approaching. After cheering them past and watching them into the distance we would return to the small screen for the finishing stages. For a glorious spell between 1969 and 1973 and again in 1975 we celebrated a string of

Light Blue victories as the Cambridge crews (coached, incidentally, by Louis Barry, whose uncle I had watched as a boy) carried all before them. It was a far cry from the days of dashing along the towpath, and rather more gracious!

Another who used to give regular boat-race parties was A. P. Herbert, who is immortalized in my mind as the progenitor of that marvellously witty description of an unhappy couple as people living in 'holy deadlock'. His house was on the Middlesex side a few hundred yards from Hammersmith Bridge near the mooring place of the famous sea cadet training ship *The Stork*. Nearby was The Dove public house where a future British Davis Cup player, Tony Mottram, used to enjoy taking an occasional pint of beer.

The hustle and bustle of London's river was so different from the country quiet of the River Orwell near Ipswich which I explored with Bertic Bray the year his parents took me away with them for a holiday, when I was about ten. This was my first trip away with another family. For the first time I saw moorhens nesting along the banks and was introduced to other aspects of country life – like the otter hunt we witnessed one morning when a large group of people carrying long poles moved slowly along the river bank. We spent one day in Felixstowe where I had my first view of the sea, and another visiting the theatre in Ipswich with Bertie's aunt and uncle. Although I had been several times to see pantomimes at the King's Theatre, Hammersmith, I had never visited another theatre or seen any other type of performance. So this was another first for me and mightily impressed I was. The play was one of those big melodramas called *The Silver King*, a show in which Henry Irving had originally taken the lead in London. This was the touring company but very convincing they were as they acted out the tragic tale of the helpless woman being thrown out by the villain into the snow as she clutched her little baby wrapped in its long white shawl. To my surprise the audience started hissing and I joined in heartily, glad to be able to give vent to my emotions.

Back home again we returned to the daily round which, once a week, meant a visit to Sunday school at St Clement's Church in Fulham Palace Road. From 2.30 to 4.00pm every Sunday afternoon we would all congregate in the hall beside the church to observe the time-honoured ritual. Occasionally I would play truant but when I did my mother would invariably ask me 'How was Sunday school today?' If I pretended I had been there she would immediately ask 'Then can you explain what you were doing in Greyhound Road at three o'clock?' Clearly I had been spotted wandering round the shops that were still open on a Sunday. The wood-turner's little workshop, between Peark's, the grocer, and the haberdasher's in Greyhound Road, was a fascinating place where the owner worked all sorts of magic on his foot-operated lathe which sat prominently in the window. There was always a marvellous smell of newly-sawn wood and the intriguing sight of partly-made articles of furniture. One day I remember watching the turner make a cricket bat from a single piece of willow, a picture of concentration as he bent over the lathe with chips of wood flying off in all directions. Years later it occurred to me that the oversize wooden racket being used by F. W. Donisthorpe, my semi-final opponent in the World's Professional Championships at Queen's Club, had probably been made in a similar small workshop somewhere in North London where he lived.

Another who was always open on a Sunday was the newsagent on the corner of Fulham Palace Road next door to the chemist. This was the home and meeting place of the Fulham Palace Athletic Football Club. The proprietor was the honorary secretary and was largely responsible for the organization of the two teams that they fielded each week. Matches were played against all the leading teams on local municipal pitches and we travelled mostly by tram or train to such venues as Ealing, Park Royal and Wormwood Scrubs.

The captain used to pay the groundsman for the hire of the pitch and we had to erect our own goalposts which had no nets. We used to change in wooden huts and then wash down afterwards at large tin bowls that stood on trestle-tables outside. These were the days before the provision of modern comforts like baths and showers! Just before I left school and for a while after joining Queen's Club I played on several occasions for the second team until a minor injury left me limping in to work one Sunday. That day Mr E. B. Noel, the Queen's Club secretary, took me aside and quietly pointed out that I had a promising career ahead of me and could not afford to risk injuring myself on the soccer field each week. Of course he was right and so I stopped playing.

Barnes Common was another favourite footballing haunt during my schooldays. The pitches we used to play on are still there today between Mill Hill road and the railway fence. One day while we were having a kick-around a man came up to me and said, 'Would you like to play for Castlenau Football Club?' I told him I was only a schoolboy who played for Everington Street School in our Saturday morning matches. 'Then why not play for us on Saturday afternoons?' he suggested. 'If you would like to come to our next committee meeting I'll introduce you to the captain.'

When I told my father I think he was quietly proud that I had been spotted by a local talent scout and it was agreed that I should attend the committee meeting. The next Friday evening I went along to the small wooden shed that sat behind the wine store, the last in the short row of shops in Castlenau just past Lonsdale Road. For the first time in my life I witnessed the ritual of procedure at meetings as I was formally introduced. The chairman sat at a table that was draped with the Union Jack. Each matter was discussed thoroughly before being proposed and seconded prior to being put to the meeting for a vote. I was to become thoroughly familiar with this formality in later life as I attended meetings of the Professional Coaches' Association, the LTA and the Wimbledon Common Golf Club where I served on the committee for twenty-two years. Subsequently I did play a few matches for the club but never became a regular member of the team.

Across the edge of Barnes Common runs Beverley Brook on its way through what used to be the Ranelagh Club and is now Barn Elms playing fields, to join the Thames a few hundred yards from Putney Bridge. This was a favourite area for us to explore as we played our make-believe games of cops and robbers among the bracken and gorse bushes which abounded. On this particular day we had walked to the Common. I was wearing a new pair of boots . . . 'a good walk will help break them in', my father had said. After a period of dashing about in the heat of a summer's afternoon, hiding behind trees to take cover from the enemy, we all sat down on the grassy bank of the brook for a welcome rest. It was time to do a little fishing for tiddlers with the improvised bamboo rods we had brought with us, so most of us took off our boots and socks to paddle in the stream. Normally Beverley Brook ran slowly and quietly but this day it was fairly tumbling along so that the tiddlers were swept past our bobbing hooks. Our jam jar, half-filled with water, remained depressingly empty. As we went to sit down on the bank again, one of my friends accidentally knocked one of my new boots into the water. Before I could act it was quickly swept along by the current and into the gulley that carried the brook beneath Rocks Lane and into the Ranelagh Club towards the river. Hopeful prodding with a stick into the waters beneath the low arch proved fruitless. The shiny new boot was irretrievably lost.

I was overcome with that awful feeling of sickness and guilt that accompanies such disasters. How could I face my father and tell him that I had lost one of my new boots? It had been clear from his attitude that their purchase had been a matter of some family sacrifice. The moment came when it was time to walk home and we set off in an otherwise happy group with me half-hopping along in my right boot and feeling thoroughly miserable. By the time we had traversed Rocks Lane and were into the long stretch of Castlenau it was already clear that I was not going to make it home without ending up with a bleeding left foot. One of the boys said 'Why don't you stop at one of these big houses and ask them if they've got a spare shoe or slipper or something?' It was certainly worth a try.

With some trepidation I entered the driveway of the next large house. As I passed through the tall, brick gateposts, on which were perched two stone eagles, my courage nearly failed me. I climbed the stone steps and rang the door-bell. A maid answered the door wearing a little lace cap and a crisp white apron over her black skirt.

'I've just lost my new boot in Beverley Brook,' I stammered. 'Do you think you could let me have a shoe or something so that I can walk home to Everington Street across the river?'

'We don't have anyone your age in the house,' replied the maid, 'but if you try next door they might be able to help you. They have three boys there, one of whom is about your size.'

Fortunately the family next door identified with my plight at once. A slipper was produced which, though rather too big for me, was kept in place by a piece of string tied round my foot by the kindly young gentleman who had answered the door. It was good enough to see me home to face my father's wrath. He was clearly angry at my carelessness but, as usual, my mother diverted the fire of his attack by sending me off quickly on some small errand. I was mightily relieved to have escaped so lightly.

I suppose of all the holiday pursuits the one I loved best was to be a part-time ballboy at Queen's Club; it always seemed to me a better way of earning pocket-money than queueing for meat or delivering bread. During the summer months when the members filled the ouside courts it was the practice to engage local youngsters to act as ballboys, both on match days and when members were having some instruction from one of the resident professionals. While the lesson was in progress we would scamper around the court retrieving the balls so that no time was wasted. In August, of course, when many of the well-to-do members were off on their holidays Queen's Club was relatively quiet. During this lull Mr Noel used to organize a bowls match between members and staff on the spare strip of grass, used as a nursery, behind the present south stand of the centre court. That was always an occasion for much leg-pulling. He also used to arrange a match for the six leading junior members against the youngest professionals and the best of the ballboys. One of my early opponents in these delightful matches was John Olliff, who later became a Davis Cup player and then the lawn tennis correspondent of *The Daily Telegraph*.

As my schooldays came to an end the idea of becoming a permanent ballboy and eventually a teaching professional grew increasingly attractive. My father had heard from a friend that the All England Club were building a huge new tennis stadium in Wimbledon Park which would seat more than twelve thousand spectators. Although he thought this would be 'the biggest white elephant that ever was', my father nevertheless recognized the increasing interest that was being shown in the game and realized that there would be a demand for good coaches.

In those days Queen's Club was recognized as the leading training school for such a profession. All over Britain and in many clubs abroad there were teachers who had learned their craft at Queen's. During my many visits to the club as a part-time ballboy I had become keenly aware of these opportunities. I had also enjoyed the sense of good breeding and orderly management that pervaded the place. Here, I felt, was an environment in which I could enjoy working.

Fortunately my father knew one of the professionals who had noticed that I always seemed to prefer to work on a court where a lesson was in progress and appeared genuinely interested in what the professional was telling his pupil. Furthermore, I had shown a natural ability to hit balls to the pupil while the professional was standing next to him giving instruction. He therefore felt that I would probably make a good teacher. Accordingly it was arranged that I would be interviewed by Mr Noel. Much to my delight, in April 1923, he agreed to take me on to the staff as one of the thirty full-time ballboys. Thus began a love affair with lawn tennis that has never faded.

TWO

The Queen's Club Years

I had just turned fifteen when I joined the permanent staff at Queen's Club as a full-time ballboy in April 1923. There were thirty of us, all local boys. We wore identical red jerseys and black plimsolls, each of us eager to be selected for duty. Members would occasionally ask for individuals by name for their social games or for the lessons given by one of the resident professionals but more usually we would be allocated to the fifteen outdoor and three indoor courts by the 'bookboy', the senior boy among us. Our wage was ten shillings (fifty pence) a week in our first two years and fifteen shillings (seventy-five pence) a week from sixteen years of age until we left at seventeen. In addition we were paid one shilling and threepence (about six pence) per session which meant an hour and a quarter on one of the three indoor courts, with their fast wooden floors, or an hour and a half on the fifteen grass or eleven shale courts. We kept one shilling of that and sometimes we would also be given a tip.

Having secured the post I moved to live with Tom Jeffery's family in a house just round the corner from Queen's Club. Tom was a ballboy like me and we both eventually became teaching professionals. Next door was another of the boys, Cyril Asling, who also became a professional and developed a classical tennis style that was used by the other teachers as a perfect model of how the ball should be hit. Cyril went on to an enviable position as the assistant to A. E. Beamish, the former Davis Cup Player who was now teaching the game professionally. Beamish's wife, Geraldine, had competed in the first Wightman Cup match that had opened the new stadium at Forest Hills in 1923. I shall always remember Mrs Beamish as one of the first players I ever ballboyed for after joining Queen's Club. She was having a practice session with Charles Cutts, the young professional who eventually had to scratch from the first World's Professional Championship that I was destined to win in rather strange circumstances many years later. But that is to anticipate events.

The Jefferys' house was even nearer to the club than The Pear Tree and provided a much better atmosphere for a fifteen-year-old than a pub – especially as our family was breaking up. My older brothers and sisters were all away and married by now and my father was finding it hard to look after the younger ones by himself. I remained with Tom and his family for two years and then in 1925 went to live with brother Bill and his wife, Marjory, who had moved to Southfields. They lived in a small but pleasant terraced house just down the road from the All England Lawn Tennis and Croquet Club which, although I did not know it at the time, would play such an important role in my later life. To get to Queen's Club I made the daily journey by train, via Earls Court, to Barons Court station.

Ever since my first visits to the club as a part-time boy in the school holidays I had been fascinated by the atmosphere of the place. Queen's Club in those days certainly had style. The members, many of them household names from the worlds of law, diplomacy, commerce, medicine, journalism and show-business, all seemed so well-groomed and affluent. Members in retirement would often spend the whole day at the club whiling away their leisure hours. Others would arrive for their friendly games or lessons in large shiny cars, often chauffeur-driven, and would dash off afterwards to important meetings that were part of a world I did not yet understand.

As I grew older I learned that the world was composed of the haves and the have-nots; the boys who went to public school and the university and those who, like me, went to the elementary school. Not that I have ever resented the lack of early opportunity. As I made progress through my chosen profession I came into contact with some truly marvellous people from whom I learned a great deal about life. I realized that education is not the exclusive preserve of schools and colleges. Furthermore, it is a continuous process. A man who is blessed with a keen intelligence and is prepared to go through life with an open mind, looking, listening and reading widely, can educate himself.

From the first I felt completely at home at Queen's Club. There was a large permanent staff at that time, all of them very friendly and helpful to the young newcomer. As I have mentioned, the secretary at this time was E. B. Noel, a Winchester and Cambridge man who had been a fine rackets and real tennis player. In fact he had won the gold medal for rackets at the 1908 Olympics, the only time that the sport was ever included in the Games. He was now the correspondent for rackets and real tennis on the *Morning Post* and had also written one or two books about the latter sport that had become definitive works of reference. Mr Noel was a tall, lean man who walked with a slight stoop. His deep-set eyes sometimes wore a worried look, perhaps because he was concerned about his health. He never looked really strong and healthy and during an illness in 1921 it became apparent that he would soon need some help. Accordingly, in 1923 – the same year that I joined the club – Vice-Admiral Sykes came in as club manager to lighten the administrative load. To me, 'Nolly' was almost like an uncle, always kind and considerate and ready to offer words of constructive criticism when he felt they were necessary.

Mr Noel's office walls were adorned with paintings and photographs of some of the great players of the past and present. His little 'museum' contained intriguing pieces of memorabilia of all the racket sports. I was always glad of an excuse to go into his office just to absorb the atmosphere of those past years.

The chief steward, Mr Platt, commanded a staff of six waiters plus the chef and his kitchen staff to cater for the steady lunch trade for members and their guests. Luncheon was served daily from 12.30pm to 3.30pm in the friendly dining-room where the half-Stiltons were always popular. Joe Richardson, one of the two senior waiters, was a splendid man, stocky and cheerful, who had been there for years and seemed almost part of the furniture. Cavers, the barman (I often wondered what his first name was – the staff were always addressed by their surnames in those days) was a quietly serious man who kept very much to himself. Perhaps this was a thoroughly desirable quality for, in his position, he must have been privy to much confidential and sensitive information, as indeed we all were at times.

Mr Symes was in charge of the dressing-room attendants. He was a large, heavy man, aged about sixty, who held court in the upper dressing-room with an assistant – Jack Shepherd in my early days. Second-in-command was Jack Jenkins, a tall, well-built man who walked in a casual, loose-limbed manner which somehow belied his very practical and alert mind. Jack was a useful tennis player and lived on the Brentham Estate in Ealing, near Fred Perry's parents' house at 223 Pitshanger Lane. Occasionally he would give Fred a hit on the local Brentham Institute court when the young man had not been able to organize a game elsewhere. Jack was also a useful golfer and some years later I played some of my early golf with him. During the war he had acted as secretary/manager and, indeed, in his thirty-odd years with the club he was a veritable 'jack-of-all-trades'.

Within about three months of joining the staff I was promoted to 'bookboy'. That meant I could enter the professionals' quarters on the ground floor beneath the dining-room. There were eight permanent professionals for the teaching of lawn tennis and squash whose quarters were situated off the eastern end of the long, dark corridor, and four for rackets and real tennis who had their own rooms at the other end of the corridor attached to the real tennis courts.

The first room for the lawn tennis professionals was the cosy lounge whose windows looked out on to the east covered court and the small piece of waste land between. There was a fireplace, a large wooden table, a couple of armchairs and some other simple furniture, plus twelve full-length lockers. The newest young professional would be allocated the locker nearest the door which made it awkward when anyone was entering or leaving the room. As your seniority increased so you progressed around the room away from the door.

Off the lounge to the left a door led to a big bathroom, containing a bath and a couple of showers. On the opposite side was the small workshop were Fred André, the stringer, used to restring and repair the members' rackets. Everyone who knew André respected the quality of his work – especially the great overseas players who came to Queen's the week before Wimbledon for the London Grass Court Championships. Men like the bounding Frenchman, Jean Borotra, and Jack Crawford of Australia, Americans Bill Tilden, Frank Hunter and Vinnie Richards; and the leading ladies – Elizabeth Ryan from the United States and Germany's Cilly Aussem – all relied on André to restring their rackets when necessary. He was certainly a great craftsman.

The head professional was Charles Heirons, a very likeable man with the courtside manner of a good doctor. When I first knew him he was aged about fifty, with greying hair and a dark moustache. He stood about five feet eight and was not obviously athletic. On court he was a neat mover. In fact everything about him was neat, from his dress to his well-trimmed moustache. The face was distinguished and the voice (which I never heard raised in anger) was pleasantly melodious. His naturally kind disposition made him a fine head professional – the sort of man that I dreamed of becoming one day.

The lady members, especially, enjoyed their lessons with Charles. I remember one Australian lady of about fifty who was reputed to be a millionairess. She used to arrive in her Rolls-Royce and Charles would always be there to greet her with an appropriate piece of patter. 'Good morning, Mrs Mills, and how are you today? You look very fit.'

'Good morning, Charles,' she would reply. 'Thank you – it's nice to see you again. Is everything ready?'

'Of course, Mrs Mills – and how was the theatre last night?'

She would be flattered that he had remembered and off they would go to the lesson with both of them already in the right frame of mind. During the lesson he might say: 'Fine shot, Mrs Mills, you've never hit a better forehand than that in your life. Now if you can do it once you can do it three or more times!' It was all a marvellous lesson for me in simple psychology.

Charles Read, who at one time was the triple champion – at lawn tennis, rackets and squash (his best game) – was the man I would eventually beat in the final of the first World's Professional Lawn Tennis Championships and then challenge for the British Professional Championships. He was of medium height, about five feet nine, was well-proportioned and a good mover in a match, though it always irritated me that in a lesson he would plant himself in the centre of the baseline and refuse to move at all. He was a cold man, somewhat insular and lacking in humour and was temperamentally defensive at games – an attitude that tended to be reflected in his social life. However, there was no doubt about his skill on the squash court. He turned the game into an art form. Instead of just driving the ball up and down the court he would devise touch shots and angles of immense cunning which would leave his opponent unbalanced or wrong-footed. Furthermore it was largely through the influence of Charles Read and, I believe, W. D. McPherson (one of the most beautiful movers I have ever seen – so light on his feet you could hardly hear him move) that the old narrow and longer court, twenty feet wide and thirty-five deep, was altered to its present dimensions of twenty-one feet by thirty-two.

The other lawn tennis professionals were Tom Jones, who always made his lessons interesting, and Len Cockhill and Joel (known as Joe) Barnett, both of whom went off to Chicago with Charles Williams, the world rackets champion, who remained in the USA until his death in 1935, still the holder of the world title. I would have gone to Chicago myself if Joel had not accepted the post (and there was some doubt about it at the time) and I often wonder how different my life would have been had I gone to America then.

There were four professionals on the real tennis side. Chief among them was the legendary Peter Latham, who had been the world champion at both rackets and real tennis. He was a fine-looking man of about sixty when I first met him, with a full head of greying hair. He was strongly built and had a firm and friendly face that was full of character. Although I never got to know him well he seemed a warm, genial man whose words of wisdom were always listened to eagerly by both the members and his fellow professionals. His pupils seemed to regard him with great affection.

Some time before my arrival Peter, who had started at Queen's on 1 January 1888, had been made an honorary member of the club, the first professional to be accorded that distinction. As you might imagine I was immensely proud when in 1955, two years after Peter had died at the age of eighty-six, I was invited to become the second honorary member from the professional ranks. It was a timely honour because, having spent the previous twenty-five years at Wimbledon, I was again based at Queen's Club as training manager to the LTA. I was equally pleased when that great

Queen's Club stalwart, Joe Pearce, a fellow lawn tennis teacher who had been a lifelong friend and colleague, became the third in the early 1960s.

Peter Latham's son, Emil, was another of the real tennis professionals; he eventually went to Lord's. Then there were Toby Chambers and Arthur Ashford. In 1932 Arthur took up an appointment at Hampton Court and taught on the ancient court built by Henry VIII who had come to love this elegant and skilful game. It was perhaps appropriate for one who had always expressed such a reverence for the game's origins that Arthur should have died on that famous court in 1958, the victim of a sudden heart attack as he bent down to play a low backhand. It was the sort of end that any serious sportsman might have chosen.

In my early years at Queen's it was the great real tennis players of the day who made the most impression on me. Real tennis, the progenitor of lawn tennis, had emerged in about the thirteenth century as a game played with the hand on an indoor stone-flagged courtyard, probably in some religious house. The French knew the game as *'jeu de paume'* and still refer to it by that name. Eventually the odd-looking court with its penthouse, *dedans*, tambours, grilles and sagging net became standardized – though no two courts were exactly the same size. Soon the game acquired popularity throughout the royal courts of Europe – hence the alternative titles 'royal tennis' and 'court tennis'. During the sixteenth century the palm of the hand gave way to heavy, strung rackets and about the same time the balls, originally made of animal hair packed tightly inside a leather cover, were henceforth made of compressed rags bound tightly with thin cord and contained within a hand-stitched melton cover.

Rackets was a game that developed in the debtors' prisons in London – the Fleet and King's Bench – during the second half of the eighteenth century. It was played at first with real tennis rackets against a high wall of the prison instead of across a net. The early game was played out of doors, of course, often as an amenity offered to customers at inns and taverns, but as the game and the rules became better organized the courts became covered and had side walls and sometimes a back wall. Following the opening of the new courts at Princes Club in Knightsbridge the dimensions became standardized at sixty feet by thirty feet. The stone floor and black plaster walls allowed good sighting for the small, hard, white ball that was hit with a light, small-headed racket with a long handle. Soon the game spread to the universities and public schools as well as overseas to British Army posts.

Soon after I arrived at Queen's there seemed to be great excitement among the members and staff about the impending visit of the legendary American, Jay Gould. He was a wealthy individual who was reputed to be the best amateur real tennis player the game had ever known. In the Olympic Games of 1908, the year that I was born, Gould had won the gold medal at Queen's. On this latest visit he was a member of the American team that was about to contest the Bathurst Cup (the 'Davis Cup' of real tennis), against teams from the British Isles and France. All the talk was of the coming match between Gould and the outstanding British amateur, E. M. Baerlein.

Every seat in the viewing gallery was taken and a lot of disappointed members never did get a sight of the match. However, Charles Heirons had arranged with Mr Noel for me to watch from the little-known gallery, hidden away near the roof, high above the *dedans*. When the players appeared I was most surprised to see that the American was a big, heavy-looking man and, to my young eyes, not very athletic. He wore a round-necked vest without a collar and white shoes that seemed to be highly polished. I later learned from Mr Heirons that they were buckskin, 'the same kind that Lord Cholmondeley wears when I give him a lesson'. Secretly, I resolved that one day I would own such a pair!

The Englishman, Baerlein, was shortish and thickset and

looked much more like an athlete. However, I soon learned that appearances can be deceptive. My recollection of the match is that Baerlein did an awful lot of running while the American had to move very little. Gould was particularly adept at volleying and chose his moments well to deliver winning shots of great firmness and precision. The American won easily without dropping a set and, afterwards, when I went to thank Mr Heirons for arranging for me to watch the match, he said: 'You have just witnessed a fine lesson – good anticipation can save a player a lot of running about. Mr Gould had time to walk into position.'

I think it was this match more than anything else that made me aware of the opportunity I had at Queen's to build an exciting life for myself. The whole atmosphere of the occasion was like something out of a book of heroic tales: two gladiators from different continents held the full attention of some of the most prominent and influential men in the land, who jostled with one another to view the proceedings. For me it was a glimpse of a world whose existence I knew not, a world where the possibilities seemed limitless.

The great men of rackets and real tennis caught my youthful imagination – men like the Hon. C. N. O. Bruce, later to become Lord Aberdare, whose son, Morys, was to become the foremost authority on the evolution and history of racket sports. In fact I am indebted to his marvellous work *The Willis Faber Book of Tennis and Rackets* for the historical facts about the two games. There was also Richard Hill, whose lyrical writings in *The Times* on lawn tennis, rackets and real tennis lifted the status of these games to a new level; and Major-General Shepperd, the 'grand old man' of rackets and real tennis. Then there was the famous left-handed rackets player, J. C. F. Simpson, whose rackets were always about an ounce lighter than anyone else's so that he broke more of them than most players. Simpson, a baronet, also competed at Wimbledon – rather unusual for a rackets player in those days. Ronnie Aird was another good player who was also a very fine cricketer and would later become secretary of the MCC; and C. S. Cutting, the American partner of Gould, with whom I later played rackets. Yet another fine sportsman against whom I played tennis on several occasions was Max Woosnam, the great all-rounder, who was awarded four blues at Cambridge for soccer (at which sport he became an international), golf, lawn tennis and real tennis. Such talented people – and to think I actually knew them all and played against them! To the young, impressionable Maskell this was a wonderful time to be alive.

Despite his age, Peter Latham had made a great impression on me, but the man whose skill I most admired was Charlie Williams, who won the World Professional Rackets Championship in 1911 when he was only twenty-two. The following year, Charlie went down on the ill-fated *Titanic* while on his way to play the first of the challenge matches for his title against the US champion, George Standing. After spending several hours in an open boat Charlie was rescued but understandably his match against Standing was cancelled.

When, in the mid-1920s, I first saw Pierre Etchebaster, the great French professional who was a master of the real tennis court, I realized that I was watching one of the game's great stylists. He stood about five feet eight, was well-proportioned and looked strong and fit – obviously trained to the minute. Although in day clothes he did not appear to have an athletic figure it was quite a different matter when he donned his long, cream flannels, picked up the rather strange curved-headed racket and stood poised to deliver that devilish rail-road serve along the penthouse. Here, clearly, was a supreme athlete. Etchebaster's stroke play was quite beautiful to behold; every shot was executed with effortless grace and absolute assurance. Another great stylist was W. D. McPherson, the great squash player who also played rackets and real tennis. On a squash court he moved like a dream and displayed the most delicate, feather-light touch that sometimes mesmerized me to such an extent that occasionally when I was 'marking' for him in a Bath Club Cup match I would completely lose the score.

I was something of a rebel over the method of 'marking'. It always seemed to me unnecessary that we should call 'play' after every shot when it was obvious to everyone that the ball was well above the tin and under the lines on the side walls. 'Surely,' I said to Charles Read, the head squash professional, 'it would be better only to call the close ones – and, of course, the initial serve.' He agreed but said that custom demanded that we continue in the approved manner. I used to enjoy watching the Queen's Club teams in those matches. Everyone was so keen to win and yet there were few occasions when any player got too physical, which is so easy to do on a squash court. We did win a lot, too. Between 1926, when the Bath Club in Dover Street put up the cup for annual competition between the London clubs, and 1985, Queen's Club was successful no less then sixteen times.

Later in life when I had become an established lawn tennis professional I was to number the graceful Spanish lady, Señorita Lili de Alvarez (who was a finalist at Wimbledon three years in succession between 1926 and 1928) among the most stylish hitters of a tennis ball I had ever seen. Later still along came that delightful American, Doris Hart, whose stroke-making technique was well-nigh perfect, despite a childhood knee injury that had left her partially crippled. Doris's classical shot-making carried her to success in all four Grand Slam singles championships and won her countless doubles and mixed doubles titles as well. More recently the gifted Indian, Vijay Amritraj, brought the same effortless grace to the courts – as well as a marvellous sense of humour. Vijay's chivalrous attitude to his opponent's winners also won him countless admirers. As he nodded, smiling, towards his adversary and clapped his free hand on the racket strings in genuine appreciation of a shot that had just beaten him, the fans would redouble their applause.

In my early years at Queen's I tried my hand at all the

games except real tennis. Being a natural timer of the ball they all came fairly easily to me. Quite soon I was 'marking' for some of the matches in the Public Schools Rackets Championships that always used to take place during the school holidays at Easter. This ancient competition had started in 1868 at the famous Princes Club in Knightsbridge where it remained until 1886. For one year it was moved to Lord's and in 1888 was transferred to Queen's Club where it has remained ever since – except for 1941 when, because of the war, the final was played at Wellington College, and 1942 when no championship was held at all.

Westminster School had entered the competition in 1908 but they had withdrawn in 1920. Accordingly, in 1925, when I was only seventeen, I was 'lent' by Mr Noel to Westminster to encourage and coach the boys who entered the tournaments held at Queen's Club each year in the Christmas and Easter holidays. My occasional visits to Vincent Square gave me an interesting insight into that charmed world of privilege whose members, staff and boys alike, were always delightfully friendly and informal. Thirteen years later the Royal Naval College, Dartmouth, also dropped out because they had recently raised the age of intake thus making the cadets ineligible to compete in the tournament.

There were some great young players among those schoolboys. I remember the 1927 final in which the Eton pair, Kenneth Wegg and Ian Akers-Douglas, beat R. H. Calthorpe and G. L. Raphael, of Harrow, 4–0. They were so good at seventeen that they could hold their own against men in the Amateur Championship which also used to take place at Queen's. I often wondered why it was that the public schools could not devote as much time and energy to lawn tennis. Somehow tennis was never given the status that cricket or rugby enjoyed – nor did it rank alongside rackets and real tennis. Sadly, in some schools, despite the revolution that tennis has experienced internationally, it is still a second-class sport.

One day at Queen's in 1925 I had seen A. C. (Aubrey) Raphael of Harrow (the brother of G.L.) playing with N. M. Ford, the son of the headmaster, against C. J. Child and T. A. Pilkington of Eton. Aubrey played a marvellous captain's part, dominating the rallies and urging on his partner, as Harrow scored a narrow 4–3 victory. Many years later I was to go and stay with the boys' uncle, E. G. Raphael. But that is a story I shall come to shortly.

The great rackets personalities of the day included some interesting characters. Leonard Crawley was a first-class player who, of course, played cricket for Essex, became a fine golfer, and, later, a highly-respected golf writer. D. S. Milford was a great hockey international while K. S. Duleepsinhji (known as 'Mr Smith' at Cambridge) was a world-class cricketer. One day in 1925 I was playing a game of rackets against him at Queen's when he tried to block an awkward shot off his chest and the ball flew off the frame at an angle and cracked me on the head just behind my left ear. I was felled like a shot stag and came round in the dressing-room. Curiously enough this was an exact replica of an accident I had witnessed in 1924 when Charlie Williams had laid out Major-General S. H. Shepperd. When he saw what he had done Charlie's eyes moistened with tears. Happily his victim recovered soon enough.

There were so many other great events that used to take place at Queen's in those days that there always seemed to be something going on. I remember watching Harold Abrahams winning the hundred yards for Cambridge in the Oxford versus Cambridge sports meeting in 1923, beating into second place Rex Alston, later to become the BBC's chief cricket commentator. In 1927 another vivid memory was of Lord Burghley soaring majestically over the obstacles to win both the high and low hurdles for the third year in succession. Then there was the glorious sight of D. G. A. Lowe striding away from his field to win the half-mile in great style. I remember, too, how sad I felt the following year watching the last of the Oxford v. Cambridge sports meetings taking place at Queen's, already knowing that they would move to Stamford Bridge in 1929. When I saw the film *Chariots of Fire* in the early 1980s, memories of those romantic days at Queen's came flooding back.

The cinder track, a normal quarter-mile track in my day though earlier it had been a third of a mile in circumference, was situated right opposite the clubhouse. Standing on the steps and looking out to the left you could see the tall, covered stand, just inside the present main gate. Off to the right, and running at right angles to the clubhouse, was the long, low 'hundred yards' covered stand, five rows deep, where the sprints used to take place. It was generally known that other more romantic things also took place in the shelter of the stand in the darkness of a warm summer's evening! Behind the stand lay four of the hard courts and the four grass courts where, each August, we used to have the annual bowls match between the members and staff – always a friendly and informal occasion when the club was relatively quiet, with many members away on holiday.

The area of grass inside the track was occupied by twelve grass tennis courts which were not laid out until mid-April or early May. It is amazing to think that the grass inside the track was also the site of the football pitch where the Varsity soccer and rugby matches, as well as some Corinthians' soccer matches, took place. This would be unthinkable today but in those days no one thought it odd. However, the ground staff, under Freddie Wilson, had to work very hard to prepare a level and well-grassed surface for the tennis courts after the area had been churned up in the winter months. The only parallel I can think of today is in Australia, where I believe the Melbourne Cricket Ground, for example, and other ovals, are used for Australian Rules Football during the winter and first-class cricket during the summer. The unusual thing about that is the fact that the whole area of the oval is run across by the footballers – there is no 'square' like there is in England on many grounds (the

Kennington Oval for example), where hockey or football is played alongside the protected cricket area.

Freddie Wilson, besides being a first-class groundsman, was also a fine athlete in his own right. When the Varsity athletes were at Queen's preparing for their meeting, Freddie would run round the track with Harold Abrahams and the rest on their training runs and would leap with the long jump men into the pit that he had carefully prepared. I never saw him run competitively but he was a beautiful natural mover and, incidentally, a charming man and highly respected.

I have often looked back on those early years at Queen's and wondered why it was that my great love became lawn tennis. There were several reasons. First and foremost I realized that the possibilities for the game itself were very much greater than were the prospects for rackets, real tennis or even squash. Lawn tennis was already a great international sport and was growing fast, with a much more varied membership at Queen's than was the case with the other racket sports. Then I always preferred outdoor games where you felt part of the natural elements. I was also beginning to show considerable promise as a player and, as I have indicated, from my earliest days I had entertained the ambition one day of becoming the head professional. To my young eyes there could be no finer achievement than to succeed Charles Heirons in that position.

We ballboys were allowed to play on the club's courts only at the end of the day – though never on the grass. The bookboy had to seek permission from Charles Heirons and special permission was necessary for the covered courts where never more than four of us were allowed to play on any one day, usually on the new number three court that was self-contained. The rest of the time we would play our own makeshift game on the large, concrete area that had been used for skating during the winter before covered courts four and five were built there. For a net we used the heavy metal crash barriers that were positioned to control the crowds during athletics meeting. We made our own small bats out of pieces of wood which we would cut into the shape of a racket.

Tennis balls were never a problem. We could always find in the hedges some used balls abandoned by members who had played without ballboys. Or we would persuade Jack Jenkins to sell us some good, once-used balls for threepence. Then there were the balls that would mysteriously disappear from the indoor courts. It was considered a sin for a ballboy to lose a ball on one of the covered courts and it was a genuine mystery how one would occasionally be lost.

Later we discovered what had happened. Under a mat on the floor of the ballboys' room, which was situated just outside the corridor leading to the professionals' quarters, was a trap-door. One day several of us decided to investigate what lay beneath. We duly removed the cover to reveal a channel, about two feet square, through which ran a pipe – presumably a heating pipe for the covered courts, for it was in that direction that the channel led. Three of us, Ernie Hunn, Fred Curl and myself, climbed down into the channel and crawled along on our bellies amid the dust and dirt towards covered court number one, the famous east court. There at the end, before the pipe turned up at right-angles, was an open space in which lay six or seven tennis balls, most of them old and dirty, some almost petrified, but two or three relatively new ones. They had obviously fallen through the narrow gap between the wall and the pipe though, looked at from above, it did not seem possible.

When we came out we were filthy, almost as dusty as we became when we were thrown into the sawdust box – a ceremony that every new ballboy went through as part of his initiation. This ancient custom got eight of us the sack. By chance Admiral Sykes was making an unannounced tour of inspection one morning and he entered the ballboys' quarters to hear an almighty din as seven of us tried to prevent the eighth, a new boy undergoing his initiation, from escaping from the box. The Admiral was not amused and ordered us to appear before him at once. We duly appeared in his office, looking suitably contrite. But we were not ready for his outburst. 'That behaviour was disgraceful and will not be tolerated,' he roared. 'Hand in your shoes and your jerseys. You no longer work at Queen's Club.' We were stunned. The other boys looked to me to sort things out, for none of them wanted to face their fathers that night with the news that they were out of a job. Fortunately, the ever-wise Charles Heirons was ready with sound advice. 'Ask the Admiral if he will see you again and make a sincere apology. Then assure him that you, personally, will see to it that the custom of the sawdust box is ended.' That is just what I did and happily we were all reinstated.

I used to organize the ballboys' 'tournaments' that we held on our makeshift court where we drew lines in chalk on the concrete surface. Not everyone was keen enough to take part but we had sufficient numbers for these matches to be taken most seriously, among ourselves at least. The rink tournament used to go on every morning and, as bookboy, I would have to come along and say, 'Right, you three are the next ones on court so off you go to the ballboys' room. I'll call you when it's your turn.' Work was allocated strictly on a rotational basis; if I had shown any favouritism my authority would have been totally lost. The only exception to this unwritten rule would be if a member had previously booked a ballboy by name – something that was discouraged – or if one of the professionals had reason to do so.

After a time I became tired of playing with wooden bats and persuaded Jack Jenkins to let me have one of the members' discarded real tennis rackets. 'Cut an inch or two off the handle, then it will be all right,' he said. That still did not satisfy me for long so a few weeks later I returned to Jack and said, 'Look, Mr Jenkins, it's about time I had a proper tennis racket.' Jack, who later became one of my best friends, replied, 'I do happen to have an old SND.' (The

Ayres model designed by the famous Australian player, Stanley Doust.) 'You can have it for a shilling. It's got thick gut in it and should last a while.'

This made all the difference. I was unbeatable with my new racket, which became a prized possession. Soon one of the other boys persuaded Jack to sell him a racket too. It was a Slazenger Demon which had a combed wooden grip with a fishtail handle, instead of a leather butt, which allowed you to wrap the little finger securely round it to prevent the racket from slipping out of your grasp even on the hardest shots. Nowadays, for the same purpose, some manufacturers attach to the end of the handle a cord loop which slips over the wrist.

Occasionally one of the members would come along and watch our rink matches and perhaps even join in. One day while we were playing the Maharanee of Baroda arrived as usual in her chauffeur-driven Rolls-Royce with two of her household staff. I had to stop playing at this point because she always wanted me to ballboy for her during her regular lessons with Charles Read, so I handed over my bookboy duties to my deputy, Fred Poulson. Before she went to her lesson, however, the Maharanee, looking most regal in her flowing sari, watched the boys for a few minutes, obviously impressed by the intensity of our play.

She must have spoken to her husband, for soon afterwards Mr Noel called us all together to announce that the Maharajah of Baroda had presented a trophy for annual competition between the ballboys of Queen's Club. When he held up the trophy we could hardly believe our eyes – it was a huge, solid silver cup that must have been worth a small fortune. The tournament was duly held some weeks later and, by agreement, was played on a handicap basis with the handicaps worked out by the professionals. I won it quite easily, beating Bill Dear in the final. Bill, who died tragically in 1930 under circumstances which led the coroner to record an open verdict, was two years older than his brother Jim, the great squash professional and great competitor. In fact I always feel that the outstanding sporting achievements of this quiet, unassuming man were never properly recognized. Jim had started like me as a Queen's Club ballboy. He spent some years coaching at Princes Club in Knightsbridge and returned to Queen's after the war in 1946. When you consider that he won the British Open squash title in 1938; was the British Open Rackets Champion three times, in 1946, 1951 and 1960; won the World Rackets Championship three times in 1947, 1948 and 1951; and became the World Real Tennis Champion in 1955, you begin to understand what an immense influence he had on these racket sports. However, in a world where only amateur sport received any publicity, Jim's exploits went largely unnoticed by the public at large.

Bill, who was a wonderful stylist and had a service as good as Mike Sangster's, could always beat me in practice but in match play he used to get too nervous to do his talents justice. It has always been a matter of some pride to me that this magnificent cup was the first tennis prize I ever won. Imagine my feelings when, on the occasion of the club's centenary dinner in 1986 – a magnificent, glittering affair attended by HRH The Duchess of Gloucester – I found myself sitting in front of the Maharajah's Cup. I still have the replica which, itself, is a very handsome trophy.

A few years later, when I had become an established teaching professional, I was approached by the Indian Trade Commissioner's office asking if I would go out to India to become his personal coach at the Palace in Baroda. At the time I felt that I would learn more about my chosen profession by staying on at Queen's so I declined the invitation. Eventually my old friend Tom Jeffery, who was now working at the Melbury Club in Kensington, decided to leave that post to take up the appointment in India where he was forced to spend the entire war.

One of my jobs as bookboy was to take in the lunches and teas to the professionals which I would carry down from the dining-room upstairs. In those upstairs, downstairs days of strict social protocol the professionals were not allowed to mix socially with the members on the club premises. They were not allowed to join them for a drink in the bar, a restriction that used to embarrass some of the younger members who loved to have a drink and a chat after a particularly exhilarating session. These meetings therefore had to take place on the steps outside the bar or in the professionals' room. It was simply the way things were in those days.

I used to enjoy sitting in the professionals' room at the end of the day, listening to all the chat as they came in from the shower to dry off and lounge in the large armchairs around the cheerful coal-fire. I hung on every word as they discussed the day's events before settling down to a few hands of solo whist round the large mahogany table which dominated the room. During the rackets tournaments at Christmas the lounge would become a gathering place for all the visiting professionals – Walter Lawrence from Marlborough, Walter Hawes from Wellington and Gerry Barnes from Haileybury with whom I would go to America in 1930.

In the winter play would finish around 3.30 because it would be too dark to play by a quarter to four and there were no lights yet on any of the courts. The electric lighting must have come in around 1927. Although they had gas lighting on the covered courts at Dulwich we never had gas at Queen's.

There would always be a few rackets to be strung or repaired – we all learned to perform this most vital aspect of the pro's art – or one of the professional's books would need to be totted up. Charles Heirons would often call out, 'Dan, check my book for me please', which meant seeing that the right amount had been entered for each lesson (the rates paid to the professionals differed according to seniority) and that the totals were accurate. I remember that the fee I was paid in June 1929, just before I left Queen's for Wimbledon, was something like ten shillings and sixpence for an hour and a quarter, of which I kept seven shillings and sixpence.

Charles Heirons used to say that there were four essential requirements that every tennis coach should always carry with him – an indelible pencil to mark the correct position of the pupil's grip on the racket handle, a penknife, a clean handkerchief and a shilling piece (this to give to forgetful members who wanted to tip the ballboy but had left their money inside!).

Much of my work as a ballboy was done for Charles Read, who was the best player among the senior professionals, though it was his rock-like steadiness from the baseline rather than any forcing qualities that kept him ahead of the rest. During his lessons he could plant himself just behind the centre of the baseline at one end and feed balls expertly to whichever part of the court was required to produce the required result from his pupil. He rarely, if ever, ran. That struck me as odd. Here was a dynamic game in which the whole object was to cover the court fast enough to give you plenty of time to play the ball without rushing your shot, and yet one of the leading coaches was not moving at all. Of course, much of the time the professionals were engaged by the older members to give them some gentle exercise. Only occasionally would a member want to play sets, though the professionals often made up a doubles four and they did a certain amount of coaching, especially in the school holidays.

One doubles match I shall never forget. It was soon after I had become bookboy that Charles Heirons and Charles Read were told that Prince Albert (he was not yet Duke of York), the future King George VI, would be coming to the club with Wing-Commander Louis Greig (later Sir Louis, and a future All England Club chairman) for a game of doubles on court three. I was told to be ready to ballboy for them. The Prince and the Wing-Commander were a useful pair who would go on to win the Royal Air Force doubles and play together at Wimbledon in the 1926 Championships – the only time that a member of the Royal Family has competed at Wimbledon.

Prince Albert was a left-hander with a beautifully natural topspin forehand. His backhand was a moderate stroke; like so many left-handers of the day he kept his elbow up and allowed the head of the racket to droop. Sensibly he tried to run round the backhand to deliver his favourite forehand – a tactic that was often possible in doubles but much more difficult in singles. Being athletically built the Prince loved to dash across the net to intercept his opponent's returns of serve with a fierce drive volley. It was probably his best shot, along with his first serve which was hit with a loose, flexible, india-rubber sort of action that was entirely natural and most effective.

I don't remember speaking to the Prince but afterwards he did thank me most courteously for ballboying for him. It was an experience I shared with all the other ballboys, most of whom had sneaked a look at the game.

Prince Albert may not have been totally orthodox in the way he hit the ball but he was extremely effective. However, there seemed to be a belief in those days that you had to be a good stylist to be a winner. It seemed to me that this over-emphasis on style could be positively harmful if, as often, it meant that a pupil was asked to sacrifice an efficient but ungainly way of hitting the ball for a more elegant stroke that was unreliable. As I got older and watched so many of the champions hitting the ball in different ways, all of them effective, I realized that the most important task as a teacher was to reinforce the confidence induced by hitting natural shots, however unorthodox they appeared to be. Then you could try to add new shots to supplement the natural ones and so increase the player's repertoire. For instance, if anyone had tried to alter Jean Borotra's extremely unusual way of hitting his backhand – almost a push with the racket well out in front of him and the thumb straight down the back of the handle – he would have destroyed the surprise element in Jean's shot as well as destroying his confidence. In those days it seemed to me most players had fairly natural forehands, makeshift backhands (which, given half a chance, they would run round to hit forehands) and, except for the few tournament players, very poor services.

However, the methods of the Queen's Club professionals were geared to the market they served. Sometimes they were beautifully subtle. One Saturday afternoon Charles Heirons had asked me to ballboy for his regular weekly session with one of the members, Mr A. J. B. Norris, known to his friends as 'Flabby' because, in truth, he was all skin and bone with not an ounce of fat on him. Mr Norris was intensely competitive and used to stride through the gates of the club swinging his umbrella playing imaginary forehands and back-hands. He was one who always liked to play sets, so after a warm-up of fifteen minutes they began. Mr Heirons won a close first set after querying several close balls. 'Out, you say, Mr Norris?' asked the coach. 'Oh yes, well out, Chas,' replied Flabby, stretching his arms wide to underline the point. Mr Norris did not enjoy losing.

With Mr Norris trailing 2–3 in the second set, they had a lengthy rally, at the end of which he got to the ball rather late (he no longer looked fresh) and played another rather poor shot. 'Oh dear, I can't go on like this,' he cried. 'My footwork is all wrong. If I can't get my feet right I can't time the ball properly.' The second set soon went to Mr Heirons 6–3. Although there were still several minutes left of the hour and a half session, Mr Norris had had enough, so they collected their things and made their way to the clubhouse. I followed with the balls.

Instead of taking his leave of Mr Norris as he usually did at the foot of the clubhouse steps, Mr Heirons said, 'I wonder, Mr Norris, if you would like to accompany us to the professionals' room as there is something I'd like to show you.' Intrigued, Mr Norris agreed. When we arrived Mr Heirons said, 'Now, Mr Norris, would you mind sitting on the edge of our large table here. And Dan,' (he never called me Maskell) 'you take a ball and go to the other side of the room. Are you ready, Mr Norris – take up your racket and when Dan feeds the ball to you I want you to control the ball so that you return it directly into his hands.' I did as I was asked and Mr Norris had no difficulty in directing the ball straight into my hands. Mr Heirons asked us to repeat the exercise twice more. Both times the ball was returned to me perfectly.

'There you are, Mr Norris,' said Heirons quietly. 'You had no difficulty in timing the ball, did you, and yet your feet are not even touching the ground. You really mustn't confuse footwork and timing – they are quite separate disciplines.'

I wondered what Mr Norris would say. He was suitably impressed. 'You are quite right, Charles,' he conceded with a smile. 'There's nothing wrong with my timing.' However, Mr Norris did not fail to add that good footwork did make timing easier in a moving ball game. That was my first lesson in clear analysis of a teaching point.

Soon after I had won the Maharajah of Baroda's Cup I think the Queen's Club committee realized that I was about ready to become a junior professional. The departure of Joel Barnett to Chicago with Charles Williams and Len Cockhill made a vacancy available and to my great delight I was appointed to the post in mid-summer 1924, and promised a contract in due course. I was sixteen and a half.

Of the thirty ballboys some twenty-five of us went on to become teachers. Amongst these was Arthur Roberts, who started his career in the Merchant Navy and then returned to live near Queen's Club while he was the assistant professional to a Miss Rhodeglia who coached in London. Eventually Arthur went on to achieve great things from his base at the Palace Hotel, Torquay where Angela Mortimer, Michael Sangster and Sue Barker were his three outstanding pupils. Tom Jeffery came back from India and eventually became the head professional at the exclusive Hurlingham Club; Joe

Pearce and Fred Poulson (my successor as bookboy) became long-time professionals at Queen's before Fred went to Roehampton. On a Sunday evening we would team up with Tom and Fred at Arthur's house and play solo whist for hours on end while we listened to records of the Mills Brothers – a wonderful close harmony sound where you would swear that the voices were really instruments – and talked shop, swapping our latest coaching experiences and learning from each other. Ernie Lowe was another who stayed for a long time at Queen's; Wig Roberts, Arthur's brother, who had a strange habit of hanging his head on one side but was one of the best stroke demonstrators I have seen, went off to teach in Biarritz; while Jack Jeffery, Tom's brother, a lovely stylist who hit the falling ball quite perfectly, fell ill and became the senior dressing-room attendant and games organizer for a period before sadly he died of cancer.

My appointment as a junior professional in 1924 coincided with the first Amateur versus Professional match that was ever played in Britain. The divide between the two classifications was absolute; professionals were not allowed to play for county or club teams as they were in cricket. Nor was there an equivalent of the Gentlemen versus Players match.

The feeling was certainly growing that the professional tennis teacher should have some opportunity to engage in competitive matches and thus an incentive to improve his playing standard. How else, it was argued, could he be expected to pass on advice to pupils about match play? Accordingly that winter the LTA secured the permission of the International Lawn Tennis Federation to hold an official Amateur v. Professional doubles match on the east and west covered courts at Queen's Club. Five of the club's coaches plus Tom Jeffery would play against a team of members – all amateurs, of course. Three matches only would be played. I paired with Charles Read as first pair, Bill Dear and Tom Jeffery were our second pair and third were Joe Pearce and Fred Poulson. Our opponents were G. R. Crole-Rees and

Cyril Eames, George Stoddart and A. E. Crawley, Nigel Sharpe and John Olliffe. The result of this historic encounter was a 3–0 win for the Amateurs, which was hardly surprising for this was the very first competitive match for four members of our team.

Despite the one-sided result the match was deemed to have been a success. Consequently it was decided by the LTA to hold up to five similar matches every year after that. The main one was to be held during the summer season at Devonshire Park in Eastbourne and the others would be at the Chapel Allerton Club in Leeds, the Northern Club in Manchester, the United Banks ground at Lensbury and the Singer Club in Paignton. Caps were to be awarded for the Eastbourne match, each with crossed rackets and the year embroidered above the peak. Also for the Eastbourne match the professionals were to be paid expenses of £11 4 shillings (£11.20) and put up at the Southdown Hotel.

There was a great sense of occasion at Devonshire Park the following August for the first of the main matches. As usual at Eastbourne there was a sizeable crowd to witness this trend-setting event. I was seventeen and playing one of the first competitive tennis matches of my life. My opponent was J. B. Gilbert, the Davis Cup player (and later captain) who beat me 6–3 6–4 after not a bad encounter. I certainly did not feel disgraced and afterwards Gilbert was most encouraging. 'Persevere, young man,' he said. 'You'll be a very good player one day.'

There is an amusing sequel to this story. Four years later, having by then twice won the British Professional Championship, I was appointed as the first professional at the All England Club, and one of the first people I bumped into at Wimbledon was Gilbert. He came straight over to me, smiled, and said, 'Dan, congratulations on your appointment, I really am delighted to see you here.' Then, with a twinkle in his eye, he added '. . . and I wasn't such a bad forecaster, was I!'

The winds of change were really stirring in 1925 for at the Gipsy Club in Highbury, North London, was held the first open professional tournament in Britain. This pioneering event was staged during the club's own regular amateur tournament. Charles Read insisted that as the Professional Champion he should be on a handicap of 'Owe 15'. Reluctantly the LTA finally agreed. Everyone else played off level. The tournament was won by F. W. Donisthorpe who beat Charles Read in the final by 6–4 6–1 6–4. In 1927 the Monegasque player, Josef Negro, who had one leg about three-quarters of an inch shorter than the other, won the singles by beating Read 6–1 6–1 6–4. His participation attracted quite a lot of publicity.

The Queen's Club committee would not release more than two of the staff to play because there would have been too few to cover the members' coaching requirements. Accordingly that first year the two senior men, Charles Read and Charles Heirons, took part. Bill Dear and I had to wait until 1926 before we could compete; I reached the semi-finals of the singles and doubles. That same year I played for Queen's in a match against the Civil Service. Although strictly speaking this was against the rules, Mr Noel called on me at the last moment because someone had dropped out without warning. There were no complaints from the opposition and I thoroughly enjoyed the chance to compete.

During the winter of 1925–26 I spent most of the time on the rackets court, marking matches and playing with members and the schoolboys who would be taking part in their Christmas tournament. There was plenty for a junior professional to do for there were always rackets to be strung or repaired and the occasional squash or lawn tennis lesson to give. Generally, though, there was a dearth of young rackets professionals at the public schools, so the Rackets and Tennis Association decided to institute a competition to be called The Junior Professional Rackets Championship of Great Britain. The senior professionals were all encouraged to enter their assistants and there was a small amount of prize money – something like £10 for the winner and, as an incentive, £20 for the senior professional who had entered the boy. Charles Read entered me along with Bill Dear.

I had not played competitive rackets before so I spent the last part of the summer persuading as many people as possible to play games against me. In the semi-final I played Bill who always used to win our friendly matches. But Bill, like so many talented shot-makers, was never a very good match player. He got too nervous. Accordingly I beat him quite easily and moved through to the final where I faced Albert Cooper, the left-hander from Wellington who had been entered by Walter Hawes, the legendary professional there. Albert was about six months younger than me but I beat him without losing a game. Freddie Wilson, *The Times* correspondent for all racket sports and father of Peter Wilson, described in glowing terms the young Maskell winning this new competition from a younger and slimmer opponent: 'It was the case of a man beating a boy', he wrote.

At about this time Peter Latham was on the point of retiring, so Queen's engaged the Harrow professional, Charlie Williams, to teach rackets and real tennis. As a result of winning the tournament I was now approached by Ernest Jones, the professional at Eton, who was within a year or two of retiring, to see if I was interested in understudying him with a view of taking over this choice position. Ernest had trained some marvellous young players – boys like Ian Akers-Douglas and Kenneth Wagg. There would have been a good living to be made at Eton but the fact was I preferred playing outdoor games and was not as keen on rackets as I was on lawn tennis. Accordingly I declined, still dreaming of one day being the head professional at Queen's.

It was this approach from Eton, I think, that prompted Queen's Club to offer me a contract at once. Mr Noel summoned me to his office one day and said: 'Young man, I'm pleased to tell you that the committee has unanimously decided to offer you an immediate five-year contract for the teaching of lawn tennis, squash, rackets and real tennis.' I was thrilled, but felt compelled to answer: 'Thank you very much, Mr Noel. I'm most honoured by your offer, of course, but I know next to nothing about real tennis. I think I would like to concentrate on just the other three games.' 'That's a pity,' he replied. 'You have just the buttocks to make a fine real tennis player!'

So that was how my full professional career began. I was paid £2 10 shillings (£2.50) per week for the first year, plus my coaching fees which were five shillings (twenty-five pence) per session for lawn tennis and three shillings and sixpence (about eighteen pence) for squash and rackets. It may not have sounded much but it was all I needed and in any case the money was secondary to my love of what I was doing. Here I was, just eighteen, working at one of London's leading clubs and surrounded by interesting people from every walk of life. I'd be on court one day with a doctor, the next a lawyer, a banker or a member of the Stock Exchange, then with someone from the theatre world or a member of the aristocracy, like Lord Charles Hope who regularly played with me when he was in London.

More important in many ways, I was now beginning to get games with some of the good international players of the day – men like J. D. P. Wheatley and Nigel Sharpe; women like Betty Nuthall and the beautiful Eileen Bennett – as well as with the promising young players and the overseas competitors who came for the London Grass Court Championships in the week before the Championships at Wimbledon. One of these was the powerful Australian J. O. Anderson; another the young Helen Wills, whom I first hit with in 1927. Little did I realize at the time that she would be the overseas player with whom I would play most over the years after my move to Wimbledon. As a result of this rich variety of opposition my own game was fast improving.

Accordingly it continued to frustrate me that there was so

little opportunity for match play. One day I was approached by a Mr Frank Mousley who lived a few miles from Queen's in East Sheen where he owned a garage behind which were four hard tennis courts. He was very keen on the game and asked why it was that we professionals had no official association.

'Why don't you form a British Professionals' Association? Then you will have a much stronger voice in the game,' he suggested.

I thought about this from the point of view of our lack of competition, and replied:

'Mr Mousley, suppose I could get eight of our professionals to come down to your courts on a Saturday afternoon, would you be prepared to advertise the matches and let us play?'

'What a good idea, of course I will,' he answered.

So began some most enjoyable sessions in which several of us from Queen's Club – Bill Dear, Fred Poulson, Joe Pearce and myself to the fore – used to arrange to be away from the club on Saturday afternoons, a quiet time for coaching when the members generally played among themselves. We were usually joined by Tom Jeffery, who seemed to have no difficulty in getting permission from Colonel Powell, the secretary at the Melbury Club, to have the afternoon off. Arthur Roberts was another who occasionally joined us whenever he was able to free himself from his usually busy coaching sessions on a Saturday afternoon with Miss Rhodeglia.

Each week Mr Mousley would put up £5 and the eight of us used to put five shillings (twenty-five pence) each in the kitty and we'd play a knockout singles tournament followed by some doubles. As the news of our matches spread we used to attract a nice little local crowd who began to know our games. From these small beginnings sprang the idea of forming the association that Mr Mousley had suggested. Harold Flew, who lived in that part of the world and was a manager with Izod's, the exclusive clothing outfitters in the

West End, became the first honorary secretary and we were all founder members. In due course the Professional Coaches' Association would embrace nearly every worthwhile teacher in the country and would become affiliated to the LTA.

One of the people who had appeared at several of our Saturday sessions in East Sheen was Gilbert Frankau, the well-known author who was about to start a new magazine called *Britannia and Eve*. Like Mousley he was very keen on seeing the development of professional tennis and the two of them hatched the idea of a World Professional Championship to be backed by the magazine which would put up a first prize of £50. The event was duly announced and entries were invited from all the important tennis-playing countries. It was a novel idea and there was no difficulty in securing the entries of ten prominent foreigners – including Martin Plaa and Robert Ramillon from France, Roman Najuch from Germany, the Wasdorps from Holland, the Irish Burke brothers, Albert and Edmund, who agreed to come up from Cannes where they were teaching, plus an American whose name I forget. From Britain there were more than forty entrants.

The excitement was considerable at Queen's Club, on whose hard courts it had been agreed the tournament would take place early in October 1927. The LTA had approved the event and good crowds were expected. However, the rules and conditions had not been drawn up too clearly and, with about a week to go before the start, it became clear that there would be no travelling expenses available for any of the overseas players save their return fares from the port of entry to London. Not surprisingly all the foreign players decided to stay away.

Thus the *Britannia and Eve* World Professional Championships became, in effect, a closed British championship. We played every match over the best of five sets without any handicaps. By Thursday the semi-finalists had emerged –

Maskell v. Donisthorpe, the man who played with a huge, oversize racket long before Prince was ever thought of, and Charles Read against Charles Cutts, who was about to set off for a new job in Canada. It rained all day on Friday so we had to play both the semi-finals and the final on the Saturday. It was still raining the next morning so it was decided to play the matches indoors on the wooden courts. Unfortunately Cutts had to leave that morning so he was forced to default against Read and departed with the losing semi-finalist's prize-money. Many of the competitors felt that this was unprofessional (though it was really no fault of Cutts). However, as a result of this episode a rule was introduced whereby a player had to complete a match before he was eligible to receive prize-money.

I began my match against Donisthorpe and won the first set 6–4. When I was leading 2–0 in the second he came up to the net and said, 'Dan, I'm going to scratch. You are going to beat me anyway and as the final is being played this afternoon and Read has not had to play at all today it would not be fair to keep you on court any longer than necessary.' 'You can't do that,' I protested. 'Oh, yes I can,' he replied. And he did. I have always thought that that was one of the most sporting gestures I have ever seen on a tennis court.

Because of the heavy rain the members were not able to play out of doors so we had a packed gallery on the famous east court for the final. Heading a large official party was Lord Desborough, in his nineteenth and last year as president of the LTA, who was there to present the prizes. The trophies stood at the side of the court on a table – the Britannia Shield itself, and a silver cup for the winner that had been presented by Mr Mousley. The press were well represented, too, with Bruce Harris of the London *Evening Standard*, Wallis Myers of *The Daily Telegraph*, Stanley Doust of the *Daily Mail* and H. R. McDonald of the *Evening News* all in attendance.

At that time I had only one decent tennis racket, a

Slazenger 'Primoris', and when I had left the court after the abbreviated semi-final I noticed that one of the main strings was fraying. What should I do? It was about midday so I had two hours before the start of the final. Should I thread a piece of gut alongside the frayed mainstring and pull it as tight as I could – an old trick among the professionals? There was still the risk that the string would break which would mean that the tension of the whole racket would be lost. Or should I do a complete restring? The problem was I did not have any gut and Fred André was no longer working at Queen's. So I sought help in the pros' room. 'Mr Heirons, could you please sell me a couple of hanks of gut?' I asked. 'I can spare you one hank,' he replied. 'It will cost you half-a-crown.' That would only do the mains but I bought it anyway and went to Charles Read, my opponent, who was prepared to sell me the only hank he had in his locker – some rather thick rackets gut, black in colour, which I knew would do for the cross-strings.

I have never been so careful with a restring in my life and had it finished with about half an hour to spare – time enough to change into my spare pair of clean white flannels and a clean pair of tennis shoes. Before I went on court for my first professional final with £50 resting on the outcome, Jack Jeffery had told me he would take down the statistics of the match so that I could study them afterwards and learn something. This was also my introduction to proper match analysis which, in my later career as the Davis Cup coach, became an essential requirement in helping the players and captain to assess our opponents.

The racket looked rather odd with white mains and black crossings, but it played well. It was not until I had spun the racket and asked my opponent to call 'rough or smooth?' that I realized I had not had time to put in any 'pearling', that very thin gut, usually blue or red, that used to be threaded round the mains to prevent them from moving in the large gaps above and below the cross-strings.

From the first ball I played like a dream. On the fast wooden court I was able to live at the net and rush Charles Read into error. I won in three straight sets. It might have been more difficult on a slow hard court where his solid groundstrokes would have posed some problems for a volleyer. But on wood there was little he could do. He was much slower than me about the court so his only real defence was to lob and to attempt disguised passing shots. Afterwards Jack told me that I had played twenty-one smashes and had hit nineteen clean winners; one I had smashed into the net and on another he had passed me a good backhand.

So in less than ninety minutes I had become Professional Champion of the World! I was in no doubt about the hollowness of that title in view of the decimated entry but at least I had won what was virtually a British professional championship. The newspapers, short of other news on such a wet day, made much of the nineteen-year-old underdog beating the reigning British professional champion to claim the world title and there were many photographs. As a result of my performace many of the members at Queen's urged me to challenge Charles Read for his British title. In those days the champion could be challenged by anyone who could raise the necessary funds. It was rather like a prize fight. There was a cup as well which had been donated in 1919 by Donald McLeod, a shipping man who was a member of Queen's. He had offices in St Mary Axe near those of F. C. Lohden, the mayor of Sutton and another shipping man, who later became the chairman of the LTA. McLeod had presented the cup to the LTA and asked them to frame the rules of the competition and administer it.

The LTA had decided that the holder could be challenged by anyone who could raise £100. But first they needed a holder, so the cup and title had been awarded to Charles Heirons as the senior professional in the country. He had then been challenged by Charles Read in 1920 who beat him and retained the title for four years. In 1925 Donisthorpe had then challenged Read but had told the LTA that he could only raise £25. Rather short-sightedly the LTA had agreed to the challenge for that amount but Read had refused to play. Since he had refused to meet the challenge Read then lost his title by default and Donisthorpe had his name put on the trophy without ever hitting a ball! Realizing the stupidity of the situation, the LTA reestablished the £100 minimum and said that the professionals could add any amount above that provided that the money was lodged with the LTA who would organize the challenge. In 1926 Read had challenged Donisthorpe who didn't accept and so Read held the championship until I challenged him in 1928.

The prospect of my challenging Read for the title created quite a stir among the membership at Queen's. One of the members, W. J. Temple, agreed to back me for £50 on the understanding that he would take £25 if I won and stand the loss if I didn't. Charles Read was making similar arrangements. Others joined in the staking in similar fashion until we had each raised pledges of £245, which was the sum we played for. The rules decreed that there should be three best-of-five-sets matches played over three weekends at agreed sites and on agreed surfaces. The defending champion would have the first choice of venue and surface, the challenger the second choice, while the third choice would be decided by lot if the players could not agree.

In the event all three matches were played during the month of October on the number three covered court at Queen's Club, the one that was on its own and stood where the new covered court building now stands. I won the first encounter by three sets to one, and lost the second by the same margin. Afterwards Mr Hamilton Price, who was the referee and umpire for all three matches, said to me: 'You know, you played a bad tactical match today – you kept playing to his backhand which is his best shot.' 'I know,' I replied, 'but my forehand cross-court approach is not my best shot.' 'Then play his forehand from the back and wait

93

for the short ball so that you can approach the net on your terms.' It was a sound piece of advice. I won the decider three sets to love.

Thus, in 1928, I became the British Professional Champion, a title I would win sixteen times altogether between that first year and 1951. All but the first one were the result of winning a conventional knock-out tournament for, even before I had played Read, the LTA had asked me if, in the event of my winning, I would consent to change the format. I had readily agreed. The second year our championship was held on grass at the Roehampton Club, in 1930 it was played on grass again at Wimbledon with the singles final on number two court (the only professional tournament ever held on the sacred turf of the All England Lawn Tennis and Croquet Club, prior to the BBC2 event in 1967 on the eve of open tennis) and in 1931 we went to Captain Rogers' hard courts at Sydenham. The final at Sydenham was a memorable affair as our umpire for the match was the former all-conquering queen of world tennis, Suzanne Lenglen, who, since 1926, had been a professional.

Later, in 1934, I had acted as Suzanne's sparring partner in a bizarre game that was played on the roof of Selfridges store in Oxford Street before a select band of Gordon Selfridge's invited guests, about a hundred in number. The great lady had been engaged for a year to promote the store in various ways – one of them an exhibition match on the loose-topped hard court that had been laid specially among the chimney pots and surrounded, of course, by high stop netting. Suzanne had been away from the court for some time when we played and took a while to find her rhythm. For three games she looked most insecure and in no time at all I was leading 3–0. I was doing my best to feed her sympathetically and wondered what else I could do to help her. Then suddenly she began to time the ball perfectly. Gliding about the court with her customary balletic grace she swept the ball unerringly into the corners and drew level at

3–3, to the enthusiastic applause of the onlookers. It was as if she was back on her beloved Centre Court, queen once more of her kingdom. Just as suddenly her touch departed and I won the set 6–3. By then the worshippers seemed satisfied. The Lenglen Magic, albeit fleetingly, had shone once more on a British court. Although we did play a second set people were moving about and talking, more concerned with planning tomorrow than remembering yesterday.

This was the age of stunts. In 1926 at the London Coliseum four professionals had played tennis on a full-size court which ran the full depth of the huge stage. However, it did not have much run back. Nevertheless Charles Heirons, Charles Read, A. E. Beamish and Charles Lockyer, with Fred Poulson as ballboy, had created quite a following. Their performance was part of a variety show that had the Irish tenor, Talbot O'Farrell, as top-of-the-bill. They all did two shows per day and the other artistes were not too pleased when, for six weeks, the tennis was promoted to top-of-the-bill.

Some years later, in fact on the eve of World War Two, I played in a short but entertaining programme devised by Bill Tilden on the huge stage of the State Cinema, Kilburn, where the court ran across the stage so that the audience was watching from the side. Teddy Joyce was the resident bandleader whose act followed the tennis and he was always complaining to the management that Tilden was over-running his allotted time. I don't think they got on very well.

Occasionally, opportunities occurred for a trip away from London and these I readily accepted as a means of broadening my experience. One such chance came in 1927 as the result of the games I used to have with Lord Charles Hope. He was a born mimic and very popular among his friends. His brother was the Marquis of Linlithgow who eventually was appointed Viceroy of India, whose estate, Hopetoun House, lay near Dalmeny on the Firth of Forth. After a knock at Queen's one March day, Lord Charles said, 'How would you like to join me at Hopetoun House for a few days to show my two young nephews how to play the game?' He had often mentioned the boys, Lord John and Lord Charles, and their younger sister, Lady Mary, and I knew how fond he was of them. 'Thank you, sir, as long as the club will release me I'd love to go to Scotland,' I replied. 'I've never been there.'

So it was arranged. Mr Noel could not have been nicer when I asked for permission. In fact throughout my early years at Queen's 'Nolly', as everyone affectionately referred to him, was like a father figure to me, always encouraging, always ready with a quiet word of advice when he felt it was necessary. Thus when he died in December 1928 it hit me rather hard. I realized with some surprise that I had become very close to him.

It was a fascinating weekend. Hopetoun House was an enormous mansion on a huge estate and they lent me a car to move around. I played tennis with the children who were marvellously energetic youngsters, though without any serious long-term interest in the game. The two boys, aged about fourteen, were keener on more violent pursuits. It frightened me one morning when I saw them on the wide terrace that ran the length of this great house which, I believe, contained the second largest ballroom in Scotland. They were charging at one another on their bicycles, like knights of old, each holding a broom-handle for a lance and issuing blood-curdling yells as they crashed into each other and fell to the ground. They seemed none the worse for their dangerous exploits and it occurred to me that some of our young tennis players might benefit from this sort of toughening up!

Besides being a keen tennis player, Lord Charles was a scratch golfer who played in the amateur championships. After our daily tennis session he would go off to practise on the nine-hole golf course that formed part of the estate. Although at this stage of my life I had not even swung a golf club I was interested to watch someone developing his technique in a different sport so I walked down the long path from the tennis court to the practice ground beside him and, one by one, he would pitch them towards the flag which stood about a hundred and fifty yards away. So grooved was his swing that each ball would climb the same gentle arc and fall beside the others on the green, perfectly grouped. The whole process fascinated me. When, the next morning, I showed interest in what he had been doing Lord Charles said, 'Well, you must experience this game for yourself. Go and see the butler, he's a keen player himself. Ask him to take you out.'

Apparently the butler had spare sets of clubs for any visitors who wished to have a round of golf and he duly accompanied me to the practice ground. 'Have you played before?' he asked. 'No, never,' I replied.

He put down a ball on a flat, mown area of grass and handed me a club. It was a number three wood which in those days we called a spoon. 'Knock the ball up towards the green over there,' he said, without any sort of advice about how I should hold the club. So I simply held the grip in the most comfortable way, took a couple of practice swings and then addressed the ball. My first shot was perfect. The ball flew straight as an arrow and swooped down towards the green some one hundred and sixty yards away. The butler was impressed. 'You were joking,' he said. 'You were pulling my leg – you've played this game before.' 'No,' I insisted. 'I promise you that was the first golf ball I've ever hit.' 'Remarkable,' he said. 'Let me see you do that again.'

He put down another ball and I took my stance again. This time I was determined to hit the ball even further. I swung at the ball and experienced an uncomfortable jarring in my arms as the club head dug into the turf about six inches behind the ball, and then parted company with the hickory shaft and went spinning away into the distance, the binding unravelling behind it. 'I see what you mean,' said the butler, as we gathered up the clubs and returned to the house. Disastrous as that first experience was, it kindled a fascination with this wonderful and tantalizing game that has never died.

Other very enjoyable tennis weekends were spent at Hall Barn, the home of Lord Beaconsfield, whose house had been rented for the summer by Mr W. G. Raphael, one of the Queen's Club members who very occasionally used to venture out for a game of grass court tennis on a warm summer's day. I would meet Mr Raphael at his home in Hill Street, just off Park Lane. On the first occasion our departure was somewhat delayed because the butler had not finished collecting together the cigars that would be needed for the stay. Mr Raphael, like Sir Winston Churchill, was hardly ever without a cigar in his mouth. Eventually we left in the Rolls-Royce with Enid, Mr Raphael's pleasant daughter, in the front beside the chauffeur, and Mr Raphael, the butler and myself in the back.

We got there in time for lunch. Afterwards I would play with any of the weekend guests who wanted to have a game. After lunch on Sunday we used to have a competition. I would play six games against each of the guests, the men receiving fifteen a game and the ladies thirty. Each would try to improve on the previous guest's score and when it came to Enid's turn Mr Raphael, who used to sit out in a big wicker armchair to watch the fun, would call out through his cigar smoke: 'Now, Maskell, no favouritism for Enid.'

At dinner-time I would go off to eat with the butler, the valets and the ladies' maids in whose quarters I was housed. Each of the guests, it seemed, had brought their own servants and there were always plenty of people about. For me it provided a genuine taste of upstairs, downstairs life.

On the Saturday evening I joined the butler on a visit to the local pub. We rode down on bicycles to enjoy a drink and, perhaps, a game of darts. I was not used to alcohol, especially the strong local ale, and after one glass I knew I did not want another. When it was time to leave, at about 10.00pm, I went to jump on to my bike but vaulted clean over it and fell into the road! The beer had made me overconfident. I picked myself up, mounted successfully, and we started to weave our way homeward. After we had cycled about four hundred yards the local bobby overtook us on his bike and stopped us. Getting out his notebook he said: 'That's not very clever of you, riding off from the pub without lights in front of all the village folk. I'd better take your names.' The butler apologized for both of us and said we were from the big house and would go quietly home. 'Off you go then,' said the law. 'But no riding, mind.'

Once we were out of sight around the corner we remounted and headed for the large wrought-iron gates and the driveway that was marked by large white stones. In the darkness I crashed into one of the stones and buckled my bicycle's front wheel. It was a long walk back up the drive to the house carrying the broken machine on my shoulder.

I once spent four days at Hever Castle at Edenbridge, the home of Major J. J. Astor, who was the chief proprietor of *The Times* newspaper from 1922 to 1966 and established it as an independent political voice that was respected the world over. He had been a very keen rackets and lawn tennis player in his youth, and a good one. In 1905 he had been in the Eton winning pair which had defeated Wellington in the final of the Public Schools Rackets Championship and, three years later, playing with Vane Pennell, he had won the Olympic gold medal for rackets on the only occasion that the sport had been included in the Games.

During the war Major Astor had had the misfortune to have a leg amputated. Despite the restriction to his movement imposed by his artifical leg he still enjoyed taking some exercise hitting balls on a tennis court, but his disability necessitated careful feeding. I used to play with him for an hour in the morning before he went off to the city and for another hour in the evening when he arrived home. In between I would return to my quarters, the little pub in the village opposite the gates of the castle, and fish in the pond at the back. All this made a welcome break from coaching at the club in London.

It was at about this time that I purchased a motor bike, a Matchless 350. Fred Poulson also owned one and we decided to spend our week's holiday motorcycling around Devonshire. We planned to do about twelve hundred miles around Dartmoor and all the local beauty spots, staying the night at bed-and-breakfast houses. We had enjoyed a wonderful week of sightseeing and were coming through Ringwood on our way back, doing about thirty mph, with Fred ahead of me by about thirty yards. Coming round a bend a car, trying to overtake me, got too close and knocked me off the bike. For a moment I was lying across the near-side wing of the car as it skidded to a stop and then I slid off on to the kerb. I lay in the road, badly shaken. As the driver peered down at me I got the shock of my life. He was the image of my father. Fortunately I was not seriously hurt, only bruised and shaken, but we had to go through all the usual police procedures of giving evidence. We also had to make an unscheduled night stop in Ringwood while the garage straightened out the bike. The accident persuaded me to give up motor bikes and when Gerry Barnes, the rackets pro at Haileybury (who lived at Hoddesden and later became a partner in the racket-making firm, Sams Bros and Barnes), offered to do a part-exchange deal for £20, trading my bike for a Morris motor car, I readily accepted.

My education regarding transport was further increased at this time when I took my first flight in an aeroplane. It was the day before the August Bank Holiday in 1928. I was due to play an exhibition match in Ostend with Tom Jeffery and we had decided to go by air from Croydon. I was not altogether happy about the prospect because on a recent flight on this same route the plane had clipped the steeple of a church near Ostend airport, an incident that had received wide publicity.

There were three flights due to leave that day and our plane was the second, a Handley Page with room for about twelve seats. While we were waiting the first plane returned, having experienced some engine trouble over Kent, so the passengers were transferred to our plane. Eventually we were boarded on the third aircraft and off we went, bumping our way across the Channel. We sat in cane basket-weave seats, six passengers down each side of a central gangway. There was no pressurization and the noise was considerable. A chap reading a newspaper in the seat behind mine could see that I was nervous, and asked if I would like to borrow it. That did help to divert my mind from the shaking and buffeting by the wind as we came in past the church steeple which, happily, we missed.

I began to wish that I could have flown down to the South of France, when I found myself still awake in the middle of the night on the Blue Train as we sped towards the relative warmth of Nice, Cannes and Monte Carlo away from the winter chill of northern Europe in January. This was a trip that had been suggested to the Queen's Club management by Sir Francis Towle and some of the other club members who regularly spent the winter months on the Riviera. It was felt that I would obtain valuable teaching experience by acting for eight weeks as assistant to Karel Kozeluh, the Czech professional who had been engaged to play with our British Davis Cup team at Wimbledon in 1928 and 1929. He was a fine athlete who had represented his country at football and ice hockey and was now attached to the Hotel Bristol in Beaulieu. In 1928 Karel had also played a series of fifteen challenge matches against America's newly-turned professional, Vincent Richards, winning thirteen and losing two. He had held the French professional title since 1926. When Karel won both the singles and doubles at the American Professional Championships in 1929 he was, at the age of thirty-four, probably the best professional player in the world, certainly on hard courts.

My years at Queen's were a marvellous experience which could never be repeated. That world has gone forever. But I shall always be grateful for the opportunity of meeting some fascinating people. Sir Samuel Hoare, who as Lord Temple-wood became the president of the LTA, regularly came for a game at the time when he was Home Secretary. He used to come down at 8.00am on his way to the House of Commons. He would always arrive promptly at 7.55am dressed ready for play clad in his flannels and one of those long, cream melton overcoats that all the leading players seemed to wear in those days. He would be driven there by his chauffeur, either in a Rolls-Royce or in a little Austin Seven. The routine was always the same. 'Good morning,' he would say, 'is the court ready?' 'Yes, Sir Samuel, the court is ready, the balls are ready and so are the ballboys,' I would reply. Sir Samuel always liked to have two ballboys, one at each end, to save time which, clearly, was precious. We never had a knock-up. It was straight into a set. I used to feed him to prolong the rallies and give him the exercise he was seeking. Actually he hit the ball quite fluently and easily – not very hard but with nice touch – as you might have expected from a man who had played rackets for Harrow and real tennis for Oxford. After exactly three-quarters of an hour he would gather his things and hurry away to the car.

I had read in the paper that Sir Samuel was due to make a political broadcast that evening, a rare event indeed at that time so, after the session, I said, 'Sir Samuel, I'm hoping to listen to you tonight on the radio. Am I right in thinking that this is the first political speech to be broadcast?' 'One of the first,' he replied. 'Let me know what you think of it.'

A couple of days later when he arrived for his game the opening routine was different. 'Did you hear my talk?' he asked. 'Yes, sir, I did,' I replied. 'I was amazed that you could be talking so calmly and quietly like that when you knew that so many thousands would be listening to every word.' 'Ah,' he said (and this is something I have remembered all my life), 'when I talk like that I just imagine I am in my own lounge at home, chatting to my friends.' That was a wonderful insight into the qualities of a good, natural broadcaster and something I remembered when I started to learn the technique of television commentaries.

Then there was the Hon. Victor Rothschild who was about eighteen and at Harrow when he used to come with his two sisters for lessons at Queen's Club. The Hon. Miriam must have been sixteen, and his younger sister, the Hon. Liberty, was about fourteen, a beautiful, fragile girl who always reminded me of a piece of Dresden china. Miriam was much stronger and Victor had a natural games player's good eye for a ball. They used to come with their chaperone or governess who sat at the side of the court while they played. They always used to send me a Christmas card but after my move to Wimbledon I lost touch with the family. I knew that Victor had gone up to Cambridge and eventually became the head of the Think Tank but I had no idea what had happened to the girls. Imagine my surprise, then, when I came home one evening – it must have been during the seventies – and turned on my television set to see the erudite Miriam discoursing with great authority about fleas, of all things! Her mastery of television technique was admirable – and so was her knowledge of her subject.

Enjoying these carefree days at Queen's Club, where I made so many friends and met so many interesting people, I little realized that my life was about to set off in an entirely new direction.

THREE

All England Professional

It was a bright autumn morning in October 1928. I was sitting
in the City office of Mr F. C. Lohden, an LTA councillor
who became chairman in 1933. He was a man I knew quite
well, who had been a first-class rugby player and was at one
time the Mayor of Sutton. He looked at me from across his
large mahogany desk and smiled. 'Dan, I've asked you to
come up here to my office because of the confidential nature
of the proposal. I think you know that all of us at the LTA
respect your skills as a teacher and your prowess as a player.
We want you to move from Queen's to become the first
professional coach at the All England Club.'

I could hardly believe my ears. In fact I was shaken to the
core. This was a totally unexpected offer. When I had had
time to recover my breath, I said: 'Well, I'm delighted. I feel
very honoured to be asked. Would you mind telling me what
the job entails?'

'Of course. You will be coaching the juniors whom the
LTA feel have the potential to become future Davis Cup and
Wightman Cup players. Then in the periods before a Davis
Cup tie or a Wightman Cup match you will be practising with
the teams and helping the captain to prepare them for their
matches. Finally, just before the Championships there will
be a need to be available for practice sessions with those
leading overseas players who feel they need them. How does
that sound?'

It sounded too good to be true. But I felt a keen loyalty to
those at Queen's Club, who had given me every opportunity

104

to further my career; in fact I'd just returned from my second South of France trip. Accordingly, I felt compelled to say: 'Of course I'd love to do the job, Mr Lohden – but I'm under contract to Queen's at the moment where I'm being groomed for the head professional's job. They've been very good to me so unless the contract can be broken with honour – and it still has two years to run – I'm not able to accept.'

'You don't have to worry about that,' said Mr Lohden reassuringly. 'We've already had discussions with the Queen's committee and they understand the importance of our request to the whole future of British tennis. You would certainly leave with honour.'

So it was agreed. A contract would be drawn up and I would start the following year, shortly before the Championships, at a salary of £750 a year – a princely sum in those days.

Soon after my meeting with the LTA chairman I had a phone call from Major Dudley Larcombe, who had taken over as secretary of the All England Club from Commander Hillyard in 1925. He came straight to the point. 'Dan, I gather you've seen Mr Lohden and that he has explained the job to you. I do hope you'll accept it – I'm sure you would be very happy here.' I told him what had transpired. 'Oh that's good, I'm delighted,' he said. I often wondered if the original idea had come from Major Larcombe because I knew him quite well and have often played tennis with him at Queen's. In fact we had played an exhibition doubles match against one another in 1925 to open the new number four and number five covered courts at Queen's that had been built for about £9,000.

Some time the following spring, it must have been in March, the Hon. C. N. O. Bruce (the future Lord Aberdare, who would soon become chairman of Queen's Club) offered the pros some tickets for his family box at the Royal Albert Hall for an evening of boxing.

I had followed what was going on in boxing ever since

Snuffy Moore had introduced me to the sport at school. Interest had been fuelled by a visit to the Holborn Stadium Club in 1927 as the guest of Mr F. H. Ayres (I never did know his first name), an affable old gentleman in his late sixties. (His family sports goods business was one of the best known in the country and had, until 1901, supplied the tennis balls and court equipment to Wimbledon, a service begun in 1879.) On the bill that night was a bout of eight rounds between 'Nipper' Pat Dailey, a highly promising lad of seventeen and a half, and Johnny Cuthbert, a vastly experienced man in the evening of his career. The Holborn Stadium Club had tables arranged in the balcony around the ring so that you could dine in style while watching the action, and the food was excellent. Opinion over dinner was divided about the likely outcome. Some thought that the bout was a mis-match and expected to see the boy murdered. Others said that Dailey would be too fast for Cuthbert, an opinion I shared. So they began. For three rounds Nipper chased the older man all over the ring and the noise in the stadium was deafening. Someone commented, 'Johnny's letting him burn himself out. He'll come back and kill him,' and that is exactly what happened. In fact the referee stopped the fight to prevent the boy from being too badly hurt.

We were all looking forward to the boxing evening at the Albert Hall. I was still giving a lesson on one of the covered courts at about 6.40pm when Fred Poulson put his head round the canvas. 'Hurry up, Dan, we'll be late for the boxing.' I quickly ended the lesson, which had already overrun by ten minutes, and dashed for the non-members' dressing-room which we were using temporarily while our own quarters were being redecorated. Most of the pros were already changed and someone else was using the only bath. As there was no shower I decided to have as good a wash as I could manage using one of the wash-basins. They were tip-up affairs on a pivot, just below waist height. Having washed my top half I lifted my right leg to wash my foot in the basin, unaware that it was cracked. I must have put some weight on it for, suddenly, the basin shattered. My foot went straight through and a jagged edge practically severed my big toe. It was a nasty moment. There I was, totally naked, with my right foot pouring blood and the other pros all impatient to be off to the boxing.

They dipped the foot in cold water but the bleeding would not stop, so one of them wrapped a towel tightly round the wound while Fred did his best to dress me. Then while the others departed for the Royal Albert Hall I set off by taxi towards the same West London Hospital in Hammersmith where I had been sent on the tram as a boy with a hand damaged in a boxing bout at school. Perhaps the fates were trying to dissuade me from associating with this violent sport! This time I was stitched up and sent home on crutches. Fred Poulson, good friend that he was, supported me throughout this whole unfortunate business and saw me safely home. Never once did he complain about missing the boxing.

My chief worry was that I would not recover in time to start at the All England Club during the pre-Wimbledon practice week which, it had now been agreed, would be my starting date. The rehabilitation was a frustrating but educative business as I discovered ways of exercising my leg muscles without putting any weight on my right foot. Although I did not know it then, it would all be very useful experience for my rehabilitation work during the war. I progressed from crutches to a stick and finally began to hit a ball again on the practice wall towards the end of May.

The contract had now been signed and I had another call from Major Larcombe inviting me to go down to the All England Club to meet the staff. That first visit as a prospective employee was a memorable one. Although the complex was only six years old there was already an unmistakable sense of tradition and history about the place. There in the men's dressing-room were the high banks of brown lockers and, between the strips of green carpet, the tall wooden benches with pegs above that had silently served the great men of the 1920s. What tales they could tell, I thought, about the French Mustketeers – Borotra, Brugnon, Cochet and 'the Crocodile', René Lacoste, who, not four months before, had won his second singles title beating Cochet in the final. The room would have memories too of the great Americans, Tilden and Hunter, Johnston and Kinsey, and of the Australian, Patterson, who had won the first title at the new ground in 1922 after the club had moved from the 'old' Wimbledon in Worple Road. That meeting had been the wettest on record and had not been completed until the third Wednesday. And we think we have bad weather today!

Of course I'd been to Wimbledon as a spectator many times since my first visit in 1924. Although I knew many of the members, who were also members of Queen's, and had played with several of them there, I'd never played on the All England Club courts simply because I was not myself a member. That was a highly-prized honour given to few to enjoy. In the social climate of the day it would have been unthinkable that a teaching professional should become a member, although it was considered acceptable for existing members who had been great players to turn to teaching as they retired from competition to provide extra income. Such were the anomalous values of the day.

Mr Noel always saw to it that the pros had a few Centre Court tickets each year and I was fortunate enough in 1924 to have one for the ladies' final in which our own Kitty McKane would be playing against the young American champion, Helen Wills. To this day I can remember the seat number – D11 it was – one of the open courtside seats on the left of the Royal Box, near the corner where the players make their entrance. Years later when I started broadcasting from Wimbledon I would often look down at that same seat just under our commentary box (before we moved to the other end) and remember my first visit. Nor shall I ever forget the match itself, a thrilling spectacle for all us Britons to see Miss McKane fighting back so courageously from being a set and 1–4 down against the relentlessly accurate Helen, eventually to win her first major title 4–6 6–4 6–4. We would not know then, of course, that this would be the only match that Helen would ever lose at Wimbledon during a remarkable career in which she won the singles title eight times – a record that Martina Navratilova equalled in 1987, though she lost far more than the meagre four sets that Helen conceded in all those years.

I had been in the open standing room for the fiftieth anniversary meeting in 1926 when King George and Queen Mary had stood on the red carpet stretched across the middle of the court to present a commemorative gold medal to each of the thirty-four former champions who attended. They were ranged in two lines down each sideline and included seventy-one-year-old Frank Hadow, the oldest surviving winner, who had been champion in 1878, Wimbledon's second year, and Maud Watson, the first ever ladies' champion in 1884, who was now sixty-three. It was a wonderful sight with all the competitors of the 1926 meeting assembled on court, the men at one end and the ladies at the other, and Commander Hillyard standing at the front of the Royal Box with his megaphone announcing each champion in turn.

Coming now to the club as an employee was an exciting prospect. From the first Major Larcombe was delightfully friendly and remained so throughout his term as secretary, which came to an end with his death during the war. He was the archetypal ex-Army officer, smartly dressed, a little below medium height and rather stocky with a crisp and businesslike manner. He had been a fine player himself before World War One and in 1906 had married Ethel Thomson who became the Wimbledon singles champion in 1912 and the mixed doubles champion two years later.

The Major introduced me to Ellis, the dressing-room attendant, who still wore the striped trousers and waistcoat of his days in service as a gentleman's gentleman. I don't think anyone had told Ellis that I was coming for he looked slightly put out that the club should actually be employing a professional. He blanched visibly when Major Larcombe said: 'Ellis, I want you to find a locker for Mr Maskell,' and then added, 'Dan, I hope you won't mind changing in the members' dressing-room – or do we have to build a special room for you?'

I could hardly believe my ears. It is difficult today to realize the impact of Major Larcombe's suggestion. When, later, I told my fellow professionals at Queen's they refused to believe me. With one blow Major Larcombe had swept away centuries of protocol, redefining the social order. I was somewhat hesitant. 'Would the committee mind if I changed here?' I asked. 'The committee?' replied the Major. 'No, of course not, and the members will be delighted, I'm sure.' I very nearly added, 'Well, the committee at Queen's seem to mind quite a lot,' but I held the thought inside. I also remember thinking at the time that this momentous decision was a small step towards elevating the status of the professional, something that, as a member of the committee of the Professional Coaches' Association, I was already keen to promote.

'Splendid,' said the Major. 'That saves us all a lot of trouble not having to build a special room. Let me now give you a guided tour. Over there is where Tilden always likes to change, that's his locker. And Cochet always goes for this corner here.' He turned again to Ellis. 'While you're about it, Ellis, you'd better find a second locker for Mr Maskell. He'll be changing two or three times a day and will have lots of clothing plus his shoes and rackets.' Ellis's protest that there were no lockers to spare were pushed aside. 'Use this one next to Cochet's, it's only old Gordon's locker – he's about ninety and he doesn't play any more, in fact his tennis clothes are going yellow with age,' instructed the Major. The raised eyebrows and almost inaudible sigh left us in no doubt as to Ellis's feelings.

Next I met Nora Cleather, Major Larcombe's assistant, whom I knew by name and reputation but had never met. She was a strikingly handsome woman with light blonde hair that was almost white. Her face was full of character and her ready smile revealed a warm and friendly personality. Nora was a fine administrator too and kept the club going during the difficult war years. She was to prove most helpful to me in arranging the timetable of visits by the juniors in the months ahead – a job that was performed with equal skill after the war by Marie Bompas. Marie joined the staff soon after I did and became the assistant to Colonel Duncan Macaulay when he succeeded Nora Cleather as secretary in 1945.

Then we went out to meet Colman, the legendary head groundsman whose family could trace their links with the club back to its very origins at Worple Road in 1870. He was a marvellous character, totally in command of his team of assistant groundsmen, all of whom took great pride in producing year after year a perfect playing surface on every court. For me this was a marvellous day. Everyone seemed so friendly and genuinely helpful – an atmosphere that I can honestly say remained constant throughout my twenty-six years at Wimbledon.

My first day of work was on Monday 14 June, the pre-Wimbledon practice week when all the overseas players started to arrive for their acclimatization and practice. My first assignment was to hit with Helen Wills, the holder of the singles title for the past two years. I remember thinking 'there's nothing like starting at the top!' Bruce Harris of the London *Evening Standard* was there, and Stanley Doust, the veteran Australian player who was now writing for the *Daily Mail*. They were there to report the form of the champion and to seek her views about the forthcoming championships. There was quite a buzz from the reporters and press photographers gathered round court four as we came out to practise under the large clock on the towering wall of the

Centre Court, with its leafy covering of Virginia creeper. Most of them surrounded Helen but one or two asked me a few questions and took some photographs. I had on a brand new pair of cream flannels and had taken care to see that my shoes were clean and white.

When it was time to go home I drove down towards Southfields station to buy the three London evening papers, the *News*, the *Evening Standard* and *The Star*, as I usually did to be sure to catch all the news of tennis and the other sports in which I was interested. The paper-seller was a regular, a man I had known for some time because in the days before I owned a motor bike I have used the station coming home from Queen's to my brother's house in Elborough Street, off Replingham Road, where I had been living for some years. As I approached him he said: 'Mr Maskell, there's a picture of you on the back page of the *Standard*.' Sure enough, there I was in play against Helen, stretching for a forehand and with my tongue out. Alongside the main story of Helen's interview was a small piece about Maskell's first day at Wimbledon.

That first week passed in a dream. I had two more hits with Helen Wills and also the first of many sessions with Jean Borotra. I played, too, with the British men, Nigel Sharpe and John Olliff, with whom I had hit on several occasions at Queen's Club, and enjoyed a work-out with Dorothy Round, the first of so many.

In no time the Championships were upon us and I saw at first hand what a fine team had been assembled to run them. The referee was F. R. Burrow, a man who, I was told, could complete *The Times* crossword regularly within half an hour. He was a warm-hearted man of about fifty, who never wasted a word. He had a donnish air, possibly because of the half-glasses he always wore. He would either tilt his head forwards and peer at you from over the top of them or raise his head and examine you through them. Mr Burrow had the confidence of the players because he was immensely experienced in the art of completing a tournament on time. Assisting him as a liaison officer with the players was Teddy Tinling, who had spent much of his young life on the Riviera as the assistant referee to George Simond and as the umpire for most of Suzanne Lenglen's matches. I had met Teddy on my two trips to the South of France and he has been a close friend ever since.

It was the custom (and still is) to allow the players who had been scheduled to play on the Centre or number one courts practice-time on the outside courts before the start of play at 2.00pm. I was available for anyone who needed a practice partner and it was fascinating for me to meet and hit against Henri Cochet, whose locker was next to mine, Cilly Aussem, the great German champion, and Lili de Alvarez of Spain. I was also available to the British players, of course, and was pleased to help Colin Gregory, Ian Collins and Gwen Sterry among others.

Gwen was a lovely person with a keen sense of humour. During one practice session shortly before the Championships a ball that I had taken on the rise and hit with an open racket shot through rather low and beat her for pace. 'Where's Colman?' demanded Gwen. 'That was a terrible bounce.' I felt bound to chide her gently by saying, 'Really, Miss Sterry, you must have noticed that my approach shot carried rather a lot of backspin, that's why the ball kept low!'

During the afternoon I would be out round the outside courts watching the British Davis Cup and Wightman Cup players in action and any others with the potential to make those teams. I would also carefully watch the foreign star performers from the wooden garden seat beside the entrance to the Centre Court, to analyse their techniques and familiarize myself with their tactics. This was all part of my tennis education. It was this knowledge that I would be passing on to any of the British players who might be meeting them in tournaments or team matches. For variety I would also make a point of spending time in the competitors' box to hear the comments of the players themselves. They were wonderfully keen observers of one another's play – and frequently uncomplimentary!

I could not have been happier. Here I was at the age of twenty-one, attached to the finest tennis club in the world and doing a job that I loved. Although as I got into the coaching routine I was often on court six hours a day it did not feel like work and I thanked my lucky stars that I had been so fortunate.

Some of the young players I started to help would enjoy considerable success on the expanding world circuit, although in those amateur days all of them needed either to have a job that would allow them time to practise and compete, or the private means to support themselves. Betty Nuthall was already an accomplished player when I started to work with her. The family owned a hotel on Richmond Hill, near the Star and Garter home, that looked down on that famous bend of the Thames that I have always loved. I can never hear that old traditional song without thinking of Betty:

> 'This lass so neat, with smile so sweet,
> Has won my right good will,
> I'd crowns resign to call thee mine,
> Sweet lass of Richmond Hill.'

Betty and her brother Jimmy used to come across to Wimbledon regularly for practice sessions and on their journey through Richmond Park Betty used to love to get out of the car to feed the deer, something that is discouraged today. Jimmy won the British Junior Championships a few months after I arrived at Wimbledon. He was a fine striker of the ball who later became captain of the Cambridge University team but did not pursue a serious tennis career after that.

Betty certainly became the 'sweet lass' of British tennis when she won three consecutive Junior Championships from

1924–26, the first at the age of thirteen. She was the only girl to achieve this feat until Shelley Walpole repeated it between 1981 and 1983. Shelley is the daughter of Brian Walpole who runs the Concorde Division of British Airways, a man who has always taken a keen interest in the game ever since Shelley and her sister, Julie (now Mrs Michael Appleton), began to show promise as juniors. Brian is now a director of the company that runs the David Lloyd Slazenger Racquet Club, conveniently situated near London Airport at Heston. Shelley is one of the teaching professionals there.

Betty Nuthall, ever smiling and always cheerful, was the Christine Truman of her day. A well-built, rosy-cheeked extrovert, she became the heroine of every schoolgirl when in 1930 she won the singles and doubles (with Sarah Palfrey) at the US Championships, the first foreigner to capture the American title. There had been advance notice of her prowess in 1928 when, in partnership with that superb American doubles player, George Lott, she had won the American mixed doubles – a title they would recapture in 1931. The same year she won a second US ladies' doubles title with Mrs Fearnley Whittingstall, the former Eileen Bennett, who was one of the most beautiful women I ever saw and a natural stylist too. She was another with whom I played in the early days at Wimbledon. It always surprised me that Eileen never seemed to understand the necessity of having a bread-and-butter game. She refused to compromise and accordingly was always exciting to watch, either hitting a succession of improbable winners or, all too frequently I'm afraid, making too many unnecessary unforced errors.

Many more doubles titles fell to Betty Nuthall's eager racket in those exciting years, including the French doubles in 1931 and the French mixed doubles in 1931 and 1932. Betty would probably have had even more success if she had ever been able completely to overcome a certain service frailty that was often her undoing. Eventually she went to live in New York and ran a very successful travel agency there.

The girl who won the Junior Championships in my first year at Wimbledon was Peggy Scriven, a very determined match player from Yorkshire with a fine left-hander's forehand and a point-winning volley. In 1931, at the age of eighteen, she reached the quarter-finals at Wimbledon where Madame René Mathieu beat her 7–5 in the final set. Peggy had glorious revenge in Paris two years later when, unseeded and not even a member of the official British team in Paris, she beat the tough French lady to win the French title. Thus she became the first British girl to win the world's greatest clay court championship. Peggy retained the title the following year by beating Helen Jacobs in the final. This was no mean achievement; very few British girls ever beat this experienced American player who, like Elizabeth Ryan, specialized in a vicious, chopped forehand but lacked a basic drive on that wing.

I always think of Betty Nuthall and Peggy Scriven as the links between Kitty Godfree and Dorothy Round. In the 1920s Kitty had let the world know that British girls could really play this game; Dorothy Round, who won her two Wimbledon singles titles in 1934 and 1937 at the time of Fred Perry's triple successes there, confirmed the fact. It was these achievements, alongside the Davis Cup victories of 1933–36, that proclaimed Britain's place at the top of the world game. It was indeed the golden age of British tennis in the modern era.

Another of that generation was Kay Stammers who came from St Albans in Hertfordshire. I spent many hours on the court with her helping her to refine her technique. She was a left-hander of infinite resource who caused something of a sensation at the Beckenham tournament of 1935 when she inflicted upon Helen Wills, who had now become Mrs Moody, the first defeat she had suffered anywhere in the world for eleven years. Kay was twice the hard court champion of Great Britain and twice won the doubles at Wimbledon with Freda James, the talented Nottingham girl who helped Betty Nuthall to a third US doubles success in 1933. Kay, in the 1939 singles final, had the misfortune to meet Alice Marble, the number one seed and one of the greatest all-court women players I have ever seen, in inspired form. The American's net game that day was utterly brilliant.

Other girls who were on the periphery included Mary Hardwick, a fine all-court player from Surrey, whose brother, Derek, was a prominent junior and later became an important figure in the game's administration – first as LTA chairman and then as a member of the Men's International Tennis Council. Mary reached a number two ranking in 1937 after pushing Alice Marble to 9–11 and always threatened to break into the topmost reaches of the game without ever quite doing so. She later married the British Davis Cup player Charles Hare and they spent the war in America where Mary turned professional and played many exhibition matches with Alice Marble.

Mary Whitmarsh was a fine doubles player who won the girls' doubles in 1932 and 1933 and the mixed doubles in 1933 and then surprisingly got through to the last sixteen of the singles at Wimbledon in 1936 when she lost to Dorothy Round. Years later, in 1958, Mary (who had married businessman Peter Halford), was a successful Wightman Cup captain, a rare thing indeed.

Another of the younger players was Pat Brazier, the junior champion of 1930; she was one of my first pupils when I started at Wimbledon. Her father was the director of Brighton and Hove Albion FC whom I have mentioned as being interested in my brother John's football ability. Then there were Rosemary Thomas, Sheila Hewitt, Valerie Scott, Jean Saunders and Mary Heeley, all of whom were fine players but not destined to become champions.

During these years the man's game in Britain flourished as never before in the modern era. Led by Fred Perry and

Bunny Austin and admirably supported by men like Pat Hughes, the doubles expert, Raymond Tuckey and Harold Lee, Britain dominated the men's game for a few brief, wonderful years – though not as completely as the Frenchmen had done in the previous decade. I shall return to British Davis Cup exploits a little later.

Among the best boys of that period, just below Davis Cup level, were John Olliff, a gifted but unreliable shotmaker from London, Charles Hare, a left-hander from a keen tennis-playing family in Warwickshire, Frank Wilde, a Middlesex man who was always happier on a doubles court than playing singles, and Murray Deloford who, though born in Middlesex, played for Kent.

Olliff had won the national junior championship twice, in 1924 and 1925, and was successful in many open tournaments without ever capturing a major singles title. He had the natural talent to have been a much greater player than he eventually became, probably because he lacked the resolve, dedication and belief in himself to become a champion. After the war, in 1946, he did at last gain a Davis Cup place but, playing with Henry Billington, lost his doubles match against the French in Paris.

Hare developed into a fine match player. In 1936 he played with Frank Wilde, reaching the final of the doubles at Wimbledon. For the first time since 1921 this was an all-British affair which resulted in a win for the Davis Cup pair, Hughes and Tuckey, in five sets. A year later Hare had the honour of replacing Perry, who had turned professional the previous year, alongside Austin as the second singles player in the Challenge Round against the Americans at Wimbledon. He served and volleyed well in a fine opening set, too, against the young Donald Budge, whose improving form and majestic game had, I am sure, been an added factor in helping Perry to make up his mind to join the paid ranks. Budge won the match 15–13 6–1 6–2 to level the tie after Austin had beaten Frank Parker in straight sets but the

Americans won the three remaining rubbers to earn a 4–1 victory and bring to an end Britain's four-year run.

Wilde was part of that defeated team. He had come in to replace Hughes in doubles and held his place for the last two years before the outbreak of war. In 1928 Wilde had been overwhelmingly the best boy of his year, winning all three titles both in the Middlesex Junior Championships and the National Championships. Good as he was, there was some element missing from his personality to translate such promise into fulfilment.

Murray Deloford was another National Junior Champion. He won the title in 1933 and developed into a fine, thoughtful player. If the war had not come in 1939 Murray would assuredly have been ranked number one in Britain but there was no ranking list that year. He was one of the clearest thinkers about the game, and about life, that I have ever met. Apart from a fine backhand, his technique was not particularly good as a youngster, yet he moved so well and concentrated so well that he was very successful. I remember sending him a congratulatory telegram one year, it must have been about 1934, when he had just won his third tournament in a row. He phoned to thank me for the message and asked if he could come and see me the following Monday at Wimbledon.

We sat in the dressing-room and he said: 'Look, I know I've just won these three tournaments, but it was only because I was a clearer thinker and had a steadier nerve and perhaps was a bit fitter. My tennis was ruddy awful and I don't want to go on playing like that because I realize how limited I am. So I'm presenting you with a problem – what can I do about it?' This was the sort of opportunity that every coach dreams about. Here was an intelligent man who was ambitious enough to consider altering his strokes, and dedicated enough to work at them. This very rarely happens. I can think of Frank Parker taking a winter off to alter a forehand with the help of the great teacher, Mercer Beasley;

and Paul McNamee spent four months with Harry Hopman learning a double-handed backhand. There are plenty of examples of players who work to add a new shot to their repertoire only to find that in the heat of battle they are incapable of playing it. Christine Truman was a good example from the post-war years. On the practice court she reached the stage where she could hit a succession of beautifully lifted backhands but she never really had the confidence to use the shot consistently in a match.

As I write these words Nick Faldo has just won the British Open Golf championship. One could not have a finer example of the dedication and courage required to alter a stroke that you know is inadequate. Faldo's success proves that if you are aiming for the very topmost heights of a sport then you must eliminate a fundamental weakness.

Of course I accepted Murray's challenge and spent many hours helping him to reconstruct his forehand. So hard did he work that in a few months the new stroke had become grooved and he was transformed as a player. It is something that I would attempt only rarely, for you have to know your man. With most people the short-term disappointment of losing control of the ball would frustrate further effort. If only Adolf Hitler had never been born! It was no surprise to me that Murray spent a very distinguished war as a pilot and that he was awarded the DFC. I had already seen evidence of his bravery. After the war Murray became the first man to fly the South Atlantic for BOAC and remained with the airline for many years.

Three others who were robbed by the war of their best tennis years were Bob Mulliken, Headley Baxter and Bobby Nichol. Bob was a very studious player whose game was virtually free of unforced errors: he had a quite beautiful backhand. Headley was a thoughtful left-hander from Middlesex who got very nervous on the match court but was one of the best athletes playing the game. Later he came into post-war Davis Cup teams though he was unlucky enough never to play a match. However, he was a great team man and a great motivator, a fact that was recognized by the selectors when they appointed him Davis Cup captain in the 1960s. Bobby and his sister, Jean (later Mrs Bostock), were both extremely talented as juniors. I remember asking Bunny Austin one day in 1938 to come and look at this boy playing in the Junior Championships and I remember Bunny's reaction. 'What an attractive player. He strikes the ball so cleanly and effortlessly,' he said. It was the same with Jean. Although Bobby never had the inclination to make sacrifices for his tennis once the war was over, Jean did give more time to it. She eventually became a Wightman Cup player and was highly ranked for several years. Jean was one of several good players of the day who had been excellent table tennis players. Besides Fred Perry there was Vera Dace (later Mrs Thomas), Eric Filby and, after the war, Ann Jones.

Another, whose best years were lost to the armed conflict, was Don Butler. A small, wiry, cheerful, stalwart, Worcestershire County player, Don was one of those I came to know well in the late 1930s. He was quiet and thoughtful by nature and mindful of the great traditions of the game. Perhaps that is why, in the years after the war, he continued to play in long, cream flannels when shorts had become the standard dress for men.

Don's home was in Sunderland and his working life was spent with the En Tout Cas company for whom he was the North of England representative. An amateur, he travelled to many of the major summer tournaments and acquitted himself well with a game of great consistency that depended on a quick eye and extremely fast court coverage. A win over Germany's double Wimbledon finalist, Gottfried Von Cramm, at the Bristol tournament in 1939, was probably Don's finest achievement, although he did reach the last 16 at Wimbledon twice. He also achieved Davis Cup honours between 1938 and 1947, was an outstanding team man, and maintained standards of behaviour that were universally admired. Playing with Frank Wilde, Don contributed a doubles win in Britain's 3–2 win against Romania in 1938, but lost his two singles against Yugoslavia that year. After the war he helped Geoff Paish to a doubles win against Poland as Britain won 3–2 in Warsaw, a match I remember chiefly for the awful shortages in the Polish capital that, nevertheless, could not quell the cheerfulness and optimism of our hosts.

When Don died in 1987 at the age of 77 another link with Britain's golden years was lost.

It was an exhilarating experience working with all these fine young players and I was totally absorbed by my work. In fact occasionally my old professional colleagues at Queen's would say: 'Dan, you take life too seriously. Really you should come out with us and enjoy yourself.' I could reply with total honesty that I was completely happy with my life the way it was, even though with hindsight I can see that it was a somewhat narrow existence. However, in a totally unexpected way, my horizons were about to be broadened dramatically.

FOUR

The American Experience

Soon after I started work at Wimbledon I received an invitation from Eddie Rogers, the professional at the New York Tennis and Rackets Club on Park Avenue, to go over to compete in the fourth US Professional Championships in 1930 which would be played at the West Side Lawn Tennis Club in Forest Hills. The letter had been signed by Rogers and Walter Kinsella, the real tennis professional and sometime American champion who, at this time, was on the committee of the American Professionals' Association. I had come to know Eddie when he had been in Britain for the rackets and real tennis championships at Queen's Club and had found him a most genial companion. He had said then that I really must go over for their pro championships, as I would really enjoy them. At the time I had not thought too much about it, so when the letter eventually arrived it came as something of a surprise. It also placed me in a slightly difficult position. No one feels too comfortable asking their employers for time off so soon after commencing a job. Yet, if I could do well, I thought, the experience would be of the greatest value in my coaching duties.

I approached Major Larcombe with some trepidation. I need not have worried. As in all our dealings he was extremely understanding, fatherly almost. 'Now are you sure of the conditions? There's nothing here about payment or expenses,' he pointed out. With some shock I realized he was right. 'Well, Eddie Rogers assured me they would send me a ticket for one of the liners and take care of me while I was there,' I explained. 'Ah yes. I'm sure he meant what he said but you must get something in writing,' he advised. 'Anyway, I'll put it to the committee and let you know what they say.'

In due course I heard from Major Larcombe that my request had been granted. However, as he explained, there were two conditions. 'I have been asked by the committee to say that you must not treat this as a precedent for any future requests and I must also ask you to be away for no more than five weeks,' he said. In fact the trip lasted for five weeks and three days and I always wondered if there was a committee debate about those three extra days!

I left from Liverpool on the SS *Cedric*, a twenty-six-thousand-ton White Star liner which was scheduled to make the Atlantic Crossing in five and a half days. However, when we eventually arrived off the American coast, we encountered a thick fog which delayed our arrival by twenty-four hours. That was a most frustrating experience, pacing the deck impatiently and gazing hopelessly at the impenetrable grey blanket while the ship's hooter sent out its mournful, sick-cow bellow every half minute. Eventually the fog lifted and I was told that the land we could see close by was Ellis Island, that historic piece of American soil that had meant freedom and opportunity for so many immigrants to the United States over the years. Then in the distance I saw for the first time the magnificent Manhattan skyline, skyscrapers pointing like the fingers of a giant hand towards the sky. Suddenly I felt a thrill of anticipation at what lay ahead.

The voyage had been an uneventful and somewhat frustrating experience because there was nowhere for me to practise, no convenient bulkhead with sufficient runback for me to use it as a practice wall. In the two weeks prior to the US Professional Championships I was due to play a series of twelve exhibition matches in the New York area with Karel Kozeluh, the Czech professional whom I had worked under in the south of France, Vincent Richards, the former US

Davis Cup player and doubles champion at Wimbledon and Forest Hills, and Charlie Wood, a professional teacher like myself who later became the chairman of the American Professionals' Association. Accordingly I tried to keep as fit as possible by running round the deck and joining in all the deck games which offered any sort of exercise. I had four of my Slazenger tennis rackets with me for the trip, two of them strung and two frames plus some hanks of gut. However, all I could do with the racket was to bounce a ball rapidly up and down on the deck to give my playing arm some sort of exercise. These were the days before ocean liners provided gymnasiums or health studios as they do today. One of my fellow passengers was Gerry Barnes, the rackets professional at Haileybury who was on a business trip for his company, Sams Brothers and Barnes, who made rackets for all the racket sports. While in America he was asked by the British amateur rackets players, who were on tour there, to practise with them. His companionship certainly helped to shorten the voyage.

Eddie Rogers was at the quayside to meet me. It was Labour Day, a public holiday in the United States that falls on the first Monday in September and always marks the official end of summer. Somebody had obviously forgotten to tell the weather gods about the change of season for a very bright, hot sun was shining and it was very humid. Eddie helped me carry my luggage to his car and we were soon driving through deserted Manhattan streets, such a contrast to the raucous bustle which I later saw on a normal weekday. Somewhere in mid-town we slowed down and parked outside a corner shop whose windows were painted on the inside with dark green paint that prevented you from seeing in. Around the corner was a heavy wooden door in which there was a grille at about head height. Eddie knocked and in a few moments a flap in the grille opened. The face that appeared seemed satisfied with whatever Eddie had said and the door was quietly opened to allow our entry.

We were in a long, narrow room and down each side wall there were alcoves with tables that could seat about six. At the far end was a bar, complete with barman in white coat. On the rows of shelves were dozens of bottles of all shapes and sizes containing every sort of beverage you could possibly think of. They sparkled in the beams of the concealed spotlights that gave the room a slightly theatrical appearance. With a start I realized that we were in a 'speakeasy', the sort of establishment I had seen countless times in American movies of the prohibition period.

There were about a dozen men scattered among the alcoves, chatting quietly and enjoying a drink together in the subdued lighting. They all seemed unconcerned but I felt distinctly uncomfortable. It would not look too good, I thought, if the professional from the All England Club, a guest of the American Professionals' Association, was arrested for breaking the prohibition laws within an hour of setting foot on American soil! Eddie could sense my unease and put his hand on my arm. 'Don't worry,' he said. 'I've been a member here for years and I've never known the place to be raided. Now what would you like to drink?' I was only partly reassured. There has to be a first time, I thought. 'I'll have an orangeade, please,' I replied. In those days I hardly ever touched alcohol as I was concerned to maintain my fitness. I'm happy to say that in later years I have come to appreciate the pleasures of the grape with gratitude! 'Orangeade!' said Eddie. 'They would not even know what that was here. You'd better have a sherry.'

I had almost finished my small glass of sherry and Eddie had consumed about half his double whiskey when the door opened. I looked up and saw to my horror that a policeman was entering. He was dressed in the familiar blue uniform of the New York police, complete with flat cap and bright silver badge, that I knew so well from my visits to the cinema. In silence the policeman walked slowly to the bar, swinging a truncheon in his left hand and resting his right hand on the

126

butt of the revolver that protruded from the holster on his hip. Without a word being said the barman poured what looked like a triple whiskey and slid the glass across the bar counter.

In my slightly light-headed state I thought I was dreaming. Any minute now, I thought, I shall be arrested. What would the movie hero do now, I wondered? Should I creep up behind the policeman and hit him over the head with a bottle so that we could all escape? Or perhaps Eddie and I should edge towards the door and try to make a run for it? No, that wouldn't work, I thought. They would have surrounded the building.

I watched, transfixed, as the policeman swallowed the contents of the glass in two large gulps and then swung round and headed straight for the door, which was opened and closed quickly and quietly as he departed. Not a word had been spoken and as I glanced round the other booths I realized that no one had taken any notice of the proceedings. 'What a strange country, Eddie,' I said. 'You can say that again,' he replied. 'Let's get ourselves moving to the races. It's time to make a little money.'

As we drove away I glanced back at the speakeasy and thought how curious it was that the outward appearance of the place gave the game away completely yet apparently the police had never raided it, and they even drank there themselves. Perhaps it was something to do with the protection racket, I thought. Little did I know that within a couple of days I would gain first-hand experience of the effects of protection in New York.

Belmont Park is a dirt track, as most of the racecourses in America are because they are cheaper and easier to maintain than grass. To someone who had witnessed three Epsom Derbys it seemed odd to see the horses kicking up the dirt as they galloped past; it did not provide the same atmosphere somehow as a beautiful green track. We sat about ten rows up in the crowded main stand and placed our bets in a most curious fashion. Down below stood the bookmakers and their representatives. If you indicated that you wanted to place a bet one of them would throw you a tennis ball that was slit so that you could place your betting slip and your money inside before throwing it back. If you were lucky enough to win you had to go down to collect your winnings. It was an ingenious way of saving time and energy.

It was still blisteringly hot and in between the races we went down to get a drink from behind the stand where there was a large grassed area milling with people. This time I did get my orangeade! The jockeys and their wives or girlfriends mingled happily with the spectators in a friendly and informal way. Eddie seemed to know some of them as well as many of the racegoers. Then it was time to return to our seats for the next race. It was a thoroughly pleasant and relaxing afternoon though, to be honest, I would much rather have been out on a practice court finding my land legs. The chief consolation, though, was that I left Belmont Park five dollars richer than when we had arrived – a spot of good fortune due entirely to Eddie's knowledge of the local scene. He had organized the betting for both of us. Our modest success helped to enliven our dinner together at a small diner near Eddie's apartment where I would be living during my stay in New York.

The next morning, on our way to the drugstore for breakfast, at Eddie's suggestion I left a bundle of washing at the local Chinese laundry and was told it would be ready later in the day. Later that morning at his club, the celebrated New York Tennis and Rackets Club on Park Avenue, Eddie introduced me to a member of the US professionals' committee who informed me that it was most unlikely that all twelve of the proposed exhibition matches would take place due to the difficulty of finding the necessary finance. These were the days of the Great Depression, a time when millionaires became paupers overnight as banks crashed and the stock market plummeted. The full horror of the situation was

Above left My father (centre), who much preferred cycling to riding in motor cars, with Harry Barker (right), the owner of The Pear Tree, where my family moved to from Everington Street.

Above right My older brother Bill, whose first love was cricket but who, like the rest of us, was a good all-round sportsman. He also used to pay annual visits to the French Championships and was a keen spectator at Wimbledon.

On my Matchless 350 during a week's tour to Devon and Dartmoor with Fred Poulson.

The boys and girls of Everington Street School gathered together on Empire Day.

The horse-drawn Fulham Fire Brigade, which I remember seeing dashing along the Fulham Palace Road.

Queen's Club staff during the 1920s, shortly before I joined. In the front row, from the fourth left are, Charles Heirons, Vice-Admiral Sykes, E. B. Noel, Charles Read, Jack Jenkins and Joe Richardson. Behind Vice-Admiral Sykes is Mr Platt, the steward, and behind him is Mr Symes, the head dressing room attendant. In the second row, sitting immediately behind Charles Heirons, is Peter Latham. Standing in the second row, second from the right, is Toby Chambers. Joel Barnett is second from the left in the back row. Immediately below Barnett is Charles Cutts and the ballboy with his right hand on the pavilion rail is Cyril Asling.

The great US Davis Cup team of 1925, winners of the Challenge Round 5-0 against France, from left to right: 'Big' Bill Tilden; Norris Williams, who survived the Titanic disaster in which his father died; Vincent Richards; and 'Little' Bill Johnston. By an extraordinary coincidence, another Williams, Charlie, the great rackets professional at Queen's Club, was a passenger who survived the sinking as well.

Above left Helen Wills (left), then twenty, and world champion Suzanne Lenglen played their celebrated match in March 1926, which Suzanne won 6–3 8–6. This was the only time these two great players met.

Above right Lawn Tennis Championships at Wimbledon; semi-finals 1930. W. Tilden (US) in his match against J. Borotra (France), which he won 0-6, 6-4, 6-0, 7-5.

The destructive backhand volley of the phenomenal Frenchman, Jean Barotra, the man from whom I learnt as much about tennis as anyone. He put the same amount of zest and enthusiasm into his practice sessions with me as most men put into a match.

The umpire of my match at Southport against Bill Tilden, which I won in five sets to become only the second Englishman to beat the great American. Eric Peters had beaten Tilden in a tournament in the South of France.

Three of the talented professional tournament players whose early decision to become teachers of the game meant that, like me, they never had an amateur competitive career. From left to right, Robert Ramillon from Cannes, Hans Nusslein of German fame, and the charming Frenchman Martin Ploa.

Above left With the ever-popular left-hander Kay Stammers, who was the runner-up to Alice Marble in the 1939 Wimbledon final and a player whom I coached from her junior days.

Above right Murray Deloford, the 1933 British junior champion, whose tournament career was cut short by the war in which he served with distinction as a pilot and gained the DFC.

Above left The British Wightman Cup player, Betty Nuthall, the first overseas woman to win the US Championships, with Charles Hare and myself.

Above right Jack Crawford (left) of Australia with his favourite flat-topped racket, and the title-holder, six-foot four-inch Californian Ellsworth Vines, before their epic five-set 1933 Wimbledon final, which the Australian won.

On the eve of the 1933 Challenge Round against France in Paris, the team relaxes after a day of golf at St Cloud. The boys look understandably happy having beaten the Americans 4–1 in the Inter-Zone final. From left to right: Bunny Austin, Pat Hughes, myself, Harry Lee, Fred Perry, accompanied by the popular secretary of the LTA, H. Anthony Sabelli.

After a very rough crossing, during which I nearly lost overboard the tray on which the Davis Cup stands, the Cup and the luggage arrived safely in the customs' shed for inspection at Dover. Major Dudley Larcombe (second from right), the secretary of the All England Club, examines the names on the trophy.

Back on familiar ground at the wooden indoor courts at Queen's Club and hitting my favourite shot during Davis Cup training in the 1930s. In those pre-war days only Bunny Austin broke free from the long white flannels that we all wore.

At Eastbourne preparing for the 1937 Challenge Round with a newly constructed team. From left to right: Tom Whittaker (Arsenal FC trainer); Raymond Tuckey; Frank Wilde; Herbert Roper Barrett (non-playing captain); Bunny Austin; Charles Hare; and myself, the only time as coach I can remember being included in an official team photograph.

vividly brought home to me one morning when, strolling through the city with Eddie near Times Square, we actually witnessed a man throwing himself out of a high office building. There was a large crowd of onlookers as he fell to his death on the sidewalk. Some screamed and others looked away. I was left feeling rather sick.

The slump had taken its toll of some of the sponsors and of the clubs too. There was no threat to the Professional Championships themselves which would take place following the conclusion of the US Championships which had just passed the halfway stage. Two of the exhibition matches would definitely take place, I was told. The first would be played in a few days' time at Ripps Hard Courts, a public facility situated on Third Avenue beneath New York's famous Elevated Railway which ran on stilts the length of Manhattan. The second was scheduled for a small private club just outside the city. I was to play a best-of-three-sets single against Charlie Wood, then Vincent Richards would play Karel Kozeluh. The final doubles match would be billed as 'Europe versus America' – Maskell and Kozeluh v. Richards and Wood.

As we came out of the Tennis and Rackets Club on our way to Forest Hills, where the Professional Association had made arrangements for me to practise, I was introduced to Tony Bertollati, one of the young real tennis and rackets professionals who worked under Eddie. He was of Italian descent and a first generation settler. It was arranged that Tony would drive me out to Forest Hills the following morning. Meanwhile Eddie and I proceeded through the dense traffic across the Triborough Bridge which links the three New York boroughs of Queens, Manhattan and the Bronx, heading for Forest Hills. I have always thought it most appropriate that the famous West Side Tennis Club, that became the symbol of American tennis might for so many years, should have been situated in Queens in view of all that my old club in London had contributed to the development of the game from its earliest years. After the move from the Newport Casino where the first US Championships were held in 1881, the West Side Club became the home of the US Championships from 1915 to 1977, except for the three years 1921–23 when they were transferred to the Germantown Cricket Club in Philadelphia while the stadium was being constructed at Forest Hills.

On our arrival I went to meet George Agutter, the legendary and highly respected professional who had been there for years after emigrating from Birmingham. George, who I'm sure said that he had at one time been a professional at Queen's Club (though I've never been able to verify this) was delighted to meet another English professional. He wished me well for the forthcoming championships and I left him to change for my practice session. The secretary took me upstairs to the locker-room where the attendant was asked to clear a locker for me. Here we go again, I thought. Will he be as reluctant as Ellis had been at Wimbledon? He showed no surprise at being asked to supply a locker for a professional – but I did when I saw him removing bottles of gin and bourbon whiskey. When I looked through the ventilation holes at the other lockers in the vicinity I was amazed to see that they all contained bottles of booze. Obviously the members of the West Side Club had no intention of allowing the prohibition laws to interfere with their social drinking habits.

After enjoying a couple of hours of practice with a young American professional on one of the grass courts that had been allocated to us, I watched some of the players warming up for the US Championships that were due to start the following Saturday. These were players who were not competing in the National Doubles at Boston that week. I was glad to see that they were having the same difficulty with the courts that I had just experienced. I had always heard that the American turf was spongier and less reliable than ours. Even so I was surprised at just how erratic the bounce was and understood at once why it was that all the competitors served and volleyed. Trying to play from the baseline was a hazardous business. One ball would come through normally, the next might shoot through low and the third would probably pop up to shoulder height.

On the way home that evening we decided to stop at the Chinese laundry to pick up my clothes. Eddie assured me that they would still be open at 7.00pm. Imagine my feelings when we turned the corner and saw a gaping hole where the laundry should have been! It looked as if a bomb had hit it – and, as Eddie explained, that is probably exactly what had happened. 'They probably refused to pay their protection money,' he said. 'But what about my laundry?' I asked. 'You can kiss that goodbye,' laughed Eddie. 'Don't worry, we can soon pick up some new clothes in the morning if you are short. Just thank your lucky stars you weren't inside when the bomb went off!'

I was beginning to understand just how precarious life was in New York in 1930. That impression was heightened dramatically a few days later. Eddie and I had just crossed a road in the centre of Manhattan when suddenly he pushed me off my feet into the gutter and landed on top of me. At the same instant a volley of shots rang out from a car that was cruising past on the far side of the road. Answering shots rang out from another car passing in the opposite direction just near us. We had got ourselves involved in a fight between two local gangs, probably a Mafia quarrel, Eddie explained later. If I had not actually heard the whine of bullets and the zinging noise as they ricocheted off the buildings I would have thought we were witnessing the making of a Hollywood gangster movie on location. It had all happened so fast that I did not have time to feel nervous. A couple of moments later, when I realized that it was all real and that we both might have been shot, I began to shake all over. Yes, life in New York in 1930 was even more dangerous than I had thought!

As arranged, Tony Bertollati collected me the next morning and we set out on the journey to the borough of Queens and Forest Hills. Again I was struck by the hustle and bustle of New York, people scurrying along the pavements clutching sandwich boxes – whether they contained a late breakfast or provisions for lunch, I don't know – and all looking as if they were late for an urgent appointment. It was at once exhilarating and exhausting to feel the throb of this mighty city, a feeling that anything could be achieved mixed with the knowledge that I could only stand the pace for a short while. Our route took us past the construction site of the Empire State Building which seemed to occupy a whole block. The gangs of workmen were swarming all over the steel framework which at this stage had reached the fifth floor. When it was completed the building would, I knew, become the tallest in the world with 102 floors. It still amazes me that five weeks later, when I was leaving New York for home, the construction had reached the tenth floor: a floor a week! For such a vast structure that seemed to me to be astonishing progress.

We drove on across the East River and into Queens. Soon after we had passed the large cemetery my foot struck against a weighty object that had slid forward from under my seat. Looking down I saw what looked like a piece of metal piping.

'Tony, you seem to have left an old pipe in the car under my seat,' I said.

'Don't touch that, it's filled with lead,' he replied. 'We might need it.'

'Whatever for?' I asked.

'In case we're stopped.'

'By the police, you mean? Surely not!'

'Good heavens, no. By the hooligans.'

Nothing much has changed in the last fifty years, has it? We tend to believe that muggings and gang disputes and violence are modern phenomena. But the New York of the Depression years was every bit as violent.

Many years later, it must have been in the mid-1970s, I was woken one morning at my home in Wimbledon by the insistent ring of the telephone. It was just after 7.00am. My wife Con woke too. 'Whoever can be phoning us at this hour?' she asked.

'It's Tony Bertollati,' I replied.

'You didn't tell me he was over here,' she said.

'I don't know whether he is in England or not,' I said. 'For all I know he is in America or Italy . . . or anywhere. All I *do* know – and don't ask me how or why – is that Tony Bertollati is at the other end of that telephone.'

'You'd better hurry up and answer it or he'll think we're away,' said Con.

I lifted the receiver.

'Hello?'

A voice said, 'Hello, Dan? Is that you?'

'That's Tony Bertollati,' I replied. 'This is the most extraordinary thing, Tony. Before I picked up the phone I just knew it was you. How are you?'

I had not seen or made contact with Tony Bertollati for more than thirty-five years; not since that first visit to America. He told me that he was speaking from London Airport en route to see his ageing parents in Italy. He said that his eyesight was failing rapidly and he had felt the need to see his mother and father for perhaps the last time. He explained that his working life had been spent at the Chicago Tennis and Rackets Club where he had become friendly with Charles Hare and his wife Mary (the former Mary Hardwick) who had been living in Chicago since the war.

'Why ever didn't you let me know you were coming?' I asked. 'We would have been delighted to see you. You could have stayed here with us. In fact why don't you stop over for a few days on your way back?'

'Dan, I would have loved to see you – but I'm going straight home from Paris. Thanks anyway.'

'Have you taken the best advice about your eyes?' I asked.

'You'll need to be able to see well enough to take aim at the hooligans with your lead pipe!'

He laughed. 'Fancy you remembering that,' he said. 'I've still got it. You never know when you might need it.'

He never did need it. Tony Bertollati died at his home in Chicago on 3 April 1983.

I spent two more days practising out at Forest Hills before the start of the US Championships there on Saturday, 6 September. In those days the tournament lasted only seven days and finished the following Saturday, 13 September, for there was not yet any play on Sunday. I did pay a number of visits to the championships but it was not the huge sporting occasion that it is today. There were only 10,600 spectators for the final day's play so that the giant bowl of the stadium was never completely full. On some days there were as few as 5,000 in the ground which meant that the atmosphere was rather subdued. There was the added problem for the players of having two matches played side by side in the stadium. No one liked it; it was too distracting. There were constant discussions among the players about how to have the scheduling changed. Actually there was room for three courts if the middle one used the tramlines of the outer two. This is what they used to do. For the semi-finals and final of the singles they moved on to the unworn grass in the centre. Thus the bounce changed again and the players had to accustom themselves to a new set of conditions.

This was the year that marked the end of Bill Tilden's dominance. Two months earlier he had returned to a hero's welcome in America after winning his third Wimbledon title nine years after his last success, a record that still stands. However, he was having some trouble with an ankle and lost his US title in a memorable semi-final battle against Johnny Doeg. The ultimate winner of that year's championship, Doeg was a tall, fair-haired Californian from San Diego who played left-handed and had a marvellous pedigree for the game. His mother was Violet Sutton, the sister of May

Sutton, who had been the first overseas player to win at Wimbledon in 1905. May, who had been born in Plymouth, later became Mrs Bundy and had a daughter, Dorothy, who was herself an outstanding player.

I was intrigued to watch Tilden's match against Doeg, in which the twenty-one-year-old reversed the result of the same round the previous year by winning 10–8 6–3 3–6 12–10. Tilden was now thirty-seven and certainly seemed less assured than of old. He did not look likely to add to his seven US singles titles, a tally he shared with Richard Sears, the first ever winner in 1881, and Bill Larned, the champion at the turn of the century. The match was played on the centre of the three courts where the grass was still green and lush. Accordingly both players wore spikes, a practice that was common in those days. Although Doeg was a worthy winner on the day there was no doubt in my mind that Tilden was still a better player than the young Californian and would probably have won if he had been able to move more freely.

Earlier, I had watched Tilden beating George Lyttleton Rogers, the tallest man in the field at six feet seven inches. I had good cause to remember this eccentric Irishman for, several years earlier in Beaulieu, I had given him a practice knock on the Bristol Hotel courts and he had left me to pay for his lunch which he had enjoyed at the hotel. I was therefore not altogether dismayed when Tilden thrashed him 6–4 6–1 6–2!

This championship was a turning point in other ways too. It was very much a triumph of youth over the old guard. Five of the quarter-finalists were under twenty, including the beaten finalist, nineteen-year-old Frank Shields, the number eleven seed, and six were under twenty-five. Besides Tilden, the other great American hero, Frank Hunter, who had been a singles finalist the two previous years, had lost to Doeg in the quarter-finals and Jean Borotra, the top-seeded foreigner, had suffered a shock defeat in his opening match against Berkeley Bell. In those days there were twelve foreign seeds and twelve seeded Americans. As title-holder, Tilden was the top home seed.

I remember the fuss caused by the extraordinary scheduling on finals day. Instead of opening the programme with the men's singles the officials put on the Centre Court, as first match, the final of the veterans' singles between Henry Bassford and 'Pop' Gill. Inevitably these two became engaged in a protracted struggle that was hardly the spectacle that most of the spectators had come to watch. There were angry calls of 'Take them off' from many of the 10,000 fans who wanted to see Doeg playing Shields. At 3.30 the old boys were still level at 11–11 in the final set and there was a very real prospect that there would be insufficient time to finish a long, five-set men's singles in daylight – and there were not yet any floodlights. In desperation the veterans' match was finally removed to another court for completion and the singles final eventually started at about 3.45pm. The extraordinary thing is that the USTA today are still making the same mistake, by scheduling a match prior to the singles final!

I do not remember a great deal about the final itself except that Doeg served particularly well. He was broken only once in the match and imposed his serve-and-volley game successfully against an opponent who, although he possessed a fine service himself, seemed happier at the back of the court. On such an erratic surface these were unwise tactics for Shields' passing shots were never consistent enough to beat as good a volleyer as Doeg. Nor did Shields lob enough – as he needed to do to prevent Doeg from hanging his nose over the net. The final took two and a half hours and was won by Doeg 10–8 1–6 6–4 16–14.

In those years the women's singles and doubles were held at Forest Hills two weeks before the men's singles there. During the intervening week at the Longwood Cricket Club in Boston were held the men's and mixed doubles events. The 6–4 6–1 win of Betty Nuthall over Anna Harper in the women's final had been as shattering to the Americans as May Sutton's success at Wimbledon in 1905 had been to the British. By becoming the first foreigner to take the title, Betty secured for herself a unique place in the game's history and also brought great reflected glory to all British players who competed in America after that. It is one of my great regrets that I had not arrived in America in time to see Betty triumph, for I always had the greatest regard for her skill and for her positive attitude.

During that week I spent most of the time out on Long Island at the home of one of the local professionals who had been engaged to coach at the nearby home of Mr John Hay Whitney, the future American ambassador to Britain. I had been invited to visit the Whitney house to use their grass courts for practice. We had a marvellous time there, practising hard and relaxing afterwards. It was one of those magnificent American mansions with a large, covered swimming-pool and beautiful grounds composed of sweeping lawns and a profusion of flowers, all neatly kept in a succession of colourful beds.

I was standing on the edge of the pool one day preparing to dive in when a very British voice said: 'That's not you, Dan, is it?' The voice belonged to one of the English polo players who were about to play a match at the Westchester Country Club, a man I had known during my Queen's Club days who was also a keen amateur tennis player. He was kind enough to offer me a couple of tickets for the forthcoming match, an offer which I readily accepted. The match itself I do not remember much about but the occasion made a lasting impression. In lovely surroundings of grassy slopes and leafy shade from the many mature trees that were scattered throughout the site, the two teams thundered across the open pitch, spurred on by the shouts of encouragement from at least 20,000 throats. The elegant attire of the glittering onlookers, as well as the timeless beauty of the setting, conjured up images of a Scott Fitzgerald world. I would hardly have been surprised if Gatsby had driven up in a large open roadster and invited us all to join him afterwards for champagne in the large, white marquee that sat comfortably on the well-manicured grass beside the fine, old, mock-Tudor clubhouse. It was hard to relate this isolated and gracious world to gang warfare, bombed out Chinese laundries and lengths of lead piping . . .

At last it was time to play the first of our exhibitions. There was a small public changing-room at Ripps Courts beneath the 'El' (Elevated Railway) and I dressed early for my match against Charlie Wood which was to be the *hors d'œuvre* to the main course – Vincent Richards v. Karel Kozeluh. After the singles we would play a doubles, Europe v. The United States, Kozeluh and Maskell v. Richards and Wood.

This was the first time that I had a chance to get to know Vinnie Richards properly. I had first seen him in 1923 when, at the age of twenty, he had come to Queen's as Tilden's *protégé*. Ever since he had won the American Boys' Championship in 1917 at the age of fourteen he had been hailed as the boy wonder of American tennis. That year he first came to England I remember so well. At that time I was the bookboy at Queen's and was summoned to Mr Noel's office. He looked at me and smiled.

'Young man, Vincent Richards will be coming to the club this afternoon,' he said. 'Now, whatever other duties you've got I want you to make sure you meet him at the gate and bring him in to the club house. You should carry his bag for him and see that he has everything he needs.' There was a pause. Then he asked, 'You'll recognize him?'

'I think so,' I replied. 'I've seen several photographs of him.'

'Good. You shouldn't have any difficulty because he'll almost certainly be wearing a straw hat . . . a corrugated straw brimmed hat.'

I did recognize Richards the moment he came into view

walking down Palliser Road from Baron's Court District Line railway station, a youthful figure wearing the familiar straw boater and carrying a tennis case. I introduced myself and delivered him to Mr Noel's office as instructed. Seeded number one, Richards duly won the London grass court tournament that year. In the final he had an easy 6–2 6–2 win over Anglo-Indian S.M. Jacob, who had upset the seedings by beating the second favourite, Frank Hunter, in a three-set semi-final. The men's doubles that year was played on a round-robin formula, with groups of six pairs playing one another. Hunter and Richards won that event easily with the loss of only one set.

Incidentally, I remember that Elizabeth Ryan won the ladies' singles from Mrs Beamish that year, and then added the doubles (played in the same format as the men's) for good measure in partnership with Mrs Lambert Chambers – who was now a sprightly fifty-one years of age.

But to return to 1930, and our exhibition matches at Ripps Courts. When I had gone out to play Charlie Wood, in my innocence I had left my bag in the changing-room. It contained two of my precious Slazenger rackets, my brother's expensive camera which I had borrowed so that I could take back some pictures to help share my great adventure with the family, and some tennis clothing. Of course, when I returned to the dressing-room after completing my 6–4 6–4 victory over Wood, the rackets and the camera were gone. I felt an acute sense of shock. It was small consolation that the thieves had left behind my spare pair of flannels, a sleeveless sweater and a singlet. With a great sense of frustration I went out before the still thin crowd to play the doubles: perhaps that was what caused me to play like a madman. Much to our own surprise, we beat Vinnie and Charlie in two comparatively easy sets.

We played only one more exhibition match, at a club on Long Island. It was not a memorable occasion in any way:

the Depression had bitten deep and there was a very real sense of gloom throughout clubland USA.

The day of the Professional Championships arrived at last. It was Tuesday, 16 September, and still sunny and very humid. For reasons that were never made clear, the tournament occupied only five days instead of the usual six so that all players in the fifty-four strong draw who did not have byes had to play two rounds on the opening day. Perhaps the cost of hiring the club was such that the pro association could only afford five days. Goodness knows what we would have done if it had rained!

Although I was the number two overseas seed behind Roman Najuch (as with the amateurs, there were two lists of seeds, one domestic and one foreign) I did not have a bye. I was lucky to play two moderate Americans on the first day, Michael Dolan and Murray Dolman, whom I beat without losing a set. I was getting used to the bad bounces by now and realized how hard it would be to play consistently from the baseline. Accordingly from now on I resolved to stake everything on a net attack.

In round three I faced the number eight seed, Ed Faulkener, a tall Californian who was to become a great 'senior' player in his later years. We had a great scrap which I won 6–2 6–1 6–8 10–8, to earn a place in the quarter finals. Although it was a long match by the standards of the day – lasting about two-and-a-half hours – I felt full of running at the end even though we did not sit down during the change-overs. No one did: there were no chairs!

On Thursday I had to play the official fourth favourite, Howard Kinsey. I had seen him at Wimbledon four years earlier where he had lost to Borotra in the singles final but had also been the runner-up in the doubles with Vincent Richards and in the mixed with Mary K. Brown. Howard was well known for being flamboyant. He was certainly an extrovert, as his extravagant gestures and frequent loud asides when I beat him with a pass or a lob demonstrated.

He was also a tricky opponent because he hit high, looping shots from the baseline, heavy with topspin, rather like Björn Borg did in a later age, but without the pace or weight of shot of the Swede. Tilden had always found Howard's game difficult to counter in their many battles. I could see why.

I won the first set 6–3 and led 5–2 and 0–40 on his serve in the second, long since soaked to the skin in the sweltering heat. Looking back, this was the moment when the match turned. Instead of finishing off the set and racing into the third, I allowed Kinsey to catch up as his touch improved. Although I held serve to lead 6–5 and then broke to take a two sets to love lead, the effort had drained my legs of precious energy and strength. A little voice within was saying 'Let's wait for the ten minutes' rest at the end of the third.' I was already thinking of the shower and the feel of clean, dry clothes. What I should have done was to make a big effort to finish the match in three sets. Instead I allowed Kinsey to win the third set rather easily, 6–2.

As we gathered our things and left the court for the break I was surprised to see Kinsey head off towards the clubhouse a hundred and fifty yards away. I had brought a bag and a change of clothes with me up to the stadium where I knew there was a small changing-room with a shower. I had showered and dressed within eight minutes and was back on court two minutes later. There was no sign of Kinsey. After a further two minutes the umpire began to ask his linesmen if any of them knew where Kinsey was. The centre service linesman was Stephen Wallis Merrihew, always known as 'Pops', who was the publisher and editor of *American Lawn Tennis*, a magnificent monthly publication that had two issues in July, August and September so that there were fifteen issues a year. After judging whether the serve had been a fault there was no other duty to perform during a rally so he used to sit with a notebook on his knee recording the salient points of a match.

'Pops' was getting quite upset with Kinsey's disregard for

the rules. 'It's disgraceful,' he said, 'to keep our English visitor here waiting like this. He really should not be allowed to get away with it.' By the time Kinsey did finally return, a full twenty minutes had passed. Although I was indignant within, I tried not to show it. It was surely up to the umpire to take any action that was necessary, not me. The fourth set, like the second, went to twelve games and, although I led 4–1 by breaking his service early, I lost my own service twice as I began to tire. In the final set my legs felt like jelly, the first time I had ever experienced anything like that. It was also the first time that I had ever played in such humid conditions and made me realize just how fit one needed to be to sustain an effort over five hard sets at this level. I could offer only token resistance as the set slipped away 6–1 and with it the match, 3–6 5–7 6–2 7–5 6–1. Altogether it was a wonderful lesson which would help me to understand the problems of our Davis Cup players in the years to come.

Unfortunately I missed out on the prize-money which began only at the semi-final stage. Nor was there any consolation in the doubles where only the finalists were rewarded. Playing with Charlie Wood I could do little to prevent Kozeluh and Najuch from winning our semi-final 6–4 7–5 6–0. Thus, after all that effort, I had no dollars to show for it, but I was immensely richer in experience. Nor, of course, had Johnny Doeg benefited by more than a few dollars paid in the form of a voucher for winning the US Championship one week earlier. I cannot help smiling at the huge rewards open to today's leading players!

The tournament was won, somewhat surprisingly, by Vinnie Richards, who reversed the result of the previous year by beating Kozeluh 2–6 10–8 6–3 6–4 in a final watched by about 4,000 spectators. That was quite a respectable gallery for the professional game in those years for there was so little public exposure for it. Richards also won the doubles; partnering Kinsey he was the brains behind their 6–2 15–13 7–5 win over Kozeluh and Najuch.

So ended a memorable first visit to the United States, a country I have always loved because of the great generosity and open-heartedness of her people and for the great tennis traditions they have established. What a pity it is that the present site of the US Open, which I visit each year for BBC Television, is such an uncongenial place to play championship tennis. It is noisy, loud and physically uncomfortable, in fact a veritable concrete jungle, totally lacking the charm of the West Side Tennis Club at Forest Hills which, admittedly, had become too crowded long before the last meeting was held there in 1977.

The countless great American champions it has been my privilege to come to know as friends over so many years have contributed enormously to our sport. In those pre-war days two great achievements stand out in my mind. First, Don Budge's remarkable feat of winning all four major championships in 1938. Allison Danzig, writing in the *New York Times*, compared this to a bridge player completing a grand slam, and it was a great landmark for tennis: here was power play at its finest. Then Alice Marble's peerless performance at Wimbledon in 1939, when she won all three events and proved that the serve-and-volley game could be performed equally as effectively by women as by men (something that the chauvinistic males of the day had always doubted!), was another evolutionary moment.

So at last it was time to take up the reins again at Wimbledon and to tackle the job of contributing to the development of British tennis. Thanks to my American experience I returned with a sharper perspective and a deeper understanding of what it takes to become a champion. I could not wait to put my new ideas into practice.

FIVE

Davis Cup Days

As well as coaching the leading juniors, I used to practise with some of the established players as they prepared for tournaments and cup matches. These included men like Charles Kingsley and Nigel Sharpe (who beat Henri Cochet so surprisingly in the first round of Wimbledon in 1931, when the Frenchman was the number two seed); Ian Collins and the man with whom he had reached the doubles final at Wimbledon in 1929, Dr Colin Gregory, a future chairman of the All England Club.

The two bright young men of the day were Bunny Austin and Fred Perry. Bunny was two years older than me and was enjoying three very successful years at Cambridge University where he was the outstanding player. He had a beautifully controlled baseline game and always seemed to know exactly what he wanted in the way of practice. Before I knew him, of course, Bunny had already raised hopes that we would at last see another British champion at Wimbledon. He had reached the fourth round at his first attempt in 1928, two months before his twentieth birthday, resisting for five heroic sets against the eventual champion, René Lacoste of France. Expectation was heightened the following year when Bunny reached the semi-finals unseeded and pressed Lacoste's fellow countryman, Jean Borotra, to four sets.

If that national yearning has a familiar ring about it today, I can assure you that in the late 1920s it was every bit as real. People seem obsessed with the fact that Britain had not produced a men's champion since Arthur Gore, who had won three times – in 1901, 1908 and 1909. At the time of that last win Gore had been forty-one, the oldest winner at Wimbledon, a record that still stands. There were plenty of people still living who remembered seeing the Australian left-hander, Norman Brookes, take the title overseas for the very first time in 1907. They were depressed, though, that we had not been able to prevent a succession of five overseas players from dominating the Championships, from Tony Wilding before World War One to Gerald Patterson, Bill Tilden and the French Musketeers – Borotra, Lacoste, Cochet and Brugnon – after it.

Fred was three years younger than Bunny and only one year younger than me so that when I started to work with him in 1930 we were contemporaries. We had an immediate rapport; from the first, too, I could see that Fred was very single-minded. He had already won the World Table Tennis Championships twice and was therefore a match player of considerable experience. He seemed to know exactly where he was going. In a sense he was not typically British, for there was an aggressiveness and dedication about him that was out of step with the contemporary amateur attitude towards sport. The fact that he came from a working-class background was a priceless advantage, though he would probably not have been able to see it as such at the time. However, it was the social chip that he wore quite prominently on his shoulder that made him doubly determined to show the establishment that he could beat them. And beat them he did.

Fred's father, Sam, was a Labour MP, a self-made man who was a prominent figure in his own right. Although he represented the constituency of Kettering, Northants, the family still lived in Ealing on the Brentham estate. I remember his father coming down to Wimbledon one day quite soon after my move there to watch the end of one of our practice days. At the time I'd played Fred only three or four times, following his debut at Wimbledon in 1929 when he had lost in the third round in four sets to John Olliff. Like all parents, Mr Perry wanted to know if his son was going to be any good. After we had had our usual work-out of about two hours I had a chat with his father while Fred was taking a shower.

'What about this young man of mine?' he asked. 'He seems determined to take this game seriously – do you think I should give him a year?'

I was glad to be able to tell him with total honesty: 'All I can tell you, Mr Perry, is that Fred is the most promising player I've ever seen. He seems to have exactly the right attitude to the game and is prepared to do whatever it takes to succeed.'

'Do you know "Pop" Summers of Slazengers? He seems to think quite highly of him.'

'Indeed I do, and Pop has already told me the same thing. I would have thought that Fred is worth every possible encouragement,' I said.

Pop Summers, the tournament director for Slazengers, was a well-respected figure in the game who knew everyone who mattered and understood the problems a young player faced in trying to break through to the top. He had spotted Fred early and had supplied him with the company's rackets from an early stage. Pop was to play a key role in Fred's development, as the father figure in the background who helped him to plan his itinerary and could always be relied upon for a wise and honest opinion when any dificult decision had to be made. I remember once going over to his house in Harrow for a confidential discussion when Fred seemed temporarily to have lost his enthusiasm for the game.

'You're absolutely right,' said Pop, 'he's over-tennised at the moment. I'm going to suggest to him that he pulls out of next week's tournament and takes a break right away from the game. I'm sure that will restore his enthusiasm.' Of course it did. The important thing about this relationship was that Fred trusted Pop and respected his judgement. Not that they always agreed – Fred's personality was much too dominating for that! But they usually saw eye-to-eye on the important issues.

Fred did not suffer fools gladly. He simply would not listen to anyone whose opinion he did not respect. Over the years he and I developed a wonderful relationship, each respecting the other's point of view and each trusting the other's tennis judgement.

These were fascinating years as Bunny and Fred developed a healthy rivalry at the top of the British game. At the 1930 Championships Bunny was seeded for the first time, at number six. This was incentive enough for the unseeded Perry to show the committee that they had erred in not according him the same recognition. In those days, remember, the seeding was not based on any computer rankings as it is today. Both the original acceptances and the seedings were done by committee. Inevitably there were disagreements about their decisions.

As it happened both players reached the last sixteen. Bunny lost unexpectedly in straight sets to an American, Greg Mangin, while Fred was beaten 6–1 in the fifth set by Colin Gregory. The title that year fell to the remarkable American, Bill Tilden, who was thirty-seven years old and had won the first of his three titles ten years earlier.

It was most instructive for me, in my second year at Wimbledon, to see again at close quarters one of the game's legends. I little thought then that in later years we would be playing against one another in professional tournaments when the great man had left the amateur ranks.

I had been most impressed by Tilden's dominating presence the previous year when he had played as a guest for the International Club of Great Britain in the first match against the newly-formed French IC on the indoor wooden courts at Queen's Club in November. The match was played on the famous old east court. In the top rubber Tilden faced Jean

Borotra, five years his junior and one of the greatest wood-court players the game has ever seen. Of course, I had left Queen's earlier that year but returned for this match which had received a great build-up in the papers. There was an unmistakable sense of occasion that day. All my old colleagues were busily occupied making sure that the court was properly swept and that the large crowd of members was marshalled efficiently. For some reason there was no temporary stand on the adjacent west court so the gallery was absolutely packed. Members and their friends stood and sat at every conceivable vantage point – I had never seen it so crowded. One row of spectators sat along the edge of the side gallery with their legs hanging over the edge, another stood shoulder to shoulder behind them, while yet another stood on the actual seats. The place was so crowded that one of the club professionals went down on court and roared out in stentorian tones a request that spectators should not smoke.

It certainly was a great match, played mostly from the back of the court, believe it or not. Borotra, the arch-apostle of the serve-and-volley game (especially on wood) had so much trouble with Tilden's return of serve early on that he was simply forced to stay back. To me the surprising thing was how well Borotra hit his ground shots, choosing the moment when he could take the ball really early, well out in front of him, for one of those characteristic charges towards the net.

Here were two dominating personalities, each casting his influence over the proceedings, so that the atmosphere was as highly charged as I can ever remember round a tennis court. The great Tilden, standing six feet four inches tall, seized every opportunity to exploit the theatrical nature of the occasion with gestures and asides that the many spectators relished; and Borotra, the long-time favourite of the Queen's Club crowds, bounded around the court to pull off spectacular lunging volleys and leaping smashes – all with a warm smile and a modest shrug of the shoulders that endeared him to everyone. It was all wonderful entertainment and the result itself hardly seemed to matter. In fact Borotra did win eventually, in two long sets, 10–8 9–7, after Tilden had served for both sets. The way Borotra wiped out Tilden's 4–1 lead in the second set was masterly, as indeed was so much of the play from both men. The real winner that day, though, was the game itself, and those like me who had been fortunate enough to be there and to witness the fine sportsmanship of both men.

Wallis Myers, the lawn tennis correspondent of *The Daily Telegraph*, had founded the British International Club in 1924. Over the years I got to know him very well. Wallis had been a fair player himself, competing in many of the regular tournaments which abounded throughout Europe in the years before and after World War One. He was also a great traditionalist and an idealist who felt keenly that the young warriors of all nations who battled so bravely on the courts should have a vehicle through which they could get to know one another better socially while continuing those friendly rivalries. I believe it was following a conversation with the former Prime Minister, Lord Balfour, that Wallis had hit upon the idea of forming the International Club. It was an idea of its time and an ideal that thrived. Today there are twenty-five International Clubs around the world whose members proudly wear the grey ties, each with a different combination and width of pink stripes. Imagine my pride and pleasure when, at the celebration dinner to mark the hundredth match between the British and French clubs, I was presented with the French tie. After dinner I went across to Jean and told him how proud I was to think that henceforth I would be able to wear the two pink stripes that I had seen around the necks of all the famous French players over the past fifty years.

'Dan, I blame myself,' replied the remarkable eighty-seven-year-old who, incredibly, had played in every one of those one hundred matches. Putting his arm round my shoulders he continued: 'We should have done this long ago, after your friendly association with us in those Davis Cup matches at Roland Garros, to thank you for your kindness to me and indeed all the French players as we have come each year to Wimbledon.'

How wonderful, I thought, as I watched Jean playing his match the next day (a special mini-game he had invented, using only half the width of the court) that the same competitive spirit still burned as brightly in that spare and sinewy frame as it had done all those years ago against Tilden.

Bill had not returned to defend his Wimbledon title in 1931, a year when both British men were seeded, Fred at five and Bunny at six. This time it was Fred who reached the semi-finals where he lost in four sets to nineteen-year-old Sidney Wood. The wonder-boy of American tennis had first played at the Championships in 1927 at the age of fifteen and had acquitted himself well against Lacoste on the Centre Court. At the Queen's tournament that year I remember hitting with him for an hour or so one morning on the grass at Queen's. He wore those distinctive knickerbockers with long white socks and he hit the ball beautifully for such a slight figure. His backhand was a dream. In 1931 Wood became the only player to win the Wimbledon title by default when his fellow American, Frank Shields, seeded three, having eliminated Bunny in the fourth round, twisted his ankle badly in the process of beating Borotra in the semi-final. Frank very much wanted to play the final but withdrew on the instructions of his Davis Cup captain, Sam Hardy, who was more concerned with the forthcoming inter-zone final against us in Paris, in which both Shields and Wood would take part, than in the Wimbledon title. After all, one of his men was going to win it. I have always thought that one of the cruellest decisions anyone ever had to make.

These were great days for British tennis and it was

wonderful for me to be involved. There was a rising tide of optimism as our leading men and women continued to improve – a feeling that at any moment we would make the breakthrough. It almost happened in 1932 when Austin, seeded six, surged through to the singles final while Perry, seeded four, fell to Jack Crawford of Australia at the quarter-final stage. Although Austin was soundly beaten by the thunderbolt serves and forehands of American Ellsworth Vines, there was universal rejoicing that for the first time in twenty years we had seen an Englishman in the final.

There was equal pleasure that year in seeing Britain supplying half of the survivors in the quarter finals of the ladies' singles. Three of them were seeded – Eileen Fearnley Whittingstall (four), Betty Nuthall (six) and Dorothy Round (eight). The fourth, Mary Heeley, was unseeded but upset Mrs Fearnley Whittingstall to earn a match against the favourite, Helen Wills, who duly despatched her in two easy sets. So passed another year.

During the winter of 1932–33 there was a new determination about Fred. We had a particularly good Davis Cup draw for 1933 with the key ties in the European Zone due to be played at home. Having reached the Challenge Round in 1931 and lost only narrowly to France in Paris, everyone had been disappointed at the 2–3 loss the following year to Germany in the fourth round in Berlin. On the slow clay courts Fred had been unable to break down the defensive wall built by the wily German number one, Daniel Prenn, who had beaten him 7–5 in the fifth set of the deciding rubber.

The sessions of hard practice were intensified. Fred was a stubborn and sometimes truculent character who believed totally in his own ability and was not afraid to speak out in criticism of anything with which he disagreed. He knew exactly where he was going and had the guts, the character and the vision to achieve his ambitions. These characteristics earned him, somewhat unfairly, the reputation of being arrogant; but also earned him universal respect.

Fred's attempts to develop an early-ball technique along the lines of Cochet and Borotra were derided by his critics as being too risky. But he knew that if he could ever perfect a running forehand with the ball taken on the rise his athletic physique and superior fitness would enable him to overcome most opponents.

Fred never saw his sliced backhand as a weakness. It was basically a table-tennis shot, a block with very little backswing, that he played soon after the bounce with an open-faced racket. Without risk, therefore, he could manoeuvre an opponent about the court until the moment came when he could run round his backhand to sweep the running forehand deep into a corner to set up his winning shot. Of course, opponents did see the backhand as a weakness. The volleyers, especially, tried to exploit it. But they did not have an easy time because Fred had perfected his touch and control of trajectory. Day after day we would practise his backhand down the line. I would thread the handle of a racket through the top of the net about six inches in from the sideline. As I came in behind a deep approach shot in the middle of a long rally Fred would take the ball early with that blocking action and aim for the racket-head that projected above the net. Eventually he could hit it almost at will.

Next Fred set about perfecting the short, crosscourt, angled pass using the same open-face, sliced, blocking action. That was an essential part of his armoury, to keep his opponents guessing. At this stage he certainly did not feel the need to develop a lifted or topped backhand. If he had ever felt unable to win his matches without such a shot I'm sure he could and would have perfected one. Many years later, when we toured Britain together with 'Focus on Tennis', organized by the Central Council of Physical Recreation, where we gave demonstrations to groups of young players, Fred used to hit perfectly-executed flat or lifted drives. However, the whole emphasis of his preparation with me at this stage was to make a world-class shot of the blocked backhand.

When we played sets Fred would experiment to discover just how early he could take the ball on his forehand side. Eventually, with his continental grip, where the palm of the hand is more towards the top of the handle (unlike the conventional eastern forehand grip where the palm is behind the handle) he was able to sweep the ball early, Cochet-like, to any part of the court so that his opponents never had time to get set for their shots. Because Fred had such a strong wrist he could also use the continental grip to deal effectively with the high bouncing ball, which had always been another of Cochet's great strengths. Few continental-grip players ever managed to drive that high shot consistently with control. Even good men like Eric Filby and Ronnie Shayes of Britain preferred to hit a drive-slice with an open-faced racket.

In those days, control was generally deemed to be more important than sheer pace. The softer ball we used then with its all-wool cover was easier to control than today's harder and less sympathetic nylon-armoured product. Also the wooden rackets in general use did not project the ball as fast as the metal, graphite and fibreglass models of today. Even the power players of the day – men like Vines and Stoefen – were unable to hit the ball hard consistently for long periods. Accordingly it was an altogether more subtle game in those days with strategy, court craft and tactical awareness at a premium.

In these respects Perry became a master. Long years of match play on a variety of surfaces had taught him just what was possible and what was not. He became a shrewd tactician. He also knew the value of total fitness. He was a non-drinker and non-smoker with a penchant for sucking at a pipe which in those days was largely a cosmetic exercise.

Equally important, he realized, was the image of fitness that would intimidate an opponent at 5–5 in the final set of an important match. So he organized regular sessions of physical training at the Arsenal Football Club in Highbury under the guidance of the trainer, Tom Whittaker. I accompanied him on a couple of occasions and could see how much he benefited. These sessions inevitably received considerable publicity as well as providing variety and mental stimulus; they also hardened his naturally athletic frame, with its God-given slim hips and broad shoulders, into an instrument of sporting destruction. By the time the 1933 season dawned no tennis player in the world was fitter than Frederick J. Perry.

Someone else who realized the tremendous potential that Perry possessed was Trevor Wignall, the sports feature writer of the *Daily Express*. His regular thousand-word column 'Daily Sportslight' was one of the best read features in Fleet Street.

One day in 1932 Trevor telephoned me to say that he was arranging a lunch party at the RAC in Pall Mall for myself, Fred Perry and the young golfer, Henry Cotton, whom Fred and I knew quite well. It was not easy to find a day when we could all be there but eventually the date was fixed. At the appointed hour we met for a light lunch beside the indoor swimming-pool at the RAC, still not knowing why we had been invited. When we saw another old friend, Jack Izod, with Trevor, we wondered if, perhaps, some clothing deal was going to be proposed. We knew that Jack's company had the Royal Warrant for supplying sports shirts to the Prince of Wales and the Duke of York. Fred and I had also helped Jack by testing some of his new tennis shirts that we both enjoyed wearing.

The conversation during a simple and pleasant enough lunch gave no clue about the purpose of our visit. Eventually we could contain ourselves no longer. 'Come on, Trevor, what's it all about?' we chorused. 'Why are we all here?'

'Well, I'll tell you,' he said. 'For my column next Saturday

I am proposing to write a piece about the three of you. Henry, you are going to win the Open Championship within a couple of years and Fred, you will win the singles at Wimbledon within the same time-scale.' Sitting there hearing these improbable forecasts I wondered what on earth I was being expected to achieve. Turning to me with a smile Trevor said '. . . and you, Dan, will coach a winning Davis Cup team for Britain – also within two or three years.' Trevor stopped talking and looked at the three of us. 'Well, what do you think of my judgement, boys?'

It was staggering that he should be prepared to put his professional reputation on the line with three such ambitious forecasts. One would have been enough. To link the three events together seemed outrageously optimistic. Perhaps he was joking?

'No,' he said. 'I'm perfectly serious. Although it will seem I'm sticking my neck out, that's what I'm paid to do in Fleet Street and anyway I know you three will give my money a good run.'

How right he was. The very next year I was sent overseas for the first time with the Davis Cup team and we did win the Challenge Round against the French in Paris. In 1934, on the middle Saturday of Wimbledon, Henry duly won his first Open Championship at Sandwich. Six days later Fred made a prophet out of Trevor by winning the first of his three consecutive singles titles at Wimbledon. I shall always think that Trevor's shrewdness that day was one of the cleverest pieces of sporting journalism I have ever come across.

During the Davis Cup campaign Bunny Austin was the perfect complement to Perry. While Fred could hustle the enemy and rush them into error, Bunny would drive them to despair with his relentless accuracy and imperturbable concentration. I did not see much of Bunny during the winter months. He would play the autumn covered court events and then, after a break for Christmas, go off to the early tournaments on the Riviera, returning sometime in March for practice prior to the start of the British season.

Apart from his service, Bunny was a lovely stylist who relied on perfect timing so that he could use his opponent's speed of shot to create his pace. He never appeared to hit the ball very hard; indeed he would have benefited from hitting a harder, faster ball. His success was built upon control and accuracy. In practice it was a joy to play against him, for his beautiful rhythm seemed to brush off on you so that you felt that you were hitting the ball particularly well yourself. What Bunny lacked was variety and a big service. I used to think 'If only he could add a heavy, sliced backhand or an occasional chopped forehand or even the odd whipped topspin pass . . .' but his was a 'pure' style of play.

Bunny played mostly from the baseline, largely because few opponents could dislodge him from that territory. He could volley when necessary as long as the shot did not need to be too acrobatic – and it seldom did, because he would only advance to the net on his terms and the accuracy of his approach shots usually produced a volleyable reply.

In the highest company Bunny's serve was a weakness. Just as Ken Rosewall's relatively weak delivery was ruthlessly exposed in the 1974 Wimbledon final by the blazing returns of Jimmy Connors, so Bunny's serve was murdered by his two final round opponents: Vines in 1932 and Don Budge in 1938. I remember a remark of Bill Tilden's as we sat together in the stand one day watching one of Bunny's matches. 'You know, Dan,' he said, 'a player is only as good as his second serve.' It was a basic truth that I've never forgotten.

No Davis Cup team can achieve ultimate success without there being a strong team spirit binding the members together in a common purpose that transcends personal rivalries. The French 'Musketeers' had certainly proved the truth of that during their six winning years between 1927 and 1932. Borotra, Lacoste, Cochet and Brugnon displayed the same selfless allegiance to the tricolour, the same attitude of

'One for all and all for one' that Alexander Dumas' famous heroes had immortalized.

The British teams of the 1930s had the same devotion to a cause that welded them into a powerful force. We were fortunate that alongside Perry and Austin there were men of the calibre of Pat Hughes, the doubles expert who was also a master of strategy and tactics, Harry Lee, the singles reserve who was sometimes pressed into doubles duty, and, later, another doubles player, Raymond Tuckey. They were all world-class performers who did not perhaps enjoy the same consistent success as Perry and Austin but who were perfectly capable of creating upsets over seeded players. After all Hughes, who was particularly good on clay, had beaten Cochet to win the second international Italian Championship in 1931 and reached the final again the following year. He had also been in the 1932 Wimbledon doubles final with Perry and would win the title four years later with Tuckey against Hare and Wilde, the first all-British final since 1906. Furthermore Hughes and Perry had just won the doubles together in Paris. It was also the perceptive Hughes who correctly forecast that topspin would come more and more into use to defeat the volleyer.

The man who must take the credit for moulding four such different characters into a cohesive unit was the captain from 1924 onwards, Herbert Roper Barrett. He had been a member of the first British team in 1900, had twice been a singles finalist at Wimbledon, and three times he had won the doubles there – in 1909, 1912 and 1913. Thus his knowledge of the game was unquestioned and his quiet authority was immediately accepted by the players. However, Mr Roper Barrett's legal work – he was a solicitor to the Corporation of London – meant that he rarely had the time to attend our practice sessions. In 1934 he was also the chairman of the LTA which provided an additional workload. Accordingly we saw very little of our captain until the draw, which was always made on the day prior to the match.

When he was absent Pat Hughes, the eldest member of the team, more or less took command.

By the time Wimbledon came round in 1933 Britain had completed four good Davis Cup wins to reach the final of the European Zone. A 4–1 victory over Spain in Barcelona had been followed by a 5–0 win against Finland in London. Then had come two victories down at Devonshire Park, Eastbourne, always a favourite venue for British teams. We had beaten Italy 4–1 and then dismissed Czechoslovakia without losing a single rubber.

In the Zone final we had to play the Australians who, with Jack Crawford, Vivian McGrath, Adrian Quist and Don Turnbull, had a powerful team. However, after an easy 5–0 win against the Norwegians in Oslo, they had struggled to beat both South Africa and Japan. The first match between the two Dominions had been played at Queen's Club in mid-June and had been decided only in the last rubber when Crawford's greater experience had brought a decisive victory against Colin Robbins. The surprise of the tie had been the doubles win by Norman Farquharson and Vernon Kirby over Crawford and McGrath, who had not played much together.

A week later, on the slow clay in Paris, the Australians had been hard-pressed again by Japan. Although McGrath had beaten Jiro Satoh and Crawford, the new French champion, had accounted for young R. Nunoi on the opening day to lead 2–0, both matches had been desperately close, ending identically at 7–5 in the final set. Then Quist had come in to play doubles with Crawford against the same two opponents and had been taken to five sets again. Not surprisingly after such an exhausting two days both reverse singles were won by the Japanese. At this time Satoh was a highly efficient clay court player and had beaten Perry in the French Championships. He would also beat Austin at Wimbledon in a couple weeks time on his way to the semi-finals and would end the year ranked number three in the world. The Australians were therefore mighty relieved to have won.

Our tie against them was played at Wimbledon two weeks after the Championships, where Crawford had played the game of his life to beat the defending champion, Vines, in a five-set final that was as good as anything I had ever seen. This was the first Davis Cup tie to be played at the new ground and rain on the first day meant that the crowds were understandably small. Crawford's four-set win against Austin was not altogether surprising although Bunny did win the first set with some glorious driving while the champion was finding his range. Perry's reply was to take apart the fragile game of the seventeen-year-old McGrath. The young man was hustled and harried to death in straight sets so that the doubles rubber became all-important.

Mindful of their two previous struggles and the fact that Hughes and Perry had beaten Quist and McGrath in the recent French final, the Australians decided to bring in Turnbull to play with Quist. This would also leave both their singles players rested for the third day's matches. On an altogether brighter day, though with fewer spectators than we would have liked, Fred played a true leader's part in securing a British victory in four sets 7–5 6–4 3–6 6–3. It was not a classic match – like so many nervy Davis Cup matches there were too many errors for that. But after the close twelve-game first set, which turned on the capture of Turnbull's serve after he had been foot-faulted for the first time, the odds were always on a British victory.

The opening match on the Saturday, Austin versus McGrath, was better attended and Bunny did not disappoint our supporters. Recovering from 1–4 in the opening set and 2–4 in the second, the Englishman deployed his skilful and accurate groundstrokes superbly to blunt the attack of the eager young Australian. McGrath's double-handed back-hand at times produced some blazing winners but all too often it projected wild and mistimed losers. This 6–4 7–5 6–3 win was enough to put us into the Inter-Zone final against the Americans; Crawford's fifth match victory against Lee was small consolation to the losers.

Naturally I had been part of the preparation for all the home matches though it had never been customary at this stage to send a coach to overseas ties. By now we had built up a wonderful feeling of invincibility that was thoroughly infectious. The powerful American team, our Inter-Zone final opponents in Paris, held no real terrors for we had beaten the USA there 3–2 two years earlier. Although we did not minimize the task, we were already relishing the prospect of tackling France again in the Challenge Round for that year they had beaten us 3–2 on their favourite clay. (Although I did not know it at the time, it was after that defeat that the players had suggested we should have a coach for matches as important as an Inter-Zone final or a Challenge Round, even when they were played abroad.)

I was totally unprepared, therefore, when on the third day of the tie against Australia, Major Larcombe had found me to explain that the Davis Cup selectors wanted me to accompany the team to Paris. 'I imagine your passport is in order?' he asked. 'They want you to leave on Monday.'

I felt a tingle of panic run up and down my spine for I suddenly remembered that my passport *had* run out, just five weeks earlier. I had intended to do something about it but there had never seemed to be the time.

The secretary took the news calmly. 'We'll have to see what we can do about that,' he said. 'We may have to enlist the help of Sir Samuel Hoare.' Fortunately, the LTA President was at the club and agreed to write a letter to the French Ambassador who had been in the Royal Box during the Championships. Early the next morning, a Sunday, I found myself at his residence, being ushered into the entrance hall by the footman. In a few moments the Ambassador himself appeared, clad in a dressing-gown and clasping a long cigarette-holder in his hand. It was all rather like a scene from a Noël Coward play.

He brushed aside my apology for disturbing him. 'So you want to go to Paris with your Davis Cup team. Do you think you'll beat the Americans?' he asked.

'Well sir, it will be a mighty close call but the Americans are not so good on dirt,' I replied, using the vernacular of the game to describe European clay courts.

'Dirt?'

I was embarrassed to think that he might consider this an insult to the headquarters of French tennis. 'I beg your pardon, sir. Of course the courts at Roland Garros are clay,' I mumbled.

'And if you do beat the Americans – will you beat France?' he asked.

It was time for total honesty. 'I think we have more chance of beating the French than the Americans, sir,' I ventured.

He seemed amused. 'Do you indeed! Well, young man, naturally I hope you are wrong,' he said, smiling.

Within a few minutes the Ambassador had given me a personal letter of explanation to put into my passport which, I was told, I should renew as soon as possible after my return.

I caught the boat train and arrived in Paris on the Monday afternoon, too late for practice. I had been told to report to the Hotel Continental, near the Tuileries, and was somewhat surprised to discover that the team was staying at the Crillon, just down the road on the Place de la Concorde. How curious, I thought, that although I had now been accepted by the All England Club it appeared that the LTA still felt the need to preserve the social differences. It was interesting that the players themselves felt very embarrassed by the situation and, after the tie against the Americans, insisted that I be housed with the rest of the team at the Crillon.

Fred had not yet arrived. He had stayed behind in London to have treatment for a painful shoulder from Hugh Dempster, the osteopath based in Manchester Square in whom Fred had a lot of faith. It had been agreed that Fred would catch the Wednesday boat train and arrive in time for a late practice with me at Roland Garros. It was almost dusk when he hurried into the club, eager as ever to hit some tennis balls. The others had gone back to the hotel after a hard day's practice.

We went out on court and completed the usual warm-up routines. Then I fed some gentle lobs so that Fred could test his suspect shoulder. He swung carefully at the first few and then started to open up. It only took a few minutes to establish the fact that all was well. There was no pain as he belted the balls into the corners. Dempster had done his work well.

By the time we had showered it was dark and Fred, like me, was pretty hungry. 'It's too late now to get back to the Crillon,' he said. 'Let's find somewhere nearby.' That sounded like a good idea to me so we made for the Café Royale, the famous open air restaurant in the Bois de Boulogne. The orchestra was playing and the tables were crowded with diners. 'I have a feeling this might cost the LTA a pretty penny,' said Fred, as we walked in and stood waiting for the *maître d'hôtel* to show us to a table. While we stood there the orchestra abandoned the piece they were playing and started to play *God Save the King*. All heads turned in our direction and we felt a little conspicuous as the beaming *maître d'hôtel* came gliding across and said, 'Oh, Mr Perry, how nice to see you here again – and the best of luck against the Americans.' As we sat down the orchestra returned to its more familiar Viennese waltzes and we tried simply to enjoy the excellent dinner. The final surprise came when we tried to pay for our meal. All our protestations that we could not possibly accept such hospitality were brushed aside and we were bowed out feeling like royalty. It was certainly a marvellous tale to tell our incredulous team-mates when we caught up with them later.

The days before the Inter-Zone final passed in a routine of practice and meals, training and sleep. Whatever we had said publicly, we knew privately that the Americans would be very formidable opponents indeed. Their number one, Ellsworth Vines, the reigning US champion and the Wimbledon champion of 1932, had just lost his title there in a classic final against Jack Crawford, 6–4 in the fifth set. We all hoped he might suffer a slight let-down after that magnificent but unavailing fight. Also, of course, we knew he was not as effective on slow clay as on fast grass where his powerful forehand and cannonball service made him unplayable at times. Above all though he was a great fighter.

Wilmer Allison, the second singles player, was really a doubles specialist, though he had also earned some impressive singles scalps and had been runner-up to Tilden at Wimbledon in 1930. His partnership with Johnny Van Ryn was one of the finest the Americans had ever produced and the two had already won two Wimbledon and one US titles together and would win another in Boston in 1935. However it was expected that Van Ryn would play the doubles rubber with George Lott because these two had beaten Perry and Hughes in the Inter-Zone final in 1931 on the same court. This would also allow Allison to concentrate on the singles. So, even though Perry and Hughes had just won the French doubles title together, we were under no illusions about the size of our task.

My role was to give the boys whatever practice they required – either feeding them to groove a particular shot, or playing tactical sets against them in the manner of an opponent they were about to face. Occasionally if someone was off his game I would try to make some constructive suggestions. I was also a safety valve, a medium through which they could release pent-up nervous energy. I enjoyed having my leg pulled and entered into the spirit of friendly banter that the boys seemed to enjoy. As I got to know the idiosyncrasies of each individual I would try to anticipate their needs. That meant making sure that Fred always had his particular type of fizzy lemonade at the side of the court for his matches, while for Bunny I ensured a constant supply of cold tea.

Herbert Roper Barrett arrived as usual for the draw on the Wednesday. First out of the hat for the singles on Friday were Austin and Vines, a repeat of the 1932 Wimbledon final which the American had won so decisively. Vines' name also came out last for the third day's rubbers, a potential grandstand finish against Perry to decide the tie.

From the first day there were respectable crowds around the famous centre court which was only seven years old. It had been built to provide a fitting stage for the Musketeers and had been opened in time for the French Championships of 1926. The problem on that slow clay court, with its deep run-back behind each baseline and wide side runs, is to hit a winning shot. A determined runner can retrieve so many apparent winners that an inexperienced player can soon lose heart and become tentative – especially when playing against a Frenchman and being intimidated by the exuberant support of a demonstrative home crowd.

If we had written the script ourselves we could hardly have improved on Bunny's performance against Vines in the opening rubber. Playing faultlessly accurate clay court tennis he spun a web of touch and control that totally ensnared the powerful game of the American. In no time at all Austin was back in the dressing-room with the centre court scoreboard proclaiming an amazing 6–1 6–1 6–4 British win.

That was just the start we needed. Riding on a wave of British confidence, Fred swept through Allison in straight sets 6–1 7–5 6–4. That night there was a wonderful feeling of elation as the team dined together at the Crillon. But the elation turned to frustration the following day when, as we had feared they might, Lott and Van Ryn proved too versatile for Hughes and Perry and won the doubles rubber 8–6 6–4 6–1, despite a 5–2 lead for Britain in the opening set. This was worse than our 1931 performance. Then we had at least won one set.

The atmosphere that night was very different. Instead of already being in the Challenge Round here we were leading 2–1 with the Americans looking much more confident. The more I see of Davis Cup ties, the more convinced I am that the five-match format is the ideal test for any team. No result is possible on the first day so that a lead of 2–0, good as it looks at the time, can soon evaporate. Time and again I have seen teams with a 2–0 or 2–1 lead slip perilously close to defeat as the tension of a revival by their opponents inhibits their performance.

Fortunately, Bunny Austin was above such frailties as he tackled Allison in the first match on the third day. A crowd of about ten thousand saw the Englishman, neatly clad in his trend-setting shorts, carrying on from where he had left off against Vines. Finding the lines beautifully with his destructive passes he pocketed the first set 6–2. Stiffer American resistance earned Allison the second set 9–7 but it only postponed the inevitable as Austin, after two hours of immaculate play, swept to victory 6–3 6–4 to take Britain into the Challenge Round for the second time in three years.

However, the tie was not yet over. Perry and Vines still had a personal score to settle. Although this was a 'dead' rubber it was a match that neither wanted to lose. It was a blistering Paris afternoon; the concrete bowl of the centre court was like a Roman amphitheatre. As the sweating gladiators ran and skidded through the soft red dust, wielding tennis rackets instead of broadswords, their faces and clothing became smeared with the red streaks of battle. And what a battle it was! An Englishman and an American playing their hearts out for the sheer glory of representing their countries caught the imagination of the huge French crowd. With both men trying to force the pace on the unfriendly slow clay it became a battle of wills. With Vines leading two sets to one and 3–2 in the fourth the American fell awkwardly and twisted an ankle. He refused Perry's offer to delay the restart and, after taping the ankle, he continued – despite the fact that this was a meaningless rubber.

But Vines was weakening. In the intense heat he began to look haggard. Perry won the fourth set 7–5 and stood at 7–6 and 15–40 on Vines' serve: two match-points. Suddenly Vines collapsed. He simply crumpled up at the baseline. He had fainted. There was a stunned silence as he lay there, unable to rise. So the match ended in mid-air with the gallant American helped off and Perry the victor by default, leading 1–6 6–0 4–6 7–5 7–6 40–15 retired. It was an extraordinary end to an extraordinary match, where personal pride had driven both men to efforts beyond the call of duty. If only today's professionals could show the same commitment to dead rubbers!

The celebrations that night were muted for we were now due to face the French one week later. With the return of the captain to London Pat Hughes was left in charge of us in Paris. We had a free day on the Monday and some of the boys wanted to play a little golf – always a sure way of ensuring some fun and relaxation. I was asked to organize a visit to the beautiful course at St Cloud, about twelve kilometres from the centre of Paris, where I knew that Percy Boomer, one of the famous Boomer brothers, was the professional. He had written what was then considered one of the best instructional books on the game and I was anxious to meet him. Although in those days the courses used to be closed on a Monday to allow the greenkeeper to restore the greens and fairways after a busy weekend usage, Percy said he would be able to arrange a game – provided that we could assure him that there would be no pressmen following us.

Six of us made the short drive to the west of Paris, the four players plus myself and Anthony Sabelli, the secretary of the LTA, whom Roper Barrett always wanted to accompany us on Davis Cup trips to look after all the financial details.

In due course Bunny, Fred, Sabelli and I had obtained our sets of borrowed clubs. Harold Lee did not play golf at this time and Pat had decided to be a spectator. We all made our way to the first tee in the company of some very attractive young ladies who, it transpired, were to be our caddies – a French custom of which we all approved. While we had been in the clubhouse I had noticed Pat engaging in a private chat with Percy Boomer and saw that he now wore a slightly conspiratorial look.

It was agreed that Fred would tee off first and the chatter died down as he placed his ball on the tee and started to address it. Just before he started his swing the voice of Percy Boomer carried across to us from the clubhouse some thirty yards away. He sounded agitated. 'Fred, quickly, there's an urgent call from America . . . something about a film, I think they said.' Leaving his ball on the tee, Fred dropped his club and sprinted to the clubhouse. Such was his popularity that he was constantly getting offers to do films and magazine articles. As soon as he had disappeared inside Pat took from his pocket what looked like a normal golf ball. He explained that it was an advertising product made of celluloid. In no time he had substituted it for Fred's ball on the tee.

A few seconds later Fred came loping back, swearing at the inefficiency of the French telephone system. 'They're absolutely hopeless,' he complained. 'When I got there they'd cut me off. That's probably cost me several thousand dollars . . . I shall have to sue them,' he said, laughing.

'Come on, Fred, never mind your business deals, let's get on with the golf,' said Pat. Picking up a club, Fred took aim and vented all his frustration in a mighty swing. There was a strange, thin, cracking sound as the club head met the fake ball and shattered it into a thousand pieces. After recovering from his surprise, Fred enjoyed the joke with the rest of us. It was the perfect start to a day of blessed relaxation.

The captain arrived in time for the draw. Roper Barrett must have had mixed emotions for this eighth encounter between the two leading European nations. He had been on the winning side in the first which had been played in

Folkestone back in 1912 and he had been the captain in the narrow defeat in 1931, two years earlier, in Paris. This would be the sixth Challenge Round to be played in Paris and by now the French almost felt that the Davis Cup belonged to them.

The ceremony, conducted in a crowded reception room at the Hôtel de Ville, was an impressive experience. The two teams sat either side of the official party, which consisted of dignitaries from the two national associations and prominent political figures. In the centre, on a large table draped in the Tricolour and the Union Jack, stood the gleaming bowl of the Davis Cup itself, the magnificent solid silver trophy that had been presented by the American, Dwight Davis, back in 1900 for annual competition between the nations. It had been worth one thousand dollars when Davis had first presented it; goodness knows what it is worth today, I thought.

Already, after only thirty or so years, the Davis Cup had become one of the best known trophies in sport. When the ceremony was over and I stood close to it for the first time I was surprised to see just how big it was. I felt a thrill of anticipation as I looked at the famous names of the teams that were engraved on the silver collar round the plinth – Davis himself and Larned of the United States, British heroes Doherty and Gore, Brookes and Wilding from Australasia, the great Americans Tilden and Johnston, and the four famous French Musketeers – Borotra, Brugnon, Cochet and Lacoste, some of whom we would soon be facing. How wonderful it would be, I thought, if the next names to be added to that illustrious band could be British!

We were more than usually expectant as we sat and waited for the names to be drawn out of the cup, as a result of an extraordinary incident that had occurred out at Roland Garros the previous day.

We had just finished the morning practice session on the

centre court, a gruelling work-out in the mid-summer sun-shine that had confirmed our growing belief that we would acquit ourselves well, whatever the result. I had left the brightness of the court and plunged into the dark tunnel beneath the main stand that led to the staircase that emerged just outside the dressing-room. At the top of the stairs I ran into Jean Borotra as he bounded out of the dressing-room, rackets in hand. He seemed slightly crestfallen which was most unusual for him.

'Dan,' he said, 'we've just picked the team.'

'You and Henri for the singles?' I ventured.

'No, I'm not playing.'

'Not playing? That's extraordinary,' I said, although I was really not altogether surprised because Jean had lost both his singles against us in the 1931 Challenge Round. 'Surely, though, you are playing doubles?' I added.

'Well, yes. With Toto.'

'So I suppose Christian Boussus is the second singles player?'

'No – Merlin.'

'André Merlin?' I said incredulously. 'But he's never played a live singles before in the Davis Cup.'

'I know. I think they had the greatest difficulty in deciding between Boussus and Merlin, but that's the decision.'

He strode off, looking immaculate in his white flannels that were beautifully creased, even for practice. But there was a little less bounce in his step than usual, I thought.

I could hardly wait to break the news to the team. 'I've just seen Jean. He says they are going to play Merlin as second singles player,' I blurted out. There was general disbelief. Roper Barrett was quick to kill any speculation. 'Let's wait until the draw tomorrow,' he said. 'Then we'll know for certain who is playing. This could be a French plot to make us over-confident.'

Silence fell on the expectant assembly as the method of the draw was explained in French and English. The two captains each handed an envelope containing the names of the singles players to the secretary of the French Federation. He opened them carefully and removed the two single sheets of paper. Then he stepped forward.

'*Mesdames, messieurs*, here are the nominations of the two captains for singles. First our visitors. The players representing Great Britain will be Fred Perry and Bunny Austin.' He turned and smiled at Roper Barrett as he placed one piece of paper on the table. Looking at the remaining sheet he said, 'For the champion nation, France, the players will be Henri Cochet and . . .' there was a slight pause '. . . André Merlin.'

So it was true! The French *had* decided to blood their young champion against us. We had all hoped against hope that this would be the selection for we all knew what enormous pressures a player had to face in any Davis Cup tie, let alone a Challenge Round. The more experienced Christian Boussus, we felt, would have stood those pressures rather better than a newcomer, however talented. There was a buzz of discussion around the room. Even some of the usually imperturbable tennis writers had raised their eyebrows in surprise. Young Merlin himself, only nineteen years old, sat there unsmiling, looking outwardly calm. Inwardly he must have been feeling the same butterflies that we all felt as we waited to see how the combatants would be matched.

The moment had arrived. Two folded pieces of paper were dropped into the cup. A hand dipped beneath the rim of the sparkling trophy and emerged clutching a single piece of paper. As he unfolded it the secretary said, 'The opening match tomorrow will be between . . .' he held the opened papers aloft '. . . H W Austin and . . .' two more folded papers were dropped into the trophy, and one withdrawn, '. . . André Merlin.'

Perfect, we thought! Bunny would give us a 1–0 lead and that would help Fred against Henri.

'The second match, therefore, will be Perry against Cochet,' intoned the secretary. 'Now for the first match on the final day.' He refolded the four pieces of paper and replaced them in the cup. After swirling them round to mix them up he invited Pierre Gillou, the president of the French Federation, to draw a name. The bearded figure stepped forward and dipped a hand into the trophy. He handed a paper to the secretary who again carefully unfolded it. 'Cochet,' he announced. 'He, of course, will play Austin, with Perry and Merlin as the last match.'

Perfect again! If by some mischance we had not already won, then we had Fred there to polish off young Merlin for the victory that we all now expected.

The secretary was making his last announcement. 'As you all know, the two captains must hand to the referee the names of their doubles teams at least one hour before the start of play on Friday. Good luck to both teams!'

At practice that afternoon there was an unmistakable sense of elation in the British camp. We all believed we could win at last and revenge the painful defeat of two years before. Roper Barrett was careful to point out the dangers of over-confidence, but I don't think any of us underestimated the task, even with two probable rubbers from Merlin. Cochet, we knew, was still capable of winning both singles and, although Fred and Pat had won the French doubles title a few weeks earlier, we were fully aware of the difficulties of beating Borotra and Brugnon in a Davis Cup Challenge Round in front of their home crowd in Paris.

The weather remained sunny and very hot. The centre court felt hotter still as it always does because of the way the concrete stands reflect the heat. It was absolutely stifling, even watching. There were no cushioned seats in those days so we all sat on folded towels and had other towels draped over our heads. These conditions would test the physical strength of anyone who became embroiled in a long match. The atmosphere was electrifying, with the twelve thousand or so spectators crammed into every vantage point.

From the first Bunny played beautifully, gliding the ball to a perfect length and frustrating the attempts of a nervous Merlin to bring him to the net; he would read the drop shots and get there early enough to hit either a winning drop in reply or drive into an empty court. When Merlin tried to prolong the rallies Bunny refused to be lured into error and allowed the Frenchman to break down first. The only hint of danger came in the second set when Merlin, trailing 1–4, threw caution to the winds and came up repeatedly to bring off some Cochet-like volleying coups that levelled the score at 4–4. Here Bunny remained calm. The Frenchman's recovery proved to be a dying kick. Looking lost and tired, the young man crumpled to defeat 6–3 6–4 6–0 to give us exactly the psychological edge for which we had been hoping.

Against Cochet, Fred began poorly – perhaps suffering subconsciously from the memory of 1931 when, with the tie balanced at two rubbers apiece, he had led 4–1 in the opening set but had been thwarted by some typically adroit Cochet magic. The Frenchman had taken the next five games and had gone on to win the match in four sets.

Pressing too hard, serving far too many double faults and finding no answer to the Frenchman's sudden and surprising approaches to his forehand, Fred was soon 1–4 behind. Although he recovered the service break he was always playing uphill as the set was lost 8–10. Another quick lead seemed to presage an easy French win. However, Cochet suddenly seemed to lose concentration and lost some easy points. With a run of four games, the last to love, Fred levelled at set-all. Hope returned to the British supporters who had come over in considerable numbers and were cheering for all they were worth.

Again in the third set Fred was behind. Cochet's touch had returned as he moved to 5–3 with two love games. Saving a set-point, Fred started to play some dazzling tennis. In the twelfth game he held and lost two set-points. On the first he double-faulted and on the other Cochet played a great winner, to tumultuous applause. In the next game the

Frenchman missed the easiest of volleys and lost his serve. It was just the opportunity Perry needed. He reeled off a confident service game and went in for the break with a two sets to one lead.

Despite a 3–1 lead in the fourth set, some expensive errors, several on low forehands, together with a resurgent effort from Cochet, cost Fred the fourth set 6–3. But instead of a climactic finish, Cochet seemed to tire and he slumped listlessly to defeat 6–1 booed, even, by some of his supporters. There was great rejoicing in the British camp at Perry's superb performance; but it turned to consternation when Fred, up at last in the privacy of the dressing-room, without any warning suddenly passed out. I was despatched to guard the door with instructions that no one should be allowed to enter. Fred, meanwhile, had come to, but was unable to remember who had won! Roper Barrett swore everyone to secrecy.

I'm sure it was that collapse, together with the fact that Fred would have to play the decisive fifth rubber if, as we feared, Cochet were to beat Austin, that decided Roper Barrett to substitute Harold Lee for Fred in the doubles.

I was sent out to find Pat to break the news. He was not too pleased, to say the least. The same thing had happened in 1931 when he had played with Charles Kingsley. In the circumstances, though, I'm sure Roper Barrett was right. Although it was tempting to try to finish our opponents off cleanly by winning the doubles, it was bound to be a long match and Fred, fit as he was, would have the edge taken off his game for the final singles which might be decisive.

Then I went out for a practice session with Harry Lee. Although most of his best results had been scored in singles Harry was a respectably good doubles player. My role on these occasions was always to build the confidence of the player who would be fighting for his country the following day. The important thing at that moment for Harry, who was being thrown in somewhat unexpectedly, was first to have a good run around to loosen up generally and then to practise the specific doubles drills. As he would be playing in the forehand court Harry rehearsed his returns of serve from that side as I delivered a stream of mixed deliveries. Then he practised serving and volleying from each side in turn, trying always to hit the first volley firmly and deep to give him and his partner the command of the net. I mixed in plenty of lobs because we knew that the Frenchmen used the lob tactically to great effect. Pat, who had already had a good work-out in the morning, then joined us for a while to get into the right frame of mind for what lay ahead.

We could not have done more to prepare what was, after all, a scratch pairing for the ordeal ahead. But it was asking too much to expect a win. Borotra and Brugnon duly despatched Hughes and Lee 6–3 8–6 6–2, to cut our lead to 2–1. Then Cochet out-played Austin in the fifth set of a magnificent encounter. Although the score, 5–7 6–4 4–6 6–4 6–4, gives an indication of the closeness of the match, I always felt that Henri would eventually find a way of winning. He looked utterly determined that day. Neither man had the equipment to hit his opponent off the court so we were treated to a fascinating battle of cat-and-mouse, a tactical stalking exercise that provided some marvellous entertainment.

So, as we had thought it might, Fred's match against young Merlin would decide the issue. I think, without being complacent, that we all thought this would be a 'routine' affair. It seemed to be a matter of when and how; certainly there was no thought of 'if'. However, as I came to discover, the Davis Cup turns boys into men overnight and produces some of the most surprising results of any tennis year.

Merlin, a *protégé* of René Lacoste, had trained for this moment with Suzanne Lenglen at a secret venue in the country away from the public gaze. He covered the court with amazing speed, hitting superb passing shots and disguised lobs to take the first set 6–4. The confidence he showed was extraordinary for one competing in his first Davis Cup tie and the momentum carried him to a lead of 3–1 in the second set. Each time he won a point the applause was loud; as he converted points into games it was deafening.

It speaks well of Fred's iron concentration that he did not let all this bother him. Even when he had served two double faults to give the Frenchman a 5–4 lead he remained steadfast. However, if Merlin had converted either of the two setpoints he held on his serve in the next game for a two sets to love lead, the outcome might have been very different. On the first of them Fred's forehand down the line was dangerously close to the line. Merlin and a large section of the crowd thought it was out. In fact they were already applauding the capture of the set, but the linesman had not called. Amid the uproar the umpire turned to the linesman and questioned him. To his eternal credit, the official refused to be swayed by the now angry crowd. The curious thing is that even among the team there was disagreement as to whether the ball had been out or in. I thought the shot had clipped the line and so did Pat and Bunny, who had by now joined us, but Harry Lee and Sabelli were equally sure it had been out. As the crowd vented their feelings on the unfortunate linesman, Roper Barrett sat seemingly quite unconcerned in his chair while Fred sat on the head of his upturned racket in the centre of the baseline and allowed the storm to blow itself out.

When play finally resumed after a break of about four minutes it seemed that Merlin had been more affected than Fred by all the commotion. Two points later Fred saved a second set-point and then broke the Merlin serve for 5–5. The crisis was over. He broke once more for the set in the fourteenth game and we all breathed a huge sigh of relief. Matters had looked really nasty for a moment.

Even then, though, Fred was not out of the wood. Although the momentum carried him to a quick eight game third set and a welcome ten minutes break, there was more drama ahead in the fourth set.

Leading 4–1 and holding a point for a 5–1 lead, Perry made no attempt to play a ball from Merlin that had fallen clearly over the sideline; the linesman was unsighted and did not call. There was nothing in the rules in those days to allow the umpire to overrule a linesman and make the decision himself. Although he asked the linesman to reconsider his opinion that official still did not call so the obvious error had to stand. Although Fred made no complaint, the incident clearly upset his rhythm and confidence. Merlin crept back to 4–4 and 5–5.

Meanwhile the French team, believing the match to be as good as over, had gone off to change for the closing ceremony which was due to take place on the court as soon as the tie was concluded. At this stage they were all in their flannels, sitting now on the stairway of the packed players' enclosure cheering on their young team-mate. They saw a brave finish as Merlin chased from side to side making Perry work for every point. Then, at last, with the tall Englishman leading 6–5, Merlin projected one last drive beyond the lines and the tie was over.

We had done it! At last, after a gap of twenty-one years, Britain had once more won the Davis Cup. The scenes on court were unforgettable. Perry was swamped in a sea of well-wishers which included most of us, who had sped down from our courtside seats. The crowd, very sportingly, had stood and cheered to acknowledge the British win, as well as to acclaim their new young hero.

Then the teams were lined up and Pierre Gillou, the president of the French Federation, was handing to Roper Barrett the famous trophy which had been in French possession ever since they had captured it from the Americans in Philadelphia six years earlier. Silence descended momentarily over the still excited crowd for *God Save the King* and the *Marseillaise*. As I stood there quietly at the side of the court, watching the men with whom my whole life was now so inextricably involved, acknowledging the applause of the crowd, I have to admit there was a lump in my throat and I could feel my eyes moistening. As anyone will know who has been part of some great team exercise that has had a successful outcome, it is a very special feeling.

At last the final speeches had been made and, at almost 9.00pm, it was time to leave Roland Garros for the last time. As we drove away to prepare for the traditional banquet I crossed my fingers for luck and offered a silent prayer of thanks to some unseen deity that my life had fallen into such a happy groove. With a quiet smile I also realized that Trevor Wignall's unlikely prophecy had now been fulfilled.

For three marvellous years after that we defended the Davis Cup successfully on the Centre Court at Wimbledon. Twice the Americans were repulsed and then the Australians were thwarted. Each year our summers revolved first around the Championships and then around the cup defence that was always held two weeks later.

By now Fred had become the dominant world figure among the men. Besides his three successive Wimbledon titles he won the US Championship three times in four years, plus the Australian in 1934 and the French in 1935. Bunny, too, was feared by everyone in a Davis Cup tie where his relative lack of physical strength was not exposed as it was over the longer haul of a major championship. With Dorothy Round's outstanding successes this was indeed the golden age of British tennis to which I have already referred.

In order to give the Davis Cup team a break away from the pressures of London Roper Barrett always liked to get them down to Eastbourne. We would go down to stay at the Grand Hotel for a few days of practice on the lovely grass courts at Devonshire Park while the Inter-Zone final was being played at Wimbledon on number one court. In earlier years, when we had other ties to play, Eastbourne was always a favourite venue for European Zone matches. Not only did we usually do well there, taking advantage of our natural surface on which so few of our European opponents could play effectively, but we also had plenty of friends down there after our many visits. In other words the ambience was good – an important consideration when preparing teams for national duty.

The 4–1 win in the 1934 Challenge Round was against the Americans, for whom Sidney Wood and Frank Shields played singles and George Lott teamed with Lester Stoefen in the doubles. The doubles rubber was the only one we lost when Harry Lee had been called upon once more to pair with Hughes after we had built the 2–0 lead. Pat was becoming resigned to his fate!

In 1935 we won even more easily against an American team that contained the young Don Budge who was just twenty at the time, Wilmer Allison and Johnny Van Ryn. To win 5–0 against men of such quality was indeed a triumph. This time Raymond Tuckey came in to replace Lee and with Hughes scored a memorable win in five sets against Allison and Van Ryn. That in itself was a major success against one of the world's great teams. It was also a great reward for Pat Hughes who had 'nursed' Raymond with such skill and understanding during his apprenticeship that led to the Davis Cup Challenge Round.

Jack Crawford and Adrian Quist played singles and doubles against us for Australia in 1936. After leading 2–0 we lost the doubles, Hughes and Tuckey losing in four hard sets. Then Quist beat Bunny, also in four sets. Thus Fred had to go into the deciding rubber against Crawford, the man he had beaten in the 1934 Wimbledon final when winning his first title there. Fred did not fail us. Playing with exemplary coolness on a dark, dismal day during which we had interruptions due to persistent drizzle, he attacked remorselessly against a slightly slower opponent who was thus forced to defend for most of the match. Perry's 6–2 6–3 6–3 win retained the cup for the third year in a row, an achievement not equalled since the earliest days of the competition when the British Isles had won the trophy in 1903, 1904, 1905 and 1906. It was a glorious moment. Britain was truly on top of the world.

However, although we did not know it at the time, the seeds of our decline had already been planted. Fred, the cornerstone of our success, had been having preliminary discussions with Frank Hunter and Howard Voshell about a contract to turn professional. I had suspected as much when I had seen Fred hesitate when leaving the Centre Court after beating Crawford. Behind the screen at the back of the court he had passed me his rackets and had returned to the emptying arena for what seemed to be a last, lingering look at the stage upon which he had played out some mighty dramas. It was a significant and emotional moment for him . . . and for me.

As the whole world later learned, it was planned that he would challenge Ellsworth Vines, the reigning professional champion, at the end of the year. But first there was one more ambition to achieve. Having won three Wimbledons, Fred had set his sights on winning a third US Championship. Now, with the impending announcement of his professional debut, it was more than ever important to finish his brilliant amateur career on a high note. He could hardly have achieved a more spectacular ending. Playing one of the coolest matches of his career under the most intense pressure he duly won his third title by beating Budge 10–8 in the fifth set.

As usual, Fred's timing was perfect. He had served his country magnificently and brought glory to Britain such as we had not enjoyed since the reign of the Dohertys at the turn of the century. The time had come for him to capitalize on all the hard work and dedication that had made him the greatest champion of his generation.

As I have described elsewhere, the team without Perry was like *Hamlet* without the Prince. Good as he was, Bunny

179

could not carry the burden alone against the Americans in 1937. Our next generation of players had not yet matured. Nor had they had the priceless experience of competing in the preliminary ties leading up to a Challenge Round. This was always the penalty for the holders in the days before 1972, the first occasion when the champion nation played through. We had benefited from this situation in 1933 when young Merlin was asked to play his first Davis Cup singles in a Challenge Round. Now, in 1937, it was the turn of Charles Hare to face the same test, against Budge.

Bunny had given him the best possible start by defeating Frank Parker, also playing in his first Davis Cup tie, 6–3 6–2 7–5 in the opening rubber. It was as good a performance as Bunny had ever produced. For a while it seemed Charles might work a miracle against the Wimbledon champion. Breaking to lead 5–4 he served for the first set. At 15–30 Charles delivered what Budge and everyone else agreed was an ace – everyone, that is, except the linesman. Clearly upset, Charles lost his serve. But he persevered with his audacious left-handed serve-and-volley game and charged the net at every opportunity on the American's delivery. If he had been able to snatch that opening set anything might have happened. As it was he began to lose his edge on service as Budge started to get more returns past him. Eventually, after an hour's glorious battle, the set fell to America 15–13 as a lob sped past the leaping Hare's racket. However, it had been a gallant fight that now clearly would have only one outcome. Once he had fathomed the intricacies of the Englishman's awkward, swinging, left-handed serve, Budge knew he could win. The champion duly completed his win 6–1 6–2 and the Americans breathed again.

At one rubber apiece the doubles became crucial. A couple of weeks earlier at Wimbledon Budge and Gene Mako had won the first of their two successive doubles titles by beating in the final the British holders, Hughes and Tuckey, 6–0 6–4 6–8 6–1. It was certain that the Americans would field the same pair for the doubles rubber so it was felt appropriate to call upon Frank Wilde to partner Raymond Tuckey. Frank was a fine doubles player who, you will remember, had been on the losing side with Hare in the 1936 Wimbledon final against Hughes and Tuckey. The gamble very nearly paid off. Combining magnificently, the British pair went down fighting 6–3 7–5 7–9 12–10 after saving three match-points in the fourth set and holding a point on Mako's serve that would have taken the match to a fifth set. But, after giving the Americans the fright of their lives, the British pair were fairly beaten by the rock-like solidity of Budge under pressure – he was the only man not to lose a serve – and the quickness at the net of Mako.

But, as we knew it would, the doubles had proved to be decisive. With the confidence of a 2–1 lead behind him, Parker accounted for the net-rushing Hare 6–2 6–4 6–2 to seal the victory for the Americans. Budge then made it 4–1 by overpowering Austin 8–6 3–6 6–4 6–3. Whether or not Budge would have been quite so relaxed if that final rubber had been live, one can only speculate. Certainly it would have been much more difficult for him against the immensely experienced Austin. However, the fact was we had been beaten by a better team. Our glorious reign had ended.

SIX

Marriage and the Professional Circuit

In my early days at Wimbledon I lived with my brother Bill and his wife at their home in Southfields. I used to get my hair cut at a little shop just around the corner from Southfields station. Another who patronized this establishment was a certain Jimmy Tompkins, who later became the captain of Fulham Football club. He was a fine, fresh-faced young man, rather like Boris Becker when he first appeared on the scene, and a good natural athlete. I knew Jimmy quite well. One summer's day in 1934 we both happened to be having our hair cut at the same time and Jimmy suggested that I should join a party of his young friends who were going swimming that afternoon at the quarry near Ashtead.

'Who with?' I asked.

'Oh, some of my chums who are down from university and three or four girls,' he replied. 'You'd enjoy it.'

I was about five or six years older than Jimmy and I felt I might be the odd one out. So I said, 'You won't want me along.'

'Nonsense,' he replied. 'We are all keen on tennis and they'd love to meet you.'

By now we were chatting on the pavement outside the barber's shop. There was a call from across the road. 'Jimmy, what time are we leaving?' A lovely dark-haired girl, aged about seventeen or eighteen and wearing a light-coloured summer dress, came bounding towards us.

'We're meeting after lunch, about two o'clock, here outside the barber's shop. By the way, this is Dan Maskell, he's the tennis coach up at the All England Club and I've asked him to join our swimming party this afternoon.'

'Oh, that's marvellous, I love talking about tennis. I only wish I could play the game,' she said.

'Dan, may I introduce Connie Cox? Actually she lives in that house just over there and she's a terrific swimmer. In fact she's terrific in every way!'

Connie threw back her head and laughed. There was something about her that immediately attracted me. There was a brightness, a liveliness that suggested a sharp mind. Her voice had a lovely lilt . . . and Jimmy was right; she did look marvellous!

I stammered something sloppy like, 'I suppose all you people who swim at the quarry are training to swim the Channel . . . you'll leave me far behind, I can barely keep afloat. In fact I shall probably drown!'

'Don't worry, I'll rescue you,' quipped Connie, flashing a lovely smile.

In view of all that happened later, hers was an ironic remark, but neither of us could know what tragedies lay ahead. At this moment our only thoughts were of the present.

I don't remember much about the swimming but I do remember the ride down and back in my wonderful Wolseley Hornet, a new twelve-horsepower car I had bought shortly before for £112 10s. I was proud of the new car but I was prouder still of one of my three passengers. I used to see 'Con', for that is what I always called her, occasionally after that, and each time we parted I realized how much I had enjoyed her bright company. She told me all about her love of drama, an interest that had been kindled at school and was now being fostered by the local amateur dramatic society which she had joined.

We began to see more of each other. On a trip to Oxford for one of our professional matches against the university, I remember going into a bookshop and buying a book of John

Galsworthy's plays because Con had been talking about him. It was the first present I ever bought her.

Con came from a musical family on her father's side and had learned to play the piano as a girl. She used to play the organ at the local church, St Paul's, for children's Sunday School. During our courting days I used to wait in my car outside the church, long after Sunday School was over, and hear the organ going full blast. Eventually I would send someone in to ask Miss Cox if she was ready yet. She always took the hint and ended her practice.

About thirty years later, long after she had stopped playing the organ, we found ourselves together in St Mary's church, just near the All England Club, for the wedding of Paul Hutchins. As we all sat there, within a few minutes of the appointed hour, the vicar came to the front of the church and said, 'Ladies and gentlemen, I have just had a telephone call from our organist to say that he has been unavoidably delayed and is still over the other side of London. There is no possibility of him getting here in time. I am appealing to any of you who might be able to play the organ. Can anyone please help us?'

There was a deafening silence. Then Con whispered to me, 'Shall I have a go?' 'But Con, you haven't played for years,' I replied. 'Well, we can't let Paul down, can we? I'm game to have a try.' With that she was off. In a few moments the first hesitant sounds could be heard, then an attempt at a quiet, slow piece as Con began to get the feel of the instrument. My palms were sweating and I felt my heart beating faster than usual. I was suffering with her. Then, suddenly, the firm, loud strains of the Wedding March burst forth and the bride walked slowly past with her attendants. It was going to be all right. Con was tremendous. Afterwards all our friends marvelled at her courage and Paul and his lovely bride, Shalimar, were extremely grateful.

There was a touching sequel to this story. Late on the Sunday night, two days after the wedding, there was a knock at our door. It was Paul and Shali, who told us that they had had time for only a two-day honeymoon and had called in on their way home to thank Con for what she had done and to give her a little present. With that they handed her a small parcel. Inside was a miniature piano with a silver plate attached to the lid on which was engraved 'To Con with many thanks from Paul and Shali'. That was one of the kindest and most enterprising acts I have ever witnessed. Just try and get some engraving done on a Saturday yourself, and you will see what I mean!

Con and I were married at Rye harbour church on 26 August 1936, one and a half months after Fred Perry's third consecutive Wimbledon win. Con's parents had a bungalow called 'Molehill' down at Winchelsea in Sussex. It was a wonderful cosy little place, just on the road that leads from the village to the sea. We had spent many happy weekends down there with her family. It was a perfect retreat with two golf courses nearby for relaxation. It was a simple, quiet wedding. My best man was Frank Henley, who was the senior representative for Gathiers, the suppliers of gut for tennis rackets.

My work inevitably kept me out of the house for long hours so that Con turned naturally to her acting to fill the absences. She was a marvellously talented character actress, well known in the district. She joined the Putney Players and performed in a string of successful amateur shows for them. Her talents were most profitably employed during the war, too, when she organized and ran concerts for the patients at the hospital where I was stationed doing rehabilitation work.

Together we saw the changes that came over the professional game in the period following Perry's departure from the amateur ranks at the end of 1936. The inclusion of Fred in the ranks of the touring professionals was part of a regular process that had begun when the game's greatest star, Suzanne Lenglen, accompanied by Vincent Richards, had left the amateur game in 1926. Suzanne signed a contract in

August and Vincent one in October to play exhibition tennis for C. C. 'Cash and Carry' Pyle. After her unfortunate experience at Wimbledon in 1926 (when she had scratched from the singles after a row with the referee, never to return) Suzanne had felt the time had come to cash in on her popularity and talent. Richards saw the same opportunity after a season in which he had beaten Tilden three times, won the French doubles title with Howard Kinsey, reached the final of the doubles with him at Wimbledon and retained his US doubles title.

Pyle's group included the leading American woman, Mary K. Brown, my 1930 US Professional Championship conqueror Howard Kinsey, another prominent American, Harvey Snodgrass, and the Frenchman, Paul Feret, who soon tired of the professional life and was reinstated as an amateur in 1929.

The American tour opened at the old Madison Square Garden in New York and, rather to most people's surprise, proved to be a great financial success with more than twelve thousand spectators paying up to five dollars each for a seat. When the tour was complete Suzanne was paid a bonus of some $25,000 to add to her reported signing-on guarantee of $50,000, while Pyle himself was said to have made a profit of over $80,000 – a huge sum in those Depression days.

In 1927 Suzanne tried her luck in Britain at the suggestion of C. B. Cochran, the theatrical impresario, but there was less scope here for a tour of this sort. However, her matches with Evelyn Dewhurst and Dora Koring, the former German champion, drew respectable crowds to the Holland Park roller skating rink, on the site of the present Kensington Hilton Hotel, where I had gone along with Arthur Roberts and Tom Jeffery to see her London debut early in July. Completing the troupe were the leading European professional, Karel Kozeluh, who had an ironclad baseline game allied to a great competitive instinct, plus Howard Kinsey.

When Pyle lost interest in tennis, Vincent Richards turned

first to Kozeluh as he himself became a promoter. There were other excellent players among the European teaching professionals in the 1920s – men like Roman Najuch, a big left-hander from Poland who lived in Germany, Josef Negro, who had been Suzanne's sparring partner at the Nice club, another Frenchman, Pierre Guidici, and the three Burke brothers from Ireland, of whom Albert was the best singles player. I knew them all from my visits to Beaulieu where we had competed in the French Professional Championships for the Bristol Cup, a superb piece of silverware that had been donated by the Duke of Connaught. He lived nearby and regularly appeared on finals day to present the trophy to the winner.

Richards realized that you could not appear year after year in the same cities with the same four players and expect to draw large gates. His own 1928 tour in America and Europe with Kozeluh was only moderately successful. An injection of new blood was required at regular intervals. The arrival in 1931 of Bill Tilden and his doubles partner, Frank Hunter, as the newest members of the group was just the shot in the arm the professional game needed. Tilden had been such a prominent world figure that the prospect of staging financially viable events in other countries became a realistic possibility for the first time. Tilden's debut at Madison Square Garden on 18 February 1931 for promoter William O'Brien was thoroughly entertaining and profitable. Tilden beat Kozeluh 6–4 6–2 6–4 in the opening match and then proceeded to win every one of their fifteen subsequent encounters. The American tour grossed $238,000 and encouraged the group to repeat the formula in Europe. Accordingly, Tilden and Hunter crossed the Atlantic and played exhibition matches in Paris, Brussels, Amsterdam, Hamburg, Berlin, Cologne and Paris again. The proposed matches in Milan had to be called off when it rained ceaselessly.

Each night Tilden played Kozeluh and Hunter played a

variety of opponents – first Albert Burke, and in Germany the young German professional champion, Hans Nusslein. Najuch also played in Berlin while in Paris the French professional, Martin Plaa, had appeared.

Tilden made two more European tours in 1932 and 1933 with the young American Bruce Barnes. The first year was basically a German tour with a last match played in Zagreb. The second year consisted of matches on Davis Cup lines against France, Germany, Czechoslovakia and Austria. It was realized that new events were necessary in the constant battle to attract new spectators. In Paris, despite Cochet's appearance alongside Plaa for the home team and his victory over Barnes, the Americans won 4–1. In Berlin the Germans were beaten by the same score with Nusslein's win against Barnes the only home success. In Prague the US team scored another 4–1 win against an amateur Czech team for whom Roderich Menzel scored the lone success by beating Barnes, and in Vienna the amateurs of Austria failed to win a match. In the light of the attitude to professionals at that time it is amazing that Tilden was able to arrange matches against amateurs.

On the 1932 tour a new tournament had been played at the Rott-Weiss club in Berlin and styled 'The Professional Championships of the World'. I had gone over with Fred Poulson to take part but neither of us reached the final stages. In a round-robin finish from the semi-finals Plaa was undefeated and, by beating Tilden 6–0 7–5 8–6, had relegated the great man to second place. The same thing had happened in 1933 when Nusslein had won all his matches but in 1934 when the event was played in Paris as a knock-out tournament, Tilden had at last won. In the final he beat Plaa 6–2 6–4 7–5.

Tilden's match in 1934 to introduce the latest amateur champion, Ellsworth Vines, was also played at the old Madison Square Garden and attracted a crowd of 14,637 – easily the largest gathering for a tennis event there had ever been. The American tour, round seventy-two cities, grossed $243,000 and so was equally successful. Vines won by 47 matches to 26.

By the time he had won his three Wimbledon and three American titles, plus the French and Australian once each, Fred Perry was the logical opponent for Vines. His inaugural match in 1937 was also played at Madison Square Garden before another huge crowd of 17,630. It was another record. Their American tour, promoted by Frank Hunter and won by Vines 32–29 was also a financial success, grossing over $400,000. In a separate Madison Square Garden promotion later the same year Perry inflicted on Tilden the first defeat the great champion had ever suffered in that famous arena. The old lion was now forty-four, Perry twenty-eight.

So the formula had been established. There was, apparently, a market for a series of meetings between the reigning professional champion and the leading amateur of the day. In 1939 Don Budge joined the circus and on tour beat Vines 21–18 and Perry 18–11 to establish himself as the new champion. Then in 1941 Bobby Riggs, the last pre-war winner at Wimbledon, joined the group. In the post-war period Jack Kramer led a regular exodus to the paid ranks that he organized and ran following his own departure in 1947.

I had been concerned in the first major professional tournament to be staged in England involving the world's top players. In 1933 I had a telephone call from Arthur Elvin who was the managing director of Wembley Stadium, the huge football arena that had been erected as part of the facilities provided for the British Empire Exhibition of 1924. Elvin told me that he was constructing a large new indoor arena to be called the Empire Pool that would be opening the following year. He had realized the potential of such an arena for swimming, ice-hockey, boxing and other indoor sports. Having seen the popularity of Wimbledon he was keen to try a professional tennis tournament. He explained that it would be a simple matter to lay a floor across the top of the pool that could be used for any sort of indoor sport or concert. I was asked how I would go about organizing a professional tournament in England. 'As long as you get Tilden you'll be all right,' I said. 'He is the place to start and he will have views about the entry and format.'

That is just what Arthur Elvin did. So it was that in November 1934 high-level professional tennis came to Britain for the first time. The first tournament was staged as a round-robin event involving Tilden, Vines, Plaa, Barnes, Nusslein and myself. It was won by Vines who did not lose a match. Nusslein was second, Tilden third, Plaa fourth, myself fifth (I had beaten only Barnes), and Barnes last.

The following year the format was altered to a normal knock-out draw for eight players headed by Tilden, Vines and the new boys to the ranks, handsome Lester Stoefen and his partner of amateur days, George Lott. Stoefen was a big hitter from California with a huge serve and had just won his second US doubles title in a row playing with Lott. In the mixed doubles final that year Lott had teamed up with Helen Jacobs to beat Stoefen and the great doubles expert, Elizabeth Ryan, 4–6 13–11 6–2. It was the only US mixed final Elizabeth ever lost.

As the British professional champion I had been invited to take part in this second Wembley tournament. My first-round opponent was the stylish Frenchman, Robert Ramillon, a man whose game I knew well. During practice in the days before the match I was horrified to discover that I could no longer hit my backhand properly – and it was normally my best shot! In consternation I turned to Joe Pearce who had joined Queen's Club as a full-time ballboy only a year or so after me. He probably knew my game better than anyone else since we often practised against each other and had met three or four times in the course of the British Professional Championships.

'Joe, if you can help me to find my backhand I'll give you

a fiver out of my prize-money,' I promised. We went out to number three covered court and started to hit some fore-hands and backhands. After rallying normally for a few shots I would suddenly lose all sense of feel on the backhand and make a simple unforced error. It was an eerie sensation – like suddenly losing your bearings in a dense fog. Joe spotted the problem immediately. 'It seems to me you are not turning your shoulders as much as usual,' he said. 'Normally when you step across with your right foot to hit your backhand you turn so much that I can see the whole of your back. At the moment I'm only seeing your right shoulder.' We went back to rallying. For a few minutes I decided to exaggerate the turn of my shoulders. Sure enough my touch started to return. Half an hour later I was at last beginning to regain my confidence.

The following day Joe and I went out again. It was still there! With some relief I hit a succession of backhands exactly where I wanted to hit them. My confidence soared. It was like greeting an old friend. At last I felt ready to face Monsieur Ramillon.

As I changed for the match I felt eager for the battle ahead. The tingle of expectation tightened my stomach muscles. It was a familiar feeling, one that competitors at all levels of any sport will recognize. Without it the adrenaline will not flow. At last we were on court, rallying. The umpire called: 'Maskell to serve. First set. Play!' I played like a dream. Far from having no confidence in my backhand it was the shot which won so many points for me and set up many others. I knew exactly what I was trying to do and, fortu-nately, was able to do it. Ramillon was a supreme stylist whose natural backhand was a slice. To pass the volleyer he could hit over the ball but it was not his natural shot and under pressure could break down. The obvious course, therefore, was to mount a volleying attack against the backhand.

On the fast wooden surface my game plan worked to

perfection. I went in at every opportunity and volleyed to his backhand corner. In no time I was back in the locker-room with a straight sets win 6–2 7–5 6–2 under my belt against the dark horse of the tournament, one whom many thought might win it. The prize-money for winning a first round match at Wembley that year was £25, so Joe got his money!

Arthur Elvin appeared to be less than ecstatic about my win. 'Thanks for ruining my tournament,' he said, but his eyes were smiling. Privately he was delighted that the lone home representative had survived to the second round. It would be good for the gate, he thought. However, I met a rather different opponent the next night, the six-foot-four-inch, cannonball-serving American, Lester Stoefen. After a good match I was beaten by three sets to one.

Certainly that second year we had respectable crowds. Wembley was, and still is, a cavernous place to play tennis. When the place is full or nearly full there is a tremendous atmosphere. As a player it is easy to respond. The adrenaline starts pumping and you feel charged up. But when it is nearly empty, as it sometimes is for those early round morning or afternoon matches, it is difficult to generate the same enthusiasm and the same deep concentration. You tend to feel flat.

The semi-final between Stoefen and Vines was a marvellous encounter, full of bold hitting and won eventually by Vines 4–6 6–2 6–8 6–1 9–7. It ended in an unfortunate scene when, at match-point to Stoefen, a Vines drive that fell well beyond the line was not called out. Stoefen lost that game and the next two in a flaming temper. Tilden, sitting next to me, said, 'Come on Dan, there may be trouble in the locker-room.' We hurried down and arrived just after the players who were arguing fiercely and already seemed about to throw blows. Bill stepped in at once to part them and did not leave until the atmosphere had improved.

Vines went on to win the tournament with another fine five-set performance in the final against Tilden. The score,

6–1 6–3 5–7 3–6 6–3, accurately reflects the greater pace and court speed of the younger man. But, as he always did, Bill gave the customers some exciting moments. 'Always remember, Dan, that we are entertainers. If the customers don't like what they see, they won't be back.' It was a maxim he had always lived by.

They were rewarding, those pioneering days at Wembley. Little did I think then that ten years later I would be commentating on the matches for BBC Television. Those London Indoor Professional Championships, as the tournament became known, were entertaining and thrilling affairs, beautifully presented by John Connell and his staff and involving most of the great players of the day who provided us with some memorable tennis matches. Of them all, the one that stands out most vividly in my memory is the final of 1956 between Pancho Gonzales and Frank Sedgman. The smouldering Mexican-American had turned professional after winning his second successive US Championship in 1949. He had played at Wimbledon only that one year and had won the doubles with Frank Parker. In the singles, seeded two, he had lost somewhat surprisingly in the fourth round to Geoff Brown of Australia.

The final, won by Gonzales in four glorious sets, was memorable for two reasons. The first was the high quality of the virtually error-free attacking tennis that these two giants of the game produced. There were hardly any unforced errors – nearly all the points were made with outright winners, a most unusual occurrence. As every tennis player knows, the majority of matches are lost, not won. The second remarkable thing was the way hardly anyone left the arena even when the hands of the clock revealed that it was now Sunday morning. The BBC created a record for an outside broadcast by remaining on the air until the match ended at 12.40 am, as Gonzales won 4–6 11–9 11–9 9–7. We won a lot of new friends that night.

By 1938 Tilden believed there was scope to enlarge our

professional activities in England. After some protracted negotiations he was able to arrange an eight-man event at Olympia in London during January. With Cochet now in his fifth year as a professional and well established in the minds of tennis fans, Bill believed there was every chance of drawing respectable crowds. I had been asked to take part to provide some home interest and Martin Plaa was another obvious choice.

By the time Bill asked me I had already booked my second skiing holiday with Con at Engelberg. He asked me to cancel it. 'Dan, you really can't go. If you fall over and break an arm we're lost,' he said. Nevertheless, I went. The pull of the mountains was already too strong to resist and in any case I certainly did not want to let Con down. It was inevitable, I suppose, that I should fall and hurt my right shoulder. Luckily the injury was not too serious but I was badly bruised. The doctor in Engelberg advised me to bathe it alternately in hot and cold water and that helped. I was able to go on skiing for the remainder of the holiday, albeit in some pain, and when I returned home it was still sore. Bill insisted that I go to see Mr Dunning, the specialist in Mount Street he always used, who prescribed daily physiotherapy treatment.

By the time the tournament began I felt more or less all right but I was woefully short of practice. Joe Pearce and Fred Poulson tried to get me into some sort of shape for my first round match which would be against Cochet. I had seen him play many, many times but had never faced him myself. As is often the case after a short break away from the game, I played like a dream. Timing the ball sweetly and moving well I took the first set and led 5–4 on my own serve in the second. With positive play I reached 40–30, match point. I thought carefully about how to play it. My serve into his body produced just the sort of return I was hoping for, a mid-court ball on the backhand side. As I came up to the ball I decided to play a forcing approach shot to the backhand corner and come in, anticipating a defensive reply. Moving forward I struck the ball beautifully, fast and low with a touch of slice. I saw Henri had no time to retreat so I checked, expecting a defensive lob. Instead of that Cochet produced one of those improvised shots that do not exist in any coaching manual, a shot of true genius, the sort of inspirational reply that we have seen more recently from that other gifted Frenchman, Henri Leconte, or from John McEnroe. Dropping the head of the racket slightly, Cochet jabbed at the ball and projected a fast half-volley that sped down the line before I had time to realize what was happening. From that moment Henri never looked back. He surged through the remaining games of the match on a cloud of inspiration that left me totally bewildered.

After the match Tilden commiserated with me. 'All I can say, Dan, is I know how you feel. He did that to me at Wimbledon in 1927.' That was a contest I had witnessed, an extraordinary affair and surely the most talked of tennis match in the days before the war. It was a semi-final and Tilden, who had won six successive US Championships up to 1925, was playing again at Wimbledon for the first time since winning his second championship in 1921. In tennis terms he was a colossus; he occupied the same sort of position in the 1920s that Borg did in the 1970s and Lendl does now. Most people expected Tilden to win, even though he had been seeded two behind Lacoste.

The match had proceeded normally for two sets. Tilden had demonstrated all the facets of his powerful game and led 6–2 6–4. Cochet, despite winning a few points with some lovely deft touches, was powerless to halt the American juggernaut. Tilden, producing winner after winner, moved confidently to 5–1. The match was as good as over. Suddenly it all changed. Tilden started to miss the lines or find the net. Cochet began to play more and more early shots to awkward angles. With a run of seventeen successive points he drew level and went through to win the third set 7–5. You kept thinking that at any moment Tilden would wake up: you expected to see the king reimpose himself (for there was a touch of royalty about Tilden). But he didn't. Maintaining the impetus he had created, Cochet coasted to an improbable victory 2–6 4–6 7–5 6–4 6–3.

I had asked Bill about that match. Everybody had asked him. 'All I can tell you is that nothing had gone wrong physically,' he said. 'And that story about me delaying the end for the benefit of someone in the Royal Box who had arrived late – well, that is just ridiculous! Instead of hitting the lines I missed them, don't ask me why. I really don't know what happened except that Henri played too darned well.'

Bill was always generous in his praise of opponents, an altogether fair performer in every way. He would never take a point that he felt he had not earned and he often threw points after a bad decision in his favour. Obviously he was a complex character, a showman first and foremost who was always the centre of attention in any company. He was a tall man and had a commanding presence which was emphasized by his definite opinions on most subjects, especially about bridge, a game he loved to play as a relaxation. However, he was not perfect. For one thing he smoked incessantly, an unusual habit for a leading sportsman, even in those days before the dangers of cigarette smoking were fully realized. Then he was one of the worst forecasters of a match I have ever known – which is a great comfort to me whenever I have picked the wrong horse during a commentary at Wimbledon! He was also sometimes an embarrassment to us with his fondness for young boys, a failing that eventually brought him two short jail sentences in America. I remember a difficult occasion during one of the professional tournaments in Southport. I was sitting in the lounge of the Prince of Wales hotel with Henri Cochet when a boy arrived with a bundle of rackets under his arm and asked at the reception desk for Mr Tilden's room. 'He has asked me to deliver them to him personally,' said the lad, who was obviously very flattered. 'I think you'd better leave them with me,' said the porter. 'I'll see that he gets them and don't worry, you won't get into trouble.' Henri looked at me and shrugged. 'What can you do, Dan? It happens everywhere.'

About a month after the tournament at Olympia I had a telephone call from Bill to ask me if I could fix up an exhibition for him somewhere at short notice. He said that he needed the money. I knew that two of my professional colleagues, Ted Millman and Doug Gresham, had recently organized some exhibition matches at local schools and clubs in the Midlands area so I approached them. With their help we had soon found a club in the Birmingham suburb of Moseley eager to become involved. The matches were scheduled for a Saturday in April. Tilden was guaranteed fifty pounds and the winner would take another fifty.

I went up on the Friday to see that everything was in order. It was a fine spring day. The club had done a good job with the court; it was nicely dressed with green canvas surrounds and there was seating for about five hundred spectators. Unfortunately a fierce gale blew in the night and left much of the canvas in tatters and the seats upturned. However, despite the violent change in the weather, we decided to go ahead. Bill duly arrived on the train and I met him. He looked pretty fit for his forty-five years, still with a lean frame that showed no sign of thickening round the middle.

I was to play Tilden first over the best of five sets and then team with Gresham against Tilden and Millman. It was unseasonably cold as we began in front of a fairly full house and many of the spectators were wrapped up in rugs or blankets – an all too familiar sight at early British tournaments. We even had one or two snow flurries as the match developed and at two sets all it was apparent that Bill was suffering from the cold. At the change of ends I suggested that we call it an honourable draw. Bill would have none of it. 'Certainly not, Dan,' he said. 'We are professionals. We have a duty to our public. We must finish.'

The final set went well for me. In a short time I led 5–0. It was somewhat embarrassing but Bill would never have forgiven me if I had not gone flat out to win. At 0–5 he staged a recovery, the instinctive reaction of an animal that was trapped or of a great champion threatened with defeat. Leading 5–3, I served a near-ace to bring the score to 30–30. On the next point a rally developed and I went for a big forehand down the line. The ball thwacked into the tape at the top of the net and fell over for a dead winner. Match point. I took my time and delivered a fast, swinging serve down the centre line. It clipped the edge of the metal tape and shot straight along the ground, a clean winner. As we shook hands I said, 'Bill, I'm sorry about that.'

'Sorry?' he asked. 'What for? You ought to be glad. I would have been if I had been at match point.'

That is the sort of man he was. Proud as I was of being only the second Englishman to beat Tilden (Eric Peters had first achieved that distinction in a South of France tournament some years before) I had to admit to a sense of sadness that such a great champion had to resort to small exhibitions like this to make a living. If open tennis had come thirty-five years earlier there would have been no need. Bill Tilden, certainly one of the greatest players ever to wield a tennis racket, would have been a millionaire several times over.

Later in the year Godfrey Winn asked me to a dinner party at his comfortable house in Ebury Street. There were twelve of us there including Billy Butlin, who had been making the headlines with his ideas for holiday camps, and Phyllis Satterthwaite, who had been a prominent tennis player in the first quarter of the century. She had twice reached the final of the All-Comers singles at Wimbledon – in 1919 when Suzanne Lenglen had beaten her, and two years later in the last year of the All-Comers when Elizabeth Ryan had been too good for her. I had played with her in my early pro days at Queen's and in the south of France. When Mrs Satterthwaite died I read she had left something like £130,000 to a cats' home. I'm sure my astonishment was shared by many others with whom she was acquainted!

The purpose of the dinner was for me to meet Billy Butlin, who had some interesting ideas for the promotion of sporting facilities of all kinds at his new holiday camp at Clacton. He asked me to go along to the opening of his 'Festival of Happiness' in the summer to play some exhibition tennis and do a little coaching for members of the public. I said I would be delighted and suggested that Fred Poulson accompany me. Billy told us that Len Harvey, our national boxing hero, would be looking after the boxing and that Joe Davis would be demonstrating the billiards and snooker. I knew Len quite well but had never met Joe, something I was keen to do for I knew that he had developed his astonishing skills despite having weak sight in one eye – or perhaps because of that fact! As a teacher and fellow sportsman I was keen to hear about his experiences.

(Much later, after we had got to know one another, we enjoyed a round or two of golf together at Walton Heath. One day I remember saying to him, 'Joe, having watched the way you unfailingly put the ball away on the table, I'm surprised you are not a better putter!'

'I would be if only they'd let me use a cue instead of this ridiculous metal stick!' he replied.)

Lord Castleross performed the opening ceremony and everyone seemed to have an enjoyable day although the public were not all that interested in the tennis or boxing. Accordingly towards the end of the afternoon Len and I decided to play golf.

It was during this period that I met for the first time one of the world's great film stars. Spencer Tracy had come to London to help promote his film *Captains Courageous*, for which he won the first of two consecutive Oscars. He was a keen tennis player who had entertained Kay Stammers on one of her visits to California when she was competing in the Pacific Southwest tournament in Los Angeles.

In order to repay his kindness, Kay had offered to organize some tennis for him if ever he came to London. The problem for her was that she was due to leave for an overseas tour with the British team on the day after Spencer Tracy arrived. She had asked me if I would be able to play with him instead.

As one of his fans I was delighted to oblige. We arranged to play at the Melbury Club in Holland Park where Tom Jeffery was the professional. The first morning Spencer played with Kay and I had as my partner his friend 'Tim' Durrant, an accomplished amateur jockey who twice rode in the Grand National.

For about two weeks after that we had a game of doubles every morning. Spencer was a useful player who showed great keenness as he chased the balls and hit them back with his own slightly unorthodox style. When I mentioned to him how much, like everyone else, I'd enjoyed *Captains Courageous* he said, 'Of course the star of the film was not me – but young Bartholomew.'

When it was time for him to leave for Paris he said, 'Dan, I've thoroughly enjoyed the tennis – if ever you are in California I'd love to have you stay with us. We have a guest house out there and it's yours whenever you want it.'

He was keen to continue with his tennis in France so I suggested that in Paris he should contact Darsonval, the famous French coach, and that in Monte Carlo the man to help him would be Pierre Guidici.

Some time later on his return to Paris before leaving for America he sent me a telegram which read: 'Thank you again for helping with my tennis and just to remind you there is a welcome for you at my place in California.' Sadly, the opportunity to visit him never materialized. Even sadder – the telegram was lost with a lot of other personal possessions during the war.

My competitive year ended with the recapture of my British professional singles and doubles titles, having lost both the previous year. At this stage of its evolution our championship was played over a round-robin format for the four players who reached the semi-finals. This was the tenth time I had been the champion but I cannot pretend that beating Fred Poulson and Joe Pearce (Tom Jeffery had retired, injured) gave me the same pleasure as beating Bill Tilden in Birmingham.

At Wembley that year Tilden had had another disappointment when Hans Nusslein beat him in a wonderfully entertaining five-set final. Whatever the outcome, the public still worshipped him. Tilden *was* tennis – as Henri Cochet discovered in the semi-finals.

The year 1939 was remarkable for the transatlantic successes at Wimbledon despite the departure of Don Budge to the pro ranks. The Americans captured all five main titles. Bobby Riggs and Alice Marble each achieved the hat-trick. They had played together in mixed doubles while in the men's doubles Riggs had played with Ellwood Cook, his victim in the singles final, and Marble with Sarah Palfrey Fabyan in the ladies'. We British could congratulate ourselves that Hare and Wilde had reached the men's doubles final, that Kay Stammers had reached the singles final, and that Wilde and Nina Brown had been the mixed finalists. As with Austin the previous year, we were again the bridesmaids. Well as Kay played there was no likelihood of her ever being the bride so long as Alice was around. She had been totally outgunned by Miss Marble. I have always thought that Alice was one of the great champions for she was the first real athlete who could successfully sustain the sort of serve-and-volley game that we take for granted today from Martina Navratilova and others. In the light of what happened later, the enforced absence of Gottfried Von Cramm from the 1939 Championships was an event of sinister significance.

Our professional tournament at Victoria Park in July had a full strength field headed by Budge, Vines, Tilden, Cochet, Nusslein, Martin Plaa and myself. Nusslein and I had reached the doubles final together. There we faced Vines and Budge. Combining particularly well and returning the big American serves with interest, we actually reached match point. I was serving to Budge at 40–30 and thought 'I won't serve to his forehand because he will be expecting it.' My tactics worked perfectly. A wide serve to his stronger backhand caught him unawares. The weak reply came floating up to Hans at the net who had the easiest of backhand volleys. But somehow he contrived to fluff the shot into the net. Our chance had gone. Once the favourites had recovered their poise they swept to victory.

As the summer faded there was more and more talk in the papers about the possibility of war. Since I had been kept pretty busy all the year I had not really given the matter much thought. But as the speculation intensified my mind went back to an incident at Wimbledon. A few days after the end of the Championships Jean Borotra had come down to the club for a game with me. As he was putting his belongings together prior to his departure he had seemed unusually serious, sad almost.

Turning to me with that earnest look he always has when he is feeling emotional, he said, 'Dan, I want to send you something with all my thanks for the many years you have been helping me here. You know it may be a very long time before we see each other again.' Some weeks later a silver cigarette case, suitably inscribed, was delivered to my home. By then it was already clear that Jean had been right.

SEVEN

The War Years

Most people grow attached to the city of their birth. However, it is extraordinary how certain other towns or cities often have great significance in the lives of particular individuals. For me Loughborough has been just such a place. Before the war I had visited the college there on several occasions for tennis events of various kinds, conferences, junior matches and so on, while during the war I was to find myself there at the rehabilitation centre. Then after the war I attended tennis conferences and played an exhibition match or two there and much later the university bestowed a degree upon me which I considered a great honour. But that is to get ahead of the story.

In the last days of August 1939 I was in Loughborough helping to run one of the LTA Elementary Coaching Award exams. Admiral Sir Leonard Vavasour was the chairman of the Professional Control Committee of the LTA at that time and we were passing out sports masters and sports mistresses as coaches at that standard.

Soon after eleven o'clock on the morning of Friday, 1 September, Doctor Schofield, the principal of Loughborough College, broke into our session and asked for silence. He looked very serious. 'Gentlemen, I do not think you need to go on with your labours. I've just heard on the radio that Germany has walked into Poland. It seems that war is now inevitable.'

You can imagine the awful pall of foreboding that descended on our proceedings. Needless to say we decided to stop at once so that we could take up our various responsibilities. Sir Leonard, who was an Admiral in the Royal Naval Reserve, went back to Gosport while most of the teachers had jobs to which they could return.

I had always resolved that in the event of war I would apply to join the Royal Air Force. However, first I had to alter my immediate plans. After Loughborough I was due to visit Liverpool where I was intending to stay with some friends while getting in touch with Mr T. E. Wolstenholme, the general manager and chief of publicity for the borough of Southport. Since 1935, we had staged a professional tournament there with Bill Tilden, Ellsworth Vines and some of the other leading professionals. I used to act for Bill to keep things moving in time for the following year's tournament. I failed to raise Wolstenholme on the telephone but I did get hold of my friends in Liverpool. I told them that in view of the seriousness of the national situation I was returning home at once.

War was declared on Sunday, 3 September. I can remember now sitting with Con in the lounge at White Corner, our house in Wimbledon, listening to the voice of Neville Chamberlain making the solemn announcement on the radio and wondering how all of our lives would be affected. My mind also went back to that day in 1918 when I had been shopping with my mother. How sad she would have been to discover that the first major conflict, with all its suffering and sacrifice, had not, after all, proved to be the war to end all wars.

That day I wrote a letter to the Air Ministry in Kingsway offering my services and asking for information about when and where to join. I had chosen the Royal Air Force because my brother John had been in the service and also because the chairman at Wimbledon, Sir Louis Greig, had always spoken so highly of his time in the RAF. In fact I had once said to him that if war ever did break out I would try to join his service.

I was soon called to an interview and told that I would be

hearing shortly of where to report for an Officer Training Course. So I went home and waited . . . and waited . . . and waited.

While waiting I returned to the All England Club which had now become an ARP Centre. In fact several other civil defence services were making arrangements to move in. One day I saw, to my horror, that workmen were knocking a hole in the wall of the men's dressing-room below the window frame. This was in preparation for the stretchers that would be needed to be passed quickly inside the building. Ellis, the old dressing-room attendant, announced soberly: 'Mr Maskell, I'm afraid your lockers have been taken – they were needed for essential supplies.' Opening them, I saw that they were now full of splints and bandages. 'I've put all your stuff in a brown paper parcel for you,' continued Ellis. It reminded me of that first visit in 1929 when Dudley Larcombe had shocked Ellis by instructing him, 'Put those things of Colonel Cartwright's into a parcel and empty the locker for Mr Maskell.'

Before I finally left to join up I saw the beginnings of the small farm that eventually appeared on the club grounds. The car parks were used both to grow crops as grazing for a group of animals that turned the club into a food producing unit, all administered by Nora Cleather, the acting secretary during the war, and Marie Bompas, her assistant. At least the sacred courts were being spared.

The period of waiting was most frustrating. Part of the time I passed by playing tennis with Bob Tinkler, a former Oxford University Blue who after the war served for many years on the All England Club committee. He had enlisted for the Army and had been told like me, to wait. Meanwhile Con had joined the ARP and was doing keep-fit classes and first-aid courses at the club. I remember one day going into the main hall to collect her and finding that they had installed a piano just inside the main door below the steps that lead to the Centre Court. Already they were having singsongs in the evenings to keep up everyone's morale.

My own morale was low. It seemed there was nothing I could do to speed up the bureaucratic process. Another letter directed to the Air Ministry resulted in an instruction to wait for a second interview. Then one evening I heard Stanley Rous talking on the radio about the process of recruitment. He was the secretary of the Football Association and I had met him on several occasions. The purpose of his broadcast was to secure the support of men with skills in physical education who were required by the Army to become Physical Training Instructors. Stanley gave an address at Aldershot to which people could apply. I decided to phone him to see if he could hasten the progress of my RAF application or perhaps arrange for me to join the Army. He said he would try to help.

Christmas came and went. Still there was no news. In January we went down to the bungalow on Winchelsea beach for a week. We spent an amusing time skiing all the way from Winchelsea on the flat straight road to Rye, being towed behind a car, and on the small hill just inland there. At last, in March, news arrived. On the doormat I found a letter from the Army instructing me to report in five days' time with my physical training kit to the gymnasium at Aldershot.

While I was preparing my things another letter arrived, this time from the Air Ministry, instructing me to attend another interview. In my dilemma I once more phoned Stanley Rous who advised me to go to the Air Ministry. He said he would square things at Aldershot. The result of that last interview was an instruction to report to Loughborough in three weeks' time to join a basic training unit. During this final period of waiting I had a call from Laurie Shaffi whom I had often played at Wimbledon and who now, thanks to some training with Bill Tilden on the wooden courts at Queen's, had sharpened his game tremendously. I could hardly believe it when Laurie told me that he had applied to join the RAF only three weeks before and was now due to go to Loughborough on the same day as myself. Life seemed rather unfair at that moment. On the day of our departure Laurie's mother drove us to Liverpool Street station where we were to catch a military train to Loughborough. The station was crowded with chaps in service uniforms, Army, Navy and Air Force, plus a lot of civilians like ourselves carrying parcels containing our service uniforms.

Laurie's mother was very tearful like a number of other parents at the departure of their sons. We might have been going off to the trenches in France at the start of World War One instead of taking a short 114–mile journey to Loughborough.

On arrival we were billeted in one of the student hostels, The Grove, where there were two other well-known sportsmen – Leslie Ames, the Kent and England cricketer, and Uberoi, the tennis player. We were all subjected to the usual basic training routines like aircraft recognition, air force law, courts martial and, of course, drill. Most of our time seemed to be spent marching up and down the parade ground learning to snap to attention at the bark of command from Corporal Green, who was in charge of our drill.

There were ninety of us divided into three flights of thirty men each. Corporal Green was determined that our flight would outshine the others. He was a fine, tall man who looked extremely fit, probably because he had only recently retired from the Guards and had been brought back in the national emergency. As we learned the intricacies of formation marching I remember thinking how beneficial the discipline would have been to some of my pupils in days gone by at Wimbledon. If only they had been prepared to work as hard as we were now doing they would surely have become better players.

Our CO was Wing Commander Sheriff who had joined the service as a cadet at the age of fifteen and risen through the ranks. At one time he had been the RAF fencing champion and had trained the PTIs who used to take part each year in the Royal Tournament at the Earls Court exhibition in London. Their gymnastic display was always a feature of the event. Sheriff was a great disciplinarian and one day, right at the end of our course, after some of us had been hauled before him for talking after lights out he pointed out the necessity of maintaining strict discipline. In fact he told us: 'There's been a hold-up in your postings. You will not be away from here for about a week so I've got a job for you all. I want each of you to give a lecture to your fellow officers. The subject will be "Discipline and how you acquire it". The Warrant Officer will arrange the times.' That was that.

I racked my brains for an original aproach to the subject. Suddenly I had an inspiration. Boxing, I thought. That was it – the discipline a boxer needs in his training and tactics. After my school boxing days I had attended training at St George's Boys Club a couple of times a week and then at Fulham Baths and Walham Green (now Fulham Broadway). I'd often heard Len Harvey, our British champion, say, 'You can never win a fight unless you have self-discipline – nor can you ever control an opponent if you can't control yourself.' So I developed that theme, relating it to other areas of life including tennis of course, and finally to our conversion from civilian to serviceman. It seemed to go down fairly well.

One of the highlights of our passing-out exam was the moment when each one of us would take charge of the ninety-man squad and drill them up and down the parade ground in front of Hazelrigg Hall, trying to get in as many commands and changes of direction as possible in the allotted time. Getting your men on to a left-hand marker was a tricky business, a skill which Laurie Shaffi never quite mastered. When it came to his turn to drill us he had us marching towards a flower-bed and seemed too tongue-tied to do anything about it. The men in the lead marked time on the edge of the flower-bed, not daring to trample beneath their feet the Commanding Officer's prize flowers! The rest of the squad piled up behind and chaos ensued. Eventually Laurie got us back on course but when he halted in front of the CO for his permission to dismiss us he forgot to salute and held up the proceedings considerably. It was something of a shambles which, afterwards, gave us all a lot of hearty laughter. However, I'm glad to say that it did not affect Laurie's future.

After the interminable drill, the day and night marches with backpacks and the exams, it was a relief to receive a posting at last. During the ten days before we were finally posted the CO gave me the task of delivering a series of lectures to our group on subjects of my own choice, including my own experiences as a professional tennis coach. It was a challenge that I enjoyed.

I was graded for General Duties and was to be posted to Hastings to join the Number 5 Initial Training Wing. Laurie Shaffi went to the Number 4 ITW at Cambridge, so our paths diverged. Another pal was Keir Hardie, a grandson of the famous politician who had been the first Labour Party leader in the House of Commons in 1906. He was posted to the Number 3 ITW at St Leonard's, just along the coast from us at Hastings.

It was a rather anxious Pilot Officer Maskell who reported for duty at Number 5 ITW in Hastings to take charge of two flights of fifty men each. Normally a new officer would be given one flight of the four that made up the ITW Squadron but we were short of trained officers so that two of us each had a hundred men in our charge.

Flight Lieutenant Morris, another retired air force officer who had been brought back because of the emergency, looked after us wonderfully. He was getting on a bit but his heart was in the right place and he nursed the new boys through those anxious early weeks with great good humour. He taught me that an officer should always be thinking about the needs of his men. Once when we were out on a march, one bitterly cold night, Flight Lieutenant Morris suddenly appeared with a large pail of steaming hot cocoa for the chaps. That was typical of him.

My senior NCO, Sergeant Farraday, was another first-rate professional, a career airman who had been in the service for ten years. Fortunately he, too, had a great sense of humour and we all got on famously. On the first occasion I had to take command of my hundred men at eight in the morning on the sea front in Hastings he took complete charge. 'I'll have them all out there ready for you . . . they'll be moving about talking but when you arrive I'll get them all lined up. Just stand by and I'll come over and give you a big salute and say "Sir, all ready for inspection".' With Sergeant Farraday's guidance I got through my first inspection without a hitch, walking up and down the lines and seeing that everyone had their hair properly cut, their shoes cleaned and their buttons polished. With some relief I asked the Sergeant to march them off to their activities – aircraft recognition, air force law, physical training and so on.

These were the boys who were going to become the new aircrews who were so badly needed in those early days of the war. They were all officer cadets and wonderfully enthusiastic young fellows. It semed tragic that some of them might never return and reminded me of the stories my brothers had told about the dreadful loss of life in World War One. One or two of them actually came to me later on as patients, having been wounded in action.

Our CO, a Squadron Leader, was an odd man, a most inappropriate choice, I thought, to be commanding a squadron at an Initial Training Wing. My opinion of him was reinforced when I was told that he wanted me to take a group of ten men to guard Hastings pier. What an absurd assignment! Of course by now the Germans occupied the whole of the French coast and there were rumours that an invasion was imminent. Thus we were issued with carbines and sent off to repel the invaders. But the rifles did not have bayonets and we were given no ammunition! From about 10.00am till 6.00pm we remained there and it occurred to me that probably all the way round the south coast, from Ramsgate to Folkestone to the east and Eastbourne and Bournemouth to the west, small detachments like ours were manning the piers, ready to thrust back an invading army! It was all rather pointless and would have been amusing but for its sheer futility.

At this time I had a little Morris 8 car which had a shrapnel wound in the boot lid. One day I parked it outside the police station at Hastings where I was calling in connection with a case in which one of my squad had become involved. The cadet and an NCO had been accused of fiddling the books concerning the laundry for the squadron, which was sent out every week to local laundries. At the court martial I was 'People's Friend' which, as I had recently learned in air-force law, meant that I was there to defend the accused.

When I came out of the police station I could not see my car and assumed that somebody had moved it. To my dismay I discovered that it had been stolen. The station sergeant took the usual step of notifying local areas of its loss and it was soon recovered by an alert policeman in Battle, just seven miles away. He had noticed a man in civilian clothes driving a car on which there was a white label prominently affixed that read 'RAF property – Reserved'. When the constable had stopped the car the driver had leaped out and run for his life. More concerned with recovering the vehicle than apprehending the thief, the policeman had not chased him. On opening the boot he had noticed a box of Slazenger tennis balls with the initials 'D.M.' on the lid plus a couple of tennis rackets on both of which the same initials were discernible. Although he had not seen a report of the loss the policeman was a keen tennis player and phoned his station to say 'I think I've found a car belonging to Dan Maskell.' In no time I had the car back.

The CO of our Initial Training Wing at Hastings was yet another prominent sportsman – Group Captain A. E. R. Gilligan, the Cambridge University, Surrey and Sussex cricketer, who played many times for England and later became president of the MCC. In charge of sport for the entire Wing – that is the five squadrons with a total of one thousand men – was Leonard Crawley, whom I had known for some years. I had played rackets with Leonard and with other members of the Crawley family when they had been at Harrow and I had been at Queen's. Leonard had been a fine rackets player and had also played cricket for Cambridge University, Worcester and Essex, but he became best known as an amateur golfer representing England on many occasions. Later, as the leading golf writer for *The Daily Telegraph*, he carved out a very special niche for himself. In his capacity as Sports Officer Leonard was in touch with the local authorities in the district to organize the hire of their sports facilities – swimming baths, football pitches, tennis courts and so on. One day when he went sick I suddenly found myself with his responsibilities thrust upon me. I then had to discover what arrangements he had made for our five squadrons and called a meeting of the officers concerned to work out a suitable programme of physical activity for everyone in the Wing. Leonard disappeared from Hastings and I seem to remember that he had to have an operation but I did not see him again before we were moved to Torquay.

Shortly before we left Hastings there were two big parades attended by Air Commodore Critchley, who was the officer commanding all the Initial Training Wings. He had earned distinction in World War One as an Army General and had now returned to the Services as an Air Commodore. The Air Ministry Orders for the week announced a church parade for the entire Number 5 Wing at which, for some reason I never discovered, I was deputed to lead the march. With some trepidation I set off at the head of a thousand men marching along the promenade with Flight Lieutenant Morris and the other officers behind me followed by the Warrant Officers, the NCOs and the officer cadets. We turned round into Warrior Square and headed towards the church. My training at Loughborough stood the test and I brought them to a halt in the right place at the right time without a hitch.

A few weeks later Air Commodore Critchley came down again to inspect the station and a march past was arranged in the town. This time I was in front of our squadron leading just two hundred men. At the appropriate moment I ordered 'eyes right' and offered a smart salute in the direction of the Air Commodore on his platform while the heads of the entire squadron snapped to the right. At the appropriate moment I called 'eyes front' and dropped my saluting arm to resume the march.

Shortly after the parade I was sent for by the Adjutant: I had to go before the Air Commodore apparently. I wondered what on earth I had done. Everyone else assumed that I was visiting the Air Commodore because I knew him. Earlier in his life he had been a well-known professional sports promoter and was the man who put dog racing on at Bellevue, Manchester. That was the first time the sport had been tried in Britain and eventually it came to the White City where I remember seeing the first ten race meetings. I would go over from Queen's in the evening and recall seeing the famous flyer Entry Badge win the Dog Derby.

However, I had never in fact met Critchley and it was with some curiosity that I appeared, shortly before lunch, with a number of other officers from other squadrons. In a fairly normal atmosphere we were all given a pre-lunch sherry and introduced to the Air Commodore in turn. When it was my turn I remember him thinking that I was a squadron commander, which I wasn't.

'What is a squadron commander supposed to do on a parade like today's?' he asked.

'Well, sir, he salutes of course and gives the command "eyes right".'

'Correct,' he said. 'And then . . . ?'

'Well, then he marches past and holds the salute until he's well past you, then gives the "eyes front".'

'No, no, no,' he said, 'not when *you* are well past me. When your *squadron* is past me. That's when you give the "eyes front". Today you gave that command before the last three or four files had gone past.'

'Well, sir, I can only apologize,' I said, and was dismissed with a curt nod of the head, suitably reprimanded.

There was an amusing sequel to this story when, a year or so ago, I met the Air Commodore's son, Bruce, at Wimbledon. Bruce, of course, is a member of the BBC golf commentary team and he was visiting the tennis in an off-duty moment. After he had introduced me to his charming wife I asked, 'Did you know that I had served under your father?'

'No, I didn't,' he replied. 'Where was that?'

'In the early days of the war at Hastings when I was a very raw young officer,' I said. 'He gave me a sharp dressing-down, too, for not letting the whole squad pass him before I gave the "eyes front".'

'Yes, he was always a stickler for detail.'

'You know I think that's the first time I've ever been ticked off so nicely by a General and an Air Commodore at the same time,' I laughed.

By now the war was hotting up. The air raid sirens were wailing more frequently, and the raids became more serious. It was particularly irksome at night when we were forced to get all the air crew cadets out of the Eversfield Hotel where we were billeted and under the shelter of the overhanging promenade along Bottle Alley, so called because of the thousands of circular bottle bases of many colours that had been let into the surface of the asphalt.

Eventually it was decided that we should move the entire Training Wing to Torquay. The CO of the squadron sent me over in my little Morris to reconnoitre the town and look at the Majestic Hotel which had been requisitioned for our use. I was given petrol coupons for the journey and allowed to take along Murray Deloford for company. As we were running into Bournemouth Murray suddenly shouted 'Isn't that Donald McPhail?' pointing to a chap in army uniform walking towards us along the pavement. Indeed it was, and we spent five happy minutes swopping experiences. Donald was the number one Scottish tennis player and it appeared that he was stationed in that part of the world. He was in as big a hurry to be off as we were so there was time only to wish each other well and go on our respective ways.

From our brief visit it was apparent that the comparative remoteness of Torquay would make it a good substitute training centre. The Majestic Hotel, some way from the front, would be perfectly adequate for the needs of our squadron. There were other officers there from Number 3 Initial Training Wing, who had been our neighbours at St Leonards, looking at other hotels which had been requisitioned in the Torquay and Paignton areas for their squadrons.

We moved into the Majestic early in July 1940. The day-to-day activities there were very much the same as they had been at Hastings. Torquay was a busy town at that time. Just about a mile away up the Babbacombe Road was the Palace Hotel which had become an RAF Officers' Hospital. We used to see them sometimes, these poor chaps encased in plaster and often on crutches, walking around the town. If we were marching cadets past them, we would have to go through the same routine as on the parade ground, a smart 'eyes right' and then a salute from the officer in charge.

Not surprisingly some of the wounded officers were not able to return the salute but regrettably others who were able to sometimes did not bother. Eventually this came to the ears of Air Commodore Critchley and he paid a visit to the officer in command of the RAF hospital to see what could be done about it.

On the day of his arrival in Torquay some of the ITW officers were sitting at a round table on the patio of the Imperial Hotel enjoying the sea view and a pre-lunch gin and tonic. The result was that the next day all officers were summoned to a meeting in a large hall near the harbour. We were ordered to wear full dress uniform which meant peaked cap and gloves plus a revolver which had just been issued to some of us a few weeks earlier (though there were no bullets!) and well-polished shoes.

In came the great man looking serious and slightly aggressive. He proceeded to deliver a superb lecture on the reasons why we were all there. He reminded us that this was not a holiday camp, that there was a war on and that we had a tremendous responsibility training the boys who would one day be flying the aeroplanes that would be defending this country. He made it clear that anyone caught lounging around and drinking in public would hear from him personally. The whole thing was short, sharp and exactly to the right point. It made a great impression on all of us.

The following day Critchley appeared unannounced at some of our activities. It was a totally different Air Commodore that we saw now, much more casual and relaxed. My cadets were on parade when he joined us. He accompanied me as I walked round on inspection and stopped to chat quite informally to several of them. 'How are you enjoying life here?' he would ask one. 'And where do you come from, young man?' to another, and, 'Well done, I hear you're doing a great job and pulling your weight in this unit. Keep it up.' It was an example of the personal touch that endears all great commanders to their men. He went off as suddenly as he had arrived and that was the last I saw of him.

I had only been in Torquay for a little over two months when one evening I was called to the Squadron Adjutant's office. He informed me that a posting had come through for me but he wasn't yet quite sure exactly where I would go. He thought it was probably an overseas posting and advised me to get my kit packed up so that I would be ready to leave the next day as soon as my destination became known. He also told me to see the CO before I left.

I saw the CO that night. He thanked me for what I'd done for the squadron and for the men and wished me well in whatever role I was asked to fill. I returned to the billet and said my goodbyes to Flight Lieutenant Morris who had nursed me through the early days at Hastings and to Sergeant Farraday who had helped me to get off on the right foot. While I was packing my belongings an airman came in to say that the Adjutant would like to see me straight away. I returned to his office to be informed that my posting had now come through. He told me that I was to report to the Officers' Hospital at Babbacombe in the morning. I was astonished. I had been envisaging a rather different future for myself and here I was moving just a mile or so up the road! 'There's no indication as to what your duties will be, but you have to report in the morning to the Commanding Officer at the Palace Hotel,' he said. 'I suspect it will have something to do with rehabilitation,' added the Adjutant.

So it was that I returned to another familiar setting, the Palace Hotel, a building which I had visited many times already through tennis and would return to often for cup events and tournaments over the next thirty years. It was 3 September 1940, exactly a year to the day after the outbreak of war. As I went through that famous entrance I felt a tingle of expectation. A new challenge seemed to be looming. The Adjutant took me in to see Group Captain Iredale who, to my surprise, was sitting there with his feet up on the table, *The Times* newspaper in his hands and his peaked cap on the table beside his feet. I saluted and wished him good morning. 'Good morning, Maskell,' he said. 'We're going to start rehabilitation here and you are the Rehabilitation Officer. That will be your branch.'

So far as I know I was the only Rehabilitation Officer in the Royal Air Force for most of the war. As we built up the rehabilitation teams to meet the demands of wounded air crew they all came from the PTI branch. The rehabilitation branch contained just me.

Iredale explained that the medical staff at the hospital had decided it was necessary for many of the patients to take exercise in a controlled way throughout the day as well as having physiotherapy treatment when necessary.

'You will report to Wing Commander O'Malley, who is on leave at the moment. But he will be back in two or three days so in the meantime, familiarize yourself with the place.' I explained that in physical terms I knew the Palace Hotel well. 'That's good – then I'll get the Adjutant to introduce you to the doctors, especially those you'll be working with. Until O'Malley returns you might as well make his office your base.'

The doctors were a marvellous team. The senior surgeon was Wing Commander John Pocock, whom I came to know well at Torquay and met again several times after the war at Bristol where he had succeeded his late father as the senior surgeon at the local hospital. I was also introduced to Squadron Leader Donald Bateman, who had read medicine up at Oxford where he had been friendly with a man named Pat Moynihan. Pat's father, Lord Moynihan, was a famous surgeon and it was Pat who persuaded Donald to write his father's life story. Donald actually completed the manuscript during his days at Torquay and *Berkeley Moynihan, Surgeon* became a bestseller during the war. An American who eventually became a patient told me that it had made an impression across the Atlantic too. Squadron Leader Cawthorne was the second surgeon and Wing Commander Bill Morris, a tall, elegant man, was the ear, nose and throat specialist. He had been the top man at the London Hospital before the war.

During the two days before O'Malley's return, I got to know these senior members of the team quite well. I also looked around the familiar setting of the Palace Hotel. Nothing seemed to have changed inside. However, the two indoor tennis courts, I saw, had become a store-house for all the beds and blankets that a hospital needs to have in reserve as well as for all the general stores. I met the quartermaster, Flight Lieutenant Fletcher, who seemed rather concerned that I was eyeing the courts with a view to using them as a covered exercise area.

Bateman suggested after dinner my first night that I join him in his consulting room so that he could explain what the team was trying to do. 'Dan, I can imagine it must be rather a change for you suddenly to be posted up here, but what we are aiming to do is to devise exercises and activities for the wounded patients who are at the moment recovering too slowly. This is not only our view but has more or less been ordered by civilian consultant to the RAF, Reginald Watson-Jones.' (He was later knighted. His counterpart in uniform was Wing-Commander 'Nobby' Osmond-Clarke, who became an Air Commodore and much later was also knighted. They had both done tremendous work in the Liverpool area and later came to London where their reputations grew enormously. Eventually the two of them became orthopaedic surgeons to the Royal Family.)

Bateman continued, 'Dan, I should gather your thoughts tomorrow about how you would like to tackle this plan so that when you meet O'Malley you'll have something to suggest to him. I think you'll like him. He came into the RAF as soon as he had qualified and he always likes to pretend that it was the only way he could lead the life of a gentleman, keep up to date with medicine and keep up with his sport! Of course, he was a fine sportsman and played rugby for the service and for a time acted as the secretary of RAF rugby. He'll certainly have some ideas of his own.'

I took Bateman's advice. The next morning found me sitting in O'Malley's office busily making notes of the things I believed might be helpful in trying to devise progressive exercises for wounded airmen. The Palace Hotel was uniquely placed to provide a wide variety of exercise. Besides the two covered tennis courts there were squash courts, a gymnasium, a swimming pool, a croquet lawn and a nine-hole short golf course. There were also four hard tennis courts out of doors. Just below the lovely gardens of the hotel was Anstey's Cove and I even visualized the possibility of the patients enjoying some swimming from there. I was busy with my thoughts when I vaguely heard the door opening. Without looking round I called 'Come in' but there was no answer. Turning round I saw a tall, well-built man standing there smiling and extending his hand. 'Dan Maskell, isn't it?' he said. 'Yes it is, and I imagine it's Wing-Commander O'Malley?' 'Right first time,' he said, still smiling. There was an immediate rapport between us as we started to discuss ways of tackling the task that lay ahead. Our initial chat turned into a two-hour brainstorm. Although he'd just returned from leave and must have had many things to do, O'Malley felt it was essential to brief me properly because we were embarking on a new and in a sense almost an experimental journey at the hospital.

O'Malley had then said, 'Well, Dan, it's up to you how you do it, but our first priority must be to get the men back into action as quickly as possible. What do you have in mind?'

'Well, sir, I've already looked at all the facilities here which seem to be very much as I remember them in pre-war days. Surely the first thing we must do is to clear the quartermaster's stores from the covered courts to give us a covered exercise area in bad weather.' O'Malley nearly fell off his chair. 'Have you met our quartermaster, Flight Lieutenant Fletcher?' he asked. 'He's a regular, you know, a man who came into the service as an Aircraftsman and he has risen to his present rank the hard way. This is going to be a hell of a problem but I can understand why you want those courts. You will certainly need all that area if we do our job properly and get them on their feet quickly. You know this is a two-hundred bed hospital. We usually have about forty chaps actually confined to bed and the rest in various stages of repair, most of them capable of taking some sort of exercise.'

I was impressed by his immediate grasp of our needs. 'The main thing is, sir, that we must conduct all our activities in a spirit of fun and optimism I think – that's the way to get the best out of people.' That surprised him. I continued, 'In my pre-war job, sir, I was doing my best to persuade my fellow professionals to make tennis lessons fun instead of just a hard, slogging sweat.' 'Yes, that makes sense,' he said. 'If you can get that over you'll have won the day.'

I was warming to my theme. 'You know that we've got Charlie Ward down here as the golf professional? He's a civilian of course but I know him well and I'm sure he'd be ready to play his part in helping us to achieve our objectives. He's employed here he tells me to cut the grass and keep the golf course in order and to look after the four hard tennis courts. I'm sure we could make use of Charlie if you'd allow us to, because like myself he's a professional teacher and I could see some of the chaps who are able to walk a little, getting a great kick out of swinging a golf club. I can't think of anything that would keep them more interested, even perhaps learning the game for the first time.' O'Malley thought this was a great idea. 'You'll probably get me put in prison for employing a civilian to do medical work for us, but I'll see what I can do.' So it was arranged. Charlie Ward did do a great deal of wonderful work with the disabled aircrew and he actually joined the RAF after O'Malley had arranged to get him out of the Army when, later, he had been called up. He was never a trained PTI but he had an instinct for teaching that made him a great asset.

When I first arrived at the hospital, Arthur Roberts, my great pal from the Queen's Club days, was still there. Shortly before the war, when Arthur had already been at the Palace Hotel for a few years, the post of Surrey county coach came up and I had suggested Arthur as the logical choice. He had come up to London to talk to me about it but eventually had turned the job down saying, 'I think I'd rather stay at Torquay as a big fish in a small pond.' Arthur would have been a big fish in any pond. He was a shrewd psychologist and had the greatest record as a producer of players of any of my contemporaries from the Queen's Club days. In a long and distinguished career he produced Joan Curry, Angela Mortimer, Sue Barker and Mike Sangster who all distinguished themselves, as well as his own son, Paddy, who won the Junior Championship and became a Davis Cup player. However, soon after my arrival Arthur left the Palace to work in a munitions factory in Bristol. An ulcer made him medically unfit to serve in the armed forces, and eventually he had to give up his work in Bristol.

The medical officers would have lunch at the top table in the famous dining-room at the Palace. In front of us at the tables all round the room were the patients, many of them Battle of Britain heroes, some of them very badly burned and many with broken limbs. It took me quite a while to grow accustomed to this for I had never worked in a hospital before and had had no preparation for my new job. On my third day John Pocock suggested that I join him after lunch for a briefing. 'I've just been talking to Wing Commander O'Malley,' he said. 'I've got your first five patients ready. They've all got burned hands and clawed fingers. You may have seen one or two of them about the place. There is nothing now that will hurt their hands. They can knock them without the risk of further damage, but they must stretch and strengthen their fingers and get the full range of movement back. They'll only do this if they're employed four or five hours every day in the attempt. See what you can think of, Dan.'

I had indeed seen one or two of these chaps trying to be conscientious about exercise. They would put a handkerchief on the table, then try to stretch their fingers out and encircle the handkerchief, then claw it up and make it into a ball. It was a sound enough activity but it was incredibly boring.

'Well, you might as well meet them straight away,' said Pocock. A batman was despatched and in a short time he returned with the five injured men. They were of mixed rank and mixed outlook. Some despondent, others more cheerful. I took them down into the gym and explained what I wanted them to do. I had a squash ball and a tennis ball and asked them to stand in a close circle ready to catch the balls as they were thrown to them. 'Let's make a game of it,' I said. 'We'll all put sixpence in the kitty and see who can win the money. You chaps will all have three lives and you'll lose a life for every time you drop the ball. I won't have any lives and we'll keep two balls going at once.'

Immediately they were keen to compete. We had a lot of fun pulling each other's legs as the ball was occasionally dropped and the lives were lost. Eventually there were just a couple of them left in; I had taken care to lose my only life early on so that I wasn't involved in the later stages. You would have thought the last remaining pair were playing the Wimbledon final, so keen were they to succeed. Some of them didn't have any money with them and as the sessions progressed, so did my list of IOUs. That, of course, was the last thing that mattered. The point was they were all exercising their hands naturally and having a great deal of fun doing it.

Their appetite for this simple pastime seemed insatiable. The word soon got around about these contests in the gym and soon we had a crowd of onlookers cheering for their favourites. More importantly the exercise seemed to be having the required effect on the fingers. Within a week the range of movement and strength of grip had measurably increased. As the weeks passed their range of activities also grew. So did the enthusiasm of the patients. We formed them into classes according to their individual abilities. There were swimming classes in groups, gym classes, golf classes and also sessions for individuals who needed more attention.

We were always looking for new ways of giving the patients appropriate activities that would both exercise the correct limbs and also provide variety and confidence. Cycling was a marvellous example of that. It became a familiar sight around the streets of Torquay to see the men toiling away on their bicycles. They revelled in the change of scene.

Archery was another activity that provided excellent exercise for fingers, arms, shoulders and even the back. But there was a desperate shortage of bows and arrows. The problem was solved by a local resident who knew of a keen archer living in Stoke Gabriel, a village on the River Dart. O'Malley suggested that I should take an RAF vehicle and visit him. A charming old gentleman answered the door and offered me a glass of sherry. On the walls of the entrance hall I had noticed half a dozen bows of various sizes and an umbrella stand full of arrows. When I explained our need he was delighted to let us have his entire collection. 'Much better that they should be used to help our fine young RAF men, rather than sit here on my walls,' he said.

The patients had a variety of injuries. There were fractures, gunshot wounds, amputees (below and above the knee) and, of course, burns. In due course John Pocock wanted me to go in and watch some of the operations so that I could better understand the problems that the patients faced. I remember seeing him operate on Wing Commander Irving Bell, who had two false feet. He used to lift himself out of the bath with his strong arms. One of his feet was not functioning properly and Pocock had to re-amputate that leg three inches above the ankle. It was a fascinating experience to see the skill of the surgeon as he did his work. This was not the first operation I had seen. That had been some weeks earlier when a fractured leg involved a cartilage with a bucket handle tear. That had made me feel a little squeamish but now I had become more used to the activities in the operating theatre.

The injuries were not all purely physical. Sometimes it was

a question of working out the right psychological approach. Pilot Officer Edmonds, a South African boy aged about twenty-one, came to us towards the end of 1940. He was one of the first patients I got to know well. Matron first told me about him. She explained that he seemed terribly depressed, very low in spirit. He had, she said, the face of a man who had suffered. She suggested that I visit him. The boy was sitting in a chair facing the window that looked out over the golf course. It was the sort of view that would normally have heartened any young man keen on sport as I knew Edmonds was. Through the open window you could hear the click of club on ball. I introduced myself. 'They tell me you've got a bit of a problem, Eddie,' I said. He showed me his legs, and they were very badly burned. His hands too had been slightly burned. He had been in a plane that blew up. 'That's the end of my days of sport,' he said dejectedly, with his slight South African accent.

This was my first experience of talking to a man who thought he had no future. 'What's that, Eddie, no more sport? Don't you ever say that here. Listen to those boys out there playing golf – every one was as badly injured as you when he arrived.'

'I can't ever imagine myself doing that,' he said despondently.

'I guarantee, Eddie, that before you leave here you'll be playing golf out there with the rest of them.'

'I've never hit a golf ball in my life.'

'Nor had many of them,' I replied.

After dinner that night John Pocock strolled across for a chat. 'I hear you had a word with Edmonds today, Dan. You have your work cut out there you know. He has real problems with those legs. If he walks again without sticks it will be a minor miracle.'

I paid Eddie several visits over the next few weeks trying to plant in his mind a seed of hope, offering enticement in the form of more individual attention in the classes that he had joined for leg injuries. All the time I was dangling the carrot of a round of golf in front of him. Gradually he seemed to acquire a purpose. In time he started to walk again with sticks, then on someone's arm. One day he said to me, 'What about that round of golf?' I knew that the battle was almost won. I arranged for him to play Charlie Ward and went out to watch. He certainly looked determined but he came back after four holes. I went to see him at lunchtime. He was still rather tense from the effort. 'As soon as you've played nine holes, Eddie, I'll take you on. We'll have a four ball.'

Edmonds was one of the great success stories. Eventually he won a golf competition. His prize, I seem to remember, was a Biro pen. To see his reaction you'd think he had been given the Open Championship trophy. He was now walking well. Pocock was delighted and had given him clearance to fly again, but non-combatant flying only. At last he headed back to a new posting at some distant station. We heard later that he'd been up to Scotland on a golf holiday and married the golf pro's daughter. If only all our cases had ended as happily.

Yet this was not the end of the Edmonds story. There was an interesting sequel in February 1943. By then I was at Loughborough doing the same work as at Torquay. We were getting a number of parachute injuries, ankles and legs mostly, from the training unit at Ringwood in Manchester. I was sent up there to make suggestions to help eliminate those injuries. I flew up to Ringwood from Wymeswold airport near Loughborough in a Dakota. Some of our patients came for the ride and to see the parachute training. There were about a dozen of us in all. As we were waiting to board the aircraft a Flight Lieutenant came over to me and smiled. It was Edmonds. He told me that he would be piloting us to Ringwood and he was clearly nervous at the prospect of flying a plane-load of battle-hardened and decorated aircrew. I was now a Squadron Leader (for some reason

I had bypassed the rank of Flight Lieutenant) and when we were in the air the Flight Sergeant navigator came back from the cockpit and said 'The Captain wonders if you would like to come up front, sir.' It was an emotional moment standing there while Edmonds piloted us expertly towards Manchester. I went back to my seat for the landing and said cheerio to him as we left the aircraft.

During that winter Flight Lieutenant Nick Zinovieff arrived at the hospital. He had been recommended by Watson-Jones and Osmond-Clarke who, as I mentioned, had worked together in Liverpool before they had come to London. Nick was to be the medical officer in charge of our rehabilitation activities. Henceforth I worked through him and he was our liaison with the other doctors. At our first meeting he said 'I think you know my sister.' 'I certainly do,' I replied. 'One of the prettiest girls I've ever seen and not a bad tennis player either.' She was a past winner of the schoolgirls' tournament at Queen's Club.

Flight Lieutenant James Brindley 'Nick' Nicolson, the first RAF VC of the war, came to us after baling out over Romsey, Hampshire, having shot down a Messerschmitt while his own aircraft was on fire. His wife, who was pregnant, came to visit him and I was able to explain to her how we were trying to help him. When his burned hands and other serious injuries had healed he returned to duty, and served in Burma. There, in May 1945, within a few days of the war's end, Nick was killed when his Liberator crashed in the Bay of Bengal.

Four years later, in 1949, I was just leaving the clubhouse with Pancho Segura at the Filey Road tennis club in Scarborough. We were about to play our first round singles in the Slazenger Professional tournament. As we came down the steps I was approached by a woman who looked vaguely familiar. She was accompanied by a young boy and a man I did not know.

'You don't remember me, Dan, do you?' she asked.

'I'm afraid I don't,' I replied. 'Should I?'

'I'm Nick's wife,' she said.

Thoughts of Torquay came flooding back.

'And this must be your youngster,' I said.

'Yes,' she said, 'and this is my brother whom you haven't met,' she added.

The boy, James, was carrying a programme and was holding it out for me to autograph. It was no easy matter finding the right words for the dedication. This poignant moment once again forcibly reminded me of the harsh realities of war.

Gradually the need to expand our staff became apparent as the workload grew. It was difficult to get permission for adding physical training instructors to our roster, but in due course we did acquire six and they were all fully occupied.

I shall always remember my days at Torquay with great humility. I counted it a privilege to be working among men who showed such depths of courage in great adversity. I remember a young Australian Squadron Leader who had a problem with his hip and knee as a result of a crash. I had never met him until Watson-Jones asked me to attend one of his clinics. I heard the prognosis. 'I've studied your case,' said the surgeon. 'Your choices are: one, to freeze the hip and knee so that you're free of pain. It means that you'll have a stiff leg for the rest of your life. Two, amputate above the knee and have an artificial leg that will bend and give you mobility. Three, stay as you are and have a painful knee and hip for the rest of your life.'

'Can I ask you, sir, if it was your leg and you were my age, what would you do?'

Watson-Jones paused and looked at him soberly. 'I would have the amputation,' he said.

'Okay – what's good enough for you is good enough for me. I'll take the amputation.'

As I sat there listening to this extraordinary conversation I wondered if I could have shown the same courage.

Squadron Leader Bill Simpson, DFC, was in his mid-twenties when he first came to us from East Grinstead, where he was a patient of Sir Archibald McIndoe, the famous plastic surgeon. He was very badly burned after being shot down during the evacuation of Dunkirk. Simpson's book, *One of Our Pilots is Safe*, made a great impression at the time and in the sequel, *The Way to Recovery*, he told a little of the story of his time with us. Another patient who wrote a moving book was Richard Hillary. *The Last Enemy* proved to be his epitaph for, after recovering from his burns and returning to duty, he was lost in action.

Throughout my early months at Torquay I was keeping in touch with Con by telephone. She was still at White Corner guarded only by a statuette of the greyhound Mick the Miller in our garden. It had been put there by the people who had owned the house before we had bought it in 1936 – presumably they were regular visitors to the Wimbledon Dog track, about a mile and a half from the house.

Con, who was seven months pregnant, was having a bad time. The nightly bombings meant that she was sleeping on a mattress under the stairs. She used to cycle to the All England Club for her ARP civil defence duties. One day late in October O'Malley said: 'I hear your wife is pregnant. I think you'd better bring her down here and if she takes a fancy to my ugly mug, I'd be more than happy to deliver the babe for her. So far, I've safely delivered 1,038 – for eight years I was in charge of the maternity wards at RAF Halton. Let me know about it in due course, but meanwhile make arrangements for her to join you here.'

I was overjoyed. I was given the necessary petrol coupons on compassionate grounds and set off to collect Con in the little Morris 8. Realizing that our absence might be quite a lengthy one, the agents let the house in Wimbledon to a war reserve policeman and his wife and two children. He had been injured by bomb blast.

It was a rule that married officers had to live out so when

we returned to Torquay we went to a small hotel near the harbour as a temporary measure. In her younger days, Con had been a secretary and with typical energy she threw herself into helping in our doctors' office. Soon she was suggesting that we should have a milk bar in the gym so she organized it and ran it with the help of Sheila Norris, who was a pupil of Arthur Roberts. In due course, Sheila's daughter became one of our best young national players.

It wasn't long before Con was organizing a variety show every two weeks and then she put on two plays, *Flare Path* and *Musical Chairs*. Both were tackled with her usual enthusiasm and energy. How she found the time to do all these things I don't know, especially in her condition, but she then added to her responsibilities by running a touring library for the bed patients – another welcome relief for them and the nursing staff. She also helped me with the *Torquay Tatler*, a magazine that we started to give the patients another interest. They contributed to it in varying degrees and we had a lot of fun with our articles that were gently disrespectful of the staff. Con, with her infectious enthusiasm, was an asset to the RAF Officers' Hospital and I'm happy to say she was thoroughly appreciated. One of her most prized possessions was a silver plate presented to her on our departure by Reginald Watson-Jones and Osmond-Clarke suitably inscribed 'To Con – in gratitude . . .' It used to stand beside the silver tankard presented to me when I was demobilized from Loughborough.

Certainly our days at Torquay, despite the serious nature of the work, were enjoyable and rewarding. However, nothing could have been more rewarding than the arrival of our first baby. As Christmas approached it became clear that the birth was imminent. Shortly before the start of the holiday O'Malley stopped me in the corridor one day and said, 'Dan, I believe you know Godfrey Winn.'

'Yes, I do, but I haven't seen him for some time.'

'Well you soon will because he's being sent down here

over the Christmas period in his capacity as a war correspondent, to do a story on the way we spend our Christmas here
at the hospital. He's due to arrive on Christmas Eve.'

Con and I were looking forward to Godfrey's visit for he
was always a cheerful person, full of good tales and good-
natured banter. As luck would have it, it was on Christmas
Eve itself that Con moved into the maternity home in The
Warren, a road that was situated near the Majestic Hotel
where I had first been billeted with the Number 5 ITW on
my arrival in Torquay.

We left a message with the duty NCO at the hospital
asking him to phone the maternity home if we had not
returned by the time Godfrey arrived. I must admit that I
was a typically nervous father as I sat that evening outside
the delivery room waiting for news from O'Malley. At six
o'clock he came out dressed in his white surgeon's coat and
red waterproof apron. He was smiling broadly. 'Congratulations, Dan, you have a baby daughter. Con is fine, don't
worry, they're both well. And always remember, this is my
1,039th successful delivery!' At that very moment a nurse
came up to me and said, 'Mr Maskell?' I nodded. 'There is a
message for you from Mr Godfrey Winn. He has arrived at
the Palace Hotel and asked me to tell you.'

'Could you please ask them at the hospital to get him a car
to drive him to the Silver Grill restaurant overlooking the
harbour, to help us celebrate over dinner.' The nurse hurried
away on her errand while I went in to see Con. I have to say
that this was the proudest moment of my life, seeing little
Robin there in Con's arms – we agreed on the name as a
tribute to the Christmas robin – and already, I thought,
looking so much like her.

It is traditional in all service hospitals that on Christmas
Day the doctors and other officers wait on the staff, the
airmen and WAAF personnel. We maintained that tradition
splendidly at the Palace. There was a Christmas tree in the
nurses' mess beyond the lift. There were presents for all the

patients which O'Malley, dressed up as Santa Claus, dug out from the huge lucky dip. The lunch itself was served in the main dining-room and for the first time patients and staff, doctors, airmen and the women of the WAAF were all together. Some of the patients even joined in serving at table.

The whole happy scene seemed to impress Godfrey Winn who, at one stage of the proceedings, asked, 'I don't suppose there's a chance of any tennis, Dan?' 'Not with me – I'm on duty. But I'm sure I can find you an opponent.' In the end he played against one of the patients, a Wing Commander, who was almost fully recovered from his injuries. It was nearly dusk when they went out to the clay courts; when they came back Godfrey was proud to tell me that he had won!

Later in the evening Godfrey started collecting material for his article. 'I hear you charge your patients a shilling for a bus ride to Dartmoor,' he said mischievously. 'Well, Godfrey, my senior instructor, Sergeant Frank Mann, is an experienced rambler and offered to take some of the boys out on the moor. Although O'Malley and the other medical officers fully approved, we couldn't get official transport so I had to hire a local motor coach.' 'Ridiculous,' exploded Godfrey. 'These are the cream of our fighting forces. How can they not provide transport for them?' Godfrey's article, *An RAF Hospital at Christmas time*, criticized this lack and with two weeks transport had magically been provided for us. It was a lovely piece he wrote and included some very flattering stuff about the work I was doing. He brought a beautiful light touch to the Christmas festivities. Later Godfrey went on a famous convoy to Russia, reporting on the bombing and torpedoing in those cruel seas. He wrote a book about his experiences and donated the royalties to the Merchant Seaman's Benevolent Fund. He was kind enough to send me a signed copy.

Now that we had Robin with us and knowing that Con's parents were coming down from Wimbledon Park to live with us for a while, we had to move. We found a house called 'Upyonda' between Paignton and Churston. Later we went on to a flat in the Ilsham valley, just near the hospital, and we employed a local girl to look after Robin.

There was a succession of distinguished visitors at the hospital, some of whom I had invited down to talk to the patients as part of our rehabilitation therapy. I persuaded Trevor Wignall to come down. He had twice been bombed out of his flat near Marble Arch and decided eventually to come and live in Torquay. He stayed at the Headland Hotel for a while until he found a house almost on the Churston golf course, between Paignton and Brixham. That was where I went to see him and suggested he might give us a talk one evening, to which he readily agreed. I knew he would interest his audience for he was a great story-teller. Sure enough he held them enthralled with marvellous tales about Jack Dempsey, Gene Tunney and other great sporting celebrities, and the famous Irish tenor, John McCormack. He also told us about his uncle, who had been the Governor of Dartmoor Prison and who in 1939 had arranged for Trevor to visit Alcatraz Prison where Al Capone was detained, so that he could write a story about his impending release. Leonard Crawley also spoke to us a couple of times and was excellent chatting to the patients afterwards.

Though none of us knew it at the time, our lives were about to be changed dramatically. On Friday, 23 October 1942, O'Malley called us all together, doctors and medical staff. 'Gentlemen, we've got forty patients going out today and none coming in over the weekend. Accordingly, I want you all to get the hell out of here for a well-deserved break. We'll just keep a skeleton staff and they'll be notified who they are. Dan, I want you to stay here for a moment.'

The others dispersed and I was told by O'Malley to take Flight Lieutenant Jimmy Rickards, our anaesthetist, who had a very heavy workload, away to Saunton Golf Club, where I had been a country member, for a weekend of golf. O'Malley was concerned that Rickards could face a possible breakdown. 'Take the whole weekend off and come back ready for work on Monday morning. Perhaps you'll contact him and tell him,' said O'Malley.

I got permission to take Charlie Ward and Sergeant Frank Mann who was being recommended for a commission, with us. I knew that Charlie would be excellent therapeutic value for Jimmy Rickards as he had a fund of golfing stories. Charlie and I set off on the Friday evening in my faithful Morris, driving once more in the blackout. I had obtained the necessary coupons for 'compassionate petrol', but we had only just enough to get us there and back. Shortly before we left I suddenly realized that we hadn't got anywhere to stay so I phoned the Preston House Hotel, a private establishment near the famous Saunton Sands Hotel, where two middle-aged sisters were the owners. I used to stay there when I went with my pals from Wimbledon Common Golf Club on golf trips before the war.

There had been rumours that the Saunton Club had been taken over by the Americans as a battle training ground so I checked with one of the sisters to make sure that golf was still being played. Of course, with war-time secrecy uppermost in our minds, I couldn't tell them we were coming but did ascertain that the hotel was closed at this time of the year. I asked them what they would do if four people were suddenly to arrive on their doorstep. 'Well,' she said, completely disregarding security, 'if it was you and your friends, I suppose we would open the hotel especially.' And that's just what they did.

Charlie and I had an excellent round of golf on the Saturday morning while Frank Mann and Jimmy Rickards came over on Jimmy's motorbike and sidecar. When we came in from the golf course there they were keen as mustard to get into action themselves. They had already checked into the Preston House Hotel so we played golf that afternoon. After another beautifully relaxing round on the Sunday morning, Jimmy Rickards said he thought he ought to go back that night because of his operating schedule the next day. Charlie and I had already decided to stay the night so that we could return to Torquay by daylight early on Monday morning. While we were having our supper that evening, we heard Lord Haw-Haw on the radio claiming that a great military establishment in the south-west of England had been bombed to pieces. We wondered where it could be and speculated that it was probably the dockyards at Plymouth or a military establishment in Cornwall. Later that evening I had a phone call from Con. It was a strange conversation. She said: 'I thought you'd like to know we've got a party on in the house.'

'What do you mean, some of the chaps?'

'Yes,' she replied, 'about eighteen or nineteen are going to stay the night.'

I could tell from the tone of her voice that something strange was going on and I remember thinking how extra-ordinary it was that the men were going to stay the night. After all, it was only about a quarter of a mile walk from our flat in Ilsham Drive to the Palace.

The conversation got even stranger. 'We're all going to be there,' she said.

'Well, I hope they all get some sleep,' I said.

'Oh yes, they'll sleep on the floor. These chaps are used to mucking in.'

For security reasons, of course, she couldn't mention the hospital and I certainly didn't tell her anything about Lord Haw-Haw's claim – but later I began to put two and two together.

The next morning Charlie and I set off in the car back to Torquay worrying about what we might find. As we came up the hill towards Babbacombe we saw the police notices, 'Bomb damage – beware' and then there were barricades. The police guided us in and I drew up under the canopied entrance to see that there was a great crowd of vehicles in

235

the forecourt. The windows on the front were out, many of them boarded up, and there was a great gaping hole in the roof. Now I realized the full significance of Con's call. She had been trying to tell me that she and Robin were all right and that she was looking after some of the patients.

Three bombs had fallen in the vicinity. One had landed on the croquet lawn outside the gym, another had gone right through the roof of the hospital and the last had dropped in the Babbacombe Road just outside Charlie Ward's house. The damage was awful. So was the toll of casualties. Twenty patients had been killed plus one nursing sister, two VADs and my new NCO, who had been with me only six weeks – one of the finest remedial gymnasts I had come across. He had been married for a couple of years and his wife was two or three months pregnant. They were billeted up in Babbacombe out of the immediate danger area. I later discovered that the bomb which killed the NCO would probably have got me if I had not been sent down to Saunton. It was the one that had come through the roof and it had landed just after eleven o'clock in the morning, at the precise time when I would have been doing my rounds instead of him. This whole episode confirmed my view that fate has ordained what our destiny will be and although we can strive to improve ourselves and look after our neighbours, there is very little we can do if our number is on the ticket.

Since those casualty figures appeared in my book, 'From Where I Sit', I am indebted to Alan W. Cooper, RAF historian, researcher and author, who recently informed me that the official list of casualties were as follows:-

Deaths: Officers 14; Nursing Staff 2; Other Ranks 3.

Missing: Officers 1.

Injured: Officers 35; Nursing Staff 2; Other Ranks 9.

We later heard that Jimmy Rickards and Frankie Mann had had an extraordinary end to their return journey on the motorbike and sidecar. They had travelled home in the blackout with only the light from the slits of the headlights to guide them. As they had pulled up outside the hospital after all those miles from north to south Devon and come to a stop, the sidecar had fallen away from the motorbike and Frank Mann was tipped out on to the ground. If that had happened when they were travelling at speed, he would have been killed. His number was obviously not on the ticket that night either.

As a result of the bombing the authorities decided that we should move to Loughborough. It was not the first experience of a direct attack on Torquay. The 'Funk Hole of Great Britain', so called by the press was far from that in reality. I personally had seen bombs fall when I was engaged on a room inspection during the early days at ITW 5 in 1940. We had even had a German plane shot down in Torbay, just opposite the Palm Court Hotel. An alert army cook had quickly manned a Bofors gun when he had heard the low-flying aircraft coming and had brought him down in the sea.

So it was that Loughborough once more impinged upon my life. I was sent ahead to meet Dr Schofield, who was still there, to see that our requests for accommodation could be met. I also met Mr Sibley, the senior lecturer in physical education, with whom I had to agree the facilities that could be made available, particularly the rehabilitation facilities. For accommodation we were given two of the students' halls, Hazelrigg Hall and Rutland Hall. So on about 10 November the entire hospital unit moved into new quarters. We soon got into the swing of things and took over the indoor swimming-pool for certain hours each day as well as the squash courts, the track, the football field and the gymnasium, which was particularly necessary to the sort of work we were doing.

The Loughborough operation was altogether bigger than the one we had at Torquay. There were two hundred officer patients and now an additional two hundred NCOs and airmen to look after, all in the technical trade branches, and it was clear that we needed more staff. Squadron Leader Harold Livingstone, a doctor from Liverpool, was the senior medical officer on the airmen's side. He had Squadron Leader Cawthorne working with him. In the rehabilitation unit we had our hands completely full and put in a request for some of the trained PTIs to be sent to help us. I suggested that the sportsmen among them would be the most appropriate choice. In due course a veritable galaxy of star performers arrived including Sergeant Griffiths, a Manchester United footballer, Sergeant Thompson who had played for Bolton Wanderers, Sergeant Peter Doherty, the Irish soccer international, and Sergeant Raich Carter, an England international footballer who would win several war-time caps. After a short period of introduction to the special needs in rehabilitation activities every one of them became valued members of our original team.

At one time we had seven professional footballers on our strength. I approached Derby County to see if they would let our boys play for them. In return I would expect the club to allow our patients to come and watch the matches from seats in the stand. The club was delighted with the suggestion. Accordingly, for every home match a bus would deliver twenty-five of our patients to watch our PTIs running rings round the opposition on the football field. Derby made a fuss of both the patients and our players. It was good public relations both for them and for us.

It then occurred to me that we could raise a lot of money for charity by playing matches on Wednesday evenings. This was early closing day in the area and in no time these matches became quite a popular feature of the season. I was talked into playing in several of the charity matches at local amateur clubs – certainly not at Derby County – smaller clubs in the district at Ashby de la Zouche and Leicester. I played as a centre-half behind Carter and Doherty, in boots I obtained from the Naafi. The matches of those two years, 1943 and 1944, were a great experience. On the left wing was

Squadron Leader Doctor Eddie Mason. During his very first match he was tackled near the left touchline and tore a cartilage. He went to Ely hospital for an operation. Later Eddie treated Frank Sedgman when he was playing at Wimbledon; another who treated him was Bill Coombs, whom I first met at Torquay. He was a skilled physiotherapist and became a regular member of the Wimbledon dressing-room treatment team in the Championships after the war.

The football was so successful that the police became worried about the number of spectators at these charity matches and asked us to take things easy. But we did raise a lot of money for the Red Cross.

When Raich Carter was chosen to play in a war-time international at Wembley in 1944, O'Malley went to watch. Although he was a rugger man he thoroughly enjoyed the experience and went into the dressing-room before the match to wish the England team the best of luck.

Our work continued with greater skill than ever as we began to learn how to help the patients with new techniques and new approaches, most of them devised by Nick Zinovieff. We tried to keep the social atmosphere as normal as possible by organizing a dance every month in Hazelrigg Hall. We saw this as part of the rehabilitation process. The patients were allowed to bring a member of the family or a friend and the parties were usually most successful. One weekend I was the duty officer of the day and welcomed Nobby Clarke on one of his periodic visits to see his patients. I was upstairs in Hazelrigg Hall listening to the news on the radio when a young duty orderly came running up to me and said, 'Quick, sir, come at once. A patient has shot someone in the bar.'

I dashed downstairs to find everyone pouring out of the mess bar looking stunned. There was a girl draped across the table with Clarke and one of the unit doctors tending her. She was taken off in an ambulance to Loughborough Hospital but died before she arrived there. The police were called

239

and they arrested one of our patients, a Flight Lieutenant who had used a small hand gun (it was not his service revolver) to fire shots in the direction of the girl. It seemed that she had been spending time with one of his friends. He was eventually given six years for manslaughter and was sent to Maidstone prison. While awaiting trial he was kept in Leicester prison. His wife was sent for, and I duly met her at Loughborough police station and then brought her to Hazelrigg Hall where the matron had prepared a room for her. From there she visited her husband. I duly made a report on the incident and tried to forget it. It had been an unnerving experience. Years later, it must have been in about 1977, one of the umpires at Wimbledon said to me that during the war he had been a prison visitor teaching languages. On one visit to Maidstone prison a prisoner said to him, 'If you're a tennis umpire, you probably know Dan Maskell.' 'Yes, as a matter of fact I do,' he had replied. 'Well, he is responsible for me being here,' the prisoner said.

Fortunately life was much less dramatic than that most of the time. For Con and me the greatest excitement came on 16 April 1945, the day that a baby brother for Robin came into our lives. John Jamie was born in Loughborough Hospital and named after O'Malley, who would have loved to have been there to deliver him but by then he had been posted overseas. However, he was always called 'Jay' by us and by all his friends.

Tennis virtually came to a standstill in Britain during the war. The junior game was kept alive by the father of Jean Quertier who was one of our finest woman players in the years immediately following the war. He founded the Junior Lawn Tennis Club of Great Britain for players under twenty-one and they played a series of tournaments in the school holidays. There were no open tournaments at all and the LTA ran on a skeleton staff, managed by a skeleton committee.

The tennis events that did take place were exhibition

matches for charity, mostly in aid of the Red Cross. I played in several of these – at Bournemouth in 1942 and in Leicester with Bobby Meredith and the South African champion, Eric Sturgess, the same year. Incidentally I remember telling Eric Sturgess that he would need a heavier service if he was ever going to make an impression at Wimbledon. He never did with the singles but was successful twice in the mixed doubles – in 1949 with fellow South African Sheila Summers, and in 1950 with that great American, Louise Brough. I remember Bill Sidwell of Australia also appeared in one of our exhibition matches. The following year I played another match at Newport in Wales and one at Queen's Club which had been organized by Nigel Sharp, a prominent international player who had not been accepted for the services on medical grounds. Even earlier than that, at Torquay, I had organized a couple of exhibition matches for the patients and the local public. Joan Curry and Tony Mottram had played, as did Sheila Norris, who later became Mrs Cooper.

For the match at Queen's, Nigel Sharp had arranged that the Air Ministry would permit me to play. I was given special leave from Friday night to Sunday night and so decided to drive down in the faithful Morris through the dark – something I usually avoided. Some of the patients scraped up a couple of petrol coupons and told me to call at a garage near Lutterworth where the proprietor occasionally let patients from Loughborough fill up their tanks in return for some cigarettes or soap. 'Take a stick and limp a bit,' I was advised. 'He always takes pity on the patients, particularly if you can find him some cigarettes or something in short supply.' I did not like the idea but decided it was the only way to make the journey both ways and be fairly sure of getting back. The matron was giving out some free 'Martin's' cigarettes which were dreadful things to smoke so I took some of those plus a couple of bars of soap and a packet of tea. I was well prepared.

It was pitch black when I knocked on the door of the small

cottage beside the garage on a dark country road. I had a torch with me and after knocking three times shone it on the ground. The door opened to a mere slit. 'Who's that?' asked a disembodied voice. 'I'm from the RAF hospital at Loughborough,' I said. He shut the door. I waited a few moments and the door opened again. 'Come in,' the voice said. When I took a look at him I was shocked. The man had only one eye, the other a gaping socket, and was unshaven. He looked most sinister I thought. Then a woman, presumably his wife, came into the room. She looked even more evil, more like a witch. The man reminded me of the old tramp you had to pass on the way to the Rye golf club across the marshes. At a gate there used to be this wizened old man with a similar eyeless socket in the sentry box. He would be huddled in an old coat and you used to throw him a sixpenny piece so that he would let you pass.

I handed over the contraband for which the garage owner seemed grateful and paid him. Then we went out in the dark and filled up the car. I was terrified that a posse of police would arrive at any moment. Then I thought I'd better protect my return journey. 'I'm coming back late on Sunday afternoon – could I call here again?'

'No, I never have callers in daytime,' came the reply.

There was nothing on the road as I set off again towards London. It was now about 11.50pm and I was driving out of Lutterworth down a road framed with an arch of overhanging trees. It was quite like being in a leafy cathedral. In the half moonlight I saw a shadowy figure ahead in the road, about seventy yards away. I stopped the car. With pounding heart I opened the door and got out. This is ridiculous, I thought, surely there aren't really such things as ghosts. But unquestionably that's what I could see standing in the middle of the road seventy yards ahead. I climbed back into the car and crawled forward about another fifty yards. The figure remained motionless, a traditional ghost shrouded in white. I began sweating. I slapped my face and hit the horn. It had no effect. I decided to drive right through the apparition so I started the engine and moved forward. My hair was standing on end as I passed right through the object. Shaking slightly I stopped the car fifty yards ahead and got out once more. Peering back I could see absolutely nothing. Was this, I wondered, the punishment for my guilty deed? No, I told myself firmly but somewhat unconvincingly: after all, my trip was in aid of the Red Cross!

The most enjoyable of the wartime tennis matches came just after the end of hostilities in Europe in June 1945. I played in the two inter-Dominion matches that were staged on the number one court at Wimbledon. The first was between the United States Forces who had been serving in Europe and the British Empire Forces. Queen Mary was in attendance and thoroughly enjoyed being back at her beloved Wimbledon. Then in July I played for the British Servicemen against the Other Allies team. We attracted a crowd of over five thousand spectators who included the Belgian and French Ambassadors, Mrs Churchill and the Regent of Iraq. It was truly wonderful to be back in familiar surroundings on that lovely court where I would never play any future matches because of the amateur rules. The only time I would hit on the court in the future would be during the preparations for Davis Cup and Wightman Cup matches.

Six months earlier on New Year's Eve we had had a party at Loughborough. The patients, instead of turning in as usual at 11.00pm, were given an extra hour to see the New Year in. I had drawn the short straw and was the duty officer again that night. I'd been reminded by O'Malley, along with all the other officers, not to forget the RAF tradition of being on parade to salute the flag at 8.00am on New Year's Day. It was made clear that the whole unit, airmen, WAAF and all the officers would be expected to turn out. After a monumental party (which involved a bit of fun with some of the patients, who at 2.30am had brought a donkey back with them from the town and led it into the fountain outside

Hazelrigg Hall), I finally got to bed at 4.30am. I remember saying to the duty NCO, 'Make sure you give me a call at 7.30,' as I staggered off to bed.

The next thing I remember was a loud banging on the door and Joe Messer, the Adjutant, calling out my name. I let him in and he asked: 'Where the hell were you? You missed the parade and the CO is not amused. Come on, up you get. I've got to march you in to the CO and that means full uniform – hat, gloves, the lot.'

He picked up my tunic and breathed on the buttons and polished them on his sleeve. I gave my shoes a quick rub and after the quickest shave of all time, I hurriedly got dressed and went down with Joe. He knocked on O'Malley's door.

'Wait,' said the familiar voice.

'Don't forget, thumbs down the seam of your trousers,' said Joe.

'Come in.'

Joe threw open the door, took three smart paces forward, snapped to attention, saluted and said, 'Squadron Leader Maskell, sir.'

'Right, bring him in.'

I marched the few steps to the table, saluted and waited. O'Malley was sitting there without his hat on; he looked at me over his glasses that were balanced on the end of his nose. I was still at attention expecting at any moment to be stood at ease. It must be serious, I thought. There will be no 'Jamie' and 'Dan' today, obviously.

Finally he spoke. 'Happy New Year, Maskell.'

'Thank you, sir. May I wish you the same.'

'Well, what have you got to say about things?'

'I feel very embarrassed about it.'

'I don't think you need to be embarrassed about it.'

'Well, I am, sir, rather.'

'I suppose you do know what we're talking about?'

'Of course I do, sir.'

O'Malley exchanged looks with Joe Messer.

'He doesn't seem to understand the significance of it, Joe.'

There was a flicker of a smile on his face. Now there was a pause, and then he said:

'So you haven't seen *The Times* this morning, Maskell?'

'I don't normally read *The Times*, sir.'

'Well, I think you'd better read it this morning.'

'Very good, sir, if you say so.'

'Well, when you do, you may be surprised to read that you've been awarded the OBE!'

I was so taken aback, it must have showed. Suddenly the atmosphere relaxed and O'Malley was smiling. 'My sincere congratulations, Dan. This is very well deserved you know.'

It was Joe's turn to break a piece of unexpected news. 'I haven't had time to tell you yet, sir, but we've had a signal from Group Headquarters sending Dan their congratulations.'

'I suppose you know what you should do now, Dan?' said O'Malley.

'I think the first thing I'd like to do, sir, is to go down to the gym to thank my NCOs. The award really is for them.' I thought for a moment and added: 'Then it would be nice to throw a party for the medical officers and the staff, some of the patients too – if that's all right, sir?'

'By all means, get things going at once.'

It didn't occur to me at the time that I hadn't seen the medal, but it eventually arrived by post. I was told that only CBEs and above were given their awards at Buckingham Palace during the war.

O'Malley came down to the gym himself later on to thank the chaps. He was keen to see that they all shared in the reflected glory. I organized a party two nights later for my instructors at a nearby village pub and O'Malley arrived to join us for a drink. They formed a guard of honour to see him back to his car when he decided to leave, while later they themselves formed up and marched all the way back to Loughborough.

Soon after the end of hostilities the process of demobilization began. I felt extremely fortunate to have been able to play a small part in helping people to restore their broken bodies and broken spirits. I would always be grateful, too, for having come into contact with Jamie O'Malley. He was one of the finest men I ever met and was a great influence on my own life.

After serving at Loughborough, he had gone on to serve as Field Marshal Montgomery's principal medical officer in the desert. When I met Montgomery in 1947 at the *Daily Mail* Schoolboys' Exhibition held at Olympia during the Christmas holidays, he'd come up to see our stand where we were hitting tennis balls with young pupils. 'What are you doing here?' he asked.

'Well, I hope I'm teaching these young people a little bit about how to hit tennis balls, sir.'

'Do you think you're succeeding?' The question was quick and sharp, as sharp as his piercing gaze. You could see why people found him so impressive.

'I hope so, sir.'

'What did *you* do in the war?' The question was fired like a rifle shot.

'I had the privilege of serving in the RAF under Group Captain O'Malley who was your Principal Medical Officer in the desert.'

'Ah – that rugger man who had gone to seed, yes, I remember him.'

Eight years later I met Montgomery again during the 1955 Championships at Wimbledon. As I came up the stairs towards the members' balcony he turned towards me. 'Hello,' he said. 'We've met before. Who are you?'

'My name's Maskell, sir, I do commentaries for the BBC.'

'Where have we met?' Then after a short pause – 'I know, the *Daily Mail* Schoolboys' Exhibition.' It was not a bad example of his fabled memory, I thought. At the time he was sixty-eight but he didn't look a day over fifty-five: a remarkable man.

The process of demobilization soon began. In due course it was my turn. I demobbed from Loughborough and was given a letter to show at Uxbridge to say that I was the only Rehabilitation Officer in the Royal Air Force. I had to collect my demob suit at Wembley and drove over in the ever-dependable Morris. With a parcel of clothes in my arms I happened to bump into Miss Evans, the secretary to Arthur Elvin at Wembley. She insisted that I went in to have a cup of tea, so I met Elvin again (he would eventually become Sir Arthur) and, sitting in his office, it almost seemed as if the past six years had never happened. The wheel, I felt, had come full circle.

EIGHT

Peacetime and a Changing Role

We faced two major problems in the period immediately
after the end of the war. Con had an internal medical
problem which required surgery and so was in hospital at the
time of my demob. The other difficulty concerned our house,
White Corner, at Wimbledon. The policeman had died but
his wife and two children still occupied it and had nowhere
else to go.

In addition, our family was split up. Robin was still up in
Loughborough, a six-year old being looked after by friends,
while Jay, a babe of two, was in the nursing home in Victoria
Drive at Wimbledon. I was going backwards and forwards
between Loughborough and London and, of course, visiting
Con in the Middlesex hospital, because there seemed little
prospect of getting the policeman's wife to move out. I had
to stay with Con's mother and father in Southfields when in
London and would go round to visit White Corner trying to
persuade the family that really we should be allowed to
repossess our own home. Eventually I was advised that the
only option was to go to the courts. In due course I attended
Kingston County Court, my first such experience. Fortunately the judge found in our favour and gave the woman a
month to move out. Unfortunately she did not comply with
this order, so we had to pay a second visit to the courts to
secure repossession. She was given another month and this
time did move out.

Long before this Con had come out of hospital and the
family was reunited at her mother's house. Robin had come

down from Loughborough and we'd collected Jay from the nursing home so, cramped as we were, we did begin to enjoy some sort of family life.

When we eventually did move back into White Corner we noticed that Mick the Miller lay in two pieces in the garden. The little statuette had been the victim of bomb blast like so many windows of the houses in the neighbourhood.

Gradually I began to pick up the pieces of my career back at the All England Club. The promising juniors selected by the LTA were sent to me once again and I began to practise with the Davis Cup players and the Wightman Cup hopefuls who themselves were shaking the rust off their games.

We had a new club secretary, Colonel Duncan Macaulay. Dudley Larcombe had not survived the war and Nora Cleather had been passed over. Thus Duncan, who had been a tournament umpire and referee and an assistant referee at Wimbledon before the war, took up the reins. There were some obvious signs of the conflict. The Centre Court had been damaged by a bomb that fell on the stand to the right of the Royal Box. When the first Championships were held, about twelve hundred seats were still out of action.

By the time it had been decided that we would try to stage a tournament in 1946, despite the shortage of time, Duncan was well installed but the prospect of making all the complex arrangements to mount the world's major tennis championships once again was a daunting one. Nora Cleather had made the decision to leave for Canada where she had relations, once the club had not reappointed her. Marie Bompas therefore acted as Duncan's assistant and with support and guidance from the committee they virtually ran the first post-war Championships together.

Food was still rationed so the catering arrangements were spartan. Labour was in short supply, too, so Duncan solved that problem by calling upon the services of the armed forces to man the turnstiles and acts as stewards, a tradition that survives.

While the preparations were gathering pace, I accompanied the team to Paris for the first post-war Davis Cup match. In Derek Barton, Donald MacPhail (whom I had not seen since running into him at Bournemouth in 1940), John Olliff and Henry Billington, we had a completely new team. No one was left from the side that had defeated France in 1939 in a third round tie played in London. Charlie Hare was still a member of the US Army, Ronnie Shayes had been killed when his training plane crashed in Rhodesia and Frank Wilde was not yet playing competitively again. However, the two French singles players, Yvon Petra and Pierre Pellizza, had been the young doubles pair for France in 1939 while Bernard Destremau, a singles player in 1939, was now playing doubles with a young left-hander, Marcel Bernard, who completely astonished the world by winning the first French Championship after the war unseeded. We were comprehensively beaten 5–0 at the Stade Roland Garros and could claim only one set during the entire tie, that in the doubles. The British captain, Mr F. T. 'Skipper' Stowe, made one of the shrewdest observations I have ever heard from a Davis Cup captain at the conclusion of the tie. Answering a press question about the prospects for Wimbledon, Skipper said very confidently that he believed Petra would win Wimbledon because, he said, 'Yvon has been fortunate to be playing tennis during the war and is relatively match tight. Furthermore he has exactly the right credentials – big serve, good volleys and booming returns.' Much to everyone else's surprise, Petra did win.

While we were in Paris, staying at the George V hotel, I had a phone call from Jean Borotra. He asked me if I would meet him in his small car outside his apartment in the Avenue Foch. He said he wanted to chat to me about his prospects of playing at Wimbledon, now just a few weeks away. After getting permission from Skipper Stowe I kept the appointment. Borotra looked just the same as when I had last seen him in 1939. There was a hint of grey hair at the temples but the lean figure looked just as trim as I remembered it and the enthusiasm was as infectious as ever.

Jean was concerned about whether the authorities would let him compete at Wimbledon since he was under something of a cloud for the part he had played as Minister for Sport in the Vichy government under General Pétain during the war. Although I had not discussed his position with the British authorities I said that personally I felt sure he would be welcomed in England by the many tennis fans who remembered him from his pre-war days. I suggested that he might test opinion by competing in the pre-Wimbledon tournament at Bristol. I was also able to tell him the extraordinary story of a certain Lieutenant Blitz, who had been a patient at the Palace Hotel in Torquay when it was bombed. He was one of the lucky ones who survived and I had visited him when the matron told me that he had asked to see me.

'I gather you know Jean Borotra?' he said.

'I know him very well indeed but I haven't seen him, of course, since 1939.'

'I'm sad to think that you have such a wrong impression of him in England,' said Blitz. 'You know that during the war when he was Minister for Sport he did all he could to preserve the youth of France by cutting down the five-day cycle races to three days, and five-set tennis matches to three sets, because everyone was undernourished.'

Blitz came from an aristocratic Parisian family whom Jean knew slightly. He was delighted to hear what the young man had said. Jean never did play singles again at Wimbledon, though after a decent interval he was welcomed back in doubles and then the veterans' doubles, much to the delight of the many Wimbledon spectators who remembered him from before the war.

Edwin Fuller, the head groundsman who had tended the courts during the war and kept them in reasonable condition, did a marvellous job with his new team to prepare the sacred turf for that first meeting. There was a wonderful team spirit among the staff as we tackled all the problems and overcame the shortages, which included tennis balls. Slazengers were asked to supply the balls, as they had done every year since 1902, but they had trouble getting enough raw rubber to make the cores. Somehow they managed it and the balls were provided on time.

The popular favourite that year was the leading American, Jack Kramer. He had been in the Marines during hostilities but had still been able to play enough to maintain some sort of form. This was the first time that I had seen him and I was impressed by his powerful, all-court game. It was a privilege to meet him and to get to know him. Our association developed into a warm friendship over the years, one which I valued particularly highly in the commentator's box. For many years Jack sat beside me there as a fellow commentator, producing little gems of information about all the players whom he knew so well.

It was a major surprise when the Czech left-hander, Jaroslav Drobny, beat Kramer on court one in the fourth round but Jack had played much of the match badly handicapped by a racket hand that was a mass of blisters. When he came into the dressing-room after the match I asked him to show me his injury. He had his fist clenched and was reluctant to discuss the matter. However he did open it to show me an almost raw palm which looked, and must have felt, extremely painful.

The number one seed that year was the neat Australian, Dinny Pails, but he fell in four sets to the powerful serving of Yvon Petra in the quarter-finals. The tall Frenchman then beat Tom Brown from California in a marathon semi-final which ended at 8–6 in the final set. His opponent in the final was another Brown, Geoff, the dynamic little double-hander from Australia, who, it seemed to me, was playing with too much inhibition. Not until he had lost the first two sets did he start to open his shoulders and really belt the ball, his natural game. It was almost as though someone had suggested to him that if he got the ball back often enough Petra would make the mistakes to beat himself. It was strongly rumoured that Australia's former champion, Gerald Patterson, who had arrived for the last few days of the meeting, had given this advice. But Petra was much too good a player and too experienced to beat himself. After all, he had competed at Wimbledon before the war. Geoff Brown was a most exciting man to watch, a real whirlwind of a player. His serve was a wonderfully explosive shot. From the moment he took his racket down to toss the ball in the air, to the end of the throwing action, the impression was of watching a blur, so quick was the swing. It was the same with the double-handed forehand. Every now and again he would meet the ball on the rise and crack it like a bullet past an astonished opponent. Probably Brown's best match at the meeting was his quarter-final against Lennart Bergelin, the Swedish stylist who later became Björn Borg's coach and mentor. Brown was at his explosive best in winning 13–11 11–9 6–4 and in fact he did not drop a set in the entire meeting until the final.

It was a joy that year to see for the first time those wonderful American ladies who so completely dominated the early post-war Championships. Pauline Betz, mainly a baseliner with an adequate net game, was a worthy champion. The beaten finalist, Louise Brough, carried on the traditions of serve-and-volley that her famous countrywoman, Alice Marble, had established as the way ahead for women's tennis during the course of her winning run at Wimbledon in 1939. It was sad that Pauline was not allowed to go on playing amateur tennis in 1947 simply because she had said publicly that it was her intention eventually to turn professional. Looking back from the distance of forty years, in the full bloom of open tennis, it does seem slightly ludicrous now to think how unenlightened we all were in those days, clinging to outmoded amateur values. The arrival of open tennis in 1968, when it finally came thanks to the leadership of the All England Club chairman, Herman David, was long overdue.

Louise Brough, one of our most underrated champions, beat the lady with whom she would form such an enduring and successful partnership, Margaret Osborne, in a close semi-final. Margaret, who would herself become the champion in 1947, had beaten in the quarter-finals another future champion, Doris Hart. Doris had the most perfect technique and style of any of those great champions. In fact we used her on one of our training film loops (they repeat the same shot over and over again) from which the next generation learned a great deal.

One of those things I wanted to achieve in those early post-war years was to improve standards of coaching and to gain greater recognition for the role of the individual professional tennis coach. That meant that our Professional Tennis Coaches' Association would have to lay down guidelines for coaching beginners. Without trying to produce stereotyped players, all with shots that looked the same, we nevertheless felt that there was a need to define the fundamentals of stroke-making which were common to all players, regardless of their individual styles. This objective provoked hours of earnest discussion over the months ahead.

The game had more or less died during the war, except for junior play, and many of our professionals did not return to coaching but took up new occupations. Some, of course, had given their lives in the six years of war and we remembered them with affection. As chairman of the Association, it was my job to pull together the thoughts and aspirations of our remaining members. We got a committee together as soon as we could which included experienced men like Doug Gresham, Ted Millman and Basil Lawrence, who helped me to organize our first conference after the war. It was held on the two indoor clay courts at the Newhaven Court Hotel in

Cromer, where Suzanne Lenglen had once played an exhibition match in the 1930s. In those days our Association had no direct connection with the LTA though that was another of my aims – to become affiliated to the LTA like the two great universities of Oxford and Cambridge, the Referees' Association and the Umpires' Association. It was a step in the right direction, therefore, when the president of the LTA, Sir Samuel Hoare, who lived in that part of the world, agreed to open the conference with a few suitable words. I remember they included an exhortation for us to improve the footwork of British players. Probably the most satisfactory result of the conference was the emergence at last of those elusive five fundamentals, something we had been striving to achieve in 1939 but upon which we had never been able to reach satisfactory agreement between ourselves. I remember discussing our ideas with Bill Cox, the golf professional at the Wimbledon Park Golf Club just across the road from the All England Club. He was renowned as a teacher but had said that the golf professionals, too, had attempted to find some common basis for teaching the game, the fundamentals as it were, but had, like us, failed to find common ground.

What we were trying to do was to unify our coaching methods. This would help the new, inexperienced tennis teachers to identify those areas of weakness in a pupil which needed most attention. After much discussion we ultimately agreed that the five fundamentals were: one, watching the ball; two, sound footwork; three, balance; four, control of the racket head through the grip; and five, control of the swing. To them we added an overriding thought about ball sense without which no one can successfully play a moving-ball game. It was felt that if a player could get all five fundamentals in harmony, then he or she stood a reasonable chance of becoming a sound stroke player. We were certainly not being dogmatic about the grip to use for particular shots or about style, though our detractors often accused us of such dogmatism.

Another of our concerns was to increase the amount of match play for professional coaches. This had been an ambition since my earliest days as a teacher. We approached the LTA, who resurrected our British Professional Championships and the Amateurs versus Professionals match which had been a regular feature of the years before the war. Thus, when Michael McMaster, the chairman of Slazengers at that time, asked me to have a chat with him about starting a new professional tournament, I readily agreed to see him. He wanted to know if I felt that the teaching professionals would support a professional tournament sponsored by Slazengers and held at one of the popular tennis venues, like Eastbourne. 'In no way do we want to undermine your present British Professional Championships, but we feel that you chaps might welcome another tournament.' How right he was. Under the direction of Slazengers' tournament director, Jim Smith, the Slazenger Professional Tournament enjoyed many successful years, first at Scarborough, then at Devonshire Park, Eastbourne. At one time or another most of the great players who had turned professional competed – men like Pancho Gonzales and Pancho Segura, Don Budge, Fred Perry and my old friend and foe, Hans Nusslein. After several losses to him on clay in Paris and Berlin it was satisfying to beat him at last on the grass at Scarborough. We played on the superb centre court that was big enough for two courts. I had always said to him, 'Hans, one day, when we meet on grass I shall have my revenge.' I taught him a lot about the drop shot that day.

Another interesting development from that first discussion with Michael McMaster was the production of a coaching tennis racket designed specifically for beginners. Michael McMaster had heard that when I was learning my job at Queen's, I used a penknife to cut grooves on the handle of my racket and those of my pupils to show where the thumb and fingers should rest for the forehand and backhand. On the racket head I had written with an indelible pencil reminders like 'Watch the ball', 'On your toes', 'Concentrate', 'Don't quit on the shot', 'Follow through' and 'Prepare early'. These six *aides-mémoire* became the basis of the new Perry/Maskell racket which Slazengers made and marketed for us. Accompanying it was a booklet in which the strokes of the game were shown in photographic sequence above a coaching text written by me. For many years this was a popular beginner's racket.

Another association with Fred came through the Central Council of Physical Recreation, a body which existed to service the needs of the governing bodies of the sport in Britain. In the early post-war years, the Lawn Tennis Association had neglected the job of extending the foundations of the game. It is true that they had resurrected the tournament circuit and tidied up the rules, but they were not trying to market the game to a wider public. The CCPR believed that we should take tennis into schools and clubs by staging demonstrations and coaching clinics all over the country. For the time it was quite an advanced idea. Thus was born 'Focus on Tennis', a tennis show that went on the road for three weeks each year for the next three years. In the morning or afternoon we would have groups of youngsters with us on the court for a clinic. They would then sit in the stands to watch us play a set of exhibition tennis. In the evening, on the same court or at the same venue, we would have the older children and one or two county players, plus the general public as spectators.

The night before our first dress-rehearsal on the courts just off Wimbledon Common, where Jim Coles was the coach, we had a piece of good fortune. Unfortunately the CCPR staff man from Wales who was going to be the tour manager and would also read the commentary, which I had scripted, had broken his ankle playing tennis in Wales the previous day. But overnight they got as a replacement Emlyn Jones, another CCPR man from the North Wales region who had played tennis for that area. This was the first time Fred and I had met Emlyn, a man who immediately understood our aims and became a very important part of our 'Focus on Tennis' team. Emlyn also became one of my closest friends and went on to enjoy a distinguished career, first as the Director of the National Sports Centre at Crystal Palace and then as the Director-General of the Sports Council.

Thus Emlyn became our tour manager and commentator and he lasted the pace as well as we did. It was a hectic tour of one-night stands at five different centres on each weekday of a three-week operation. We motored thousands of miles to cover the whole country, an exhausting experience. Whilst playing down in Cornwall at Carlyon Bay there was an amusing incident. Our hotel was situated in a remote part of the countryside where there were no street lights. As I went through the narrow gates of the drive, I caught the wing of the car on one of the gate-posts. I stopped the car just inside the gates and got out to see what damage I had done. Sticking his head out of the window of the following car, Fred called: 'Dan, fancy doing a silly thing like that. How did it happen?'

'Well, there's not much room here, Fred. If you come and look you'll see what I mean. The concrete post is disguised by these bushes that grow out and conceal it. I thought I was just brushing the foliage. But I'll show you what I did.'

So I climbed back into the car, intending to back out and make a second pass at the entrance, but in doing so I backed the off-side rear wing into the post. There was a crunch of folding metal and a loud peal of laughter from Fred and Emlyn, who have been pulling my leg about my driving ever since!

The person we had to thank for suggesting 'Focus on Tennis' was Phyllis Colson, the lady who ran the CCPR. She was a remarkable woman who gave her entire life to the organization. She and her technical staff had come up with the original idea but Bill Latto it was who worked with me to script the programme. Bill set up the organization for each venue through the CCPR regions in the cities and towns we visited. It really was a great success, the forerunner of tours like it in other sports. Harry Crabtree, the director of education for Essex and a former cricketer, set up a similar tour for cricket, and the Golf Foundation did something similar for young golfers. The Lawn Tennis Foundation, established in the 1950s, ran a similar tour under the title 'Spotlight on Tennis', organized by Bill Penney. They always say that imitation is the sincerest form of flattery, don't they?

In 1953, much to my surprise, I was made a member of the All England Club. The news was broken in the most delightful way. After practice during a Davis Cup tie versus Belgium at the Waterloo Club in Brussels, the captain, Herman David, called us all together. With him was the club secretary who handed him a telegram. Herman opened it as Geoff Paish, Tony Mottram and Roger Becker gathered round. 'My goodness, listen to this, gentlemen. I shall read the contents to you – 'Please congratulate Dan who was made an honorary member at last night's meeting' – and it's signed "Duncan".' Then Herman, with a wide smile, produced from his pocket a faded club tie. 'You'll get the new one when we get back. In the meantime please have mine – it's the very first one I ever had.' That day the drinks were on me.

This was the first time that a teaching professional had ever been accorded such an honour and, except for those members who had been re-elected after the arrival of open tennis in 1968, no professional had ever been allowed into the charmed circle. For me it was a dream come true for I had always revered the ideals for which the club stood, and indeed for which it still stands.

It was about this time that I realized that my days as an active, tracksuit coach were nearing an end. I was now forty-five and could no longer hold my own in practice matches against the new young tigers challenging for places in the

British Davis Cup team – men like Billy Knight, Bobby Wilson and Mike Davies. I felt that these boys deserved somebody younger as their player/coach. Duncan Macaulay was most sympathetic when I explained my views and asked me whom I would recommend as my successor. I told him I had already discussed the situation privately with three of my senior professional colleagues. We were all agreed that there was no one in the country who was either a good enough player or an experienced enough coach at the level required. Like me, they thought that the Australian, George Worthington, if available, would fill the bill.

George was highly prized by Harry Hopman as the ideal practice player for his all-conquering Australian Davis Cup teams of the 1950s. I remember once asking Harry how it was that he never played George in a match, though he always seemed to be in the teams or squads of the period. I knew from locker-room chat that George often used to beat Lew Hoad and Ken Rosewall in practice matches leading up to the Challenge Rounds each year.

'Dan, I would always have George on the squad. He hits the balls so well and plays practice sets so well that it brushes off on the other boys.' What a compliment, I thought, when you considered the strength of the Australian teams – men like Hoad and Rosewall, Rose and Hartwig, Anderson and Cooper. But Hopman was a shrewd judge of character. 'I would sometimes go up and see whether George was in bed at 12.30 at night and quite often he wouldn't be.' There were no half measures with Harry.

George was indeed a likeable man and someone of whom I became very fond. I knew that he got on well with young people and would have the respect of British players at all levels of the game. George liked the idea of taking over from me when it was first suggested to him, but it took us two years before he felt ready to leave the amateur game. Accordingly, George Worthington became the All England Club coach in 1955 and I moved over to work for the LTA as their first training manager, a rather misleading title for the post.

I had been approached a couple of years earlier by the LTA to fill this void. They felt the job needed someone who understood the whole spectrum of the game in Britain. I agreed to take it on the understanding that I would have a free hand to overhaul the entire amateur coaching set-up. I particularly wanted to change attitudes at the teacher training colleges where, I felt, tennis was regarded as a very low priority. I also wanted to rethink the schemes for the training of coaches, for both amateurs and professionals, and present a full report and plan to the LTA Coaching and Professionals Committees.

I realized that if I was to do the job properly I would need to have some sound coaching films to take round the colleges with mc. Thus I came into contact once more with Bill Latto, who had now left the CCPR and set up his own film unit, 'Town and Country'. We made two films together under the title *The Way to Wimbledon*; they covered the strokes of the game and basic tactics. A little later, we undertook an ambitious project by making a doubles coaching film, something which as far as I knew had not been attempted before. It had been inspired by a remark from Kitty Godfree while we were standing together watching the girls' doubles final at Junior Wimbledon: none of the four players seemed to have much understanding of what doubles play was all about. We also made some film loops which were particularly useful for analysing the mechanics of stroke production. We used the good young players of the day as models: Billy Knight demonstrated his excellent left-handed forehand; Bobby Wilson displayed his flowing serve and leaping smash that were the hallmarks of his exciting game; Michael Davies hit the most perfect early-ball running forehand and Christine Truman showed us a slightly topped backhand. For those who remember Christine's game, that may sound surprising, but I can assure you that in practice she could hit the most beautiful lifted backhand drives imaginable. However, she never developed the confidence to carry that shot into her match play and always relied on her safe, sliced backhand.

For the next twelve months I set off on a voyage of discovery, visiting the farthest corners of the kingdom and covering something like 28,000 miles, lecturing, showing films at teachers' training colleges and visiting clubs and schools. Sometimes I would take with me some of our best junior players. Young Stanley Matthews, Graham Stilwell and others would play exhibition games while I commentated upon them – all part of giving variety and substance to the lectures. It was quite apparent from this trip that people felt the LTA were not terribly concerned with the development of the game. Park superintendents felt that they were being neglected, some schools felt much the same and all too often some of the counties were not really trying to spread the game to a new generation of players. It is sad to think that despite my reports at the time and the similar views of other experienced individuals since, the LTA is only now, in the 1980s, beginning to market the game properly to widen the base of the playing pyramid. This surely must be the first step in raising national standards.

As I have said, the teachers' training colleges particularly interested me. Visits to Carnegie and Loughborough, Bedford and Lincoln, Derby and Matlock, Anstey and Dartford, Nonnington near Canterbury and the I. M. Marsh College in Liverpool convinced me that, given the right approach, the future schoolmasters and schoolmistresses of this country could be persuaded to give tennis a higher priority than it enjoyed. With a few shining exceptions there was little follow-up to my lectures. The LTA had no machinery then to exploit the greater interest of the teachers. It is sad to think of those thirty lost years.

Not that there was any shortage of competition or training opportunities for juniors. The LTA Schools Committee and

Juniors Committee administered a large number of tournaments ranging from national and county championships down to the smallest local affair. There were courses in the school holidays at Christmas and Easter for selected players at residential venues where covered courts were available. Ted Robbins, chairman for so many years of the committees running junior tennis, worked tirelessly on these matches and courses and travelled with me on many occasions. He always showed great enthusiasm and vision. Tony Mottram was another whose contribution was immense. He was the LTA's development manager and over the years I spent hours with him watching junior matches and making notes. However, the basic job within the schools themselves was never tackled.

One of the improvements that I was proud of concerned the restructuring of the coaching exams. With the help of a dedicated and experienced teacher, Jack Moore, we overhauled the old Part One Elementary course for amateur coaches and the Part Two Advanced course so that the teaching of tennis would be much more fun for the pupils and more rewarding for the teachers. That seemed to me an essential requirement if one was going to retain the interest of any young player. Then Jack and I tackled the twelve-day residential Full Professionals' course which, at that stage, had a rather inadequate exam at the end of it. Encouraged from the LTA side by Charles Wright (a fine man from Cambridge of advancing years but young ideas, who had been a great mountain climber in his youth), we totally reorganized the written exam which concluded the tests. Charles was a wonderfully clear thinker and brought a refreshing breadth of vision to what we were trying to achieve. His was a tremendous contribution. Another who gave us great support was Derek Penman, whom I eventually persuaded to become the president of our Association. This further strengthened the bond that was growing between the teaching professionals and the LTA for, as a councillor,

Derek was extremely active. When accepting the presidency, though, Derek did say, 'If it ever comes to a conflict or a division of opinion, remember that my first loyalty must always be to the LTA.' For that I admired him. Derek led us with wisdom and with action. In five years he totally changed the attitude of the LTA towards us which made a great impression on all our members. Experienced men like Dudley Georgeson, Basil Lawrence, Bill Moss, Michael Evans and Jim Lee were now prepared to devote more of their time as instructors and examiners to the LTA training of Coaches scheme.

There have been four major personal tragedies in my life, two of them concerning men I had come to respect and admire and two involving my own family.

Dr Colin Gregory had become chairman of the All England Club in the same year that I had joined the LTA, 1955. I had more or less grown up in tennis with Colin. He was five years older than me and I had always admired him and respected his athletic ability. He was a great all-rounder, a fine rugby player, a good squash player and an outstanding doubles player whose best years were in the 1920s. He had represented Britain in the Davis Cup between 1926 and 1930 and in 1929, captaining a team to Australia, had won the Australian Championships. That same year he had reached the final of the doubles at Wimbledon with his regular partner, Ian Collins, and just lost a memorable five-set match to a great American pair, Wilmer Allison and Johnny Van Ryn.

It was quite natural therefore that Colin should have been appointed our Davis Cup captain in 1949 when Tony Mottram and Geoff Paish were beginning their extraordinary run of nine unbroken years representing Great Britain. The years 1947–1955 were ones of consolidation for British teams, an era in which Headley Baxter played an unselfish part in 1948,

1950 and 1951. Although Headley never played a representative Davis Cup match, he did contribute greatly to the team
spirit of our squad. Later he would become an energetic
captain.

I was the coach to those teams when Colin Gregory was
the captain and always found him a shrewd and understanding manager of men. He had an extraordinarily difficult
decision to make in 1952, when we were playing Yugoslavia
in Belgrade. Geoff Paish had injured an ankle in training
and, with Mottram having a difficult reverse singles to play
on the third day against Palada, Colin decided to play himself
in doubles with Mottram instead of seventeen-year-old
Roger Becker who was in the team for the first time.
Remember, Colin was then forty-eight years old and had not
played a Davis Cup match for twenty-two years. In a rubber
that would decide the tie, the tension was considerable but
Colin played his part magnificently as the British pair beat
Palada and Laszlo 6–4 1–6 9–11 6–2 6–2.

Colin proved to be a fine chairman of the All England
Club. He was a man of decision, a man with a great feeling
for tradition and for the welfare of all the club staff. Above
all he was a visionary and a tremendous leader who was
appalled by the hypocrisy that existed in the amateur game
at that time. He, it was, who really inspired the move to
bring about open tennis, a banner that would be successfully
carried by the succeeding chairman, Herman David, whose
own efforts finally opened the door in 1968.

One day early in 1959 I had a call from Duncan Macaulay
to say that Colin was coming to the club the following day to
have a hit with his son and daughter. He wondered whether
I would make up a four with them. It was a Saturday and
bitterly cold. I hadn't seen Colin for some time but when he
arrived he was recovering from a cold which left him feeling
a little bit low. We had a light-hearted family game on the
new covered courts which Colin was largely instrumental in

having built. He and I had actually played an exhibition set on the day the courts had been opened.

In the family doubles I played with Colin's son, Ian, who is now a distinguished doctor himself, while Colin played with his daughter Sarah. I remember that Colin's wife, Phyl, sat on a bench at the side of the court wrapped up in a blanket. It was so cold that I remember Phyl had difficulty in carrying on with her knitting.

We had played about a set and a half when suddenly Billy Talbert, the great American doubles player with whom Colin had always been very friendly, made an unexpected appearance accompanied by Duncan Macaulay. Billy and his son, Pike, had just called in on his way home to America from a skiing holiday in Switzerland – the last stop on a round-the-world holiday undertaken during the boy's Christmas holiday from school. After an exchange of greetings Colin said, 'Billy, it's too cold to hang about here. Why don't you all go back with Duncan to the lounge while we finish this set and then we'll join you there?' As they were about to go, Pike said, 'I wonder if I could take a picture while you're all here.' So we all stood at the net while Pike went to work with the new camera of which he seemed so proud. That proved to be the last picture ever taken of Colin.

When we had finished the set, Colin and I walked back to the dressing-room, leaving the youngsters behind to play a little more tennis. As we walked in I saw Colin rubbing his chest and asked him if anything was wrong. 'Oh no, just a touch of indigestion,' he replied.

Colin sat down on the seat and seemed preoccupied. This was unusual because normally he was one of the quickest men I can remember to get out of his tennis clothes into the bath and back into his ordinary clothes. He always seemed to be in a hurry, always rushing off to some appointment or other.

'Are you sure you're all right, Colin?' I asked.

'Yes, it's just a touch of this indigestion. It'll pass off in a moment.'

'You doctors, you make the worst patients,' I said. 'Anyway, let me go and find you some McLean's tablets.' I always used to have some in my locker, not that I used them often. When I opened the locker the packet was empty and I came back and apologized.

'Never mind, Dan, would you mind just asking Bulley to run me a bath?' he asked.

As the bath was being run, I said, 'It looks as if we're going to be a bit late, Colin. I have been invited to lunch with friends in the town at 1.15 and if we're going to have a drink with Billy, I must go and phone my friends to tell them I shall be a few minutes late.'

'Fine,' he said.

I went out to the phone which was in the entrance hall and when I came back, barely a minute later, Colin was lying on the floor turning blue before my eyes. Obviously he had had a heart attack. Bulley was still attending to the bath and hadn't heard him fall. I shouted to him and quickly got some blankets from the massage-room to wrap round Colin. Then I rushed up to fetch Phyl whom I knew had been a nurse. My agitation was apparent as I ran into the bar calling her.

'Dan, what's happened?' she asked.

'Come quickly, it's Colin,' I said.

It was the saddest moment of my life, watching Phyl cradling Colin's head in her lap as he died.

I left them and rushed up in my car to the doctor's surgery at the top of the hill in Wimbledon village. I actually ran in while one of the doctors was in consultation. 'Forgive me,' I said, 'but one of your professional colleagues, Doctor Colin Gregory, has just had a heart attack at the All England Club and needs attention urgently.' The doctor dropped everything and came back with me to the club. It had taken only about ten minutes but, of course, we were too late.

Duncan, quite rightly, closed the club for the rest of the day and lowered the flag to half-mast.

The second loss was less of a shock, but much more harrowing. George Worthington had adapted to British conditions extremely well, although he never quite got used to our chill British winters, especially on the unheated covered courts at Queen's Club. His arrival in 1955 had coincided with the change in our Davis Cup team. After the nine-year reign of Mottram and Paish, the younger brigade had been asked to take over – Roger Becker, Billy Knight, Michael Davies, Bobby Wilson and Tony Pickard. The competition for places was intensified by the arrival of John Barrett in the upper echelons of the British game. He had been up at Cambridge University from October 1951 until the summer of 1954. I had seen him on the many occasions when he had helped us with the training of some of the leading juniors. I had also been impressed by his enthusiasm when leading the Cambridge team in 1954 to another resounding victory over Oxford. In those days poor Oxford seemed to attract none of the better players; for some reason Cambridge would get them all.

At that time George and I used to take junior teams up for a short stay at Cambridge to play matches against the university. I remember the young Mark Cox being on one of those teams and so impressed was he by Cambridge that he determined to become an undergraduate there himself one day, which of course he did.

George greatly admired Herman David, who had been the Davis Cup captain in the early 1950s. For his part, Herman greatly respected George's ability to bring the best out of the new young players. I always felt that this generation had also benefited from the period of National Service that each of them had to complete. The discipline did them no harm and they had plenty of opportunity to play tennis. Barrett went into the Royal Air Force and won the RAF Championships in 1950 and 1951. The two previous years Paddy Roberts had been champion. Paddy, Arthur's son, never really made the progress that he expected of himself and, like his father, became a teaching professional.

Like Cambridge, the Royal Air Force seemed to be more successful than the Army or Navy in getting the better tennis players. After Barrett, Roger Becker became the RAF Champion in 1952 followed by Billy Knight in 1954. Tony Pickard, always a shrewd timer of life's moves, elected to go into the Army where he knew there was less opposition and he duly became the Army Champion for two years in 1954 and 1955. The RAF scored again with Alan Mills who became their champion in 1957 before moving into the Davis Cup teams of that period. Later, of course, he was destined to become the referee at Wimbledon, a post he is occupying with distinction at the time of writing.

When John Barrett succeeded Herman David as the Davis Cup captain from 1959 to 1962, George was the driving force behind the scenes, practising assiduously with all the players and showing a healthy irreverence for authority that they all liked enormously. At times during the Davis Cup contest I would be invited to eat with them. To hear the way they tore apart those in authority with verbal barbs that were often amusing, and usually accurate, was an education. They knew, or thought they knew, exactly how to put the tennis world to rights – but any young man worth his salt in any generation is always able to do that.

Now that I was based back at Queen's Club as the LTA training manager, I saw less of George on a day-to-day basis. One day early in 1963 John Barrett came to find me at Queen's to say that he was worried about him. Apparently the prominent birthmark behind George's knee had started to weep. Not liking the sound of this I insisted that he should see a medical specialist. George resisted but eventually it was arranged through Duncan Macaulay who sent him off to see Guy Cooper, one-time captain of Oxford University and a member of the club who was a doctor. As soon as he had examined George, Guy arranged that he should visit Sir Stanford Cade at Westminster Hospital. An operation was advised. Apparently the birthmark had turned malignant and speed was essential.

George was surprised that so much flesh had been removed from his leg, but recovered with amazing speed and in fact later the same year won the Slazenger Professional Tournament at Eastbourne. The following year George had to go back into Westminster Hospital and after examining him again Sir Stanford Cade realized that nothing could be done. George never left Westminster Hospital and for the last few weeks of his life all his tennis friends used to pay him regular visits. Whether or not George actually knew at that stage that he had cancer we shall never know. All I do know is that he bore his misfortune with extreme bravery. I was reminded of some of the fellows I had seen enduring great suffering during my rehabilitation days in Torquay and Loughborough. Somehow, though, this was different. As he got thinner and the voice weaker, I realized that a great and dear friend was slipping from my life. He remained cheerful to the end, talking about booking his return passage home even when he was looking like a skeleton. Almost the last time I saw him he held out his hand and said: 'Dan, I want you to take these. This was the first tennis prize that I ever won. I want you to have them.' In my hand lay a pair of gold cufflinks with the letters G.W. engraved on them. At that moment I realized that he did know. Feeling a lump rise in my throat, I said, 'Thank you George. I'll always wear them.' I have done so faithfully at every black tie function since.

The void left by George's death was filled by John Barrett. His plan for a national training squad was adopted by the LTA in 1965 and for four years the 'Barrett Boys' set new standards of fitness among British players. Among the eleven members of this squad were Gerald Battrick, Peter Curtis and Graham Stilwell, who later became members of the 1969 Davis Cup team that reached the International Zone final under Headley Baxter's captaincy when the team was sponsored for the first time by Rothmans. I shall always think that Stilwell's two singles wins against Tiriac and Nastase in the 2–3 loss to Rumania at Wimbledon were among the best performances by a British man in the post-war period. The others would be Roger Taylor's three appearances in the semi-finals at Wimbledon – in 1967 when he went down in five sets to Wilhelm Bungert of Germany, in 1970 when he beat the holder, Rod Laver, and then Clark Graebner before Ken Rosewall beat him in four sets, and finally in 1973, the year of the ATP boycott, when he had that thrilling finish at 5–7 in the final set against the eventual winner, Jan Kodes.

Alongside Taylor's achievements I would place Mike Sangster's performances in 1961 when he, too, was a semi-finalist, both at Wimbledon (losing to that year's runner-up, Chuck McKinley) and at Forest Hills where Rod Laver beat him, and in 1963 when he led Britain to the Inter-Zone final of the Davis Cup and reached the semi-finals of the French Championships, the first Briton to achieve as much since Bunny Austin in 1937. I was the manager of that team and was impressed by the quality of Mike's serving on the slow clay, and by the solidity and consistency of his ground strokes.

On the evening before his semi-final Mike and the others persuaded me to buy some expensive tickets for *Lawrence of Arabia* which was showing at one of the cinemas on the Champs Elysées. Within five minutes of the start I was surprised to see that all the boys were fast asleep in their comfortable seats. Having woken them at the interval and enjoyed a breath of fresh air with them I was even more surprised when, within minutes of the resumption, they were all sleeping peacefully once more. At the end of the film, which I had thoroughly enjoyed, I remonstrated with the lads.

'Fancy letting me spend the LTA's funds on those expensive seats and then sleeping throughout the entire performance,' I said.

'Well, Dan,' said Mike, as their spokesman, 'we had all seen *Lawrence* before but we knew you were dying to see it . . . and, anyway, it was a great place to have a nap!'

The other post-war highlight, for me, of course, was the three Wimbledon successes by our British girls – Angela Mortimer in 1961, Ann Jones in 1969 and Virginia Wade in the year of Wimbledon's centenary, 1977.

Angela had worked long and hard for her success away from the spotlight with Arthur Roberts at Torquay on those same wooden courts where we had carried out our rehabilitation activities. Her final against Christine Truman, a thrilling rain-interrupted three-setter, was the first all-British affair since 1914. Angela was the first British winner since Dorothy Round in 1937. On the Monday following Angela's victory, I happened to be at the club when she came in to collect some rackets. As she was leaving I rushed out and said, 'Angela – quickly, come and look at this.' Together we hurried into the main hall, where the honours boards hang on the walls, to the right of the entrance to the Centre Court where Kipling's immortal words challenge every competitor who plays there:

'If you can meet with triumph and disaster
And treat those two impostors just the same.'

High on a step-ladder, the signwriter was painting in Angela's name in gold letters, 'Miss A Mortimer'. It was the first time I had ever seen a champion witness that moment when his or her name was being recorded among the immortals of our game.

Angela's Wimbledon win crowned a most successful career which had brought her the French and Australian titles in 1955 and 1958. With her patience rewarded, Angela's 1961 win provided great impetus to the women's game in Britain. Thus when Ann Jones achieved her success eight years later, with magnificent back-to-back wins against Margaret Court and the holder, Billie-Jean King, no one was really surprised.

Ann, like Fred Perry, had been a world-class table tennis player and her left-handed game was beautifully controlled. She had previously won twice in France in 1961 and 1966 and twice reached the final of the US Championships to emphasize Britain's high place in women's tennis at this time.

Virginia's win at Wimbledon in 1977 was a complete fairy-tale. Here she was, the tigress of British tennis and the first US Open Champion in 1968 (when she beat Billie-Jean King in the final), playing for the sixteenth time at Wimbledon. Besides being the centenary year of the Championships, it was the Queen's Jubilee year and the Queen herself was there on finals day when Virginia played Betty Stove.

I shall never forget the scenes that followed Virginia's shaky win. She had wobbled nervously as she so often did but came through eventually with forthright attacking tennis to claim the title she most wanted. Spontaneously the crowd started to sing *For she's a jolly good fellow*. For the first time at the microphone on the Centre Court I felt momentarily too emotional to speak.

It took me a long time to get over George Worthington's loss. We buried him from our house and marvelled at the courage of his wife, Barbara, and the three young children, Jan, Kim and little Paul, who can't have been more than six at the time. I kept in touch with Barbara when eventually she went back to Australia to work once again with Vic Edwards, the coach of Evonne Goolagong, for whom she had worked before she had met George. At various times since I have seen the three children on their visits to this country. Paul was here in 1987 working at the Championships at Wimbledon as a member of one of the court covering teams. When he came to see us in our BBC lounge, a fine bronzed young fellow looking so much like his father, the memories came flooding back of those days in the 1960s. George would have been proud of him.

I was often conscious of not being able to spend enough time with my own children while they were growing up. To give us all more room we had moved in 1948 from White Corner to Steeproof, a beautiful, detached, four-bedroomed house in Watery Lane, Merton Park, a conservation area. Robin was eight and a half and Jay four. The house had been designed by an architect for his own use and was full of character with an oak-beamed lounge, leaded-light windows and a cosy inglenook fireplace. It was a large, airy room with enough space for our grand piano in the corner, which Con loved to play. Outside an old wistaria encircled the house to provide a beautiful mauve covering every spring. The secluded garden was an ideal place for growing children to play. It was also a perfect place for a summer party. For several years in the 1950s we used to have a get-together on the Friday evening after the men's singles final for some fifty colleagues and friends in the tennis and broadcasting worlds.

Harry Hopman always used to bring his Australian squad. In 1952, after he had won the singles, Frank Sedgman, by now well into his celebration and thoroughly relaxed after a glass or two of Pimms Number One, the favourite refreshment at these parties, grabbed a microphone that someone had brought and recorded a very amusing story on the tape recorder.

That same year the two seventeen-year-olds, Lew Hoad and Ken Rosewall, on their first visit to Wimbledon, disappeared for a while. They had wandered into the kitchen and, finding a few bottles, had decided to mix their own drinks. Harry swore that he had discovered them drinking secretly behind the piano!

At the party a few years later John Newcombe met for the first time Con's doctor, Sir Brian Windyer, who had been at medical school in Australia with John's father.

Robin went successfully through school and eventually decided she wanted to make a career in the Wrens, an idea that appealed to me because it would mean she would learn to be independent and might also have the opportunity of seeing something of the world. Jay was at King's College school in Wimbledon and went through each stage successfully always intending, he once told me, to become a civil pilot. Whether this had been anything to do with his early years when he had met several of my air-force friends I'm not sure, but eventually he changed his mind and decided to go into accountancy. Jay had a great head for figures and was marvellous at picking his way through balance sheets – with the same careful skill that he showed sweeping down mountain sides on skis. The few skiing holidays we had together when the children were young I look back on with great fondness. We used to go out by boat and train, a journey that took us one and a half days – by rail from Victoria to Dover, by ferry to Boulogne, on the train to Paris, and another train via Basle to Zürich. Then we would take another train to Lucerne, across the lake by boat and finally on the cog railway up to Engelberg.

Con and I had caught the skiing bug in 1937, a year after we were married, when we went on our first visit to Switzerland. We fell in love with the mountains, with beautiful Engelberg perched high above Lake Lucerne where we were staying, with Mary Hess, an Englishwoman who ran the Hess hotel with her Swiss husband, Freidl, and with Edy Kuster, our skiing instructor, who had a farm in the valley and was a mountain guide in the summertime. Con became a particularly good skier and I was not too bad either. Under Edy's guidance we soon left the nursery slopes and moved on to runs of greater difficulty. We noticed that others who, like us, had never skied before, could soon do the same. There was a couple who had never been very active in their lives who soon left the nursery class with us to come a thousand feet up in the funicular to ski down the Gerschni Alp – a most exhilarating feeling the first time you attempt it. When Con and I moved into a higher class we were often tempted to move off the piste into the challenge of deep powder snow. However, Edy Kuster constantly warned us all of the danger of avalanches so we resisted our impulses. In view of the tragic happenings at Klosters and St Anton in 1988, he was obviously right.

During that first holiday we came to love the long, fast run down from the Joch Pass through Paradise on the piste that led through the three avalanche fields and on to the picturesque little log cabin restaurant at Unter Trubsee. Finally you swooped down the Gerschni Alp and the steep funicular station slope at the bottom. Then it was into a sleigh and a ride, jingle bells and all, back to the bar at the Hess Hotel for *glühwein* in front of the log fire. It was sheer heaven. When conditions were good, the most exciting piste run was down through the 'Gun Barrel', a two-hundred-yard or so slalom-type run through a steep cleft in the rocks that had been part of the 1936 FIS Championship course. It was a severe examination of one's technique and courage.

Years later I remember being asked on a radio interview in the company of five or six other well-known sportsmen what I would do if given just one more day of sport. The other fellows all answered fairly predictably. When it came to my turn the interviewer said, 'What about you, Dan? I'm sure you would like to have one more day of tennis on the Centre Court at Wimbledon.' 'No,' I replied, and even as I answered I realized perhaps I ought to have said 'Yes,' in public. But it was time for honesty. 'No, not tennis at Wimbledon,' I said. 'Oh, really?' said the interviewer. 'Well, I suppose because you're a very keen golfer it would be golf then?' 'No,' I said, 'I'm afraid it wouldn't be golf either, it would be skiing.' They were all very surprised. However, anybody who has experienced the thrill and exhilaration of skiing and the majestic beauty of snow-covered mountains would I'm sure understand my feelings.

Although I have never enjoyed the thought of being a mountaineer, I came to love climbing on skis. I often relive a wonderful early morning climb just before dawn when Edy took a small group of us from the Trubsee Hotel up to the Titlis on skis, under-lined with adjustable skins, that gripped the snow. Nowadays, you take this route in a couple of lifts, but all we had was leg power. Until dawn broke the only light we had was from the lanterns we carried. It took us something like five or six hours to climb to the top of the Titlis at ten thousand feet. We achieved this in stages of fifty-five minutes climbing and then five minutes of rest, rather like a military cross-country exercise. During the breaks Edy would take out a cigarette while the rest of us sucked our oranges and consumed whatever we'd brought with us in our rucksacks. Then on we went again for another fifty-five minutes until the climb was completed. At the top there would be that wonderful feeling of achievement as we rested and sunbathed in the crisp air and just nattered among ourselves or even fell asleep. There was no hut up there in those days; now there is a beautiful restaurant but we were happy enough with the sandwiches out of our rucksacks. Edy had his bread and dried sausage and then would choose the moment when the surface of the snow was getting like butter so that it was perfect for our descent – slightly wet on top and frozen beneath. The finest skiing, of course, is in powder snow which plumes up behind you as you *schuss* and turn, but the snow on which we skied in the early spring was almost as good. Edy led us down with three or four stops on the way. The long hours of climb were quickly consumed in thirty minutes or so of sweeping descent. Edy chose a route that would not overstrain the standard of his class and we followed in his tracks for about four hundred yards at a time before stopping for a rest. Edy was always careful to warn us, 'We don't have to catch a train,' conscious of the dangers lurking behind every innocent-looking slope for those who are over-ambitious.

It was wonderful to be able to be with Con on these trips. She loved her skiing and was so good at it. So was Jay when he started to go regularly on skiing holidays in the 1950s. As my job began to occupy more and more of my time it became difficult to get leave in the Christmas holidays and the spring when there was so much tennis activity. Accordingly Con would go off with the children by herself and they all became proficient skiers. In fact Con and Jay both earned their gold standard award quite quickly. Even if it snowed heavily when we were at home, which didn't happen often, we would go out on Wimbledon Common, to Richmond Park, Ham Common or Box Hill, near Dorking in Surrey, and ski down the gentle slopes. In fact very early in 1944 when Con was pregnant carrying Jay there was a fairly heavy snowfall in the Loughborough area and Con insisted on going out with me to ski on the small slopes nearby. I even managed to ski on Dartmoor a couple of times at the very end of 1940 and once, at the suggestion of John Pocock, skied down from the top golf tee at the Palace Hotel, Torquay, to inspire the patients into getting back to full fitness. I zigzagged through the bunkers and ended up on the croquet lawn outside the gym, much to the surprise of our new CO who had arrived just two days earlier!

In Switzerland, Freidl and Mary Hess became good friends. Mary was a lovely skier who almost used to dance round on her skis, when turning at speed. She knew the mountains around Engelberg intimately as did Freidl who, twice a year, used to set off on the 'meter run'. Because the family was connected with the electricity company, he had to go round on his skis to read the meters at the various ski huts and small restaurants that lay dotted around the slopes of the mountains. Con and I joined Freidl and Mary once for this task which meant getting up very early. We stopped first at the Gerschni Alp at the top of the funicular where there was a little restaurant. That was at about a thousand feet and we had a drink there whilst waiting for the cable car to swing us up to the Trubsee Hotel. We called in to see the woman who owned the restaurant. She had not been too well and was actually still in bed when we arrived, but she was delighted to see Freidl and they embraced and had an animated conversation. By this time Freidl had been given a couple of large brandies and I remember throwing an orange to her as a parting gift. Then it was up in the cable car to the Trubsee Hotel at about seven thousand feet, run by another part of the Hess family. The meter was read once more and that meant more drinks and chats. Then it was across the frozen lake on our skis through the deep snow that covered some twelve feet of ice. Across the other side of the lake at the foot of the Joch Pass there was a drag lift. You sat on a T-bar and it pulled you up to the ski hut at the top at around eight thousand feet. This was the hut where you could stay the night and sleep on the mattresses they provided and enjoy hot soup and wine. Freidl had to go in and read their meter. By now he had enjoyed a lot of hospitality and I had to be very careful too, not being used to these sort of quantities. Time had flown and by now it was so late that I was worried we would not be able to ski down again in daylight. Freidl seemed to be quite unbothered; perhaps the inner fires were burning brightly by then, for he seemed fine as we skied back in the moonlight. Fortunately we made it home quite safely. It was not always so, though; on one of these trips Mary had broken a leg coming down a heavily-wooded slope on the outskirts of the village.

As Jay became more proficient as a skier on trips to Engelberg with Con, the representative of the British Ski Club wanted him to train out there at other times. She told Jay he had the potential to become an international skier. At that stage of my career there was no way that I could have afforded that and so I had to say no. Jay did not seem too disappointed. In fact I am sure he much preferred the social side, skiing with his friends and enjoying the camaraderie that always surrounds skiing holidays, to the hard work that would have been involved in trying to become an international skier.

Eventually Jay qualified as an accountant with a big London firm who, a year or two later, sent him out to the Bahamas. So he went to Nassau, a bright young accountant with the world opening before him. Jay loved the life in the Bahamas and, by all accounts, was most popular among his wide circle of friends. He was a good swimmer and loved water skiing and could knock a tennis ball around in a natural way that enabled him to enjoy the game socially. When he came home on his first leave to England after about a year he was full of the fact that he had got his single-engine pilot's licence. He told us he used to fly every Saturday to an island about twenty-eight miles away to pay the workmen who were building an extension to lengthen the runway of the small airport. The aircraft belonged to the senior accountant of his firm and Jay was the only one allowed to fly it, probably because he was such a conscientious individual who took no risks and made sure that everything he did followed all the rules. They used to call him 'MM', standing for 'Meticulous Maskell'.

Jay told us that his firm would be sending him to Tokyo when he had completed his tour in Nassau and this he was looking forward to very much. He was also excited that he was shortly hoping to take his test to gain a twin-engined pilot's licence, which would enable him to fly larger and more powerful aircraft. On the fateful day his flight to the island had to be delayed as there was a very strong wind blowing. The midday take-off was postponed and they told him that the weather would have improved by 4.00pm. Two of his friends in Nassau were with him as he gave in his flight plan and took off. All went well on the outward journey and he received clearance to land from the controller on the island. But as he was on his final approach he was unaware that a twelve-seater passenger plane was taking off towards him. The Bahamians had recently taken over airport control on the island and apparently lacked experience. The aircraft taking off had obviously not been warned about Jay's impending landing. At the last moment Jay appeared to have spotted the other plane rising towards him. He tried to take avoiding action, swung sharply to the right and crashed into some trees. Immediately the aircraft burst into flames. There were no survivors. Jay was exactly one month short of his twenty-fifth birthday.

By an extraordinary coincidence Fred Perry was in Nassau on business at the time. The colleague he was meeting said to him: 'We had a very sad crash here yesterday, Fred. A young accountant, about twenty-five years of age, named Maskell. His plane came down in some trees and all three of them were killed.'

'You don't mean Jay Maskell surely, do you, Dan's son?'

'Yes, that's right, it was Dan's son.'

Fred was deeply shocked. He had seen Jay growing up from babyhood and he felt an almost personal loss because of our own friendship.

I heard the news on the golf course at Hindhead. It was a Sunday, 15 march 1970. We'd finished our round and I had just come out after tea to enjoy a little practice putting when my golfing friend, Reg Curtis, told me there had been a phone message from the police to break the sad news. Having got no reply at home because Con was in Switzerland on a skiing holiday and Robin was in the Wrens stationed up in Arbroath, they had traced me via the All England Club. David Mills, the club secretary, had suggested that Emlyn Jones would know exactly where I was. He did. When Reg told me what had happened I was overcome with shock. There was a numbness, an emptiness that I was quite powerless to oppose. Suddenly I felt at one with the brave parents of a tennis player who had been killed during the war. They had evacuated to Torquay and I had been given the difficult task of telling them officially that he had been lost in action. It had been one of my most difficult moments in the war.

Three years later I retired from the LTA. I had reached the age of sixty-five in April but they asked me to stay on until the end of the junior season in September. Accordingly I did my television as usual at Wimbledon, went down to watch the juniors at Eastbourne which I'd always enjoyed, and then attended the Junior Championships at the All England Club in the first week of September. It was on the court there on finals day that I was presented with a trophy, a beautiful decanter, by Joan Rowsell, who at that time was chairman of the junior's committee. They asked me to say a few words. It was a very hot day and I felt rather sad. At the end of a short speech I said something like, 'I'm afraid from now you'll have to put up with me in the freelance seats as it were . . .' and then put down the microphone. I had been watching the Junior Championships from the mid-twenties, even before I went to Wimbledon in 1929. I don't think I'd missed a meeting in all those years and felt part of the scene. From the mid-fifties onwards I used to go round with George Worthington and Jim Cochrane, a schoolmaster and the referee of several junior tournaments in the north (who later would become the president of the LTA), helping to spot the players whom we felt might have international potential with some coaching. In retirement I have made a point of visiting the juniors at least once or twice each year. The simple truth is, I enjoy watching them play and like to keep in touch.

The big event in our lives the following year was Robin's wedding. In August 1974 she would marry Chris Charlton, a former naval officer whom she had met during her years in the service. We planned to hold the reception in a large marquee in the garden at Steeproof so there was plenty to think of in terms of guest lists, the marquee itself, catering and so on. We were lucky that 14 August was a beautiful day. It was a lovely wedding with Chris attended by naval officers at the church which made a really lovely picture. Seven months before they were married, Chris had decided to leave the job he had taken immediately after leaving the Navy, to run a chalet complex up in Scotland which combined residential accommodation with holiday bookings. He is still happily installed as the manager of Barend Farm, Sandyhills, in beautiful country on the Solway Firth, near Dalbeattie. Robin keeps herself busy by spending three or four mornings a week as a receptionist and clinical secretary to a team of doctors nearby and by joining in the local activities.

Another passion of mine, second only to skiing in intensity, is golf. Ever since I hit my first golf ball all those years ago at Hopetoun House on the Firth of Forth, I have been smitten by golf fever. In the years when I was living with brother Bill at Southfields, we would occasionally go off to play in Richmond Park, or at Home Park near Hampton Court. One or two of the chaps I got to know when I was living with Bill used to play on the Common at Wimbledon and I remember the first time I was invited to join them. It seemed rather odd to have to put on the pillar-box red jacket of the Wimbledon Common Golf Club that a local byelaw demanded so that the other members of the public could see the golfer clearly. The steward used to hire out the jacket for sixpence a round.

I must have been about seventeen or eighteen the first time I played there and I soon grew to love my rounds of golf on the Common. However I didn't join the club until after I started working at Wimbledon in 1929. In spare moments I used to pop across to Wimbledon Park with a seven iron and a few golf balls to practise my pitching. This was not at Wimbledon Park Golf Club but in the park itself, where in those days they didn't stop you playing.

Over the years I've had some marvellous fun and relaxation with my friends at the Wimbledon Common Golf Club where now I have survived as the oldest playing member. For twenty-two years I served on the committee and they were kind enough to make me an honorary life member some years ago. In 1988 they invited me to become a vice-president.

The thing that attracted me to golf was not just the game itself. As a teaching professional, it was fascinating for me to experience the problems of learning a new discipline. Occasionally I would ask Fred Leach, the golf pro at the Royal

Wimbledon Club, to give me a lesson at our club where he was an honorary member. Fred was a lovely man, a traditional teaching professional who used to play with James Braid, Harry Vardon and the other great golfers of the day. While he was teaching me I would be analysing my reaction to what he was saying and trying to feel the experience of learning new things. Whenever I could I took part in club matches and competitions simply because it was so difficult to obtain match play in tennis if you were a professional like I was. Later on I used to pop across to Wimbledon Park Golf Club to talk at length to Bill Cox. He was a wonderful analyst of a player's technique. Bill had been the first assistant to Henry Cotton and it was through him that I got to know Henry. Each year I would travel to watch them play at Walton Heath in the *News of the World* tournament there, and at other places where our paths crossed.

It interested me that Bill Cox found it beneficial to come across to the club to watch me giving a lesson. He arrived one day when I was trying to help Kay Stammers to develop a topped backhand to add to her naturally good slice. Bill and I chatted for hours about all aspects of getting across to pupils new techniques. I was a regular visitor to Walton Heath and got to know many of the leading golfers like Alf Padgham, Harry Weetman and Dai Rees and of course Henry. Bobby Locke was another whom I got to know quite well through my association with Slazengers, for he always used their clubs and was often in the Slazenger office on his visits to this country. Bobby used to play with a set of shallow-faced woods, just like a club that Bill Cox had given me years before in gratitude for finding him a Centre Court ticket for a friend at short notice. The loft of the wood was between a brassie and a spoon, what we would now call between a two and a three, and he explained, 'With this you'll be able to pick up those tight lies on the Common for your long second shots.' When I saw the way Bobby could use these woods, I knew that Bill Cox had been right. My first new clubs, a set of Slazenger Bobby Locke's, were as good as any I ever had in my life.

In 1934 through a friend named Harry Clegg, who was a member of NALGO (the National Association of Local Government Officers), I had a delightfully cheap and enjoyable golfing holiday at Saunton down in North Devon. NALGO had a holiday camp just round the corner at Croyde Bay and by going late in the holiday season we got special rates. Jack Jenkins from Queen's Club and another friend joined us for what proved to be a wonderful golfing holiday. They were lovely people at Saunton – none nicer than John Goodban, the secretary, who eventually became the president of the English Golf Union. He always reminded me of Henry Longhurst whom he knew so well, of course, having been up at Cambridge during a part of Henry's time there. I came to know Henry quite well before the war and while we were at Loughborough at the Rehabilitation Centre, I had persuaded this famous golfing scribe to come down to give a talk to the chaps. He had recently left the army to become the MP for West Acton and his subject was 'A New Boy in the House'. He so impressed his audience of aircrew officers that they insisted that he come back after a drink at the bar to talk to them again. Generously, he did. His second subject was the surprising but visionary one 'The Future of Education in Britain'. What a man! It was a riveting evening, one that anyone present will never forget. He had said to me then: 'If ever this war ends you must promise me you'll go and play these great courses – Ballybunion in the west of Ireland, a majestic course, one of the truly great links courses; Royal Dornoch up in the Scottish Highlands, another great links course which you will adore; Newcastle County Down under the mountains of Mourne in Northern Ireland, so beautiful you won't believe it; and, of course, the old course at St Andrews.' I have now played all those courses except Newcastle County Down so, to keep faith with Henry, I must try and repair that omission, even at this late stage.

Every golfer has a favourite golf hole. For me it is the first at St Andrews. Standing on that tee is like standing on the Centre Court for the first time. Behind you rises the famous Royal and Ancient club house and in front of you the vast expanse of fairway. The first at St Andrews shares the fairway with the eighteenth; there is no rough in between. Simply being there was the fulfilment of a dream and I was determined, the first time I played it, to make par which is four. The Swilcan Burn is the main hazard at this famous hole and you have to carry it with your second shot to land the ball on the green just beyond the burn. With Bill Moss, my playing partner, already out of bounds in the car park, I was lucky enough to hit as good a drive as I'd ever hit, absolutely straight on the line I wanted. When I reached my ball I found it nestling on a very slight hump, a rise about as big as a soup plate. It was resting on the downhill side of it, an awkward lie. This left me with an iron shot of about a hundred and fifty yards to clear the Swilcan Burn and hold the green. I had always vowed that if and when I played St Andrews for the first time I would certainly never land in that burn. Short maybe, but never in it. Now I was faced with an awkward lie, and surprisingly chose to cut up a high five wood! I took the club out of the bag and with a very open stance managed to cut the ball high in the air hoping that it would pitch over the burn and make the green. I could hardly have played a better shot. The ball carried the water by a couple of feet but being very high dropped almost dead and spun right. I was left with a nasty little pitch and run. I played a shot I often quit on but this time I timed it well and left myself with a five foot putt which I had to make to get my par. Concentrating as never before, I willed the ball into the hole – but it missed by half an inch to the right!

Con had never really been interested in playing golf. Her first and last loves were her skiing and her amateur dramatics.

The Putney Players were doing marvellously well. One of the social members was Roy Plomley, the man who made his name on the radio with Desert Island Discs. I came home one evening and Con told me that Roy had phoned, asking me to go on the programme in about three or four weeks time. He wanted me to ring back the following day to suggest two or three records so that they could be doing the research. I remember I selected among them *The Royal Air Force March*, to remind me of those wonderful war-time days in rehabilitation; *I Could Have Danced All Night* from *My Fair Lady*, and *The Sound of Music* from the musical and film of the same name. It was great fun doing the programme, especially choosing which books and which luxury item to take with me. I seem to remember that I persuaded Roy to let me take both Churchill's *War Memoirs* and a selection of Henry Longhurst's golfing books. For the luxury item I selected a number five iron and a dozen golf balls. Roy asked me why I had chosen them. I replied, 'Well, I've always believed that I could more or less make a tennis ball talk but I've never been as successful with a golf ball. I felt that given plenty of time on my desert island, I could happily hit golf balls and learn to slice and draw the ball intentionally instead of by accident as I do just now.' I was surprised at the extent of the fan mail resulting from *Desert Island Discs* – hundreds of letters, rather like my mail each year around the Wimbledon period. Henry Longhurst was kind enough to write thanking me for mentioning his books on the radio. With his letter he enclosed a copy of *Around in 68* which, deceptively, is not a specialist golfing book at all but the fascinating story of a working tour around the world that he completed in sixty-eight days.

In 1978 I was asked by the makers of the film *Players* to act as the commentator on the fictitious Wimbledon final between the film's hero, Chris Christianson, played by Dino Martin, and Guillermo Vilas. So it was that on the Wednesday following that year's championships I found myself back in the commentary box watching an empty Centre Court staging the Wimbledon final – empty, that is, except for the two hundred and fifty or so extras, all appropriately dressed, who sat together in that section of the stands which appeared in the background of each shot. It was an eerie sensation. The 'crowd' had to move around several times to cover all the shots that were required so it was a very time-consuming business. For a week the club was virtually taken over by the film crew. There were all the extras, the technicians, the directors and producers, the make-up people, the caterers and their vans, the lighting men and their equipment plus the cameramen and the cameras. They seemed to be everywhere. All the normal club rules were waived. But one of our members, Gus Holden, had forgotten that the men's main dressing-room had been taken over as a dressing-room for the stars. He had wandered in at the moment when Ali McGraw, the main lead, was standing totally naked as she prepared to dress for her next scene. Mumbling an apology, Gus beat a hasty retreat but said that Miss McGraw had not seemed in the least disturbed by his intrusion. Being a perfect gentleman he would reveal no more facts about Miss McGraw's finer points.

I was due to go to California to do the actual commentary on the match once the film had been cut and edited early in March 1979. In February Con had been invited to spend a couple of weeks with our mutual friends, the Days, in Antigua where they had a house. We had known Barbara and Frank since our courting days. She was the daughter of Walter Merricks whose wife, Barbara's mother, had died. He had married again, his second wife being Chrissa Tyrell who played at Wimbledon from 1923–1931, reaching the quarter-finals in 1926 when Kitty Godfree had beaten her quite easily. The Merricks lived in Icklesham, between Hastings and Rye, in a big farmhouse called The Manor. They were a most hospitable family. Barbara's father was a great sportsman and despite a limp he was most proficient as a billiards player and a bowler and played a very decent game of tennis. Barbara married Frank Day, the son of a farming family in Kent, so there was a union of two great farming families. The Days lived at Marden. Frank was a great cricket lover and some years ago was the president of Kent County Cricket Club. I remember going down with him one day to the Canterbury cricket festival where I met a couple of friends – Colin Cowdrey, who had dropped in for the afternoon, and Les Ames, with whom I shared my early days in the RAF. On the Canterbury ground they had a stand named after Les and another after Frank Woolley. The match that day was against Gloucestershire and Colin took me round and introduced me to some of the Gloucestershire players. It was a most enjoyable occasion.

The Days loved to spend some of the winter at their house in Antigua where Con had been twice before. I had never been able to clear enough time to join her because of my work. Con loved swimming and was always ready for her pre-breakfast dip. According to what Barbara and Frank told me later, Con had gone down from the house before breakfast announcing that she would be back for breakfast after her usual swim. When, after a longer time than usual, she hadn't returned, the Days went out looking for her, and around a headland she was found floating on top of the water. They pulled her out and tried all sorts of resuscitation drills but it was too late. She had drowned. On the beach in their usual place lay her dry towel, another costume, her lipstick and the other little bits and pieces that she always took with her.

To this day, nobody knows what happened. Con was a strong swimmer but did have a slightly troublesome hip that she was thinking of having replaced eventually, but there was no clue as to whether this had had any bearing on her death. They wrote on the death certificate 'Asphyxia due to drowning'. Frank had the difficult job of breaking the news to me. I shall never forget that telephone call. I could not believe what I was hearing. First Jay, now Con. There was the same terrible shock and a numbness which took months to disappear.

Con's ashes are buried in the graveyard of St Mary's Church at Merton Park, where Lord Nelson once worshipped. On the small gravestone there is a plaque in memory of both Con and Jay.

NINE

Behind the Microphone

In spite of the personal tragedies that I have suffered I have always considered myself a fortunate man – fortunate in my work, fortunate in my friends and fortunate in the path that destiny chose for me behind a microphone. It all began in 1949. The BBC asked me if I would like to join Max Robertson in the radio commentary box to act as the summarizer while he performed with marvellous verbal dexterity to describe every shot that was played with his quick-fire, ball-by-ball commentaries. Knowing as I did so much about Wimbledon, the Championships and the performers, it was a job I found relatively easy and quite fascinating.

In fact I had performed on television even before that. In 1938, the second year of regular television broadcasts, I was asked to do a coaching feature for *Picture Page*. Incidentally I well remember the very first broadcast, in November 1936, with the Postmaster-General opening the proceedings in the afternoon and at night a collection of celebrities being introduced. These included Kay Stammers, our leading tennis girl, representing sportswomen; two years later she would be in the final at Wimbledon against Alice Marble.

I was asked before the 1938 broadcast what props I would need. I had simply said a wall or backboard to hit against, with a line on it three feet from the floor sloping slightly upwards from the centre to resemble the net and a run back of about twenty-one feet so that I could show that tennis was a game of fast movement. I remember T. M. Mavrogadato, who was on the committee at Wimbledon, saying to me one

291

day in the dressing-room: 'I see you're going to do some stuff on the new television.'

'How did you know?' I asked.

'Well, I saw it announced on my new television set.'

Mavro rose even higher in my estimation after that, for he must have been one of the first of only about two thousand people who owned sets at that early stage.

Come the day of the performance I tramped up the hill to Alexandra Palace carrying the tennis bag that Percy Portlock had given me after we had won the Davis Cup. Eventually somebody showed me where I could change and I was taken on to the set. It appeared that I would be working in among the paraphernalia of a drawing-room set that was part of the scene from Dickens that they had just finished, *The Pickwick Papers* it was. There was a mock bookcase that was turned round for me to use as the practice board. There was no net line on it nor did there appear to be very much run back. I wondered if we were going to move the bookcase to a more open area. The producer appeared. I asked him.

'What are these crosses on the floor?'

'Oh, that's where you must stand,' he replied. 'If you move outside those marks the camera won't be able to pick you up.'

'But you've only given me about fourteen feet,' I said. 'It won't be easy to make it look convincing in these conditions.'

It hadn't occurred to anybody to provide any tennis balls but fortunately I had brought a box with me. I dropped a ball and knocked it against the back of the bookcase which promptly tottered and almost fell over. A stage-hand was despatched to find some supports for the bookcase which was eventually propped up. The programme itself consisted of a demonstration of the three basic shots of the game – the ground strokes, the service and the volley. In extremely cramped conditions I somehow got through the programme, emphasizing the swinging nature of ground strokes, the throwing action of the serve and the punching racket-head of the volley. In recalling this episode it has occurred to me that this was probably the very first tennis instruction that was ever broadcast anywhere in the world. Looking back, it was a pretty ordinary little item but at the time we all thought we'd achieved something rather special.

Soon after that I remember making an instructional gramophone record, a 78 of course. To be accurate there were two records in the set and I recall going through the lessons with H. P. T. Wakelam and Colonel Brand who had been the first radio commentators at Wimbledon when that had all begun in 1927.

After two years with Max Robertson in 1949 and 1950, Peter Dimmock, who was then running BBC Sport, suggested that I should have a trial with Freddie Grisewood, the man with the golden voice. He was married to Peggy Scriven's elder sister, who was a very beautiful woman. Peggy herself was a pupil of mine and had won the French Championship twice, in 1933 and 1934, beating Madam Mathieu and Dorothy Round in those two finals. Peggy, a Yorkshire girl, was one of the toughest competitors we had at that time and one of the most intelligent, too. I had met Freddie once or twice with her sister so I knew him slightly when we started working together.

I could not have had a better or kinder mentor. I literally sat at his feet in the tiny commentary box and learned the business of television commentary. The box itself, in those early days of black and white television, was situated slightly below the Royal Box on the left-hand side. To get to it you had to climb an iron ladder and emerge through the concrete floor of the platform on which the box stood. It was difficult to do this and many years later Paul Fox, who was then associated with BBC Sport, had a nasty fall from the iron ladder and broke some ribs. Because there was so little room in the cramped quarters the only place to sit was on the ledge where Freddie's chair stood, so that my nose was almost on the desk. I could only just see through the window to the court.

The box's position was perfect. We looked straight down the sidelines past the umpire. It provided almost as good a view as the Royal Box and was in a better position than our present television commentary box which is at the other end alongside the scoreboard. The change came when we converted from black and white to colour in 1967 to televise the BBC2 tournament, the first professional one at Wimbledon involving the world's leading players. It was held in August as part of the All England Club's orchestration of the build-up to open tennis. That was the first outside broadcast in colour.

For the first part of the Championships in 1951, I was summarizing for Freddie until one day towards the end he suggested that I ought to have a crack at the ball-by-ball commentary. I did a day or two of that and he said, 'You're ready now to do this on your own, you know.' I was astonished that he should think so.

In 1951, of course, there were no recordings. Everything was live and when you were off the air you simply had a break until you came on again. It was during one of these breaks that the producer came through on the talk-back and said to Freddie, 'We've just had a message, Freddie. The office want to get hold of you so shall I ask them to ring you now?' He said, 'Yes, of course,' and in a moment the phone rang in the commentary box. I could not help hearing Freddie's end of the conversation which went something like this:

'Yes, that sounds very interesting. Yes, I would like to think about it . . . Perhaps we could talk about details after Wimbledon. You know how to get in touch with me?'

He put down the phone and turned to me. 'Rather interesting, Dan,' he said. 'They've just asked me whether I'd be interested in doing a new series they're starting on radio. It will move all over the country, beginning down in the West Country. It's a series that I think they intend to call *Any Questions* or something like that,' he said. 'The idea is to have four or five people sitting round and talking about topics of the moment. The questions will come in from a studio audience. They've asked me to be the chairman. It all sounds rather fun and I'm looking forward to hearing more about it after Wimbledon.'

I said just now that I feel that I am a fortunate man. Another piece of good fortune is the fact that ever since that first broadcast with Freddie Grisewood in 1951 I have not missed a single day's play, or a day's broadcasting, during the thirty-six Championships that have taken place. That is surely lucky. Not to have caught a cold or had a family engagement of a pressing nature, not to have been injured or taken ill and sent to hospital, is luck of the very highest order. The fates have certainly smiled upon me.

From the start, I realized that the commentator's role is merely the sharp end of a huge team effort. That is probably one of the reasons why I have thoroughly enjoyed the challenge of each new broadcast. I was always at my happiest in team situations, with the Davis Cup and other teams with which I have been associated over the years. The BBC team at Wimbledon is magnificently professional. From the producer and editors to the directors and their assistants, to the cameramen, engineers and stage managers, all work together in harmony to produce the end product.

When I moved from radio to television there was, of course, an abrupt change of pace. Quite obviously one must speak all the time – or most of the time – during a radio broadcast because the listener depends utterly upon your word picture to give him an idea of what is happening. With television, the picture tells the greatest part of the story and I have always believed that economy of words is what most viewers enjoy. I try to help them understand what is happening by adding to the picture things that they cannot or might not know. Instead of describing in words a winner that they have just seen anyway, I try to say why it was a winner. Or if Jimmy Connors misses a low forehand approach shot, I tell viewers why I am astonished that after all these years Jimmy, with his vast experience, has not eradicated this failing which has cost him literally hundreds of points in his career. There is a delicate balance between being informative and lecturing to an audience, something I always try to avoid. Yet you will never satisfy everybody. Newcomers to the game who know nothing about technique, or the personalities of the performers, would probably enjoy a little more talking than we usually allow ourselves. The keen followers of the game, who are perhaps players themselves, probably feel that they need next to no comment. You may be surprised that, despite our comparatively low-key approach, we still get letters saying that we talk too much!

We do now use many more replays during the course of a game than we ever used to do. I believe we have now got the balance about right though I'm sure not everyone would agree with me.

The fact is you can never please everybody. For instance, in the 1961 all-British ladies' final between Angela Mortimer and Christine Truman, I had introduced the players by saying that I had played with Angela a few times and had coached Christine since she was thirteen. I expressed the hope that, since we were assured of a British champion at long last, they would both play at their very best. Despite that statement of my position, I nevertheless had thirty-four letters about that match alone – seventeen criticizing me for favouring Angela and seventeen being just as critical for my support of Christine! You can never win, can you?

The art of sports commentary – for at its best it is indeed an art – is partly acquired and partly instinctive. All the best commentators that I have ever heard immerse themselves in the match they are watching to such a degree that they are part of it. They feel what the players feel and use words sparingly to communicate those feelings. At the top of my list I put the late Henry Longhurst, who once said to me, 'A second's silence is worth a minute's talk'. Not far behind are Richie Benaud and Peter Allis, both of whom bring to their commentaries the authenticity of people who have experienced what they are talking about. To have performed at a relatively high level gives you the inner understanding that helps you to interpret what is happening in front of you. But we all depend on the skill of our directors.

All tennis commentators need to have two golden rules, I think: first, never talk during a rally; second, always keep one eye on the monitor. Nor must a commentator forget that he is there to inform and explain when necessary. As a viewer I feel a little bit cheated if a great performer suddenly does something quite brilliant, or makes a glaring mistake, and the commentator doesn't enlighten me.

I have worked with some very gifted executive producers. Peter Dimmock, my first, was a dynamic man who knew what he wanted and how to get it and set a high standard for others to follow. Bryan Cowgill was certainly one of the great men of broadcasting who helped to keep BBC Sport at the top. 'Ginger', as he was always known to his friends and colleagues, had the reputation of being something of a tyrant. Grown men were supposed to tremble in his presence, dreading the moment when he would explode and castigate them for some minor misdemeanour. All I can say is that I found Bryan one of the most reasonable and stimulating of men. He may have barked often but he also knew when to pat people on the back. Just before the 1972 Wimbledon final, when Stan Smith played Ilie Nastase in what proved to be one of Wimbledon's great matches, Bryan came into our commentary box and asked the stage manager to give him a headset. He wanted to listen to the communication between the producer, who sits in the scanner directing, and his team of commentators and cameramen. (I was working with Jack Kramer in those days, a marvellous companion and in my view a fine broadcaster, who sadly fell victim to a political decision in 1973. After leading the Association of Tennis Professionals in their dispute with Wimbledon it was felt that he would no longer be welcome as a commentator.)

We had expected Bryan to stay for five or ten minutes to see the match under way before returning to the control room. Although we hardly noticed his presence, he became so gripped by this absorbing match that he stayed for the whole three hours and ten minutes. When it was over he simply stood up, tapped each of us on the shoulder and said, 'Gentlemen, that's the best sports commentary I've ever heard. Well done.' Coming from Bryan, who didn't throw too many bouquets about, that was quite an accolade.

Slim Wilkinson was another who contributed greatly to the development of our coverage at Wimbledon over a long spell. He it was who introduced the idea of having temporary buildings in the compound behind number one court, where the vehicles are parked, an area that was soon christened 'Slimsville'.

Since 1951 my own view of Wimbledon has inevitably been restricted in one sense. For much of the time I am ensconced in the commentary box and therefore can no longer wander round the outside courts on the early days, getting a look at some of the fine, new, young players making their way in the game. Nevertheless, I keep in touch watching them in other tournaments, matches and practice sessions and, like other commentators at Wimbledon, watch much of the play on the monitors in our 'rest room' when not on the air myself. I also have a few good vantage points for looking at the play on the outside courts.

Television is an intoxicating medium in which to work, expecially at Wimbledon and, even after all these years, during the minutes before I step into the box, take off my jacket, loosen my tie and settle down with my headset on and my pen poised over my notepad, I still feel the thrill of anticipation. It is not unlike the feeling you get when preparing to play an important match. The day I no longer feel the adrenaline pumping will be the day when I know it is time to stop.

Despite the years of practice and my familiarity with most of the players and their records, I never go into a match without having done my homework. I was taught a short, sharp lesson once. Believing that I knew all about the four players whom we would be seeing later in the day in a men's doubles, I did no research. When the time came to broadcast the match I found myself hesitating when describing the records of these men, groping for the facts. Had Vic Seixas ever been in an Australian final? Had he been in the US doubles finals once or twice with Tony Travert? And so on. In no time I was floundering. It was a most unpleasant experience and one which I have never allowed myself to be subjected to again.

During the course of the match, I like to make notes on a special type of score-pad which my present colleague, John Barrett, produced some years ago for the juniors of the BP International Tennis Fellowship. The pads were designed for them to record every point that a future opponent played during the course of a match that they would be watching as preparation for their own likely meeting with the player. As well as recording the number of double faults and aces, the sort of basic information we all require, the pad is designed like an umpire's score-pad but with space on the right-hand side for notes. I use that space for all the biographical information which I have worked on in the hours before the match. In the squares of the umpire's pad which mark every point won and lost, I record with my own shorthand the type of shot that has been hit. Thus, b.v.n. in the little square means backhand volley into the net. A large A means an ace has been served, while d.f. denotes double fault. If the server comes in and makes a winning volley I record it as S/V. If he misses his volley it is either S/VO or S/VN, the meaning of which I'm sure you can deduce. In this way not only do I keep track of the match, but I also know exactly what has happened on every point. The difficulty about all this is to maintain concentration but I can honestly say that if I am enjoying a match and am thoroughly involved in it, concentration is never a problem. It is those rather dull, lifeless matches which test you in that respect.

Things do not always go smoothly on our broadcasts. When we arrived with a complete outside broadcast colour unit in Barcelona to televise the 1972 Commercial Union Masters (the Spaniards could not supply colour equipment), our producer Slim Wilkinson was appalled to find that there was no suitable position for the main camera. 'We must get further back from the court,' he said to the operators of the Palau Blaugrano, the hall owned by the Barcelona Football Club where the tournament was being staged. 'You'll have to knock down that wall to give us a longer shot,' he added, more in jest than anything else. To his surprise, within an hour they had demolished enough of the dividing wall to give him the camera position he needed.

All went well until the final stages when the Spanish Broadcasting Company announced that we would have to use Spanish cameramen instead of our BBC men who had been operating the equipment up to then without fuss. There was nothing we could do. Unfortunately Slim did not speak Spanish so, with an interpreter, he organized a crash course in basic communications with the cameramen so that he could direct the programme. Jack Kramer and I were very conscious of the problems during our broadcast, but by some miracle we got by without any major disasters – though Slim lost a few more hairs! However, when it was all over, in the early hours of the morning, the Spaniards stood Slim on a table and cheered him while they drank his health.

It was also in Barcelona that one night, on the stroke of midnight, all the stadium lights went out while we were in the middle of a match. Apparently the caretaker had decided that it was time to go home so he had turned off all the switches, locked his office and left for home . . . with the key! We had a twenty-minute delay before power was restored.

It had been even worse in Tokyo for the first Grand Prix Masters tournament in 1970, sponsored by Pepsi-Cola. The same Slim Wilkinson had had to use a great deal of tact to explain to the host broadcasters, who had never covered tennis before, that normally the main cameras are placed behind the end of the court, not alongside the net where the Japanese had installed them!

Before you laugh too heartily at the Japanese, I must tell you that the very same thing had happened in Torquay when the BBC were due to televise a Davis Cup tie against Denmark from the covered courts of the Palace Hotel. The young assistant producer, whose first experience of tennis this was, had a very red face.

The same sort of problems occur with radio broadcasts. When Britain reached the Davis Cup final against the Americans in 1978 the tie was played at the Mission Hills Country Club in the Californian desert in Palm Springs. BBC Television did not have the rights to the event so I was invited by BBC Radio to join their team, which included Gerry Williams and Max Robertson. Our commentary position was a temporary structure built on the roof of the club house. When we saw the position before the matches had begun we were all conscious of the lack of a screen to shield our voices from the players. The inevitable happened. After about three games John McEnroe, playing against John Lloyd in the opening rubber, came down to serve at our end. As I was describing the scene he turned his head and snarled in our direction 'Shut up!' When Gerry Williams recounted this embarrassing incident on my *This is Your Life* programme he ended by saying, 'Imagine anyone expecting Dan to shut up!'

That was a difficult tie in many ways. We had not realized just how great the drop in temperature was in the desert once the sun had disappeared behind Mount Jacinto. It seemed that one minute we were boiling under the desert sun and the next we were freezing to death. I had taken with me to Palm Springs, purely for fun, my Russian astrakhan hat. Of course that first day it was sitting in my hotel bedroom whilst we all shivered. But on the second and third days I was the envy of all my friends who had been forced to rush to the local stores to purchase some warm headgear (as well as some longjohns!)

On a similar occasion at the Monte Carlo Country Club one year when Björn Borg was making his comeback, we were again in an open-air commentary position high up above the club house looking down across the three main courts to the deep blue Mediterranean beyond – surely one of the finest views at any tennis club. Again it got very cold when the sun set and we were in shadow. John Barrett, who was commentating with me, was not suitably dressed for the weather and could not hold his pencil to make his notes as his hands began to turn blue. In fact it was so cold that neither of us could hold the lip mikes steady in our hands and our teeth began to chatter. To John's rescue came Con, who lent him her tigerskin coat and her gloves. They were much too small of course, but at least they kept him reasonably warm. I can assure you he was a lovely sight!

I had my problems one year at Wimbledon when, due to a shortage of commentators, I found myself working in the box for most of the afternoon. Shortly before we went off the air it became apparent that I was losing my voice so the producer had me relieved. Knowing that I would need to be in action again the following day I telephoned the ear, nose and throat specialist who lived just behind the All England Club. He agreed to see me at once and by 7.00pm I was in his consulting room. Fortunately his examination showed that it was nothing serious but he prescribed a gargle and warned me not to speak unless it was absolutely essential. When I got home Con could see the funny side of it. 'It's about time somebody gagged you,' she said. But she was marvellous and for the next few days she mixed the honey and lemon drink that the specialist had advised me to take into the commentary box. I never could convince John that there was no whisky in the mix!

Our BBC style of commentary is very different from that of the Americans where, on all the major networks except the Public Broadcasting Service, there are commercials. Therefore the commentators in the USA have to cram all their information into the periods between the points of a game – and sometimes even during the play which tends to irritate viewers. Thus with constant replays of even quite ordinary points plus a plethora of statistical information the whole effect is somewhat frenetic. By BBC standards there's far too much talking and it is all far too busy – although the American public is conditioned to this approach.

One year at Wimbledon the NBC coverage was switched to our BBC sound output for the purpose of showing this difference in technique to American viewers. Bud Collins had been making the point that the Brits spoke very little during the forty-five seconds of silence that followed whilst a point was completed and we saw the players preparing for the next, without any comments from me (simply because there was nothing to say that would enhance the broadcast for the viewers), Bud had to keep saying: 'Don't worry, folks, we really are tuned to the BBC commentary – they just don't happen to be saying anything at the moment!'

I had an interesting reaction to the difference between the two treatments one year in Dallas. It was during the WCT finals, played indoors in the Southern Methodist University stadium. The BBC had been allocated six seats in an open position among the spectators halfway up one of the stands. Because of the shortage of seats we had agreed to allow guests of Lamar Hunt, the owner of WCT, to sit in the vacant places alongside my own. We had warned them that they would have to put up with my chatter but at least they would have the chance to watch the picture on my monitor if they wanted to. Afterwards they all thanked me and were most generous in their praise of the commentary, adding what a pity it was that the American commentators were not similarly restrained. In fairness I pointed out that we did not have the problem of commercials during each change of ends so that we could use the time when the players were at the chair to make most of our comments.

These last thirty-six years working from the 'best' seat in the house have given me as much pleasure as anything that went before. I consider that the luck I spoke of must include the fact that I have been earning a living by doing something that is really not work at all. Every match, every set, every game, every point has been a source of enjoyment for me and I do indeed bless the guardian angel who has allowed me to carry on for so long.

One of the most interesting aspects of a long and rewarding life has been to coach some members of the Royal Family in a relaxed and natural setting. At one time or another I have had the privilege of playing with four of the Royal children – Princess Alexandra, Princess Anne as she was then, Prince Charles and Prince Andrew.

It all started quite informally. Princess Marina had approached the All England Club to ask if I would be able to give Princess Alexandra a few lessons prior to her visit to Australia. Discretion was of the utmost importance, to avoid media attention. Accordingly it was arranged that I should give Alexandra her first lesson at Lord Iliffe's covered court at Yattendon near Newbury. I took care to arrive early and went out to see the court, which was a beautiful wooden-framed building on low ground. The butler took me down and I noticed that a table had been laid for tea. The Royal car had been delayed in the traffic and when they arrived a few minutes after the appointed hour Princess Marina apologized and explained that they had had to enlist the help of

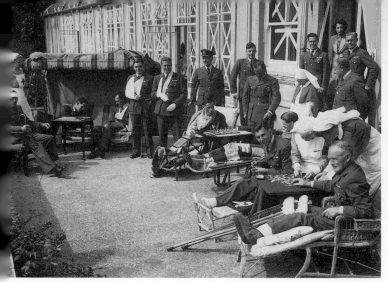

In 1940, on the terrace of the Palace Hotel, Torquay, which had become the RAF Officers' Hospital.

Supported by Matron Coulhurst, the senior medical officer, Wing Commander Jamie O'Malley, dressed up as Father Christmas, enters the spirit of the occasion at a Christmas party in 1940.

One of the wartime exhibition tennis matches held to raise money for the RAF Benevolent Fund, this one for Loughborough 'Salute the Soldier Week'. Front row, from left to right: Natalie Zinovieff, Diana M. Wood, and myself; back row, Doug Snart, Andrew 'Nick' Zinovieff, Edmund Burke and Frank Shields.

Helen Wills and Eileen Bennett; two of the most beautiful women to grace the world of tennis.

Above right On parade with Field-Marshal Lord Montgomery at the *Daily Mail* Schoolboys' Exhibition in 1947 – a meeting, which to my surprise, he recalled many years later at the All England Club.

Pilot Officer Uberoi, Lauri Shaffi (after the war a member of the British Davis Cup team), Lesley Ames, England's famous test wicket keeper and batsman, and Dan Maskell. New recruits at Loughborough 1940.

Charles Hare, British Davis Cup, Dan Maskell, Sergeant Hank Quinn, famous American tennis coach, and Frank Shields, American Davis Cup player who, in the 1931 Wimbledon semi-final, injured himself playing Jean Borotra and could not contest the final, giving Sidney Wood, fellow American, the only walk-over in a final in Wimbledon's history.

During our 'Focus on Tennis' visit to Carlisle in July 1950, Fred Perry demonstrates the backhand to a class of juniors while I give the instruction over the public address system.

A session in 1956 with some amateur coaches who were among the first I addressed after reconstructing the LTA coaching scheme, in which I was loyally supported by Jack Moore (far left). He later did tremendous work as the manager of the Lawn Tennis Foundation.

Above left Jay, Robin and Con skiing in Engleberg in the late 1950s.

Above right My daughter Robin, our nanny Charlotte Babbington, son Jay and wife Con in the garden at Steep Roof, with Nick the labrador.

Above My daughter Robin was the Officer in Charge Wrens, when HRH Princess Alexandra, to whom I had given a few tennis lessons in her teens, visited HMS *Condor* in Arbroath, Scotland.

Above right Bill Moss (left) and George Worthington during the British Professional Championships at Devonshire Park, Eastbourne, Bill, who was a pupil of mine when he was a junior, became the Scottish National Coach and is now the President of the Professional Tennis Coaches' Association, George succeeded me as coach to the All England Club in 1955 and also became coach to the Davis and Wightman Cup teams.

Robin's marriage to Chris Charlton at St Mary's Church, Merton Park.

Above left In the Centre Court commentary box at Wimbledon where our proximity to the action allows us to become completely involved.

Above right At Fred Perry's memorable party held in the members' enclosure at the All England Club to commemorate the fiftieth anniversary in 1984 of his first win at Wimbledon, some old friends get together. From left to right: Fred Perry, Colin Snape (then executive director of the Professional Golfers' Association), Henry Cotton and myself.

A moment of nostalgia for Charles Hare and myself taken at the final of the 1978 Davis Cup in Palm Springs, California, when the British team were beaten 4–1 by the Americans. Charles had been in the 1937 Challenge Round at Wimbledon when I was still the coach.

My wife signing the visitors' book at Alton Hospital; Kay's book *Give Us the Chance* has become a standard work on sport and physical recreation for people with a mental handicap.

Above left The Chancellor of Loughborough University of Technology, Sir Arnold Hall, conferring my honorary MA degree in July 1982.

Above right A proud day at the Palace after receiving the CBE, from left to right, Kay's daughter Susan, myself, Kay and Robin.

Trapped for *This is Your Life*! The moment of truth when I realised that Eamonn Andrews had caught me. The chief conspirator was John Barrett (centre). After the initial shock, I resigned myself to enjoy the programme.

A happy gathering at the end of the show. From left to right: son-in-law and daughter Brian and Susan Killip; son-in-law Chris Charlton; Kay with granddaughter little Héloïse; daughter Robin; myself; Emlyn Jones; Virginia Wade, Geoff Paish; Kitty Godfree; behind Kitty Godfree is Christine Janes (née Truman); Angela Barrett (née Mortimer); (partly hidden) the famous England footballer Raich Carter; John Barrett; and Mark Cox; Grandson Ross, with teddy bear 'Wimbledon', is in the foreground.

Reading police to get a motorcycle escort to help them through the dense traffic.

Alexandra was about sixteen at the time and was a very apt pupil. She quickly adapted to suggestions that I made to her but was having a few problems with the rather old racket she was using. Once or twice when she struck the ball off-centre the racket head sounded most odd and gave way at the shoulders after a few more shots. I suggested that she borrow one of my rackets, even though the handle was really a little too big for her. It wasn't too long before she enjoyed hitting a few well-timed shots with a tightly strung, top-class racket. By the time we had completed our first lesson, Alexandra was making contact with the ball quite well but, like most beginners, was sometimes too close and sometimes too far away from the ball, making it difficult for her to develop a grooved swing on the forehand drive. Her judgement of flight and bounce, I explained, would be greatly improved if she had the opportunity to use a practice wall, which almost every great player I knew had done in their very early days. When we had finished, Princess Marina thanked me and suggested that because of the difficult journey it might perhaps be better to have the next lesson at their home at Iver Heath in Buckinghamshire.

After two visits there, it was decided that it would probably be more appropriate still if, for future lessons, Alexandra came to Wimbledon. After one of our sessions there the topic of skiing came up and I told the Princess how much I enjoyed my visits to Switzerland. 'It's very much part of my life, not merely skiing but being in the mountains,' I explained. 'After a skiing holiday I feel refreshed and invigorated and altogether fitter.'

When I played with her again Princess Marina came too. I had just returned from a skiing holiday. It was a lovely spring day so we were able to play outside on the hard courts. As we strolled down towards the courts Princess Marina said to me, 'Mr Maskell, I gather from Alex that you are a keen skier and have just come back from a skiing holiday.'

'Yes, ma'am, I have. It was wonderful.'

'Ah, a wonderful sport, yes, but a dangerous one I should have thought for somebody like yourself who has to be able to run about all the time.'

The problem for Princess Alexandra was that there was little opportunity for her to practise what we had been learning in between her lessons. However by the time we had finished over the course of two seasons she was hitting the ball reasonably well, well enough to be able to enjoy the game socially on her impending visit to Australia.

It had all been delightfully friendly and informal and I was very touched when Con and I were invited to Alexandra's wedding. She had invited six of us from the All England Club – Duncan Macaulay went with his sister and Herman and Mavis David also attended. It struck me then how fortunate we are at the club that the Kent family have taken such a deep and lively interest in the club's affairs ever since the first association through Princess Marina's husband, the Duke of Kent, who had been the president in 1929. Marina herself had strengthened that bond as the president from 1961–68 and her son, the present Duke, staunchly maintains the family tradition. It has been obvious by watching her excited reactions, that Princess Alexandra has also thoroughly enjoyed her visits to the Royal Box at Wimbledon.

The next time I met the Princess was on the occasion of the BBC *Sports Review of the Year* in 1969. She was due to present the award to the year's sports personality, Ann Jones, who had won the Wimbledon ladies' title that year. Just before the programme began the house lights were dimmed and a spotlight picked out the Princess standing in the theatre box at the side of the stage. She was wearing a lovely dark evening dress and the whole effect was like something from a Gainsborough painting. It was a delightful moment, with the packed audience full of expectation. At the end of the show she came down to present the trophy and after it was all over a party was held on stage. While I was having a drink with some outside broadcast friends Peter Dimmock came up and said, 'Dan, the Princess would like you to go up and say hello to her and meet her husband. I'll take you up.'

They were chatting with some of the other guests when I arrived but she broke off and came over smiling to say, 'Hello, nice to see you. You've never met my husband have you?'

'No, I haven't had that pleasure,' I replied. Angus Ogilvy joined us and said, 'Well, it's nice to meet you at last. I have a special thank you that I'd like to pass on to you.'

'Really, sir?' I said, wondering what on earth he was going to say.

'On the day that I proposed to Alex she had just come from having a lesson with you . . . and I was accepted!' he said, smiling.

Many of our friends used to say that Robin bore a strong resemblance to Princess Alexandra. Her fellow Wrens at Arbroath used to pull her leg about it, especially on the day when Princess Alexandra went up there on an official visit. Robin had been in the line-up at the reception when the Princess was inspecting them and somewhere in our family archives there is a photograph of her curtseying to the Princess. Some time later when I was playing with Alexandra at Wimbledon I said, 'My daughter had the pleasure of meeting you when you were up in Arbroath at an official inspection at the station.'

'Oh, why ever didn't you tell me beforehand? I would have loved to say hello to her.'

'That's the last thing my daughter would have allowed me to do. If I'd mentioned her name to you she would have been furious.'

The first time I met Princess Anne she was about ten and a half. Once again an enquiry had come through the club and I was asked to report to the Privy Purse entrance at Buckingham Palace one Monday where I would be directed to Miss Peebles, Anne's governess. When I arrived and presented myself to the policeman on the gate I found I was expected. After he'd asked me who I was and on what business the officer said, 'I shan't need to ask you for any identification, Mr Maskell, your voice is enough.'

I was taken up to the nursery where I met Miss Peebles. Anne and two other girls about her own age were just finishing their lesson. I could see from the papers on the table that they had been drawing weather-charts. I was offered a drink. The girls were given a glass of Ribena so I joined them. Miss Peebles then sent them off to change while I was taken down to a bedroom on the garden side of the palace near the swimming-pool. When I had changed I went through another larger bedroom adjoining the pool and waited on the patio ouside. The three youngsters, dressed now for tennis, soon appeared and we proceeded to the court. At that first lesson it was obvious that Anne was blessed with natural ball sense. Her companions were less gifted but I took care to see that there was no favouritism. I paid about half a dozen visits to the palace on Monday mornings in the spring and early summer that year, mostly with three young people on the court. Anne quickly outstripped the other two and it was clear that she would have benefited from individual lessons.

The following year she did have lessons by herself. Anne was a natural athlete and a good, strong mover around the court. Quite soon her forehand became a very sound stroke, and she quickly showed good footwork in positioning and adjusting to balls of varying heights and speeds. When she had acquired a satisfactory grip on the backhand that stroke, too, began to show improvement. We were now rallying and enjoying keeping each other on the move.

It was during this period in the second season of lessons that Herman David, the All England Club chairman, was invited by the Queen to attend one of the private lunch parties that she and the Duke of Edinburgh give for people from all walks of life. Herman went to one just after the Championships. Yuri Gagarin, the Russian cosmonaut, was also one of the guests. A few days later Herman told me that while they were waiting to go in to lunch, before the Queen and the Duke of Edinburgh had arrived, Anne came into the room and talked to some of the guests. When she approached Herman, whom she knew from her visits to the club, he said: 'Hello, Your Royal Highness. Mr Maskell is very pleased with your tennis. He tells me that you had a rally of thirty strokes the other day.' 'Thirty? It was thirty-two!' I remember that particular rally because she had played five backhands during the course of it. And if you included the two balls that I low-volleyed standing on the baseline then she was right – there really had been thirty-two strokes and not thirty. The fact that she had remembered the incident impressed me, for she was obviously very keen.

The service proved a little more difficult, as it does with so many girls. I started by explaining that the service was a throwing action and demonstrated by throwing a ball, releasing it from above head height, to the far baseline and asked her to do the same. Her very first throw hit the bottom of the netting behind the baseline. I then challenged her: 'Throw it as hard as you like,' I said. 'Throw it over the fence if you can.' Her next attempt hit the netting a foot from the bottom. When I came the following week I asked how her service was going. 'Have you had a chance to go out and practise it?' I asked.

'No, but I can throw better,' she said, and proceeded to show me just how much better. She stood near the stop netting at one end of the court and threw the first ball straight over the top of the netting at the far end, leaving Miss Peebles to retrieve it from the grass beyond. Then I said, 'Well, that's excellent but show me if you can do it with a racket.' After a few tentative efforts, tending to guide the racket head to the imaginary ball over her head, Anne was soon producing a fine throwing action with the racket. As is always the case at this stage of a player's development, synchronizing the placing of the ball in the air and the timing of the hit did not come easily. 'What you need to do now,' I said, 'is to come with a dozen or so balls and simply practise the throwing of the racket-head and the toss so that they blend together and feel comfortable. It's simply a matter of repetition. Then try serving and count how many you get in out of twelve – but pushes don't count.'

After another two or three lessons Anne was beginning to get the feel of it. When we came to try the volley on the forehand she immediately grasped the need to punch the racket-face at the ball, meeting it at the side and well out in front of her. It had not been necessary for me to demonstrate the stroke more than twice. Our last session that year took place during the week of the British Professional Championships at Eastbourne where I was competing in the veterans' event, having retired from the singles. I remember asking Mike Gibson, the referee, if I could play two matches on the Tuesday because I needed to have the day off on Monday to visit the Palace for the last time. In the course of those few sessions it had become clear that Anne had the ability, if she so wished, and if it had been appropriate to spend the necessary time at the game, to compete on the international circuit. When we had started to play a few actual games in our sessions, I was aware of a keen competitive spirit which was later revealed in her riding activities.

On some of my visits to the Palace I had enjoyed a swim with Anne and the other children in the indoor pool. This had been Miss Peebles' suggestion originally. Before returning to Wimbledon it was most refreshing to take a dip and I remember what a strong natural swimmer Anne was. At one end of the pool there was a diving board with the top platform about eight feet high. At the foot of it was a pile of aqua diving equipment which I imagined belonged to Prince

Charles. I had by now given several lessons to Charles. The first of these had been at Windsor Castle. I had arrived at the appointed hour and been allowed past the sentries into the inner quadrangle. I had changed and was waiting in the garden for Anne who was to have her lesson before Charles. It was a rather miserable sort of morning – dull, overcast and rather windy. While I was standing there the Queen came along. She was wearing a mackintosh and a headscarf and greeted me, 'Good morning.'

'Good morning, Your Majesty.'

'Charles is with us today and would like to play if that's all right with you.'

'Yes, of course, I'd be delighted, Ma'am.'

'Would you prefer to have them on court together or separately?'

As I hadn't seen Charles play before I suggested that it would probably be better if they had their lessons separately. I could give Anne her usual hour and then have a session with Charles.

'Very well, I'll tell Charles to come down after about forty-five minutes then,' said the Queen, before turning to walk back the way she had come.

Anne and I had our usual session during which she coped quite well in a very troublesome wind. After about three-quarters of an hour Charles came down, walking quietly round the side of the court to the gate. Anne seemed surprised to see him and I said, 'Oh, I forgot to tell you – your mother said that Charles would have the second half of the lesson.'

While Anne was collecting her things I introduced myself to Charles.

'What would you like me to do?' he asked as he walked on to the court.

'Well, as I've never seen you play before I suggest you go down to the other end and I'll hit some balls to you.'

I noticed that he had a full Western grip on the forehand

and he enjoyed trying to hit the cover off the ball. The first few shots didn't go too near the court but when I hit some wider balls to him he moved quickly to the side to crack those as hard as the others. I stopped hitting balls and went up to the net.

'Well, you looked as if you were enjoying that, but the object of the exercise of course is to hit the ball over the net and inside these lines. Just try to get the ball over the net and into the court.' I didn't say any more than that because I wanted to see how he would interpret my suggestion. Immediately, with a great deal of concentration, he pushed and guided a succession of shots into the court, and we had quite a few rallies. There was little pace on the shots, of course, but he was doing exactly as I had asked. We had a short breather before I said: 'Well, you certainly got the ball into the court without too much difficulty but let us see if we can add to the fun by rallying. Somewhere between these two extremes, belting the ball and pushing it over the net,' which I demonstrated as I spoke, 'there is a halfway stage that would allow you to keep the ball under control and yet hit it firmly. Something like this.' One after the other I just dropped a couple of balls on to the court and swung the racket head at them to hit firm shots deep to the far end.

He got the idea at once of what we were trying to achieve and we had some rally play of a much higher standard. He was beginning to find that middle ground between pushing and guiding and a swinging hit; the swing had adapted itself naturally. Without warning it came on to rain. The wind was gusting up and it appeared that the rain would be coming down harder any minute. As we came off court and headed for the little quartered shelter with a thatched roof that stood nearby, I tucked the heads of my rackets under my sweater. 'Why have you done that?' he asked.

'To keep the rain off the gut,' I said.

'Why is that necessary?'

'Well, rain or any sort of dampness is very bad for gut. Eventually the strings will break.'

'Oh,' he said. 'Well, I'd better put mine out of sight too,' and he tucked his own racket under his sweater.

'I don't think it will matter too much with yours because you've got synthetic strings in your racket. The dampness won't affect them,' I said.

'What's in your racket then, catgut?'

'No, not catgut, though it is often called that. Actually it comes from the intestines of sheep or cows,' I said. 'The most resilient gut comes from sheep – especially from sheep that haven't grazed on pastures where there is any sand in the soil.'

'What's that got to do with it?'

'Well, if they get sand in their intestines the gut is slightly affected so when they come to prepare the gut for rackets of the highest class, they try to get gut that is absolutely perfect.'

'What happens if it breaks?' he asked.

I could see that he was leading me on and noticed the sparkle in his eye. I was gently having my leg pulled. 'Well, when it breaks, I cut the strings out carefully and send them to Yehudi Menuhin for his violin,' I said. He gave a quiet little chuckle.

By now it had stopped raining and we were able to return to the court. By the end of that first lesson Charles was producing some nicely controlled shots. His ball-sense was not as well developed as Anne's but nevertheless he responded well to this initial instruction.

Some time later I gave him a lesson at the All England Club, on court four, the one facing the main entrance to the club-house and under the famous clock. This was his first visit to the club and he seemed to enjoy it. On another occasion Anne and Charles came together so I arranged a mixed doubles for them by inviting Herman David's daughter, Penny, to join us. As the two young Royals chased about the court I felt how nice it was that they had this opportunity

313

to experience the grass courts of Wimbledon where their grandfather had played in the Championships soon after I had ballboyed for him in my early years at Queen's Club.

I think I played with Charles on the court at Buckingham Palace on only a couple of occasions. On the second I went in once more for a swim and this time Anne and Charles were both there. They seemed to me to revel in the water, swimming around like fishes. It was obvious that I was no great swimmer myself but nevertheless they insisted that we should have a race the length of the pool.

'How much start do I get?' I asked.

'You don't want a start, surely,' said Charles.

'Well now, if I was playing you at tennis I'd give you quite a big start, a few points a game at least.'

He seemed to see the point. 'All right, you go first then Anne will go and then I'll chase you both,' he said.

I heard the two splashes, one after the other, as they dived in after me but they had both passed me before I was halfway down the pool. All I wanted to do was to have some gentle exercises and relaxation. I had just got out, acknowledging my defeat, and was standing at the side of the pool when Charles swam towards me. As I made ready to dive in again he turned on his back beneath me, floating on the water and, pointing towards the diving board, said, 'Have a go off the top board there.'

Looking down at him I said, 'Oh I really couldn't do that, I can't dive.'

'Oh, do have a go off the top,' he said.

'No, really. I'll break my neck if I try to go off there.'

'Well then, jump off like this,' he said, holding his nose between thumb and forefinger.

I looked down at him again. 'No, I can't do that. Really I can't.'

'Well, if you don't, I'll send you to the Tower!' he said laughing.

Many years later Prince Charles came to the BBC Television Centre to make the presentation at our *Sports Review of the Year*, just as Princess Alexandra had done in 1969. Before the show began Cliff Morgan, the head of BBC Sport, had invited a few guests to a small party to meet Prince Charles. As they came up to us Cliff said to him, 'I don't think I need introduce this young man to you, sir.' Cliff had emphasized the 'young'.

'No,' said Charles. 'We've met before. How are you?'

Then Cliff introduced Con and Charles asked her, 'Do you have any problems with him at home?'

'Not at all, Sir. Whenever he gets a bit uppish we remind him of what you threatened him with once.'

Charles was very surprised. Raising his eyebrows he said, 'Oh, what was that?'

Con reminded him of his threat to send me to the Tower. Smiling broadly, Charles said, 'Did I really say that? I must have been a most precocious young man!'

I played only twice with Prince Andrew. He came to the All England Club one day shortly after the Championships. His tutor was with him and introduced me to the young man who was then about nine years of age. We did the usual thing, hitting a few balls to see what natural ability he had and how he shaped up to a moving ball. He had no strokes at this stage, but his good ball-sense and timing were very promising and he was a most energetic young fellow. As he cracked the ball over the net, somewhat erratically, it was obvious that he enjoyed the sheer physical experience. Once I had suggested to him that inside the swing of a ground-stroke is the hit, the moment of impact, he got the idea and started to swing the racket into the ball. Here obviously was an adventurous young spirit and if he had had the chance to play regularly he would have been a most presentable player.

The Duke of Kent I have met on two or three occasions and have always found him to be most interested about the club and concerned for its welfare. He has been an exemplary president. He was also very generous about praising my part in the film *Players*. At the reception after the première I found myself talking to Group-Captain Douglas Bader. The Duke came over to us and said, 'Well done, Dan. That was a very good effort – the commentary certainly kept the film together.'

In 1986 I suddenly got a message via the committee that the Duchess of Kent wanted to see me. It transpired that she was about to be interviewed by Peter Ustinov for American television and wanted to check on some facts of past Championships. I answered all her questions and remembered being most impressed by her own wide knowledge. One of her favourite moments concerned Ilie Nastase. It was the year when the magic eye was introduced to help the service linesman decide whether a serve had been good or a fault. The first time he appeared on the Centre Court that year, Nastase was querying some of the decisions made by the magic eye. After another call that he thought had been incorrect he went across to the box and got down on hands and knees, turned his head upside down and peered into the inner workings of the machine while waggling his finger at it in admonition. It was an incident that had much amused the Duchess and the Centre Court crowd.

The Duchess of Gloucester is also very fond of tennis. She plays regularly at Queen's Club and has often visited our commentary box on finals day at the Stella Artois tournament. As the patron of Queen's Club, she was the guest of honour at the magnificent banquet that was the highlight of the club's centenary celebrations in 1986.

I could hardly believe my eyes when I went in to the gallery of the two old covered courts, one and two, at Queen's that evening. The courts had become a festive fairyland with bunting and gaily decorated tables covering the entire area. It was hard to believe that this was the same austere court where Borotra had thwarted Tilden all those years ago in the first IC match between France and Great

Britain; the same court where the great George Caridia had half-volleyed his way to many wins and much admiration. Caridia was the honorary treasurer at Wimbledon and was the man who gave me my monthly cheques. At the reception before the dinner the Duchess of Gloucester had spoken with me in animated terms about the Championships, Queen's Club, the players and about the business of broadcasting. It was obvious that she had a deep and genuine interest in the game.

I met the Queen twice more. At the end of the Centenary Championships, that marvellous day I have referred to when Virginia Wade set home hearts singing, I was asked to join the champions and one or two others up in the committee area behind the Royal Box. I was standing next to Neale Fraser, the 1960 champion, and it seemed to us that the Queen was not feeling one hundred per cent that day. She seemed to have a heavy cold.

In between that brief meeting and the next, had come the traumatic experience of Con's death. I had been pretty low in the months afterwards and went on living by myself at Steeproof. Several of my friends paid regular visits to keep an eye on me but I felt unable to accept the many invitations I had to go out and socialize with them. At times I seemed to have lost all reason for living. Looking back I suppose I was in danger of sliding down a dangerous slope but fortune smiled on me once again as she had done so often in my life.

Heavy with depression, I found myself one day at Queen's Club in the lounge talking to my old professional coaching colleague Jack Moore, the manager of the Tennis Foundation. I was surprised to see Kay Latto, Bill's wife, whom I had met on many occasions during the days of 'Focus on Tennis', walk by. Kay had been the CCPR representative in the Nottingham area and had done a superb job organizing our 'Focus' visit there.

'Hello Kay – what are you doing here?' I asked.

'Helping Jack reorganize his office, he's away such a lot,' she replied.

'How's Bill?' I asked.

'I'm afraid we are not together any more,' she answered. 'We are divorced.'

I expressed my regret. So many of my old friends, it seemed, had suffered the same painful experience. Kay had known Con and had seen the children growing up. I had met her young daughter, Susan, at their home in Nottingham. Although we were old friends and Kay had written a letter of condolence at the time of Con's death, I had not seen her for many years.

On a later visit to Queen's, I saw Jack Moore again. He said, 'Dan, I hope I haven't let you in for something, but Kay Latto has asked me if I thought she could write to you about borrowing any material you had concerning rehabilitation you had done during the war.' He told me that she was now writing a book on the rehabilitation of people with a mental handicap for the Disabled Living Foundation and had reached the stage of describing the practical activities they might undertake. 'I've told her to write to you because I thought it would be good for you to get your teeth into something,' said Jack.

Eventually Kay's letter arrived but I was in no mood to answer it at once. About two months after that casual meeting I took the opportunity of a rain-cancelled golf morning at Wimbledon to telephone her. I offered to take down some papers and photographs that afternoon to her home in Surrey. Kay was most grateful and invited me for tea.

I can honestly say that this first visit there totally changed my life. Instead of living in the past, I now had the opportunity to think of the future. They were constructive thoughts, healing thoughts, and in helping Kay to help others less fortunate than most of us, I was at last thinking positively again. Quite unexpectedly, and unsought, love bloomed between us and in a short time we decided to get married. We were married on 20 September, 1980, at St Martin's Church, Dorking. It was a quiet family affair with only close relatives in attendance. Kay's daughter, Susan Killip, was there with her husband Brian, and Robin and Chris came down from Scotland. You could say that I have been twice blessed, for few men can have had the good fortune to have two such wonderful partners.

Eventually Kay's book, *Give Us the Chance*, was published and was well received in the medical world. It has become a standard work on sport and physical recreation for people with a mental handicap. A revised edition was published in 1989. I marvel sometimes at Kay's energy which involves her in so many voluntary activities. Her work with the Disabled Living Foundation alone would keep most people busy but she also somehow finds time to serve on the committee of the Outward Bound Centres at Aberdovey in Wales, another wonderful organization helping young people to plumb the depths of their own personalities and experience new areas of life that they would otherwise probably not see. For good measure Kay is also on the fund-raising committee of the Cheshire Home in Dorking. Kay's love and understanding have brought me back to full health and vigour so I can honestly say that in my eighty-first year I feel as eager as I ever did to welcome the next match on court.

The news in the birthday honours list in 1982 that the Queen had bestowed upon me the CBE was another surprise. The award was given for 'services to tennis'. Certainly I had devoted my life to the game but I did not feel that I had done anything out of the ordinary.

The investiture itself was a memorable experience. You are allowed to take your spouse and two others so, of course, Robin and Susan accompanied me on that November day. It was a typical November day too, chilly and wet with the rain lashing down as we drove through the gates of the Palace. I felt rather grand driving through the main arch this time. In the old days of lessons with Princess Anne I had always parked round at the side, near the Privy Purse entrance. When we'd parked the car we followed the signs, 'CBEs and Knights this way' and assembled with everyone else ready to be taken through the forthcoming routine by an experienced member of the household staff. There was a stool for the Knights to practise kneeling on – always the left knee – and they practised walking backwards afterwards, just six steps and then a bow to the Queen. Then it was the turn of the CBEs.

'You will all be waiting outside the investiture room and called individually by name. As soon as the person ahead of you has been decorated and is leaving, walk in right opposite the Queen, turn left and move forward to the edge of the carpet facing the Queen. Remember that Her Majesty will be standing on a dais just above you. You chaps remember that the Queen will be placing the ribbon round your neck so lean slightly forward.' We rehearsed it a couple of times until everybody knew exactly what to do.

The investiture was taking place in the ballroom and Kay, Susan and Robin were already in their places on the rows of chairs that faced the dais. Kay was familiar with awards ceremonies because she had been a steward for the Duke of Edinburgh's Award Scheme and had been one of the ten or twelve ushers who were in attendance when the young gold award-winners came to be presented to the Duke. So the ceremony began. One by one the Knights preceded us through the door into the ballroom. Then the CBEs followed. Once or twice a courtier came along to make sure that we were all still in the correct order. It was all so quietly efficient and dignified, there was no fuss. Soon my name was called and I went through the door where I paused until the recipient ahead of me moved away and then I stepped forward a few paces to bring myself in front of the Queen. I turned left, took a couple of steps and leaned forward. The courtier on her left announced my name. As she put the ribbon round my neck the Queen said quietly, 'I do hope that you are going to go on with your tennis.' 'Thank you very much indeed, Ma'am, I hope so too.' We had been told to answer the Queen if she spoke to us and on the spur of the moment I said, 'Dare I ask if Princess Anne ever hits a tennis ball these days?' The Queen leaned forward again and said very quietly, 'Time is the great enemy.'

About ten days before the day of the investiture, I had had a phone call. It was about 9.30pm and a cultured voice said 'Mr Maskell?'

'Yes, this is Dan Maskell.'

'Good evening, this is a call from Buckingham Palace. I hope you don't mind my ringing. I am the housekeeper here at the Palace and first I'd like to congratulate you on your CBE.' She continued, 'I was in the Wrens and looking at your guest list for the investiture I wondered whether either Mrs Charlton or Mrs Killip is in fact Robin.'

'Yes, Mrs Charlton is,' I said. 'She's my daughter, Robin.'

'Well, Robin served with me at Greenwich and I'm phoning to ask if you and your party would like to come to my apartment after the ceremony for a drink. It is underneath a place which I'm sure you know well, the Privy Purse arch,' she said.

After having our photographs taken by the official photographers outside the main entrance in the inner courtyard we made our way to the housekeeper's flat. It was still pouring with rain so we all got in the car and I drove as near as I dared to the arch and parked the car there. It was a very pleasant visit, during which I learned that a member of the housekeeper's staff was the daughter of a lady whom I'd heard had rescued the Bexhill Lawn Tennis Club when it was near to collapse. By the time we left, about an hour and a half later, my car stood all alone, the last vehicle there, with a policeman waiting beside it. 'We were wondering who this belonged to,' he said.

We all got in and I drove us back to the Grosvenor Hotel,

where we'd stayed the night, for a welcome lunch. I had been careful not to sample too much of the housekeeper's sherry. But Robin had been less abstemious. At the start of the day, in front of Kay, Robin had said, 'Now, Daddy, do be careful with the drink because these may be naval-sized drinks and you've got to drive back to the hotel.' Ironically, it was Robin who got a bit tiddly!

It seemed to be my year for honours in 1982. In the spring I had a letter from Loughborough University saying that they would like to award me an honorary MA degree in view of my long association with them. They gave me a date in June. About this time I was due to go into hospital for a minor internal operation and so had to decline the date. Accordingly I was asked for the next degree-giving ceremony which was to take place in November, shortly after the investiture at the Palace. Kay and I went up to Loughborough the day before and stayed with a former CCPR colleague, Robert Newton, who had just retired as a lecturer at Loughborough University.

When I had been demobbed in 1946 I had said to Doctor Schofield, the principal of what was then called Loughborough College, that I would be pleased to return if they ever wanted me to give a talk on tennis or to conduct a clinic. Some years later they did ask me to return and I spent a very pleasant evening with the students after delivering a lecture and showing a film. My topics had been 'The Art of Coaching' and 'The Skill of Learning' which, I thought, suited their needs since they were all there taking education diplomas. They gave me a wonderful night and we went up to the pub near Charnwood Forest to unwind afterwards. I remember getting to bed at about three or four in the morning.

Although I had not returned to Loughborough since that visit I was always suggesting the university as a suitable place for tennis events and many courses were held there.

It was a nostalgic return. Now the place was a university it was almost unrecognizable because there were so many new buildings. As I went into the large ceremonial hall memories came flooding in from every side – of the teacher's course I was examining during the week before war had been declared; of my initial training experiences; of the strenuous days of rehabilitation work; and, finally, of my demobilization.

The degree-giving ceremonies occupied two days and I was asked to attend on the second one. There was another honorary degree being given that day to a man in engineering, Dr D. E. Broadbent, OBE. He gave the speech of thanks for us and made a fine job of it. This was my first experience of such an occasion and I was impressed by the solemnity of the ceremony. It is difficult not to be serious when you are weighed down with the robes and caps which each one of us wore. The balcony was crowded with the relatives and friends of those receiving their degrees. The Public Orator, Dr A. M. Duncan, had written to me well before the day to ask for a few personal details to add to the many notes he told me they had already collected about me. It was certainly a glowing citation that he read out and it was very gratifying that when I stood to receive the degree itself there was prolonged applause. I felt very humble in such distinguished academic company.

Susan and Brian came up from London for the ceremony but it was sad that Robin could not attend as she was too busy with her team of doctors and could not be spared. She had been suitably irreverent when I had told her about the original invitation. During our telephone call to Scotland she had said: 'Oh Daddy, that's wonderful. At last somebody realizes you've got some brains as well as brawn!'

We were given a marvellous lunch after the ceremony and then returned to spend a second night with our host before making our way home.

The surprises were not yet over. Early in April 1985 Johnnie Watherston, our senior BBC tennis producer, called to say that he was asking the entire tennis commentary team to attend a dinner at the Savoy Hotel to discuss the following season's coverage. 'The Savoy, Johnnie?' I said. 'I thought the BBC was broke.' 'We are,' he laughed, 'but we've never done this before, Dan, so they're allowing me to do it properly – and it's about time we said thank you for all that you've done for us over the years.'

He gave me the date, 19 April, and explained that en route to the Savoy we would be calling in at a pub on the river for a pre-dinner drink so that the photographer from *Radio Times* could get a group picture of us. He suggested that I should drive over to John Barrett's house, as I usually did for any evening functions in town, so that one car could be sent to collect both of us. I readily agreed and began to look forward to the evening.

I still suspected nothing when, sitting in John's lounge waiting for the car to arrive, his son, Michael, popped his head round the door and said, 'Dad, there's a huge limousine pulling up outside the Mottrams.' John got up and said: 'Oh, they must have got the wrong house. They're always mixing up The Oaks and Coombe Wood Oaks. I'll go and sort them out.' Little did I realize then that both families were involved in the conspiracy.

On our way to town John asked the driver to divert to the All England Club where he had to deliver something. We still had plenty of time so there seemed to be no problem. On we went over Wandsworth Bridge and along beside the river. We were due to meet Mark Cox and Gerald Williams at a pub there. Johnnie had said he would see us at the Savoy. In a few moments the car drew into the courtyard.

There was an attractive bar, welcoming and cosy, with a marvellous view of that busy reach of the Thames. The others had already arrived and we ordered a drink and sat on the bar stools waiting for the photographer. I was busy speculating with Gerald Williams about the likelihood of us covering the semi-finals at the French Championships that year as well as the finals which we always did, when, suddenly, I was aware of someone at my elbow. I turned and to my surprise I saw the smiling face of Eamonn Andrews and behind him four lovely young ladies, attractively clad in short tennis dresses and holding tennis rackets. Suddenly everywhere was brightly lit and there was a whirr of cameras. Eamonn was completing his preliminaries and turning to me he said, 'Dan Maskell, this is your life.' I had been trapped.

I had always said that if ever I was confronted with this situation I would refuse to go on with the show. Danny Blanchflower had been the only person I believe to walk out on a programme some time before and I had always admired his courage. However, when the moment arrived, I was more stunned than angry and John assured me that all the research had been meticulously prepared and that I was in for what he thought would be a few pleasant surprises. How right he was.

I discovered later that Kay and Robin had been acting as conspirators with John to help the producer with all the background information they required. Kay had been rather worried that I might not perform when the moment arrived and Robin had some doubts too. John reassured both of them. 'No, he's a professional – of course he'll do it. He'll resent it at first, but then he'll do it.' He had judged the situation accurately.

Going back in the car to the theatre with Eamonn, whom I knew quite well, I sensed his anxiety. 'Dan, I'm so relieved that you're going to help us today. We knew you weren't very keen about this but I'm glad that you're happy to do it.' Then we talked a bit about golf and I told him one or two of my golfing stories. By the time we arrived we were both in exactly the right frame of mind.

Kay told me afterwards that she was worried the whole thing might prove to be an emotional strain for me. It was indeed emotional but there was so much goodwill from all the people who had taken enormous trouble to take part that I felt I had to stay in firm control. To see Mary Hess again was marvellous and brought back so many memories of happy days on the mountains in Engelberg. I had only seen her once in the last seven or so years. Then to have Buzzer Hadingham and Kitty Godfree saying such wonderful things brought back all the days at the All England Club since 1929. It was so good to see Raich Carter again – which opened another floodgate of memories from Loughborough and the days of rehabilitation there. Then there were all those film tributes from Fred Perry in Florida, Rod Laver and Jack Kramer in California and Bunny Austin, who was also over in America at the time of the programme. The whole of my life came flooding past me. I can assure you it was a most moving experience.

It was particularly moving to see little Ross, our grandson, playing tennis with Mark Cox, and then, during the programme, producing his teddy bear which we had given him at Christmas. I'd bought it from the museum shop at the All England Club, so it was called 'Wimbledon'.

The whole occasion brought home to me the importance in everyone's life of family. It made me wish that I had remained closer to my own brothers and sisters. Largely because of the wide spread in ages we had drifted apart and not kept in touch. Dorothy had become Mrs Faulknall and had moved with her husband, Walter, to the other side of London. They had both died a long time ago. I had not seen anything of them for some years. Bill, who was closer to me than any of the others, had died in 1981 after he'd retired to Worthing with his wife, Marjory. Up to a couple of months before he died he was playing golf four or five times a week and cycling to the golf club at Worthing. He was very proud of the hole-in-one he had done at Worthing and left me the golf ball that he had used to achieve the feat. Then about fifteen months after Bill had died Marjory had a heart attack in the kitchen of their flat. A neighbour had found her. During that fifteen-month period Kay and I used to go down every two or three weeks to take her out to lunch. She used to enjoy a drive round the local district. Now she, too, had gone.

Bert had run a pub in Somerset when he had left the police but we had lost touch with him, too, and he had died in about 1963. John is still alive and lives on his own in Hayes since his wife, Win, died in 1981. I had sent my condolences to him when she died and he had written back to thank me for my thoughts. Very recently we have resumed contact.

Lilian is still alive and lives in London over near Ravenscourt Park. She is eighty-five now and is suffering from arthritis which makes her virtually immobile. She gets about on a frame. Elsie lost her husband some years ago and was eighty-three when she died in 1984. I knew her son and daughter, my nephew and niece, and went to the funeral in Putney Vale where her ashes are now.

That accounts for all of them who were older than me. Jean, the only one younger, is now seventy-two and recovering from a hip operation. She lives at Southend-on Sea. Her husband Frank, retired some time ago from his own business as a nursery gardener and they've just moved into a new cottage. On 28 November 1987 they celebrated their golden wedding anniversary. Their daughter, Pam, is really the only member of the family we have kept up with. Her husband, Malcolm, is a pilot who flew Boris Becker back home after he won his first Wimbledon singles title in 1985. Malcolm invited Boris up to the cockpit and mentioned his connection with Wimbledon through me.

The friendship extended to me by members of Kay's closely-knit family I value very much, and Robin, too, keenly feels the need to pull the strands of the families together. A couple of Christmases ago she kindly entertained all of us at Barend Farm in Scotland. There were fifteen of us altogether – Kay and me with Susan and her family, Chris and his naval officer son with his wife and child and his mother. We had a marvellous Christmas reunion with the grandchildren keeping us all on our toes.

The older you get the more you realize that the most important things in life are human relationships. What I have been through is as nothing compared with the awful burdens of suffering that some families have to bear. I can look back over these eighty years and count myself a lucky man indeed.

TEN

The Best of All Time

In selecting and ranking the ten best men and women champions I have seen since my early apprenticeship at Queen's in 1923 and my first Wimbledon the following year, I realize only too well what a hazardous enterprise it is. My lists would certainly not be everyone's choice. When you look at the players I have had to leave out – men like Lacoste, Crawford, Gonzales, Kramer, Sedgman, Hoad, Newcombe and Emerson; women like Godfree, Jacobs, Marble, Betz and Brough – you begin to realize what an impossible task I have set myself!

There are so many difficult judgements to make. There have been so many changes within the game itself that it is difficult to decide how a champion in one era would have met new conditions and new situations in another. For instance, the tennis ball itself has changed markedly since I first started playing. The old stitched-seam ball with its much smoother melton cover was an altogether gentler animal than the harder, fiery products that today's players use. The rackets of today, made of space-age material like ceramics, boron, graphite, and fibreglass are far more efficient in transmitting energy to the ball than were the one-piece frames made of ash or the laminated wooden frames of the 1920s and 1930s. Competition today is so much more fierce than it ever used to be, resulting in a much greater depth of standard. The improvements in international travel now make it easy for players to compete throughout the year. No longer does one have to spend a week on a boat to reach

America from Europe or six weeks to reach Australia. Today you can whisk yourself to the other side of the globe in twenty-four hours. Then there are the refinements of training and diet – an altogether greater professionalism in the approach of the modern player – that make comparisons with the great players of yesterday so difficult.

Indeed, one of the questions I am most often asked is how the great players of former days would fare against today's champions. I have no hesitation in suggesting that, given the same playing conditions and equipment, they would have fared every bit as well against today's players as they did against their contemporaries. The point is that champions dominate by the force of their personalities as well as by the technical and physical attributes they possess. Yet, when you come down to it, inevitably you still have opinions about the relative merits of all the great players you have seen. I have been privileged to watch and play against most of the great champions of the period before World War Two from the game's first superstars, Bill Tilden and Suzanne Lenglen, to Fred Perry and Alice Marble.

Since the war I have seen all the men and women who have conquered in Paris, at Wimbledon, at the US Championships and in Australia – the Grand Slam Championships. Between 1946 and 1967 there was a regular procession of champions from the amateur to the professional ranks. This is probably the area, therefore, of greatest difficulty in making comparisons. Undoubtedly in competing against one another the champions of succeeding years did produce some wonderfully exciting tennis to watch. Yet they were playing against a very small group of players whose games they came to know so well that anticipation became second nature. Many observers believed that this group of players, from Kramer to Newcombe, had lifted the game to new heights of perfection. In a sense they certainly had, for their speed of reaction and movement were every bit as good, if not better, than the amateurs of the day and their technical qualities were refined with the need to play 'percentage tennis', i.e. the most effective shot for each situation they faced. And yet when the first open tournament took place at Bournemouth in 1968 we found that lack of variety in opposition had dulled the ability of these great players to improvise and alter well-tried tactics. Also much of their play had been in the sheltered, flattering conditions of indoor arenas so that the outdoor setting at Bournemouth was unusual for them. At first sight it was impossible that Mark Cox, a fine young amateur but by no means the best of his generation, should be able to beat both Gonzales and Emerson. But that is what he did.

It was those results that reinforced my belief that the game has been advancing imperceptibly all the time. A visit to the qualifying tournament for Wimbledon would soon convince you of that. The strength in depth today is quite astonishing. The one outstanding difference in comparing the majority of the pre-war and early post-war players with those of today is the speed at which the ball is hit. Thanks to the greater efficiency of modern rackets, today's champions can project the ball so much faster and (thanks to the large-headed and mid-headed rackets) with greater control than any of yesterday's men. However, given the opportunity to play in today's conditions, the great men and women of the past would, I am confident, hold their own.

Accordingly my choices, like all such lists, are a subjective judgement not only of the skills of the men and women I have seen but also of the effect they have had on me while I have watched them. All twenty of the champions on my lists have at some time or another lifted my head and my heart into the clouds. Some of their performances have been so electrifying that I have woken at night hardly believing what I have seen.

Here, then, are my two lists. When you look at the players therein you see a group of men and women who learned to dominate. None of them, having reached the top, allowed themselves to fall below that high standard so that, for their period of dominance, they performed consistently well and had very few losses to inferior players. This is one of the marks of a true champion in any sport.

MEN		WOMEN	
1	Rod Laver	1	Martina Navratilova
2	Don Budge	2	Helen Wills-Moody
3	Bill Tilden	3	Margaret Court
4	Fred Perry	4	Billie Jean King
5	Björn Borg	5	Maureen Connolly
6	John McEnroe	6	Suzanne Lenglen
7	Henri Cochet	7	Chris Evert
8	Jean Borotra	8	Maria Bueno
9	Ken Rosewall	9	Doris Hart
10	Jimmy Connors	10	Evonne Cawley

ROD LAVER

I doubt if there has been a player in the history of the game who came nearer to being the complete champion than the wiry red-head from Rockhampton, Queensland, who was inevitably christened 'The Rocket'. Rod Laver's record is quite remarkable. The jewel in his glittering crown surely must be the second of his two Grand Slams. Having won the four major championships as an amateur in 1962, Rod repeated that feat in 1969 the second year of open tennis. This unique achievement, which can never be equalled, suggests that if open tennis had come in 1962 Rod would probably have won even more than the eleven Grand Slam singles titles that already stand against his name, four at Wimbledon, two in the USA, two in France and three in Australia. If you add to that his five Grand Slam doubles titles and the victories he scored while representing Australia in their unbeaten Davis Cup teams between 1959 and 1962, plus the three rubbers he won when he returned to that competition as a profesional in 1973 when Australia defeated the United States 5–0, you begin to understand his versatility.

Technically faultless, from his richly varied serve to his feather-light touch on drop volleys plus a backhand drive carrying destructive top spin when needed or controlling slice when the situation demanded it, you realize why he is considered to have set new standards for left-handers. Even as great a player as Jaroslav Drobny did not have a forcing topped backhand drive. He relied on slice and control of trajectory against the volleyer. Moreover, Laver set a fashion for left-handers who followed – men like Vilas and McEnroe – who could certainly take the ball on the rise and counter-attack with top spin on the backhand side. At his peak Rod was unbeatable. Tactically mature and with a disciplined and enviably shock-proof match temperament, he could mount a devastating attack or the most resolute defence to suit the occasion. Being compact and light on his feet Rod's footwork allowed him to move quickly and easily into the correct position to make his strokes as well as enabling him to cover the court very fast. Moreover he proved himself to be a winner on all surfaces – a quality which has affected my judgement of the entire list.

Furthermore, there was a humility about Rod Laver that made him a most admirable example for the young players of his generation. Always in control of his emotions, which nevertheless must have been boiling away inside that cool exterior, he never in my experience embarrassed court officials or anyone else by the manner of his queries. A polite raising of the eyebrows or a slight turn of the head would be the only indication to show that he felt the call might have been wrong.

It was always a pleasure commentating upon any of Laver's matches. On one occasion at Wimbledon on an overcast day Rod did not appear to be keyed up. It was an early round match and I remember making the point several times that Rod was not taking advantage of his opponent's short length second serves. Instead of stepping in confidently and hitting a forcing shot as he usually did, he was letting the ball come to him. In mid-set rain interrupted the match and the players retired to the dressing-room. When they resumed Laver was his usual sharp self, now moving forward and punishing those bad length serves. I was able to say: 'The break seems to have done Rod a power of good. This is more like the champion we all know.' He soon completed his win.

That evening, when play had ended and I had gone into the dressing-room for a refreshing shower after a full afternoon in the box, one of the Australian players who had engaged in a late doubles was getting dressed. He approached me. 'Dan, you really did Rod a favour today. We'd all been watching the match here in the dressing-room and when Rocket came in from the rain we told him you'd been giving him a bit of stick about his lack of confidence on returning bad length serves!' It had never occurred to me that the players listened to our comments; it was a rather sobering discovery.

As you enter that changing-room at Wimbledon you have to open two doors. Inside the first is the area which leads you one way down to the press interview room used during the Championships and the other into the changing area. I have always thought how appropriate it is that as you pass through the second door you see facing you, on the wall opposite, a single photograph. It is a portrait of Rod Laver.

In every department, then – his record, his temperament, his technical ability – Rod Laver is indeed a champion among champions.

DONALD BUDGE

Tall and with the easy grace of a natural athlete, the red-headed Californian, Don Budge, became the greatest of the pre-World War Two champions. By winning all three titles – singles, doubles (with Gene Mako) and mixed (with Alice Marble) in successive years at Wimbledon in 1937 and 1938, Don set a record that will probably never be equalled. After winning in Paris, at Wimbledon and in New York that second year Don decided to make an assault on the fourth great championship of the time. Accordingly he made his first and only visit to Australia where he duly captured the title, so that he then held all four major championships in the same year. It was this remarkable achievement that caused the American tennis correspondent of the *New York Times*, Allison Danzig, to compare the feat to a bridge player taking all thirteen tricks and scoring a 'Grand Slam'. The phrase immediately passed into the tennis vocabulary.

Don was essentially an attacking player. At its best his spectacular serve-and-volley game was as good as anything I have seen since, as was his fierce, controlled backhand drive, hit with a wonderful turn of the hips and shoulders and a straight arm that drove the racket-head like a ramrod through the path he intended the ball to take. One felt he could do anything with his backhand. He had a glorious approach shot to the forehand corner of a right-handed opponent, hit with a touch of side-spin as well as controlling back-spin so that it faded away much wider than expected and took the opponent out beyond the sidelines.

Before Budge had matured, he was a member of the 1935 US Davis Cup team beaten by Great Britain on the Centre Court after the conclusion of the Championships, where Budge had reached the semi-finals, unseeded, after beating Bunny Austin, the fourth seed, in four hard sets. But despite all his power the young American could not overcome the experienced German, Baron Gottfried Von Cramm, the number two seed, who won their match in four sets. Even then Budge's great backhand was evident but so, too, was a comparative weakness when forced deep into his forehand corner.

In their Davis Cup meetings both Fred Perry and Bunny Austin made use of this knowledge to score valuable points for their country. However, as he became more experienced and more familiar with Wimbledon's fast lawns, the weakness was eliminated and Don Budge became one of the most complete attacking players it has been my pleasure to watch.

Budge's backhand and Ellsworth Vines' service and forehand were the three greatest single shots of the 1930s, with Perry's forehand only slightly behind them for quality and effectiveness. The day before his final against Jack Crawford in 1933 Vines asked me to hit with him. He was anxious to practise against a sliced backhand like Crawford's that kept low so that he could adjust the swing on his flattish forehand, which he realized would be a key factor in trying to retain his title against one of the greatest ground-stroke players of the day.

Interestingly, Jack then asked me to hit some balls with him – he wanted to face some very flat, hard-hit forehands – a shot which I explained was not my normal one. 'I can't guarantee to get too many in court,' I said. 'Don't worry – as long as some come in!' he replied. The match later proved to be one of Wimbledon's greatest finals, won by Crawford in five sets.

Budge was equally meticulous about his preparation and such was the confidence of this modest champion that once, when asked what tactics he would be using against a Davis Cup opponent (Henner Henkel of Germany, I seem to remember) he is alleged to have replied that tactics did not concern him once he had got his own game going. He believed in trying to make an opponent play on his terms. Don turned professional in 1938 after winning the singles and doubles twice both at Wimbledon and at the US Championships and once each in France and Australia. Between 1935 and 1938 he played in eleven Davis Cup ties winning twenty-five of his twenty-nine rubbers.

Totally devoid of histrionics, Don Budge set about the

business of winning tennis matches with a directness of purpose that was never blurred by doubt. Never once did I see him quit on a shot, no matter what the pressure.

BILL TILDEN

Many have claimed that this tall Philadelphian was the greatest player of all time despite the fact that he never won the French or Australian titles. In those days, of course, players travelled much less so that missing those two great championships was nothing unusual. Certainly his contemporaries considered him to be the greatest because of his tremendous versatility. Such was his commanding personality, his great variety of stroke, his deadly use of spin, his keen sense of strategy and tactics, that whenever he stepped on to a court he brought to it a real sense of occasion. Though not by any means a natural volleyer, he worked hard to become an adequate one, as I knew from my many hours of practice with him in our professional days. So good was the rest of his game that he was able to choose the moment to volley with such precision that he nearly always won the point. He would come in behind heavily sliced drives or viciously kicking top spin serves or sometimes behind a raking forehand drive into an opponent's backhand corner. But above all his commanding personality seemed to dominate each opponent across the net.

Tilden had had physical problems in early life and matured as a tennis player later than most. He was twenty-seven when he won his first major title at Wimbledon in 1920. He won it again the following year and came back to capture a third Wimbledon title in 1930 at the age of thirty-seven. He was the US Champion every year from 1920 to 1925 and claimed the title for the seventh and last time in 1929. During these years he won the doubles five times and played in the Davis Cup competition from 1920 to 1930, winning thirty-four rubbers of the forty-one he contested. Twenty-one of these rubbers were won in twenty-eight Challenge Rounds and between 1920 and 1926 so consistent was his form that he triumphed in thirteen successive Challenge Round singles. The remarkable thing about this record is that in 1922 Tilden had lost the top of the middle finger of his racket hand. He simply adjusted his grip to compensate.

Bill turned professional in 1931 when he was thirty-eight years old and became a promoter as well as a player in professional tournaments and tours all over the world. He maintained his form wonderfully well in the company of the succeeding champions like Ellsworth Vines, Fred Perry, Henri Cochet and Donald Budge and held this form almost until the outbreak of war in 1939. During this later period of his tennis life he became an energetic entrepreneur, never missing an opportunity to promote himself and the events with which he was associated. The fact that all his life he was keen on the theatre helped him to understand the mechanics of publicity. During the Southport professional tournament I have described elsewhere he immediately spotted the potential of the show that was on at the local theatre – named 'Carol Levis and his Discoveries'. This talent show, Bill realized, could be used to help the tennis tournament. 'Why don't we arrange with Carol Levis to bring his "Discoveries" to the tennis where we will introduce them to the crowd and we can go to the theatre for him to introduce us to his audience. That way we both win!' It was a simple but effective idea which Carol Levis immediately accepted. Bill and I were presented to the theatre audience and hit a dozen autographed tennis balls into their midst. It was a promotion that seemed to be most popular.

Some of the plays that Bill wrote were actually performed professionally but received no critical acclaim. His one appearance in a feature film and the numerous stage performances, including two appearances on Broadway in shows that he backed himself with financial help from friends, were universally panned. However, he certainly brought to the court a sense of theatre.

I always felt it was a pity that Tilden came into conflict with the USLTA over his contributions to the press. As an amateur he was bound by the strict code that existed in those days, preventing players from writing about events in which they were participating – unless, of course, they were professional journalists, like Stanley Doust of Australia and Wallis Myers, the *Daily Telegraph* lawn tennis correspondent who founded the International Club movement.

Bill loved to write. His books on tennis were classics of their kind, for example *Match Play and the Spin of the Ball* and *Tennis A-Z*. His one attempt at a novel, *Glory's Net*, convinced no one that a new Hemingway had appeared. His other great love was bridge and during a rubber he would smoke continuously. He saw bridge as a perfect companion to tennis and thought it was the ideal way to pass the time between matches and a wonderful form of relaxation in the evenings.

I have always felt sad that this great champion should have ended his days a lonely and forgotten man who had lost many of his friends after spending two short periods in jail. He died in June 1953 at the age of sixty.

FRED PERRY

No one would argue about Frederick John Perry being the greatest champion that Britain has produced in modern times. You have to go back to the Doherty brothers at the turn of the century to find records that compare with his. How fitting, then, that in 1984 the All England Club not only renamed the Somerset Road entrance gates 'The Fred Perry Gates' but also erected a threequarter-life-size statue of the great man on the concourse between the Centre Court and the club's main gates, that commemorate the famous Doherty brothers. This memorable and, for many of those present, emotional occasion was conducted by the club's president, the Duke of Kent, and took place just fifty years after Fred had won the first of his three successive Wimbledon singles championships in 1934.

Fred was no stranger to sporting success for he had won the World Table Tennis Championship in Budapest at the age of twenty and two years later, in 1931, had played his first Davis Cup match against Monaco at Plymouth. That first round European Zone win was the starting point for a run of five more British victories that year before losing to France, the holders, in Paris in July. The Challenge Round was desperately close and went to the fifth rubber. Fred lost there to the man upon whose game he'd tried to model his own, Henri Cochet, who prevailed in four sets. I have always thought that it was the invaluable experience of the Davis Cup ties we played that year that formed the solid foundation upon which Fred's spectacular career was built. By winning eleven singles rubbers of the thirteen played and, with Pat Hughes, four doubles out of five, Fred was gaining experience of playing pressure-laden matches in different countries on different surfaces and against some really testing opposition – all in the company of a wily and respected non-playing captain, Herbert Roper Barrett. Moreover, there was the experience of team-mates Bunny Austin and Pat Hughes always available to call upon in moments of doubt.

As I have described already, Fred was always brimming with confidence in everything he attempted, superbly fit with a God-given physique for tennis and with a rapidly improving all-court game, the spearhead of which was a well controlled early-ball forehand drive. Already he was at the very forefront of the world game. By the time he left the amateur scene to turn professional after Britain's third successful defence of the Davis Cup in 1936, Fred had built an enviable record which included (as well as the three Wimbledon titles) three in the United States (1933–34–36) and one each in France (1935) and Australia (1934).

Davis Cup tennis always had a warm place in Perry's heart and between that first tie in 1931 and his farewell, after beating Adrian Quist and Jack Crawford in our Challenge Round triumph against the Australians on the Centre Court in 1936, Fred had played in twenty ties. He had won thirty-four of his thirty-eight singles rubbers and eleven of his fourteen in doubles, all with Pat Hughes. Fred was wonderfully loyal – to his country, to his county, Middlesex, and to his club . . .

In those golden years for British tennis in the 1930s when I was the coach at the All England Club and travelled with the team to their matches, I would sometimes go to teachers' training colleges and other educational establishments and tennis clubs to lecture on the game. Whenever Fred knew I was about to set off on one of these missions he took an impish delight in reminding me: 'Dan, don't forget to tell them that I also played doubles and won the French and Australian titles with Pat Hughes and the Wimbledon mixed twice with Dorothy Round, plus the French mixed twice with Betty Nuthall!' Fred was a great believer in competing in the doubles events at Grand Slam Championships. He felt that it kept him tuned up without imposing too great a strain.

There are so many memories about Fred that I could fill a separate book with them. One I must mention here is the wonderful party that he and his wife, Bobby, gave to his close friends from every sphere of his life held in the Members' Enclosure at Wimbledon on the occasion of the fiftieth anniversary of his first Wimbledon singles win in 1934. It was a dazzling occasion and so nostalgic for me as I hosted one of the tables where the other guests were my old friends Henry Cotton, Denis Compton, David Miller, Colin Snape and Henry Cooper and our ladies.

For the past sixty years I have been proud to call Fred Perry one of my closest friends. We have been through many trials and tribulations together but never once has our respect for one another diminished. He is one of those men, sadly all too rare today, whose word is his bond.

BJÖRN BORG

A boy of fifteen, playing his first Davis Cup tie for Sweden against New Zealand, lost the first two sets against Onny Parun, an experienced tournament player who had been a quarter-finalist at Wimbledon. The boy clawed his way back to win in the fifth set. A few months later on Wimbledon's fast lawns the same boy was 2–5 down in the third and deciding set of the junior final against Britain's Buster Mottram, but fought back to achieve a splendid victory.

We could hardly have known then that nine years later, when he was only twenty-four years of age, Björn Borg would already be hailed as a living legend. The highlights of Björn's remarkable career make fairy-tale reading. He led his country to its first Davis Cup triumph in 1975 when Sweden beat Czechoslovakia a year after taking the first of his six French Championships. He was to win five Wimbledons in succession – a modern record – and was four times the defeated finalist in the US Open, losing twice to Jimmy Connors and twice to John McEnroe.

At first sight it might seem surprising that a player with such a pronounced Western forehand (where the palm of the hand is underneath the handle) and a heavily topped two-handed backhand, should have succeeded on grass. These are usually the attributes of a successful clay court player or one who has grown up on the high-bounding cement courts of South Africa or California (where the description 'Western' originated). In this method of hitting the ball the racket is swung up and over the ball with a wristy movement that closes the racket face, instead of forward through the ball with a lifted finish, as with an Eastern forehand. It is not easy to perform this shot on grass because you are always hitting across the flight of the ball.

However, there have been other champions who have succeeded on grass with a Western forehand. One was Billy Johnston, the 1923 Wimbledon Champion, who had beaten Bill Tilden in the 1919 US final (also on grass) but had spent the rest of his career in the great man's shadow. Others have been Vic Seixas, the Wimbledon winner in 1953, who had a semi-Western forehand and Guillermo Vilas, the left-handed Argentinian who confounded us all on the grass in Melbourne during the 1974 Masters by top-spinning his way past Newcombe and Nastase to capture the title.

Time and again on his triumphant way Björn had to demonstrate rich match-playing qualities. The equable temperament, resilience in adversity, the powerful will to win and the stubborn refusal to admit defeat were outstanding features of his teenage tennis. This was apparent most notably at Wimbledon in 1977 against the Australian Champion, Mark Edmondson, who, in the second round, led Björn by two sets to love out on court fourteen. But the Swede prevailed. The following year Björn was in deep trouble in the first round against the giant American player, the left-handed Victor Amaya. Serving from his full height of six feet seven inches Amaya projected cannonball serves and many spectacular winners off the ground and on the volley. Unable to find any rhythm or timing against this fierce bombardment on a still-soft and sappy Centre Court, Björn was one set to two down and just one point away from a 1–4 deficit in the fourth set. Perhaps Amaya sighted victory too soon and slightly lost his grip on things so that the title-holder was able to surge back to take that set 6–3 and the fifth by the same margin. It was the only time that year that Borg was threatened on his way to equalling the record of three successive Wimbledon singles titles won by Fred Perry between 1934 and 1936.

The 1979 Wimbledon Championships had reached only the second round before the Swede, notwithstanding an improvement in first service power, heavier top-spin on the forehand and fierce early-ball counter-attacking from the baseline against the volleyer, found himself out-manoeuvred again and again by one of the games greatest stylists – the ever popular Indian Vijay Amritraj. Only Björn's greater competitiveness and will to win that day gave him the fourth set tie-break and the fifth set at 6–2.

Dropping just one more set in reaching the final, Borg found the left-handed American and number five seed, Roscoe Tanner, awaiting him. Three years earlier he had beaten the husky man from Lookout Mountain, Tennessee, in straight sets in the semi-final before beating the gifted Rumanian, Ilie Nastase, in the final. That had been his first Wimbledon triumph.

His meeting with Tanner in the 1979 final was a very different affair. There were few rallies of any length – Tanner saw to that, by serving his bullets and taking risks with his returns. Again two sets to one down, Borg produced solid ball control to win the fourth set and battled on to lead 4–3 in the decider with his own serve to come. It looked as good as over but the champion had one more crisis to overcome as Tanner blazed away to reach 15–40. Here Borg showed again how resourceful and defiant he is when really threatened by taking that set 6–4 to win his fourth consecutive Wimbledon singles.

His sterling fighting qualities and wonderful temperament would be needed more than ever against the number two seed, John McEnroe, the American singles and doubles champion who was Björn's opponent in the 1980 final. This was destined to become one of the most exciting matches in Wimbledon's history and indeed can rank with anything that other sports could provide for sheer sustained excitement.

McEnroe had had a 7–6 set victory over Borg in 1979 in the semi-finals at New Orleans but this was their first meeting at Wimbledon. At the start this eagerly awaited clash hardly lived up to expectations. Borg, overpowered by the American's service and consistent net attack, lost the first set, winning only one game. Not until the Swede saved three break-points to lead 5–4 in the second set did the match really come alive, with both men now playing well at the same time. Borg broke the service for the first time to lead 6–5 with superb controlled aggression – especially on his renowned two-handed backhand. It was now one set all.

Borg won the third set 6–3 but not before he found himself 0–40 when serving at 4–2. He saved that game and edged to 5–2 after much industrious chasing and many deuces. The play had now reached genuine championship class with a fascinating fourth set in prospect. Who then thought that we were to enjoy the most remarkable set of tennis that I think I have ever seen? It is one that will live in the memory of all those who witnessed it – either in person or on television.

Borg was the first to break service to lead 5–4 – the feature, a murderous cross-court backhand drive. He was now serving and held two championship points at 40–15. Now it was McEnroe's turn to produce not one but two breathtaking point winners, the first an uninhibited but accurate backhand pass and the other an instinctive forehand drive-volley that seemed to surprise even McEnroe. It certainly dismayed Borg but the Centre Court audience rose to acclaim McEnroe's incredible courage. A somewhat bemused Borg now suffered the loss of the next six points which eventually led to six games all and the tie-break.

As they prepared to play their never-to-be-forgotten decider of thirty-four points that lasted a full twenty minutes, the tension was more comparable to that which I had experienced when Fred Perry was within two points of being two sets to love down against André Merlin in the fifth and deciding rubber of the Davis Cup Challenge Round in Paris in 1933. To their eternal credit, Borg and McEnroe now played the most positive tennis of the match. Their physical and mental speed, plus their controlled power and accuracy – the result of perfect timing – was almost beyond belief. The whole heroic stanza was played in the most sporting and indeed chivalrous manner and it made for compulsive viewing and complete involvement. The seesaw nature of the contest is shown by the tie-break scoring. At 6–5 Borg had his third championship point. He was to hold four more and was denied each time. McEnroe had his first set point leading 8–7, his sixth at 16–15, his seventh at 17–16. Borg was now serving and at last made an unforced error on the volley – unforced that is except for the degree of tension that now existed – to end the most memorable twenty minutes of championship tennis that I have ever seen. If ever you needed to support the introduction of the tie-break, this surely was it. (How long, I wonder, will it take before it is made part of Davis Cup tennis too? However, I also hope that the US Open will come into line with the other three Grand Slam Championships over the final set, which should never be a tie-break.)

So, after three hours and three minutes, it seemed to be anybody's title. However, the defending champion was to raise his own game, particularly on the serve, to new heights. After losing the first two points to open the final set he then produced a series of well-disguised and beautifully struck first serves that completely tied McEnroe to a defensive role. Borg lost only one more point in his next six service games and finally broke the American to win the set 8–6. This gave him the modern record of five successive Wimbledon titles.

I have always thought that Borg's character more than his technique rewarded him with such outstanding success. It was his inability to adapt his technique to the fast and excessively high bound of the ball on American hard courts in three US Open finals that prevented him from beating Connors in 1978 and McEnroe in 1980 and 1981. Had he done so, and also improved his volleying by competing more frequently in doubles, he must surely have won a US title. His best chance had been in his first US final on the clay at Forest Hills. Still slightly inhibited by an injured stomach muscle sustained while water-skiing he had lost to Connors in four sets. As with Rosewall at Wimbledon in 1954 there still seemed ample time for the young Borg to succeed eventually in New York. As we now know, he never did.

Eight weeks after Borg had won his fifth Wimbledon title McEnroe had sweet revenge at Flushing Meadow but the Swede came back in 1981 to beat Ivan Lendl in five sets to win his sixth French Open. This was destined to be his last Grand Slam title for, a few weeks later, he lost at Wimbledon in a four-set final to McEnroe and two months later lost again to the same player in the US Open, also in four sets. McEnroe had now won their last three Grand Slam final meetings.

There was no doubt about Borg being a living legend. He was still only twenty-five but had amassed six French titles, five Wimbledons and had been runner-up in four US Opens. He had led Sweden to their first Davis Cup triumph and inspired a whole flow of first-class players who, like him, have taken the game by storm with disciplined play, a two-handed backhand and impeccable behaviour.

JOHN McENROE

In 1984 John McEnroe produced the finest tennis that I have ever seen in a final on Wimbledon's Centre Court when he beat fellow American Jimmy Connors, the champion of 1974 and the man who had beaten him in a great five-set final in 1982. John lost just four games to the number three seed who had looked so good himself in the semi-final when he had ripped through a seven-game set against the second favourite, Ivan Lendl.

McEnroe had started his Grand Slam that year looking certain of winning the French Championship, a title that had always eluded him. When he won the first two sets against Lendl 6–3 6–2 and led with a service break in the third, he seemed sure to break the hoodoo. But his concentration was disturbed by the sound of voices emanating from a spare headset that one of the courtside television cameramen had left hanging down beside the camera. After a typical outburst and a short stoppage John was never the same player. He lost that third set 4–6 and thereafter was always struggling against a very determined Lendl who won the fourth and fifth sets 7–5 7–5. When it mattered John was simply not fit enough to sustain his effort on slow clay courts. Perhaps he had never admitted to himself that it was necessary to train for a two-week championship on such courts where every match was decided over the best of five sets.

John's disappointment may well have been the trigger for the outstanding Wimbledon performance a few weeks later. He utterly dominated the tournament, winning it for the third time with a display of near-genius against Connors, the like of which many of the past champions confessed they had never seen.

In highly confident mood he later took the US Open for the fourth time, beating Connors again and then Lendl in a superb three-set final. For good measure John also repeated his Wimbledon doubles victory with Peter Fleming.

Indoors that year John strode triumphantly to his fourth WCT title and his third Masters crown at New York's Madison Square Garden. The only blemish on an otherwise outstanding season was John's defeat in the first rubber of the Davis Cup final in Gothenberg when he lost to Henrik Sundstrom 13–11 6–4 6–3 as the Swedes scored their surprising 4–1 win over the Americans.

Though he had lost that all-important rubber, McEnroe had led his country to four Davis Cup victories in five years between 1978 and 1982. Couple that with his three Wimbledon singles titles from five appearances in the final, four US Open titles from five finals plus one French final, and you begin to see what a great singles player he was. His doubles record with Peter Fleming is equally impressive. Four Wimbledon and three US Open titles fell to their excellent teamwork and seven times running they took the Masters title, a feat unlikely ever to be equalled. However there are gaps in John's record and without any singles successes in France or Australia one cannot think of him as the equal of a Laver or a Budge. Yet I suspect that in his later years he will be as proud of the first Grand Slam title he ever won as any of his later victories. It came in Paris in 1977 when John was a junior. Partnering Mary Carillo, who, like him, came from Douglaston, New York, he won the mixed doubles with a display of doubles artistry that revealed his instinctive grasp of that area of the game. This win must have given him tremendous confidence for his first appearance at Wimbledon where, after winning three qualifying rounds, he advanced to the semi-finals and there pressed Connors to four hard sets.

Yes, John McEnroe was always exciting to watch. There were things about his game that were quite remarkable. His service, delivered from an unusually closed stance, meant that he had his back to his opponent as he prepared to deliver the ball. Thus it was very difficult to pick the direction of first and second serves. Incidentally, as he attempted his comeback in 1988, against continuing back problems, it appeared he was now paying the penalty for such an exaggerated stance.

His ground strokes were so natural and delivered with so little back swing that the element of disguise here too was considerable. At times his forehand looked dangerously wristy but when his timing was sharp he could swing the ball impossibly early to remarkably sharp angles or fire his passes, bullet-like, into the corners without any apparent effort – all the result of perfect timing. John's reflexes at the net were as fast as any player's have ever been and he could perform on the instinct level so perfectly that he would suddenly produce the unexpected stop volley or lob volley that no one would have attempted . . . and bring it off! He was rather like Henri Cochet in this respect. No amount of coaching or instruction can produce these effects. They are the stuff of genius.

How sad it is then that this extraordinarily gifted player is more likely to be remembered not for his tennis but for some truly appalling behaviour which echoed around the world. If only the authorities had made him pay the penalty when it was all beginning he might have cured this errant behaviour.

Increasingly I find myself referring to John in the past tense. This, too, is sad for he is still under thirty years of age and retains the ability to make you gasp with his audacious shot-making. However, after such a lengthy break from the game I shall be amazed – and delighted – if John can return to the heights he once touched.

Perhaps for everyone's sake it would be better if he decided to retire now. I would hate to have to remember him as a once-great champion struggling to beat second-class players.

HENRI COCHET

In the days when covered court tennis invariably meant that the playing surface would be wood, those who learned to play on that surface usually acquired an easy effortless game and in some cases an attractive style.

One who did was Henri Cochet, who was to become a great French sporting hero, especially for his play when appearing for his country in the Davis Cup. He played altogether in twenty-six ties, winning forty-four rubbers out of fifty-eight and was successful in six Challenge Rounds. He took the Wimbledon singles and doubles twice each, won the American once and the French four times in singles and three times in doubles.

Unlike most great players, Cochet never really hit the ball hard except occasionally when smashing. There was no sign or display of physical strength, no great winding up of the body when he produced his service and moved in for his ground strokes. He really did make the game look easy and effortless because he was a hand and arm player. He still threw the racket head at the ball when serving, and swung the racket head through the ball on the forehand. But his backhand was not a swing at all. It was a prolonged pushing of the racket head through the ball with a locked wrist. This was rather like his basic volleys but he could loosen the wrist when he needed to caress the ball on his backhand drop shot or stop volley.

How then did he generate such speed and weight of shot on his ground strokes? He told me one day while we were relaxing after dinner at the Prince of Wales hotel in Lord Street, Southport, during the big pro-tournament there just before the war where Bill Tilden was also competing: 'The difference between Bill's game and mine is that he is a big man who revels in his strength but he is essentially a baseliner who has no instinctive net game. He opens his shoulders on the forehand and backhand with a very full swing and hits the ball hard. Even when he changes his style to slicing and chopping he's still brutal with the ball. He sees the possibility with his power of winning the point with the first stroke of every rally, whether service or return of service, like he did all those years ago against me at Wimbledon in the semi-final (1927) when he won the first two sets and led 5–1 in the third before he blew up. I am a much smaller man – French, not American – and not a violent man, so I just take my racket back and lean on the ball and try to take it early in the bounce and use the speed of my opponent's shot. I don't think tennis should be played in a state of mental and physical fury. I prefer just to be mentally and physically aware; perhaps that is why I used to win so many matches in the fifth set. It was also probably why I lost to a few players not in my class early in a tournament because their play did not stimulate me so I didn't make myself aware until it was too late.'

There was never a more sensational upset at Wimbledon than that day in 1931 when Cochet, the number two seed, lost in the first round to the British Davis Cup player, Nigel

Sharpe. The Centre Court was stunned. So was I, when I went into the dressing-room and ran into Henri whose locker was next to mine. 'Henri, I'm sorry about your defeat. Whatever happened to you?' I asked. With a typical Gallic shrug he replied, 'I was dead – I never had that little windy feeling under my heart'. As all competitors in every sport know, it is impossible to produce a top level performance without being keyed up. When the adrenaline is missing, the performance is flat.

Normally Cochet did not talk a great deal about tennis but when I got to know him personally in his professional days he opened up. I was fascinated by his views and while he was in this mood I questioned the wisdom of the amount of half-volleying he did. His answer was totally reasonable: 'I enjoy it more than any other stroke – except perhaps blocking a cannonball service on Wimbledon's fast grass or on wood down the line against the incoming server – and is there any better way to counter-attack the incoming volleyer's deep approach shot, before he gets into position and settled at the net?'

Little did I know then that some time afterwards he would do that to me when I had a match point against him myself in the big pro-tournament at Olympia in London. I had hit a perfectly placed backhand approach deep into his backhand corner. I felt he was bound to retreat and play a lob or a low trajectory reply to make me volley from below the height of the net. So, instead of closing right in on the net, I held back just a little in case a lob came. He stepped straight in to my shot and played a brilliantly timed and accurately directed half-volley down my forehand line and that was that.

The last time I sat with him was in Paris in the mid-1970s. We were watching Argentina's Guillermo Vilas playing on the very slow centre court at the Stade Roland Garros. Henri soon got up and excused his departure, exclaiming, '*Mon Dieu*, technically illiterate!'

Perhaps Bill Tilden summed up Cochet best: 'Henri's game was quite perfect, he was the connoisseur's player.'

JEAN BOROTRA

Anyone who was lucky enough to see Jean Borotra at his entertaining best would understand why he is universally acclaimed as the most popular player ever to walk on to a tennis court. Jean played tennis competitively or socially as games were meant to be played. His infectious enthusiasm, his bubbling spirit and his adventurous all-court game never failed to communicate itself to audiences all around the world, but most especially at Wimbledon. He only had to put on one of his famous berets for the crowd to burst into an explosion of applause. He would do this at key moments in a match, for he was fully aware of the value of crowd support!

When he was driven wide of the court he would be so fast off the mark, like the release of a coiled spring, that he often could not stop and was forced to leap over the courtside barrier. Again, at critical moments, it seemed he always used to finish up in the lap of an attractive girl, much to the amusement of the crowd! Yes, beneath the devil-may-care veneer on court there was a tremendously clear strategic and tactical tennis brain at work.

I remember watching the Wimbledon semi-final he played in 1930 against Bill Tilden, the number two seed that year. Borotra opened spectacularly and won the first six games. Tilden came back to win the second set 6–4 but lost the third by the same score. In losing the fourth set 0–6 Borotra appeared to be harbouring his resources for the struggle in a final set. Borotra, at thirty-one, was six years younger than the American. The Frenchman's strenuous style of play was exhausting and he had been known to throw sets tactically before. He must have thought that the longer the match went on, the better his chances would be.

Halfway through the fifth set, with Borotra leading by the odd game, Tilden came round the far side of the net at the change of ends to avoid Borotra and the chatter in which he would often engage his opponent. Tilden stood waiting to serve; the knuckles of his left hand holding the balls were white with tension, as I could clearly see from the garden seat at the players' entrance on which I often sat in company with the referee and the head groundsman. The umpire chided Borotra and reminded him that play must be continuous. Full of apology, the Frenchman hurried towards the far baseline, still towelling himself with the large white bath towel supplied by the club and beckoning the ballboy to follow him. When he had reached his position he turned and tossed the towel over the ballboy's head, completely enveloping the lad so that he looked like a ghost. The crowd's reaction was spontaneous. The laughter echoed round the stands. A lesser man than Tilden might have crumbled. But the tall American remained impassive. Waiting for the amusement to subside, he set about holding his serve, which he did successfully. Tilden eventually won that set 7–5 and with it the match. Two days later he would beat fellow countryman Wilmer Allison to win his third Championship, ten years after his first. This is still the biggest gap between wins for any champion.

I have practised and played as much with Borotra at Wimbledon as with any of the overseas men. Every year on the Saturday before the tournament began he would arrive at the club in his chauffeur-driven Hispano-Suiza carrying a long racket press from which protruded the handles of six rackets, each one numbered. He would want to play for an hour or so before going off to that evening's International Club dinner.

I have seen Borotra battling away in the French Championships and in Davis Cup matches at Roland Garros and, of course, at Wimbledon. I have seen him play on the indoor wooden courts at Queen's Club on which for so many years he was virtually unbeatable. In fact one of my most imperishable memories, which I have described elsewhere, was in 1927 when he played Tilden in the inaugural match between the International Clubs of Great Britain and France. Borotra won in two long sets and most of the points were gained with positive shots rather than by his opponent's errors. I shall never forget the lengthy, standing ovation they received from as knowledgeable an audience as was ever likely to gather round a tennis court.

Jean had a marvellous physique for the game with a spring in his step that exuded vitality. He came from the Basque country in south-west France and as a youth had played pelota, the popular game of the region which requires great footwork and lightning-fast reactions. He had also played rugby at school. These pursuits had helped him to develop the ball sense that was most apparent later when he took up tennis. He always gives credit to his English 'holiday mother', Mrs Wildy, for awakening his interest in the game from the age of fourteen when he used to stay with the family at their home in Kenley, Surrey, during the school holidays.

I once asked Jean when he first competed in tournaments. 'It was after World War One, Dan,' he told me. 'I was posted to Baden Baden as a young officer in the army of occupation. A tournament was being organized locally and the CO ordered us to enter. He thought it would be good for our public relations. So I played and won the mixed doubles. It was at the Wiesbaden Club that I sought advice of the local professional. He told me to grip the racket with the thumb down the back of the handle to hit my backhand drives and volleys. It was the only piece of coaching I ever had.'

The Borotra backhand volley was a truly remarkable shot. Even when caught in mid-court around the service line, he would punch sensational winners off any ball above net height. I have never seen anyone else, not even Lew Hoad, produce such amazing shots. For low backhand volleys, hit always well out in front of him with a firm wrist, Jean was a model of getting down low with bent knees. Of course, it was his extreme grip that made this absolutely necessary if he was going to hit a controlled shot.

Borotra's overhead was another spectacular shot. He was so quick to get back and leapt so high that he had time to make unexpected winners at awkward angles. He never seemed to hit the ball particularly hard but his smash was a flat shot that was beautifully timed and was invariably too good for his opponent.

Jean Borotra's record is an enviable one – two Wimbledon singles titles and three other appearances in the final plus three doubles wins there; an Australian singles title; plus a fine Davis Cup record. Between 1922 and 1947 Jean played fifty-four rubbers in thirty-two ties and won thirty-six of them.

But you cannot measure the effect that Jean Borotra has had on our sport by mere statistics. His personality stamped itself indelibly upon the game over a period of twenty years and such is his enthusiasm that still, at the age of ninety, he is competing in those annual IC matches between Great Britain and France. What a man! I doubt if we shall ever see his like again.

KEN ROSEWALL

It is easy to say that Ken Rosewall never won Wimbledon because his service was not strong enough. That may be true but I am tempted to wonder if the level of the rest of his game would have reached such near perfection if the service had been stronger. Nevertheless it is quite remarkable that a player in today's competitive conditions, containing a relatively weak delivery, should force his way into world class and stay at or very near the top for over twenty years.

Let us reflect upon Ken's record. At his second Wimbledon in 1953 he was seeded number one at the age of eighteen, having won the French Championship a few weeks earlier.

Perhaps he found the weight of responsibility attached to his top seeding something of a millstone. That has happened to others. He was beaten by the powerful Dane, Kurt Nielsen, in the quarter-finals after leading by two sets to one. Nielsen went on to become the first unseeded player to reach the final where he lost to Vic Seixas, the American whom Rosewall had so recently conquered in the French final. Winning the doubles title at Wimbledon with Hoad that year was some consolation and there was no question that here was a superstar in the making.

Rosewall had flawless ground strokes – compact, soundly-produced forehand and a backhand that has become, like that of Donald Budge, a legendary shot. The quality of his volleys below the height of the net were remarkable and anything above that height was despatched to eternity. His overhead was a consistent point winner by virtue of angle or, more surprisingly, its power. This was achieved by perfect timing and early preparation. Although standing only five feet seven inches, Ken covered the net with exceptional anticipation and speed and rarely failed to get up to the best of lobs. His temperament and match discipline were a model and few players made fewer unforced errors – a tribute to his superb sense of balance, his concentration and timing. The gut in his racket always seemed to be singing.

Ken's first Wimbledon final came in 1954. He lost to the crowd's favourite, Jaroslav Drobny, the former Czech, in four sets. This was Drobny's eleventh challenge and at the age of thirty-two his time seemed to be running out. It was a match to be savoured, with rallies full of glorious strokes of touch, feel and artistry. Two years later in the 1956 final Ken's tennis 'twin', Lew Hoad beat him in four sets only to lose to him two months later in the US final where Rosewall won by three sets to one and robbed Lew of the Grand Slam.

A new era began for Rosewall after he had turned professional in 1957. He quickly rose to the top of the pro game and stayed there until 1963 when Laver left the amateur ranks.

When open tennis arrived in 1968 at the British Hard Court Championships in Bournemouth Rosewall, not thirty-three years of age, beat Laver in the final. They both showed that age had not withered them. A few weeks later Rosewall regained the French title that he had first won fifteen years before. He beat Laver in four sets in Paris during the student riots that accompanied a wave of strikes and, with Fred Stolle, regained the doubles title that he had first won in 1953 with Hoad. Before retiring from serious competition in 1979, an incredible twenty-seven years after his first appearance at Wimbledon, Ken's overall record of Grand Slam titles reads: French Championships, two singles and two doubles; Wimbledon, four losing finals, two doubles titles; US Championships, two singles and two doubles; Australian Championships, four singles and three doubles. Nor must we forget how well he served his country in the Davis Cup. He appeared in four Challenge Rounds between 1953 and 1956, playing ten rubbers and winning seven.

One of the most impressive displays amongst all my memories of classic performances occurred at Wembley. It was 1959. The Peruvian-American, Alex Olmedo, had won Wimbledon that year beating Laver in three sets. Turning pro after the US Championships, Olmedo was still playing like a young tiger. But on the wooden court at Wembley the Wimbledon champion could hardly believe what was happening to him – nor could the spectators – as Rosewall's clinical efficiency took his game apart. For fifteen flawless games Rosewall was supreme. He led 6–0 6–0 3–0 with as perfect a display of tennis as I have ever seen. The measure of its quality can be judged by the fact that all the other professionals in the tournament came out to watch, some sitting in courtside seats, others leaning on the top of the balustrade that surrounded the court. When the massacre was over the Slazenger representative, Dennis Coombe, went to see Ken in the locker room afterwards to congratulate him. 'Unbelievable,' said Dennis. 'Do you know that in those first fifteen games you made only four unforced errors?'

'Three, you mean,' laughed Rosewall.

I had sat watching this match with John Barrett from our courtside seats. The thing that had impressed both of us was the depth of Rosewall's concentration that day. It was almost as if he had set himself the target of beating the Wimbledon champion in three love sets. The accuracy of every shot he played was millimetre perfect; the speed of his reaction on the volley was astonishing; the depth and variety of his second serve was better than I had ever seen it.

Like Laver and the other great players of this period, Ken's best years were spent in the wilderness of professional tennis. He had been forced by circumstance to spend many years on the road, mostly in America, away from his wife and family. But when, in 1970, he qualified for the first Masters tournament in Tokyo he brought Wilma and the boys, Brett and Glenn, with him to Japan where I met them for the first time. They were a delightful family. The boys were approaching some important exams and Ken had had to promise their headmaster that they would conscientiously attend to their daily studies. I always thought how surprised his millions of fans would have been to see this Peter Pan of tennis acting the strict schoolmaster.

It seems unfair that the fates have denied this great Australian ambassador the Wimbledon singles crown. Along with Baron Gottfried Von Cramm of Germany, who was three times a beaten finalist, Ken must rate as the finest player never to have won that title. Obviously the All England Club committee felt the same way because in 1971 they took the unusual step of awarding him honorary life membership. It was a fitting recognition of the tremendous contribution that he made not only to Wimbledon, but to the world game.

JIMMY CONNORS

Jimmy Connors was taught to play tennis by his mother, Gloria, and her mother, Bertha. Whoever had the greater influence, mother or grandmother, matters not for they were both determined that Jimmy Connors would become a champion. His grandmother lived long enough to see Jimmy put his feet on the first steps of the championship ladder when he won the National Inter-Collegiate (NCAA) title as a freshman at the University of California, Los Angeles, in 1971. This was a path trodden by so many great American players both before and since.

The following year, 1972, Jimmy won his first professional title in Jacksonville, Florida, and made his Wimbledon debut. It was a warning of what was to come when he beat the number seven seed, Bob Hewitt, 7–5 in the fourth set in his first match. Taking immediately to Wimbledon's fast grass which suited his attacking style, Jimmy won three more rounds before losing in the quarter-finals to Ilie Nastase, the number two seed. Nastase went on to play one of Wimbledon's greatest finals against Stan Smith which the American won 7–5 in the fifth set. The following year Jimmy would team up with Nastase to win his only Wimbledon doubles title.

Jimmy's fierce competitiveness was already evident. So too was his double-handed backhand and his attacking service returns on both wings. At times he would launch himself against the serve (no safety-first blocked returns for him) and hit the ball with both feet off the ground in order to keep the pressure on the server. At this stage he volleyed rarely and showed none of the true volleyer's instinct for the low volley. He seemed to have little of the natural net player's ability to maintain the initiative with angle or depth. His best shot in this area was a sweeping drive volley off the shoulder-high ball. His game was essentially built on controlled power from the back of the court with low, fast passing shots against the volleyer. Jimmy's left-handed service in those days lacked speed through the air and penetration off the ground so that it was not exactly conducive to a dominating serve-and-volley game. In essence his game remained unchanged through the years and when he played his sixteenth consecutive Wimbledon in 1987 it was technically the same player. However the service now was much improved, the result of throwing the ball a little further forward. This had helped him to win a second Wimbledon title quite brilliantly in 1982 against John McEnroe. He had served quite well in his first Wimbledon final in 1974 when he had destroyed Ken Rosewall 6–1 6–1 6–4 and two months later beaten Ken again, losing only two games to the little Australian in the US Open final. In both matches his uncertain forehand approach shot, especially against a lowish ball, behaved impeccably. But it was this shot that was always his Achilles' heel, a shortcoming cruelly exposed in the 1975 Wimbledon final by Arthur Ashe.

Sadly, Jimmy's behaviour too often offended audiences who had the greatest respect for the zest and enthusiasm that he brought to the match court but less affection for his often vulgar gestures. Rarely though did he fail to provide anything but a hundred per cent effort. Towards the end of his career in a fourth round match at Wimbledon in 1987 against the Swede Mikael Pernfors he gave a performance that was a fascinating match to commentate on and will never be forgotten by those who saw it. Jimmy was now just short of his thirty-fifth birthday and had been taken to four sets in each of his previous two matches. Against Pernfors he had lost the first two sets 1–6 1–6 and was 1–4 down in the third to a twenty-four-year-old opponent who was running rings around him. This was Jimmy's sixteenth consecutive Wimbledon where only twice since 1971 had he failed to reach at least the quarter-finals. One felt that a glorious career was about to come to an ignominious end. Perhaps, one felt, he was content with his two Wimbledon titles, his five in the United States and his one in Australia. But we had reckoned without the fighting heart of Jimmy Connors, surely the toughest competitor in the business. By sheer willpower he won the third set 7–5 but he was soon down 0–3 in the fourth. Somehow he pulled it out at 6–4 and amazingly went on to lead 4–1 in the decider. But this brave recovery had taken its toll. When the ATP trainer, Bill Norris, was summoned to the court it seemed the old warrior might yet be denied the victory that he had worked so hard to achieve. But the leg muscles he had injured responded to Norris's treatment. Amid scenes of unparalleled excitement and noise Jimmy finally won the set and with it the match 6–2. As the old warrior limped away the ovation was as great as any I have ever heard on the Centre Court since my first Wimbledon in 1924. The match had lasted three hours and thirty-eight minutes. It was hard to believe that the American could recover in time to stand a chance of beating the cannonball serving Yugoslav, Slobodan Zivojinovic, in the quarter-finals for the bad weather had meant the normal rest days between matches in the second week had been sacrificed. The following day Connors walked on to court one without any visible signs of weariness. The limp had gone and there was a spring in his step. That he won in straight sets 7–6 7–5 6–3 was extraordinary and later in the dressing-room he enjoyed reminding those around him that he was the only former champion left in the Championships as Becker had been beaten in the second round. This was Jimmy's eleventh Wimbledon semi-final.

The warm sun had shone on the match and indeed on Jimmy's glorious career which was now surely coming towards its end. But what an immense contribution this swaggering American had made to Wimbledon's history.

MARTINA NAVRATILOVA

I have no hesitation at all in placing Martina at the top of my ladies' ranking list. Her record, of course, is tremendous but it is her style of play that is so appealing and so successful. She is a very strong woman, an athlete to a degree, but is also intelligent and courageous. All this she brings to her aggressive and severe, adventurous, all-court tennis. When she decides to play the serve-and-volley game she is fully committed and when counter-attacking against the volleyer she never quits on the shot, whether going for the pass or the attacking lob.

When she first came to England at sixteen to play for Czechoslovakia in the BP Cup (an international under twenty-one team event) on the wooden courts at the Palace Hotel, Torquay, it was known that she was a very promising teenager. After the first day's matches I was interviewed on Western Television about the competitors and the event. I made the forecast that Martina could be a Wimbledon winner before her twenty-first birthday playing all-court tennis on Wimbledon's fast grass which is so much like wood. She failed me by some eight months, winning there for the first time in July 1978 when seeded number two. Her run of eight singles titles there has now equalled the record of Helen Wills-Moody. That first victory against Chris Evert in three sets was sweet revenge for her semi-final defeat by the same player and by a similar score two years earlier.

I have often been asked why I made such a confident forecast of Martina's future after having seen her play only one match. There were at least three good reasons.

The first was that I had been watching her practise before the matches started and on the wooden covered courts at the Palace Hotel which were new and strange to her she settled down at once. These courts are nearer to Wimbledon's grass in speed and bounce than any other indoor courts I have ever played on. Martina was timing the ball, judging the length and speed of the bounce, and moving around fast with confident, strong footwork as though she had never played on anything else. What particularly impressed me was that whether she was half-volleying under pressure on the base-line or half-volleying following her serve to the net, her timing was near-perfect. This is one of the most difficult shots in the game but Martina always controlled the ball and placed it purposefully. There was no scrambling and hoping that it would be an effective shot. Here, I knew, was a natural quality that could not have been taught.

The second was on a more personal note. I was to discover the depth of personality and range of interest in this still young teenager in a most delightful way. I was asked by Vernon Weaver, one of the LTA Counsellors for Devon, if I would take Martina and her team-mate, Renata Tomanova, for a drive around Torquay to show them something of the resort and the attractive coastline. My car was available and it gave me the opportunity to refresh my own memories of the place that had been so much a part of my life during the early days of the war. It was also a fine opportunity to talk to the girls and get to know them. Shunning the opportunity to visit Mike Sangster's sports shop, they persuaded me to buy them an ice-cream cornet at the foot of the hill near the harbour. We then got back into the car and toured the Paignton and Churston area and eventually returned to the Palace by way of that lovely coastal road that runs from the Imperial Hotel past Thatcher's Rock. They were much impressed for it was a gloriously warm sunny day in February. I pulled the car into the car park at Daddyhole Plain at the top of the cliff so that they could get a full view of Torbay, Churston and Corinne Molesworth's home town, Brixham. Almost at once Tony and Joy Mottram who were also down for the BP Cup matches, pulled into the car park. The introductions and pleasantries over, we set off once more towards the hotel and the girls asked me to tell them about Joy's and Tony's tennis careers. I also told them of Tony's fine RAF record, a turn of conversation which led, of course, to the bombing of the Palace Hotel, then the RAF

Officer's Aircrew Hospital in 1942. To my surprise all this seemed to hold their interest.

Martina spoke quite good English and I was much impressed by her mature conversation and her views on a number of other things apart from tennis. This, I felt, was very much a young lady of character. Back at the courts, after thanking me, Martina led Renata straight to the gallery overlooking the covered courts to watch the other competitors in action. That was the second sign, I felt, that she was a lady with a purpose.

The third came on the match court where she fulfilled in every way what she had practised. So often we are disappointed with promising young players who, when the chips are down, fail to show belief in their game or themselves. With some it is a lack of fibre for competition but there are numerous other reasons too. Martina showed in her first match that she revelled in being in a competitive situation. The court was her theatre and the match something to enjoy.

Obviously our paths have crossed many times since that first meeting but never so closely as during that week in Torquay. Martina knew that during the week I had forecast that one day she would win Wimbledon. By the time she had equalled Helen Wills-Moody's record of eight titles in 1987 she also knew that a year or two earlier I had said publicly that I doubted if anyone would ever beat that record. At the Champions' Dinner that year Martina came over to me during the reception before we all sat down and said, with a suggestion of a smile, 'Well, Dan, I'm on my way aren't I?'

A genuine superstar, Martina has collected titles on all surfaces in the Grand Slam circuit. Apart from the eight she has won on grass at Wimbledon there are two in Paris on clay and two on Melbourne's grass plus three on asphalt in New York. Being a lover of doubles I also rate her the best I have ever seen in that exhilarating department of the game. As I write I wonder whether Steffi Graf will prevent Martina from attaining the ambition that is dearest to her heart –

namely to add a ninth Wimbledon singles title to her already wonderful record.

HELEN WILLS-MOODY

I must have played against Helen Wills-Moody more than any other overseas player. Every time we went on court it was an interesting and very pleasant experience. The press dubbed Helen 'Little Miss Poker Face' or 'The Ice Queen', tags that amused this very beautiful and, as I always found, delightful Californian. She had a natural dignity and an almost regal presence that added much to the image of the game.

She was involved in the first final I ever saw at Wimbledon. It was in 1924 and Kitty McKane came back from a set and 1–4 down to beat Helen in the third set. This was a remarkable performance because Helen had already won the US Championship. It is even more remarkable that in eight subsequent visits she was never again beaten. Her eight singles titles stand as a monument to her concentration and flawless accuracy from the back of the court. However, in 1935 she was rather lucky to beat fellow American and near neighbour Helen Jacobs. She had faced a match point that year but 'the other Helen' had failed to convert it when she fluffed a relatively easy overhead – more in excitement than anything else many people thought at the time, though I wondered if she had taken her eye off the ball whose flight seemed to me to have been disturbed by a gust of wind. After that she never won another game. The Wimbledon final had had the same outcome in 1929, 1932 and 1934. In 1938 the two Helens met yet again but this time Helen Wills (who had become Mrs Moody in 1930) had looked much more convincing as she beat her old rival 6–4 6–0. But she had not felt as confident as she looked. After the match, as I congratulated her and said goodbye for the last time, she had said, 'Thank you Dan, but you know I wasn't really playing at my best.'

Winning the US title at Forest Hills seven times showed Helen's ability on grass but, like all great champions, she also mastered the difficulties of European clay to win the French Championships in 1928 and 1929.

Helen's game was built on solidly hit ground strokes carrying very slight controlling top spin. It was a base-line game *par excellence* with superb control of length and powerful diagonal cross court driving to the extreme corners. The service was also firmly struck with a strong throwing action, mostly carrying a touch of controlling slice. Her volleys were adequate but there were never any acrobatics at the net. If she came in it was only because she had prepared her advance so well that it made the volley a logical finish to the point. She had a large frame, but excellent anticipation more than compensated for her somewhat heavy footwork.

In our practice sessions we always followed a similar pattern. We would rally for a full fifteen to twenty minutes to get the feel of the court and to warm up. Then, at her request, I would play like a steady woman from the back of the court, driving and playing long rallies. I did not volley or use spin or vary the tactics. I would serve fast enough, but not at full power, and would vary the direction. Playing like this I would usually win about 6–4 6–4. After a short breather at the net post she would remind me, 'Now it's your turn to have some fun.' This meant that I could now play all out and do what I liked. So for some points I would serve and volley, on others play drop shots and slices and on others try to wrong foot her on the drive or volley. Then I might play some slow highish balls in the middle of a rally and suddenly rush to the net. Or perhaps I would bring her in with short balls in which case I would either go for a fast pass, a disguised lob or make her deal with a slow, feather-light ball to test her low volley. These she would deal with very well and I once said to her: 'I'm surprised you don't

volley a little more – it might shorten some of your rallies.'
Her reply was so beautifully logical: 'While I'm hitting a
good length and finding the corners, I can't come to much
harm, Dan.' Dorothy Round has confirmed that basic truth.
She once told me that she found the weight and accuracy of
Helen's drives – especially when she tried to come in against
her – so difficult to deal with, even though she herself was
one of the best volleyers of the day. Like Chris Evert today,
Helen never minded anyone coming in against her. In fact
she always liked a target.

After practising for about a set playing my own way we
would finish for the day. By then Helen had had a complete
workout. The two sets of rhythmical play had grooved her
normal shots, then the set when I had free rein had sharpened her anticipation and tested her timing and ball control
under pressure. In these sessions I was always impressed by
her judgement of what was possible and what was not. She
would never chase a ball she knew she could not reach. It
was the same in her matches where, usually, she had so much
in hand that there was little point in her wasting energy.
Maria Bueno had a little of this about her.

I treasure indeed my hours with Helen Wills-Moody on
Wimbledon's immaculate lawns.

MARGARET COURT

One of the greatest matches in the history of women's tennis
was the 1970 Wimbledon final between Margaret Court and
Billie Jean King. Expectation of a great match was high, in
spite of the fact that both players were nursing injuries. Billie
Jean had a troublesome knee that had been worrying her for
some time and needed attention while Margaret's ankle
required treatment right up to the moment of leaving the
dressing-room.

The match had an international flavour – Australia versus
America – and both players were at the height of their

careers. They were two vastly experienced champions. Mrs Court had been the winner in 1963 and 1965 while Mrs King had won in 1966, 1967 and 1968.

Of the increasing number of women now playing all-court tennis, these two finalists were the best that the women's game had yet produced especially on Wimbledon's grass. Both could play solidly from the baseline if necessary and both were wonderful examples of the attacking all-court player. Even more intriguing was their record at Wimbledon against each other. In 1962 Miss Smith, as she was then, was seeded number one and had been beaten by the unseeded American teenager, Miss B. J. Moffitt, in her first match after winning the first set. Margaret lost the second and third sets 3–6 5–7 to become, incidentally, the first number one seeded player ever to be beaten in the first round at Wimbledon. The two met in the final again the next year when the Australian had sweet revenge with a two sets win, 6–3 6–4. In 1964 they met yet again, this time in the semi-finals (Margaret seeded one and Billie Jean seeded three) and once again the score was 6–3 6–4 to Margaret. Their last meeting, in the semi-final of 1966, had brought their head-to-head record at Wimbledon level as the American won 6–3 6–3.

Thus, the 1970 final promised a great tussle. Finals do not always fulfil themselves in that respect but this one certainly did. Nobody could have foreseen what a titanic, heroic contest it would be. The match will certainly live in the memory of all who were fortunate enough to see it. More than that it will forever be written of by the game's historians as one of Wimbledon's greatest finals.

Margaret Court was a supremely athletic woman, tall and well proportioned and with an exceptional reach. She was very strong and a disciplined mover, especially under pressure at the back of the court. There were no unnecessary acrobatics at the net. Her service was powerful, penetrating and heavy, like the rest of her shots – except on those days when she could not find the purity of her timing on the forehand drive. Rarely did she find this difficulty on her backhand side or on the volley. Throughout her career there had been days when her nerve had wavered on the match court in moments of crisis. Never did that frailty appear in this match. Margaret was behind in both sets. Her will-power and raw courage could not have had a more severe test from Mrs King who, time and again, produced rapid tactical changes: sometimes playing from the back of the court, then darting unexpectedly to the net. The American showed a thoroughly professional understanding of how to approach the net when the opponent had lost her length. The rallies were fascinating in their variety, particularly near the end when only the courage and sheer guts of two great match players kept them going. It was unbelievable that they could maintain such accuracy and consistency of return for so long. At last, after two hours and twenty-seven minutes the Australian prevailed 14–12 11–9. So ended the longest women's final that Wimbledon had ever seen. While they received a standing ovation I could not help feeling a moment of sadness for the loser. Even in losing Billie Jean had made a tremendous contribution to women's tennis.

I well remember the time that Margaret came to play in the popular pre-Wimbledon tournament at the Northern Club in Manchester. It was 1962 and the BBC were there to televise the semi-finals and final of the ladies' singles. The producer decided, late on Thursday evening, that he wanted me to interview Margaret Court in the BBC studio in Manchester so that we could use it as part of our build-up to the following day's semi-finals.

I was surprised at Margaret's hesitancy when the question of the interview was being discussed. She did not seem at all keen to talk about herself. However, after I had assured her that my questions would be concerned solely with her tennis and particularly with her much publicized training routine, plus her thoughts on the forthcoming Wimbledon, she began to look more relaxed. In front of the cameras she was perfectly confident.

This slight hesitancy reflected, I think, the occasional lapses in confidence that she showed in her matches. For somebody so well trained and with so much experience it was extraordinary that at times Margaret would, for some inexplicable reason, suddenly lose her confidence and fritter away a string of games against a player who was well within her compass.

The other relative weakness I had noticed on her first visit to the Northern Club a year or two before our interview. I had sat watching that match with Ted Tinling from seats behind the court. After watching almost a set I remarked to Ted what a beautifully athletic attacking player she was but suggested that there seemed to be an uncomfortable look about the forehand stroke on occasions. The timing of it was not as good as on the backhand. Ted agreed immediately and was interested to hear my comment because it coincided with the opinion he had already formed of her game.

However, we are talking here of 'relative' weaknesses. In the fullness of time Margaret became one of the finest attacking all-court players I have ever seen and I doubt whether anyone will ever equal her record of sixty-two Grand Slam titles in singles, doubles and mixed doubles – sixty-six if you count the two singles and two doubles she won in America in 1968 and 1969 when they had two championships, the amateur as well as the open. Yes, I fancy that Margaret Court will remain the most prolific champion there has ever been.

BILLIE JEAN KING

Miss B. J. Moffitt, a seventeen-year-old American, made her debut at Wimbledon in 1961 and lost her first match against the number five seed, Yola Ramirez. This loss raised a few eyebrows, for Billie Jean had won a hard first set from the

Mexican 11–9 before losing the next two 1–6 2–6. Eyebrows were raised a bit higher still when, partnered by fellow American Karen Hantze, this bubbling tomboy won the ladies' doubles beating the Australian pair of Jan Lehane and Margaret Smith in the final 6–2 6–4. However, nobody could possibly have imagined what lay ahead.

By the time she had completed her twenty-second Wimbledon in 1983, when she had reached the final of the mixed doubles with Steve Denton, she had played her 265th match on the lawns of the All England Club. The former Miss Moffitt, Mrs King since 1965, had become Wimbledon's most prolific winner and was by now one of the great sporting personalities of the world.

Her playing record is quite awesome. By winning the ladies' doubles in 1979 she had fulfilled an ambition to break the record of nineteen Wimbledon titles she had shared with fellow Californian Elizabeth Ryan since 1975. Fate had decreed that Elizabeth would not live to see that proud record broken for she had died the day before the final, after collapsing in the ladies' dressing-room. Six times Billie Jean won the singles title, ten times the ladies' doubles and four times the mixed doubles.

In the US Championships Billie Jean won thirteen titles – four singles, five ladies' doubles and four mixed doubles. In Paris she won the French mixed doubles twice, in 1967 and 1970, before finally winning the ladies' singles and doubles there in 1972. By winning in January 1968 in Melbourne she became Australia's last amateur singles champion and added the mixed for good measure. Her total of Grand Slam titles was thirty-nine.

Wonderful as her record is she will, I think, be remembered as much for her contribution to the cause of women's liberation as for anything else. Her determination to succeed, not only on the court, but in building up worldwide support and public interest in women's tennis, received enormous publicity. She was the driving force behind the establishment of the Women's Tennis Association and their professional tour.

Rarely if ever has tennis attracted so much interest as the match she played in September 1973 at Houston's Astrodome in Texas against the 1939 Wimbledon men's champion, Bobby Riggs. This 'battle of the sexes', as it was called, was the second such encounter. Riggs had beaten Margaret Court some time earlier but that match had not attracted anything like so much attention as his battle with Billie Jean. She was in her thirtieth year, had just won for the second time the Wimbledon triple crown, and was playing for a cause as much as for the $100,000 prize. It was the crusade that mattered and victory was everything. Defeat would have destroyed all she had worked so hard for through the years. When the moment arrived she was magnificent. She could not wait for battle to commence, her extrovert personality perfectly suiting the extravagant razzmatazz of the occasion. Bobby Riggs was now fifty-five. It was thirty-four years since his dramatic debut at Wimbledon where he had won the triple and then, two months later, had confirmed his match playing skills by winning his own National Championship on the grass at Forest Hills before turning professional in 1941. But Riggs was still very active in the game. After a short professional exhibition career in the post-war years Bobby, with the reputation of a gambler and a hustler, had continued to play in veterans' competitions and there were many in his own age group who thought that his tactical skill would compensate for his age against Billie Jean and that he would win this best of five sets extravaganza.

Before a record-breaking crowd of 30,492 and an estimated fifty million television viewers around the world, Billie Jean gave a brilliant display of the art of match play. Bobby Riggs, the great tactician, was outwitted – sometimes with controlled aggression but at other times by finesse and touch shots of delicacy and angle. Time and again he was wrong-footed until he must have felt dizzy. The score tells it all – 6–4 6–3 6–3.

Great all-court player that she was, with one of the most dominating personalities of any of her contemporaries, Billie Jean nevertheless realized early in her career that her forehand was a relative weakness. When she first came to Wimbledon as a teenager I could see that this was an unreliable shot. She could not maintain a rally of consistent drives on that wing which was nothing like as powerful and well controlled as her backhand. There was a certain inhibition about the forehand. Typically, thorough professional that she was, Billie Jean decided to do something about it. While in Australia she sought help from Mervyn Rose and when I next saw her there was a marked improvement. The forehand was now grooved and she hit it with much more confidence. This was apparent in that marvellous final at Wimbledon against Margaret Court in 1970 – admittedly a losing final for Billie Jean but one in which she nevertheless distinguished herself.

Throughout her career, Billie Jean has shown great courage in overcoming physical setbacks that would have daunted lesser women. She had a series of operations on both her knees that must have tested her resolve to the full. She has also shown great moral courage in espousing causes that were not always universally appealing.

When the history of the game comes to be written in the next century, Billie Jean's name will be remembered as one of the greatest single contributors to its growth. As player, visionary (Team Tennis was one of her ideas), as first president of the Women's Tennis Association, as entrepreneur and as spokeswoman for fair treatment for her sex, Billie Jean's influence has been unequalled.

MAUREEN CONNOLLY

Affectionately known the world over as 'Little Mo', Maureen Connolly made her Wimbledon debut in 1952. Her famous coach, Eleanor 'Teach' Tennant, introduced her to me and asked me to 'have a look at her game, like you did with Alice'. Teach had coached Alice Marble, the last Wimbledon champion before the war in 1939.

Maureen had won the previous year's US Championships on the grass at Forest Hills and was about to be seeded number two behind the holder, Doris Hart, at Wimbledon. Having been asked by Eleanor to have a good long warm-up and then a set or two, we began. I had heard and read a lot about this dazzling American teenager's relentless baseline game, her concentration and avoidance of unforced errors, so I was surprised to see – after at least fifteen minutes or so – that, whereas her timing and ball control on the backhand were trouble free, on the forehand side the reverse was very much the case. The occasional sly glance I gave Teach revealed a slightly worried look. A few minutes later she suggested to Maureen that we should play a few games. We had completed just four when Maureen suddenly said to both of us, 'My forehand's a joke.' Teach turned to me and said, 'Any comments, Dan?'

I thought my reply was pretty obvious when I said, 'I know Maureen's forehand is meant to be a rather flat drive but at the moment it's carrying unintentional slice. I think the preparation is too late; the racket needs to be taken back earlier, especially against the fairly deep ball, so that she doesn't hit the ball too late and can meet it more out in front of the body.' The response from Eleanor was immediate: 'So it's back to basics – as it was with Alice.' To the enquiring look from Maureen she explained what she meant. 'Dan will throw you some underhand, threequarter-length and waist-high balls to your forehand, while you wait for them just behind the baseline. Hit them first to the back hand corner and when you feel happy try the cross court. Then we will go from there.'

This was absolutely basic, beginner's work, with the pupil under no pressure of any kind and with the chance now to rebuild some timing, rhythm and confidence. In no time at all the gut was beginning to sing in Maureen's racket. The stroke was no longer slightly cramped and the ball carried no unintentional slice and had the right flight for a flat, lifted forehand, with a low trajectory that carried to a length.

Soon we were on to cross-court forehands. It took a little longer before we could progress to feeding the individual ball with my racket. We then rallied at medium pace followed by my shots being hit alternately to Maureen's backhand and forehand. Finally we concentrated on maintaining rallies of twenty strokes or more. No outright winners were being attempted but we were swinging the ball about and using the full length and width of the court. We took a short breather before playing some serious games. Little Mo, happier now, asked: 'Did you really have to do this with Alice Marble?' I answered with a slight smile, 'Yes, just like you, she used to get a bit mentally lazy on her slightly topped forehand.'

When Maureen left to go on to Queen's Club we were not to know that she would injure her shoulder slightly. It was a difference of opinion about how to deal with the situation which finally and completely ended her relationship with Teach Tennant. Teach insisted that the medical opinion she had taken convinced her that for Maureen to play at Wimbledon would result in permanent damage that might end her career. But Little Mo had taken medical advice, too. This diagnosis was completely different from the first. She was told she had only a minor injury which some regular heat treatment and massage would soon put right. She insisted that she'd come to play Wimbledon and would do so.

That she did, and won it too, but only after a really tough 7–5 final set quarter-final win against Great Britain's Susan Partridge. Not only did she beat fellow American Louise Brough 7–6 6–3 in the final but she also reached the ladies' doubles final with her too. She was to retain her singles title in the following two years to equal her three successive American titles. In 1953 and 1954 she won the French and in 1954 the Australian crown. But 1953 was a truly great year when she became the first woman to achieve the Grand Slam.

How sad it was that this great champion, who after her first US win in 1951 lost only four times, all in minor events, should have had her brilliant career cut short by a riding accident. Thereafter she was forced to restrict her tennis activities to coaching and, on one occasion, assisted the British Wightman Cup team during their preparation for the annual team match against the Americans. Interestingly I had done the same thing in reverse – when asked, helping US teams prepare for the match when it was played at Wimbledon – such was the spirit in which these contests were played.

Maureen's marriage to Norman Brinker, the Olympic showjumper, was a happy event for the entire sporting world. The creation of the Maureen Connolly Brinker Foundation by her friend Nancy Jeffett and the girls' matches they promote have perpetuated Maureen's memory in a most appropriate way.

Before she died in 1969 we had the pleasure of Maureen's company one day during the build-up to our BBC television coverage of the day's Centre Court programme. She had lost none of her youthful generosity of spirit and showed obvious enjoyment in the success of those following in her footsteps.

SUZANNE LENGLEN

In 1925 I saw the great Frenchwoman, Suzanne Lenglen, play Mrs A. E. Beamish, a British Wightman Cup player and the wife of a former Davis Cup player who had turned to professional coaching. She won their Wimbledon quarter-final 6–0 6–0. After she had turned professional in 1926 Suzanne embarked upon a series of matches in the United States. Eight years later I played with her twice on gas-lit wooden covered courts at Dulwich. I teamed up with the reigning French champion, Peggy Scriven, against Suzanne and Blair, a British professional. The next day Suzanne and I played an exhibition match to open the newly-laid hard court on the roof of Selfridges in London, to whom she had been contracted to do some tennis coaching and promotional work.

In my early days as a young assistant professional at Queen's Club I had read and heard so much about Suzanne both from the club members and from the senior professionals that I was not unduly surprised at the way she played. When I met her for the first time I was nevertheless impressed by her easy natural manner. She was unassuming and friendly, in fact the right description, I think, would be affable.

At Wimbledon I was impressed by the ease with which she moved into position to play her strokes – at times fluid and velvety and at others, when going for a winner off a waist-high ball short of a length on her forehand, more like a cat. She would spring off the ground and leap at the ball, swinging right through it with a long follow-through. It was all very spectacular but perhaps somewhat wasteful of energy. Her service was basically sound in that she threw the racket head at the ball but unless she was following it to the net she allowed her weight to fall slightly backwards so that in reality it was really an arm action with a very free wrist producing racket-head speed. However, it always carried the ball to a good length or an awkward place for the receiver.

Her net play fascinated me. Technically it was as sound as a bell. She had sensitive racket-head control and a firm punching action on the ball. It seemed as if she was always looking for a chance to play a drive-volley and make a spectacular display of a straightforward stroke. It was delightful to watch but again wasteful of energy and would have been risky in less capable hands. Overriding everything, however, was her masterly ball control with hardly an unforced error. This had been instilled from an early age by her father, Charles, who was her only coach. The family lived adjacent to the Nice Tennis Club in the south of France and Suzanne played there every day. She was made to aim for targets put down in the corners of the court. This helped her to develop a deep concentration. She also showed complete confidence when dealing with the unexpected drop shot or a wrong-footing ploy. Time and again she was able to produce a winner from quite unexpected places and always her timing was perfection. Her speed about the court and her graceful movements had been developed through attending ballet lessons.

Suzanne died in 1938 on the fourth of July – two days following Wimbledon finals day. For seven years following the end of World War One she was invincible. She won the Wimbledon singles six times between 1919 and 1925 and the French title as many times between 1920 and 1926. She also won the ladies' doubles at Wimbledon six times with Elizabeth Ryan. Her only defeat during this period occurred in New York in 1921 on her only visit to the United States. Having lost the first set of her opening match against the American champion, Molla Mallory, Suzanne, who was clearly unwell and in distress emotionally, defaulted. The incident caused a sensation at the time as did Suzanne's eventual departure from Wimbledon in 1926 when she scratched from the tournament after a misunderstanding with the referee over the scheduling of her first round singles match. Despite that she will always be remembered as Wimbledon's most popular lady champion.

However, many will remember her more for her great contribution to the emancipation of women when her daring calf-length dresses that emphasized the female form first started to take Wimbledon and the sporting world by storm in 1919 just after World War One. Her influence was immense and her premature death was a sad loss to the world.

CHRIS EVERT

In February 1988 I read that Chris Evert had announced to a wondering world that, having been undecided, she had now resolved to play a full year of tennis. This was good news for us all. She was now thirty-three years old and some weeks earlier, in the Australian Championships, she had just beaten Martina Navratilova 6–2 7–5 in the semi-finals before losing in the final 6–1 7–6 to the official world champion, the eighteen-year-old West German, Steffi Graf. Chris had also reached the final of the ladies' doubles there with Australia's thirty-five-year-old Wendy Turnbull, losing to one of the greatest pairs of all time, Martina and Pam Shriver. The record crowds of 245,000 at Australia's new National Tennis Centre, in Melbourne, with its unique retractable Centre Court roof, could not have had a better finish to the ladies' singles championship. Chris Evert had already won the Australian singles title twice and had now become a four-time runner-up.

The decision of Chris to continue competing set me thinking once again of the tremendous contribution she has made to the history of tennis and the development of the women's game. Her remarkable career in world-class tennis started in 1970 when she was just fifteen. With a sensational two sets victory over Margaret Court, who some weeks earlier had achieved the Grand Slam, Miss Evert served notice of her precocious worth. Now here she was, eighteen years later, the world's number three, and still good enough to surprise Martina Navratilova and everyone else in the Australian semi-finals and still able to reach the doubles final. These were remarkable performances.

Her Wimbledon debut was in 1972, and in 1987 she was playing for the sixteenth consecutive time; during this period she had won the singles title three times and was a finalist on seven other occasions. Only once did she fail to reach the semi-finals; that was in 1983 when she was unwell and lost in the third round to fellow American Kathy Jordan 6–1 7–6.

It was ironic that in the same year England's John Lloyd, whom she had married in April 1979, won the first of his two mixed doubles titles with Wendy Turnbull. This was the first Wimbledon title to be won by a British man since 1936.

Chris Evert's achievements at Wimbledon are certainly impressive. But she had a wonderful record elsewhere too. She won the US Championships six times in nine appearances in the final; she was the French Champion seven times and a finalist twice; in Australia she was the title-holder twice and runner-up four times.

So much for actual competition. In other areas, too, Chris found the time and energy to support causes she believed in. She has never failed to be complimentary about, and fully supportive of, Billie Jean King's crusade to ensure that women's tennis would take its rightful place in the world. Nor has she shirked responsibility. Six times she has served as president of the WITA. Throughout her career she has shown dignity and sportsmanship and has never lost her gracious femininity. This is a considerable achievement in a commercial world where the leaders of sport are so much under the media microscope. Chris Evert's integrity has indeed been a model for all and has won her universal respect.

When you watch the great players in action as regularly as I do from my commentator's seat, you come to recognize small defects in the delicate machinery of a player's technique.

I well remember being in the lounge of the Grand Hotel, Eastbourne, after dinner one evening during the warm-up tournament the week before Wimbledon. Chris came into the lounge and we greeted each other. 'I notice that you had a sticky patch out there today,' I said.

'Yes, I did rather.'

Although I don't usually talk to players about their play unless asked, which does happen frequently, I said: 'Do you mind me mentioning something about your play?'

'Not at all,' she replied.

'Well, it appeared to me that you were reaching for the ball on the forehand side on shortish balls, instead of stepping in to meet them. You seemed to lack the confidence to positioning yourself properly.'

'Did I really! Thank you for mentioning it.'

The point had only occurred to me because Chris's footwork and preparation for all her shots, all so well instilled by her father and coach Jimmy, was normally perfect. Eventually that year she beat Martina Navratilova in a marvellous final on one of Eastbourne's windiest days. The control and consistency of the play of both women in such difficult conditions was amazing.

Chris's timing has always been near-perfect. I remember comparing the sound of the ball on her racket with the sound made by Tracy Austin's racket when, aged sixteen, she had played Chris in her first appearance on the Centre Court in the third round at Wimbledon in 1977 – a kid with braces on her teeth and dressed in one of those Shirley Temple creations. Whereas Tracy's racket sung sweetly, there was a definite thwack as Chris struck the ball. People do not realize what a heavy ball she hit, rather like Dorothy Round, who, for all her flowing strokes, still hit the ball hard.

In her later years, Chris has hit the ball even harder than she used to and has a better trajectory now against the volleyer – perhaps because of the fierce but friendly rivalry with Martina Navratilova whose own weight of shot is considerable. The great contribution to the evolution of our sport by Chris and her fiancé of 1974, Jimmy Connors, has been the way they have legitimized two-handed backhands. At that time players using two hands were thought of as unusual if not freakish. Subsequently the advantages of power, control and disguise have become more apparent through the development of the two-handed theme by men like Björn Borg and Mats Wilander, and women like Tracy Austin and Andrea Jaeger.

The thing about Chris and Jimmy is that, like Henry Cotton hitting a golf ball, there is a concealed hit within the swing. Without apparent effort there is a moment when the ball is given an almighty blow, the result of weight being transferred into the shot with perfect timing.

For all great champions like Chris Evert there is never a perfect time to retire. Personally I hope she will go on competing for as long as she feels the same enthusiasm and excitement that has sustained her career so gloriously for the past seventeen years. But when that moment finally does arrive, I, for one, shall feel that an era has ended.

MARIA BUENO

In 1958 a girl of eighteen came to Europe for the first time. Maria Bueno won the Italian Championship, then reached the semi-finals of the French Championship and a few weeks later found herself on Wimbledon's fast grass for the first time, seeded number four.

By the time she had reached the quarter-finals that year she was variously described as 'the most stylish player since we first saw Doris Hart just after the war' or 'more like a ballerina' or even 'beautiful and artistic to a degree'. One writer said: 'She has the star quality of Spain's pre-war Centre Court favourite Lili de Alvarez.' Praise indeed.

Carrying such tags may have been a burden for a young Brazilian making her debut at Wimbledon, especially as we had yet to applaud a Wimbledon champion from South America. The undoubted flair and brilliant shot-making was evident when Ann Haydon (later Mrs Jones) beat her 6–3 7–5. Although unseeded, Ann, aged nineteen, was not short of match experience for in 1956 she had won the Wimbledon girls' invitation event, had reached the third round of the Championships the following year and in 1957 in the World

Table Tennis Championships had battled her way to three finals. Unluckily she finished as runner-up in all three events.

That 1958 defeat against Ann's disciplined tennis must have impressed Maria with the necessity for ball control. This basic ingredient was much more evident when, in partnership with Althea Gibson (the first black player ever to win at Wimbledon) she won the ladies' doubles.

Although a somewhat private person, on court Maria was wonderfully spectacular and never appeared to lack confidence. She was full of that priceless quality for the next two years during which she won Wimbledon and the US title in 1959, won Wimbledon again in 1960 and was runner-up in the American Championships. Clearly now she was accepted as the world's number one but sadly she became a victim of hepatitis and was out of the game for many months. This magnetic twenty-one-year-old had been fêted in her own country. Stamps were issued and a gigantic statue erected to honour the daughter of a veterinary surgeon who had left her comfortable home in São Paolo at the age of eighteen to conquer the world. She had more than fulfilled those descriptions of her so plentifully bestowed at Wimbledon only three years earlier.

I remember interviewing Maria for BBC Television on the eve of Wimbledon in 1962. I welcomed her back and wished her a happy and successful championship. Her response was somewhat subdued. However, she was very sincerely appreciative of the messages of sympathy she had received about her illness and her absence from Wimbledon the previous year.

Maria's bold, imaginative, all-court game depended so much on perfect timing and control. She never compromised by using spin of any sort. Purity of stroke was her trademark but when her eye was out or her concentration was patchy she paid a heavy penalty. In 1962, seeded three at Wimbledon, she lost to the unseeded Czech Vera Sukova in the semi-final, 6–4 6–3. However, later in the year at the US

Championships she won the ladies' doubles title with Darlene Hard.

After a quarter-final defeat at Wimbledon the following year by the unseeded Billie Jean Moffit, Maria enjoyed a victory in the ladies' doubles with Darlene Hard which must have brought some consolation. But the winner of the singles title at Wimbledon that year was Margaret Smith, who beat Maria's quarter-final conqueror, Miss Moffitt, 6–3 6–4, ample revenge for her astonishing first round defeat by the American twelve months earlier.

Who could have foreseen then that current form would be turned upside down in the US Championships that followed. In the title match Maria beat the favourite, Margaret Smith, 7–5 6–4. This was the first of the five Grand Slam finals they would play in the next two years which thrilled and illuminated world tennis. They were fascinating contests designed by the gods. The two best players in the world; the first Australian woman to win Wimbledon against the first Brazilian to do likewise; two champions alike in their aggressive all-court play but Bueno all artistry and grace and Smith strong, athletic and masculine with her consistent power and weight of shot.

Of their five finals, Maria won the US title in 1963 and Wimbledon in 1964 while Margaret won the French in 1964 plus Wimbledon and the Australian in 1965.

Plagued by ill-health and injury, Maria still managed to win the Wimbledon singles three times, the ladies' doubles five times with four different partners, and the US singles four times and ladies' doubles four times with three different partners. You can add to that record for she won the Italian title three times as well.

This supremely stylish player, always strikingly dressed by Ted Tinling, was a joy to watch. On reflection I cannot ever remember her playing an ugly shot even under the severest pressure.

DORIS HART

One of the greatest stylists who ever played tennis stepped out of a Pan American aeroplane at the new Heathrow airport in 1946, the first American plane ever to land there. Her name was Doris Hart. She was nearly twenty years of age and was accompanied by other members of America's first post-war Wightman Cup team. Margaret Osborne, Louise Brough and Pauline Betz were among the others there – a better Wightman Cup team than this there has surely never been. So good was it that Doris, who would become the Wimbledon finalist in 1947 and 1948, the winner of three events in 1951 and the finalist again in 1953, managed only to get into one of the doubles pairs.

Doris had suffered a severe illness as a child that had weakened a leg and had started to play tennis as part of her rehabilitation routine. Her brother encouraged her and, it is said, insisted that good style was more important than trying to hit the ball hard as no physical strain should be borne by the weak leg.

So perfect was Doris's all-court game, from the beautiful service action to the lowest of low drop-volleys and the accurately placed smashes from deep in the court, that I and many other coaches used films of these shots when lecturing and teaching. This universally popular and highly respected girl always attracted a full house in the players' gallery when she was on court. They came not only to admire her classic style but to marvel at her anticipation and her ability to vary her tactics when it was necessary.

I well remember practising with her one day at Wimbledon and commenting on the freedom, fluency and rhythm of her forehand drive. I suggested that, like all classic forehand drives, hers seemed to emphasize the early forward return of the hips which had pivoted almost before the forward swing of the racket had started. Forehand drives that lack such quality result from starting the forward swing and not allowing the hips to unwind early enough. (My golf has been suffering from this defect for the last forty years!)

Doris replied that she did not consciously emphasize the hip action but at Rollins College, where they were very keen on tennis, she seemed to remember it being given much importance. I asked if she would mind playing some more forehand drives if I hit a few individual balls to her so that I could concentrate closely on the actual stroke production which you cannot do so thoroughly when rallying. Four glorious drives followed, but the interesting thing was that, because I had raised the point, she now seemed consciously to exaggerate the early hip return so that they had a pulling effect on the start of the forward swing and the point of impact with the ball was a little more forward than normal. We both had a laugh when I told Doris that I would relate this demonstration to my professional colleagues when we gathered for our forthcoming annual conference. If they ruined their forehand drives as a result she would have to take the blame!

My own forehand, which has never pleased me as much as my backhand, took on a new lease of life after practising this, not only on the court, but against a practice wall-net. What I have regarded as a basic movement ever since that interesting session with Doris, had to be implanted into a stroke that was in the evening of its career. What a pity that I did not meet Doris Hart when I was seventeen!

It always interests me when a group of tennis players start to discuss style and technique. It will not be long before the name of Doris Hart is mentioned. Those who have seen her play or have played against her become almost lyrical in their praise of her style. Today the players admire Ken Rosewall, Vijay Amritraj and Ramesh Krishnan for the same reasons. Most people who saw Doris Hart felt that by merely watching her, the style would brush off on their own games. They felt motivated to get on to a court at once.

Then in this sort of discussion inevitably some Jeremiah will say that style doesn't win tennis matches. At this point I find myself saying that neither does speed, strength nor any other virtue on its own. But a combination of these, plus fitness, courage and stamina, together with tactical appreciation, will result in a pretty effective match winner. Doris Hart certainly had all those qualities and made the game of tennis a thing of beauty.

But Doris also knew how to win matches. She was one of only seven women ever to win every Grand Slam singles title at least once. In fact she won Wimbledon in 1951 without losing a set and also won the ladies' and mixed doubles that year. Three times she was a beaten finalist. In New York she won the singles twice and was runner-up four times; the French title came to her twice and she was a beaten finalist three times; on Australia's grass she was triumphant in 1949, the only year between 1946 and 1955 she did not compete at Wimbledon. Add to her record the fact that she was one of the greatest doubles players of her generation and there you have a great champion indeed.

One of my most vivid and recurring memories of Doris is of her 1953 Wimbledon final against the young Maureen Connolly. Although Doris was beaten 8–6 7–5 she gave a display of stylish tennis against the relentlessly accurate baseline drives of her opponent that was delightful to witness. It was a match of beautiful contrasts of styles and personalities with a consistently high standard of play that was remarkable. Doris tried every known way to break up Maureen's fierce driving. She used drop shots to bring her forward, lobs to test her overhead, a great variety of serves to keep her guessing. Clearly she felt that Maureen's forehand was the shot most likely to break down. However, she was not allowed the luxury of too many attacking chances against that wing. Doris's anticipation that day was particularly good – though in the end she was forced to succumb to a supreme match player.

Doris turned professional in 1955 and became a tennis teacher in Florida. What a privilege for anyone to have had lessons from one of the most outstanding women ever to grace a tennis court!

EVONNE CAWLEY (née Goolagong)

Evonne Cawley has been shown more affection by tennis lovers all over the world, especially at Wimbledon, than any other player I can remember. This was most evident in 1971 when, in Paris, she won her first major title, the French Championship. It was overpowering some four weeks later at her second Wimbledon. Player after player was brushed aside, then in her seventh and final match she demolished Margaret Court, who had so gloriously won the title the previous year, 6–4 6–1.

It was all done so naturally and effortlessly and was such a joy to watch. There seemed to be no physical or mental strain. Her enjoyment of the actual tennis and the occasion shone on her face and, it seemed, through the whole of her being. This magic and the spirit in which it was displayed transferred itself to the entire Centre Court audience. Here we were, transported back to the gracious and sporting days of amateurism.

After an early supper one night with Evonne and Vic Edwards her coach, at my home at Merton Park during the first week of the 1971 Wimbledon, we chatted about the All England Club, the Championships and the Australian players I had known through the years. Evonne and Vic seemed surprised when I told them I had been a ballboy for Norman Brookes in 1924 at Queen's. Later Brookes became Sir Norman and was chairman of the Australian LTA. He had, of course, been a former Australian Champion in 1911 and Wimbledon's first overseas male winner in 1907. He had also won Wimbledon in 1914 and played in the first final after the Great War in 1919 when he had lost to fellow Australian

Gerald Paterson, who won again in 1922 at the first Wimbledon where the Challenge Round had been abolished after the move to Church Road.

But what really impressed me that night was how relaxed Evonne was. She seemed completely at ease and natural. I mentioned this to Vic the next day at the club and he told me how he had picked her out of some athletic-looking youngsters he had seen at her very small home town of Barellan in New South Wales. She was part aborigine, thirteen years of age and had five brothers and sisters. Her father, an itinerant sheep-shearer, agreed to Vic's offer that he should bring Evonne up with his wife and family in Sydney where, in his tennis school, she would combine a tennis education with a formal one. Vic emphasized to me that although everyone now regarded her as a perfectly natural player, what he had first seen in her was the effortless movements of an athlete with natural hand and eye co-ordination and ball sense of a high order, plus an easy-going, malleable disposition. Like all the other youngsters who joined Vic's clinics and mass-group coaching classes, Evonne had learned the basics of stroke production by shadowing the strokes. Not until she could repeat and produce the grooved strokes in good style was she allowed to play on the court. I mentioned that Suzanne Lenglen had used such a method in Paris after she had turned professional and I had given a public demonstration of the same thing at the Festival of Britain in 1951 on the South Bank using a class of promising LTA youngsters, who included Billy Knight, Bobby Wilson, Tony Pickard and some of the leading junior girls.

Vic agreed with me that unless the pupil has reasonable ball sense and can judge and react to the flight, speed and bounce of the ball then positioning, timing and stroke production are of no avail. In Evonne's case no problem arose. Her selection at Barellan was based on these qualities. Her early days revealed timing of high class, unlike the wayward concentration which, in Vic's words, 'still gives me a headache'.

That, then, was Evonne Goolagong's very earliest tennis education. There followed hours, days and months of hard and varied practice, years of ceaseless travel to compete at the highest level. All that effort eventually produced an enviable record.

Apart from 1977, Evonne played every year at Wimbledon between 1970 (when she won the Plate) and 1980. That year she won the singles title nine years after her first victory in 1971, thereby equalling the nine-year break between titles of Bill Tilden (1921 and 1930). Incidentally, Evonne became the first mother to triumph at Wimbledon since the legendary Dorothea Lambert Chambers who had won for the last time in 1914. Evonne was the finalist three times and a losing semi-finalist three times and she won the ladies' doubles once. Grass was her native surface and she won the Australian title four times and the ladies' doubles four times. To her great delight, and that of the French, she won their championship in 1971 but lost it the following year to Billie Jean King. Sadly Evonne could never surmount the last hurdle in New York. Four years running from 1973 to 1976 she lost in the final – first in three sets to Margaret Court, then to Billie Jean King in a twelve-game final set. In 1975, now Mrs Cawley, the wife of a former very promising English junior player, Roger Cawley, Evonne lost to Chris Evert, this time by 2–6 in the final set. Lastly in 1976 she was again beaten by Chris 6–3 6–0.

Here was a glorious career in every way and in spite of suffering more than her fair share of injuries never did Evonne Cawley complain or fail to please. She now leads a happy family life with her two children and her husband at their home in America.

In my book, '*From Where I Sit*', published just before Wimbledon in 1988, the last chapter was headed, 'The Best of All Time', and included my ten best men and ten best women players. Since then, Steffi Graf of West Germany has achieved a unique record. She is the only player, man or woman, in the history of the game to win the traditional 'Grand Slam' (the Australian, French, Wimbledon and US Singles Championships) – and the Olympic Tennis Gold Medal. And to have done it all in the same year, 1988, at the tender age of nineteen years and three and a half months is, indeed, remarkable.

No tennis was played in the Olympic Games after 1924 until 1988, a sixty-four-year gap, so Rod Laver, Donald Budge, Maureen Connelly and Margaret Court, all Grand Slam winners, never had the opportunity of winning an Olympic Gold Medal.

As I write, Steffi Graf, the Official World Champion, has successfully defended her Australian title and has now won the last six Grand Slam titles in a row, thus equalling the records of Don Budge, Maureen Connelly and Margaret Court. If, as she should, Steffi wins the French Open in June 1989, she will stand alone with seven Grand Slam Crowns. With a game that is still improving one wonders how long it may be before she heads the list of the 'Best of All Time'.

EPILOGUE

EPILOGUE

It has been an extraordinary year. I had always realized, of course, that the publication of *From Where I Sit* on 9 June 1988, and the transmission, a few days later, of a BBC television programme to mark my eightieth birthday, would probably stir the clouded waters of memory among those of my readers and viewers with whom I had some sort of direct connection. But I could never have foreseen the avalanche of letters and postcards (dozens of them), as well as phone calls and personal approaches, many of them from complete strangers, that have assailed me ever since.

Perhaps the most moving letters were those from men like Gordon Hayhurst who had passed through our officer aircrew rehabilitation unit at Torquay in 1941. Gordon, a fine athletic young man (he and his younger brother Roger, who also served in the RAF, were both keen cricketers, I later discovered) was twenty years old when he arrived at the hospital. Like so many in those perilous days, he had been badly smashed up physically and was inevitably depressed about the future. Our job was to get him back into action as soon as possible. He writes:
'You may not know even now how much your influence had on us young officers trying to overcome our injuries. I was one with a broken spine and I remember how constantly you repeated to me – "you will recover, you are a survivor". And that is why, although I was offered a

395

ground job, I went back to flying and flew night fighters for the rest of the war.'

How well I remember Gordon – and so many other wonderful young fellows like him. Their indomitable spirit was a great inspiration to me. However, it was not always easy persuading them to undertake painful exercises. As he remembers:

'You always insisted on my gymnasium treatment – three hours a day weight-lifting, swinging weights on my feet and even riding the medicinal horse, just to keep my muscles active. Then, in the afternoons, you would take us all to your house for afternoon tea – always welsh rarebit done with mustard and beer, a recipe we use to this day'.

Those were marvellous moments for me too, seeing the spirit returning to these determined characters.

It was that sort of spirit that enabled badly injured men eventually to play energetic games and to give vent to their naturally competitive natures. Gordon Hayhurst again: 'You also taught me to play squash and I still proudly guard the Nuffield Trophy (a pewter mug) which you presented to me on winning the squash championships – and I was still in a plaster jacket!'

Ah, the plaster jacket! It was responsible, I seem to remember, for getting Gordon into trouble on the snooker table . . . 'and occasionally I leant over the table and crushed the chalk. You fined me half a crown every time I did it – mainly because the chalk was very scarce.' How right he was!

Gordon enclosed with his letter a copy of the programme for the 1941 (and only) production of 'Alladibara and His Red Riding Boots', a Christmas pantomime put on by the patients and staff masquerading as the 'Sub-Rosa Opera Company'! I have already referred to those marvellous occasions, which Con used to enjoy so much in so many different roles. Until I looked again at the programme, with the beautifully drawn caricatures of the medical staff – John Pocock, Malcolm Campbell, Bill Morris, Wing Commander Gillespie, Wing Commander Skeet, Matron Coulthurst and me – I had forgotten that Godon Hayhurst was the man responsible for the music. He is credited thus – 'With music by Pilot Officer G. A. Hayhurst and Second Lieutenant R. I. Fraser. Slung together by the former, who directs the noises'. As I recall the noises were mostly quite melodic.

Gordon also enclosed a cutting from the *Evening News* of January 1945 which detailed his amazing recovery and his distinguished record afterwards that had resulted in his promotion to the rank of Squadron Leader. A bright young trainee engineer, he had volunteered at the start of the war and had been sent for flying training to Canada where he earned his wings. One month after seeing active service he had been thrown out of his plane and broken his back in a crash in Ireland. After a miraculous recovery he returned to night operations and bagged six enemy aircraft.

Gordon is one of the lucky ones who lived to tell the tale. Happily he is in retirement now after twenty years as Managing Director of an engineering company. However, there is a legacy of those wartime days. 'Unfortunately the old injury is catching up and I am becoming less mobile', he says. 'Sports are now out – except for snooker at which I am now reasonably competent (and no crushed chalk!).' What spirit! It is thanks to men like this that we survived.

One who helped Gordon survive is Grace Alexander. Now widowed, Mrs Alexander was a sergeant nurse at Torquay and tells me of the lucky escape she had on the day of the bombing. 'While I was practising some table tennis in preparation for our inter unit matches, some Polish patients arrived and stood watching. They were waiting to play so we relinquished our bats and left. Ten minutes later the gymnasium suffered a direct hit. The Poles were all killed.'

Another survivor is John Hallett whose path crossed mine at Loughborough after we had left Torquay following the bombing. John had two spells in the Rehabilitation Centre during 1943 and 1944 and remembers so many of the characters who were there at the time, men like Jamie O'Malley, Joe Messer, Nick Zinovieff, Raich Carter and Peter Doherty. He also remembers the more colourful characters like 'Joe the Dutchman' and the well-known trainer Chub Leach. John tells the delightful story, which I had not heard before, of the time we treated Chub whose stables were nearby, even though he was not in the Service. 'He had suffered a badly broken leg, not through enemy action but by falling off a couch when he was drunk. Most nights in the bar he was to be found drinking steadily but one day, through his alcoholic haze, he gave me a tip for the 1943 Derby – Garden Path – and it duly obliged at 40–1!'. You would remember a story like that wouldn't you!

John Hallett also mentioned the great evening that was organized at Loughborough by Nick Zinovieff to impress Fleet Street of the importance of the job we were doing. Having seen all the active work the reporters wanted to see how we all let our hair down. So, for the benefit of the press photographers . . . 'In the afternoon the Officers' Mess was turned into a nightclub. Curtains were closed to give the right atmosphere, there was loads of beer, loads of girls (all imported from the Army Camp nearby), lots of music and flashing cameras. The result? A centre-spread story in the *Sunday Pictorial*. Fame at last!'.

It was sad to learn from Sir Ian Gourlay, who had married Nick's sister Natalie that, unknown to me, her brother had died while I was completing the text of *From Where I Sit* in 1987. There had not been space then to mention what a fine war Nick Zinovieff had. He was always cheerful and popular and so very competent professionally. If he had not been unlucky enough to suffer from an unusual skin condition which affected his hands I am convinced he would have become an outstanding surgeon. I know Sir Reginald Watson Jones felt the same.

The last time I worked with Nick was towards the end of the war when we were asked jointly to advise on the suitability of Headley Court, near Leatherhead, Surrey, as the site of a permanent RAF Rehabilitation Centre. Our favourable report (and doubtless others, too) led to the conversion of that attractive old Jacobean house which opened in its new role in 1950. About ten years later we had a reunion party there, a get together for the old medical team – Watson Jones, Osmond-Clarke and the staff from Loughborough. It was a splendidly nostalgic occasion and we were all pleased to see that the facilities had been considerably enlarged. Today, of course, it is bigger still and serves as a medical Rehabilitation Unit for personnel from all the armed services.

Sidney Rose was a member of that staff for a time, but I had not heard from him since those days. It was the BBC television programme that prompted him to write and remind me of the occasional games of tennis we used to play together at Loughborough. Sidney still plays tennis regularly at the Northern Lawn Tennis Club in Manchester, scene of the big tournament that takes place annually three weeks before Wimbledon. Now, of course, Sidney is well known as the Chairman of Manchester City Football Club and expresses a worry about the falling standards of behaviour among today's footballers. We think alike here.

Another from the Loughborough days who contacted me is Kenneth Hills. He writes:

'I was one of your inmates at Hazelrigg Hall in the Autumn of 1943, a twenty-year-old Pilot Officer with numerous broken bones, who was so ably looked after by you, Connie and Nick Zinovieff – and doubtless many other good people – I went back to flying some ten months later and survived, happily with few clinical complaints in the following years.'

That was good news indeed, but even more encouraging from my point of view was his next comment. He continues:

'You will no doubt be pleased to hear that I have been playing tennis almost non-stop since then and still play twice a week now (winter and summer) with chums fifteen to twenty years my junior, none of whom will take me on for three sets of singles for £50!'.

Joe Messer's widow Billie was another who made contact. She sent me a lovely photograph of Joe together with a note explaining that when Joe had died she had felt unable to go through the painful task of sorting out his papers after forty happy years together. When eventually she did, she had come across a picture of O'Malley and the shot of Joe which she felt I would appreciate as I had been quite close to him in those far off days. Her kind gesture was a reminder that there are so many versions of pain. We have enjoyed several chats since.

There have been several other contacts from the war years. O'Malley's elder daughter, Lynn Barrow, has been in touch with her 'Uncle Dan' on several occasions. She is divorced now but sees her three married daughters and numerous grandchildren on frequent visits to Zimbabwe, Malawi and Botswana where they all live. Otherwise Lynn is at the cottage in Sussex to which her mother moved from Africa when Jamie died. Happily I have spoken to her on several occasions during her visits to this country. She still has the same lively mind that I remember in her as a girl.

It was such a pleasant surprise to hear from Alan Cooper, an RAF historian, who sent me a copy of the original signal that had recommended me for the OBE in the 1945 New Year's Honours list. We have since been in touch and I am glad to have been able to help him with some details of the Torquay and Loughborough days.

Then a Mr Gordon Somerville wrote to say that O'Malley's wife Althea had been a bridesmaid at his mother's wedding in London in 1920. After attending Merchiston College in Edinburgh (like Sir Louis Greig, he reminds me), he had joined the Marines at the age of eighteen at Lympstone, near Exmouth and had later served on the cruiser, *HMS London*. Gordon's mother used to live near Largs, on the Clyde and was a neighbour of Angus and Winnie Shaw whose daugher, now Winnie Wooldridge, I used to coach in the days before she became a Wightman Cup player. The world is smaller than I thought!

Some of the letters are very sad. Let Mrs Nan Barry, an Australian visiting Britain with her husband Hal, tell you her story in her own words:

'During our stay we visited the Palace hotel, Torquay, where the Manager and staff were kind enough to allow me to examine their records in connection with the tragic events of 25 October 1942, the wartime bombing of the then RAF Officers' Hospital.

'My particular interest is in Flying Officer Alan Henry Wood who died on that day. He was an Australian who had joined the RAF in England just before the war. He was injured when his plane was shot down and was sent to the Palace for convalescence. Alan was the 'big brother' of my best friend and the only son of a widowed mother and I had a great 'crush' on him – although I was only about thirteen to his twenty, at that age almost a generation gap. I remember his farewell party in Sydney before he left for England and my sadness – especially that he had no idea of the adoring heart beating in the freckled friend of his kid sister, Peggy.

'In October 1942 I was in the WAAAF at Headquarters

401

in Melbourne. My job was to receive the signals reporting the deaths of Australian Air Force personnel, search Records for the next of kin (or persons to be informed), then write and send the awful official telegram and all the follow-up correspondence. Just two days earlier I had received a letter from my mother in Sydney full of the wonderful news that, although injured, Alan was safe and well and would soon be returning to Sydney and, to his mother's great joy, would probably be out of the war.

'You can imagine my shock and horror when I read the signal reporting Alan's death (among all the others) as a result of (and I can still see the words) DIRECT HIT CONVALESCENT HOSPITAL TORQUAY UK. After I had checked and then double-checked that it was indeed *our* Alan, I went to my Commanding Officer – a lovely, caring man named Wing Commander Neesham. He decided to break a very strict rule that we were never allowed to contact anybody in connection with any information in our possession, and telephoned my mother (a very close friend of Mrs Wood) asking Mum to be there with her – but she was sworn to secrecy about her knowledge. It was a terrible ordeal for my mother listening to Mrs Wood joyfully planning and anticipating Alan's long-awaited return and knowing the awful reality. Incidentally, 25 October 1942 was my nineteenth birthday – one of the saddest.

'Among the archives at the Palace was an official RAF photograph taken of two of the patients receiving physiotherapy – 'Lifting Weights', according to the caption. To my amazement and delight, one of them is Alan in uniform, looking exactly as I remembered him all those years ago.'

* * *

It is stories like this that bring back the brutal realities of war, the sacrifice and the suffering, the anguish and the loss, that so many brave families had to endure. Obviously we were all fully conscious of the dangers at the time but tried to ignore them as we went about our daily business. It was the only way.

Mrs Barry had enclosed a copy of the photograph and wondered if I remembered Alan Wood. When I looked at the smiling young man, with a weighted bag over his right ankle to exercise his injured leg, I did indeed recognize him and realized that, but for the chance decision of O'Malley to send me off to Saunton for the weekend, I would possibly have been with him when the bomb fell. Such are the inexplicable twists of fate that have caused me to believe that . . . 'there is a destiny that shapes our ends, rough hew them how we will'.

Kay and I spoke to Nan and Hal Barry during their 1988 visit to England and found we had so much in common. Having originally remarked to Kay what a marvellously compassionate letter Nan had written, it was no surprise to discover that she had spent many years working with handicapped children in Sydney. Since Kay herself is something of an authority in that field, they found plenty to talk about.

The other person who has good reason to remember the visit to Saunton that fateful weekend is Jimmy Rickards, our conscientious anaesthetist at Torquay who had been under strain because of an excessive workload.

We had last met shortly after the war in Birmingham so it was particulary nice to hear from him again after so many years. His wife, he told me, had given him a copy of the book which had reawakened so many memories for him. He insisted that if I ever had cause to visit North Wales I must look him up in Abersoch, where he was living in retirement. By an extraordinary coincidence, in two weeks time I was due to accompany Kay on one of her regular Outward Bound visits to Aberdovey which is just across the bay from Abersoch. A quick 'phone call, and a meeting with Jimmy Rickards was arranged.

When Kay and I arrived at his farm Jimmy was out in the fields flying kites with his grandson who had a little friend with him. He came in and showed us round, explaining that some twenty-five years ago he had bought the property which had been virtually derelict then.

That seemed hard to believe when we looked at the beautifully restored old farmhouse – until we discovered that his elder son, who lived there with his family, was a builder by trade. Jimmy lived in a picturesque building that had once been the stables. In the old pigsty, which now was a superbly appointed small cottage, lived Jimmy's disabled sister. The old cowshed had been converted into a well equipped workshop where Jimmy indulged his favourite hobby – making high class furniture (in pine mostly). All around the three houses there was ample evidence of his skill as a furniture maker.

Jimmy's other passions were golf and sailing. He was now on the committee of the local golf club and also had a boat which he sailed on the waters of the bay. I remembered, when he told me that, that he and John Pocock had occasionally gone off sailing in Torquay harbour in those far off war days. Knowing of my interest in golf, Jimmy suggested . . . 'Let me know in good time before your next visit to Aberdovey and I will arrange to sail across to have a round with you on the Aberdovey course'. That is something I look forward to very much indeed!

Among many other letters connected with the war there were two from former WRENS who had served with my daughter Robin. Anne Cleary, who is now Mrs Tuite, lives in Somerset and has two teenage daughters. Winifred Robinson was the Regulating Chief Wren on *HMS Daedalus* at Lee-on-Solent when Robin was her Third Officer. It was nice to think that those friendships, made so long ago and forged in the furnace of conflict have been reawakened.

Then there were so many letters connected with my tennis past. Michael McAfee wrote from the Wirral to recall the occasion when, as a small boy during the war, he had gone to the Hoylake Tennis Club with his father to watch the exhibition matches that I had participated in to raise money for the Red Cross. He also remembers my visit to the Bertram Lawn Tennis Club a few years later with Stanley Matthews Junior, Graham Stilwell and some other promising juniors, to open the newly installed Tennisquick courts. It was a pleasant occasion that I am reminded of every time I enjoy a pint of beer from the suitably inscribed silver tankard they gave me that day.

The porous cement Tennisquick surface, developed by old Mr Ewbank in Belgium, helped to revolutionize winter play at many clubs after that. They were certainly a great improvement on the clay courts that were out of action for much of the winter. Although the new surface was impervious to frost and drained wonderfully fast, even after the heaviest downpour, the courts were too hard on the legs for some people and the solid surface made the ball bounce rather too high for comfort.

I have already written about the immense contribution made by Fred Perry on our promotional tours together. One who remembers Fred with great affection is Barbara Holland. 'His father, S. F. Perry, worked under my father (also an OBE) in his Liverpool Ministry of Health office', she wrote. 'Later Samuel (Perry) left – to become Secretary to the Co-operative Society, I believe. Fred had to amuse me, aged five, for a day while my brother Alastair was born. We had a free fight erecting a tent in his back garden with his sister Edith. What a small world!'

All my life I have been astonished by the number of extraordinary coincidences that seem to occur in everyone's lives. But how about this one for being more extraordinary than most. Mrs Nora Colley had been watching the BBC birthday programme from her home in Wilmslow, Cheshire, and was moved to put pen to paper thus: . . . 'and when you showed to the camera the gold cigarette case with the inscription that meant so much to you (from the winning Davis Cup team of 1933) it recalled an incident my late husband had told me of over fifty years ago. There were two young men waiting for a train at a station in Switzerland. You had chatted and had then offered a cigarette to my husband who could not help remarking upon the beautiful cigarette case and its inscription. As a keen tennis player he had been so pleased when you were kind enough to explain it to him. How I wish he had been with me watching television that day to relive that brief but very pleasant encounter.'

One day towards the end of July an oddly shaped small parcel arrived at my home. My wife Kay was as intrigued as I was to know what it contained. When we opened it we found, carefully wrapped in a polythene bag, a very old tennis ball. With it came the following letter from Mrs Daisy Brown of Tanworth in Arden, in Warwickshire: 'Surprise, surprise – I'm sure you never expected this to come bouncing back to you after fifty years! You hit this ball into the audience at the Garrick Theatre, Southport, in 1938, and my big brother caught it for me. I was twelve years old and so excited about it. There were two signatures on the ball but I cannot decipher the other one – would it be another tennis player? It almost looks like "Carol Gibbons".' I have since telephoned Mrs Brown to explain that it was Carol Levis, of 'Discovery' fame. It was that occasion I have already described when Bill Tilden and I went to the theatre to promote our tennis matches in Victoria Park where we, in turn, promoted the Carol Levis show. Mrs Brown continued: 'My children were hunting through my treasures long ago and unfortunately I allowed them to play with the ball. It soon became soiled so I hid it away again and was reminded of it when you recently celebrated your birthday'. It is an odd feeling, I assure you, to have your past paraded in front of you like this.

I was reminded again of those pre-war years when two former pupils made contact. Peter Graves had been a fine junior player before becoming a distinguished actor and singer with Ivor Novello's company. Now Lord Graves, I was delighted when he eventually married my favourite leading lady, Vanessa Lee, whose golden soprano voice melted my heart with those fabulous songs from the Novello musicals – Perchance To Dream, King's Rhapsody, and the others. On Desert Island Discs years ago Roy Plomley asked me what was my favourite song of all. Unhesitatingly I replied 'Someday My Heart Will Awake, sung by Vanessa Lee', It was a song I used to sing heartily in the shower at The All England Club after a hard day of coaching – much to the dismay of the members!

Peter was a pupil of mine during my pre-war days at Wimbledon. One morning he arrived for his lesson on a day when scudding clouds and intermittent showers threatened to prevent us from playing. Peter, who had walked through the rain from Southfields station, was not about to give up. Even though there were still puddles on the court he said optimistically, 'Come on, let's go out and hope it dries up – we can still serve and volley, anyway'. So out we went.

Knowing that Peter needed to improve his service, I suggested that he start by hitting some practice serves, thinking that he would first use a few shadow swings. But, without even bothering to loosen up Peter tried to smite the very first delivery as hard as he could. There was a yelp of pain as he clutched his right shoulder and allowed the racket to drop with a clatter on to the court. 'That's torn it – literally', he said with a grimace. 'I only took up this bloody game because I thought there was no pain attached to it!' The lesson was over before it had even begun. We have often laughed about it since. Hence the sting in the tail of Peter's recent letter of birthday greetings. 'I haven't forgotten how you drew blood teaching me to serve!', he wrote.

The other former pupil was Sheila Hewitt who, you may remember, I have already described as being one of a promising group of pre-war players who were never destined to become great champions. However, Sheila did have something special. So natural was her game and so fluent her strokes that it did not surprise me when one year in the South of France she seemed to beat everyone who mattered. Had the war not come when it did, and had Sheila not been dogged by indifferent health, I honestly believe that she could have been among the best of the pupils I have been privileged to coach over the years. We shall never know. It was so nice to hear from Sheila again and to discover that she is living in Wimbledon. Kay and I spent a most enjoyable and nostalgic day visiting her last year.

There was an echo of even earlier days when a letter arrived from Dennis Turner, who I have already identified as the man who produces the weekly programme for the Fulham Football Club. He had kindly enclosed an excerpt from the Club's book of biographical sketches of their former stars. There, on the left hand page, was the cheerful grin of Jimmy Tompkins, the man who had introduced me to Con, my first wife, outside the barber's shop in Southfields. It was surprising to read that between 1933 and the outbreak of war Jimmy had represented the Club on 163 occasions and had scored five goals from his regular position at right half. After joining up early (because of his experience in the Territorials) Jimmy had seen active service and had risen to the rank of major. How sad, then, that like so many other brave young men he should have lost his life on 'D' Day, a fact of which I had been unaware.

Another link with those war years came from 'Dick' Whittington at Nottingham University's Department of Physiology and Environmental Science for whom I had signed a programme of the wartime Charity Football Match in which I had participated in 1943. In his letter of thanks 'Dick' had said . . . 'At the time of the match I had just joined the RAF and was guarding Torquay from enemy invasion'. It reminded me forcibly of that ridiculous occasion when I had guarded Hastings pier – without a weapon! Enclosed with 'Dick's' letter was a delightful cartoon that had appeared in the *Nottingham Evening News* in 1944. It showed the players and club officials who had taken part in an afternoon of exhibition tennis at the Western Lawn Tennis Club to raise funds for the Red Cross. With Squadron leader Dan Maskell are the Nottingham County players, Freda Hammersley (née James), Miss F. M. Burton and Miss E. A. Middleton, and the former Polish Davis cup player, Flight Lieutenant Ernest Wittman. Incidentally, I had a nice card from Mr W. B. Garnowski of the Polish Air Force Association and a former air crew member who wanted me to know that the Poles in Britain had much appreciated the fact that I had seemed to care about them. It was most touching.

Inevitably there have been golfing letters too. Brian and Maggie Dove-Meadows, former members at Wimbledon Common Golf Club, wrote to remind me of the happy pre-war days we shared with mutual friends. I was pleased to hear again from John Goodban who, I was delighted to learn, became Captain at my beloved Saunton Golf Club in 1987. He tells me that Donald Steel has been brought in to advise them on the restructuring and resowing of the greens. In 1987 nine were relaid and the other nine were completed in October 1988. It is good to know that the club continues to flourish.

At the top of my list of places to visit, you will remember, is the Royal Newcastle County Down Golf Club – the only one of the four great courses recommended by Henry Longhurst that I have not yet played. Well, help is at hand! A member there, Mr Stratton Mills, has kindly offered to organize a round for me. Perhaps it should be in 1989 when this famous Club celebrates its centenary.

* * *

Lasting friendships like these are the true rewards of a long and satisfying life. It was through the BBC television programme that another old friendship was reawakened. One day in July I received a letter at Wimbledon from Rex Alston, that master of the spoken word, whose sporting commentaries on BBC Radio are part of the folklore of British broadcasting. I had met Rex years ago in the course of our joint involvement with sports broadcasts. He wrote 'Somebody once told me you lived near Dorking in which case you can't be far from here . . . We would like you and your wife to come to lunch sometime before you go off to Seoul . . .' It was a pleasant surprise to discover that Rex and his wife are near neighbours. His letter led to a happy reunion, and a most enjoyable meal at his picturesque house deep in the Surrey countryside near Guildford.

Soon afterwards I left with the rest of the BBC team for Seoul – my first visit to an Olympic Games meeting. It was an unforgettable experience in so many ways. The Koreans had done a wonderful job in providing first class facilities – not just for the tennis events where the 10,000 seater stadium and outside courts provided a perfect setting for a sport that was making a return to the Games after a gap of sixty-four years.

Some observers had doubted the wisdom of re-introducing tennis to the Games. I was never one of them. It had seemed to me that sport in general had become increasingly professional, and thus increasingly honest. The Olympics, surely, was about having the best performers in all sports competing at the highest level. I saw no difficulty in re-admitting tennis which, since 1968, had been open to allcomers, with ability the only yardstick upon which entry to tournaments was based.

In the event, tennis came out of the Olympics with flying colours. We had four spectacular finals; the players themselves were enthusiastic about life in the Olympic village, a unique experience for all the tennis players and the organization by the International Tennis Federation was first class. We even had an official delegation visiting our closing ceremonies to see how we contained the photographers and prevented them from overrunning the entire arena as they tended to do elsewhere.

It seemed to me that tennis provided quite a shot in the arm for the Olympic movement – though perhaps that is an unfortunate way of putting it in a year when the IOC faced major problems of drug abuse that tarnished an otherwise memorable meeting. Not one tennis player tested positive and if anyone doubted the ability of the competitors to give of their best when there was not a penny in it for them, they need only have watched a first round women's doubles between Canada and Argentina to be convinced. For four hours and thirteen minutes Carling Bassett-Seguso and Jill Hetherington battled against Gabriela Sabatini and Mercedez Paz before eventually winning an exhausting encounter 7–6 5–7 20–18. It was the second longest women's doubles match in the history of our sport!

I was entirely captivated by the Olympic spirit – as were, I feel sure, the vast majority of competitors of all sports and all nations. It was wonderful to see so many young people of different colours, religions and nationalities all enjoying one another's company in the great brotherhood of Olympic sport. I shall be eternally grateful to the BBC for including me on their team.

My love of being involved in team situations is well documented, and I am grateful to the reader who sent me a cutting from the *London Evening News* in 1940 that recalls the Maskell family team effort during the war. Under the heading 'Four Maskells', appears the following: 'A Royal Engineer, on leave in London, calls attention to the fine record of the four Maskells in sport and war. A note of mine announcing the entry of Dan Maskell, the professional lawn tennis champion and well-known All England coach, into the RAF with a commission has apparently prompted my soldier friend. 'I have known all the Maskell boys', he says, 'since they were kiddies.'

'The eldest Maskell, Bill, served in France and 'Mespot' in the 9th Lancers from August 1914 to March 1919 and was mentioned in despatches. After the war he played in the Evening News Tennis Tournament for several seasons. The second Maskell, Bert, who served in France with the 7th London Regiment, was a good footballer who occasionally turned out for Fulham when Andy Ducat managed the team. He is now taking wickets in police cricket. John Maskell, the third brother, is the best known of the quartet as a footballer. After three years in the old RFC in India he attracted much attention as centre-half in the Wimbledon Isthmian League team. Going across London to Hayes, he played for that club at right full-back in the FA Amateur Cup Final of 1931 against Wycombe Wanderers who won by a goal at Highbury. This season he has played some excellent cricket for West Drayton.'

Ever since receiving that cutting I have been speculating about the identity of the mysterious Royal Engineer – without any success I'm afraid.

There was nothing mysterious about the communication from Lord Rothschild who had watched the BBC programme and wondered if I remembered coaching him as a young man. As I told him, those early Queen's Club years were etched firmly in my memory simply because they were some of the happiest days of my life. Those lessons with Victor, his sisters Liberty and Miriam, and many other youngsters of varied backgrounds, were so fulfilling to the young Maskell and are well documented in these pages.

The Dowager Marchioness of Cholmondesley was another who was kind enough to write with birthday greetings. She reminded me of the games of tennis my Queen's Club colleague Charles Heirons used to play with her late husband, who, I recall, as always most punctual for his sessions. He was not a bad performer on the tennis court either, and played three times at Wimbledon.

The one correspondent who has defeated my memory is Emily Ansell who is ninety years old and lives in Saltdean, in Sussex. As you will see, however, it is hardly surprising that I have no recollection of the incident she described. After watching the BBC programme she wrote . . . 'Your family and mine were good neighbours at 9 Everington Street, Fulham and my dear brother was your little playmate at the age of four. He met with a tragic death – falling over the fireguard onto the fire. They took him to St George's Hospital but he died of pneumonia. Before the funeral, I can remember you standing in the parlour with your sad look, carrying a bunch of narcissus, so shyly.'

Not surprisingly I cannot remember the occasion. Even if it had been possible to bridge the seventy-six-year memory gap in other areas I would probably never have been able to recall that particular incident for the brain seems to have a protective way of blocking out unhappy memories of that sort – like my mother's death. However,

Emily Ansell's letter was a marvellous link with my early days. I shall always be grateful that she took the trouble to write, for it seemed to bring my long life full circle – back to Armistice day, 1918, when I was out shopping with my mother.

INDEX

INDEX

418

Still Dancing

Lew Grade

Performer, entrepreneur, raconteur, founder of Associated Television, film and stage producer, Lord Grade's dynamic personality, as perenially conspicuous as the king-sized cigars he smokes, pulses through every page of his fascinating and long-awaited autobiography.

Spanning almost eighty years – from the inception of the nickelodeon to the advent of video and such high-tech musicals as Andrew Lloyd-Webber's *Starlight Express*, which Lord Grade co-produced on Broadway – *Still Dancing* has a cast that includes such heavyweight names as Jack Benny, Bob Hope, Edith Piaf, Judy Garland, Lena Horne, Mario Lanza, Maria Callas, Franco Zeffirelli, Laurence Olivier, Frank Sinatra, Shirley MacLaine, Roger Moore, Tony Curtis and Sammy Davis Jr, and offers a privileged insight into the wheeler-dealing world of international show business through the eyes of a man who is himself a living legend.

'It bubbles with life and – a much rarer commodity – honesty.'   *Daily Express*

'I read it at a sitting . . . Lovely stuff.'   *Screen International*

James Callaghan

Time and Chance

James Callaghan's career has been unique: no other British politician has held the four great posts of Chancellor of the Exchequer, Home Secretary, Foreign Secretary and Prime Minister. In these long-awaited memoirs he writes openly of the issues and crises of the times, and conveys vividly what it is to be in the front rank of politics in a modern democracy.

He describes his relationship with the trade unions and the struggle to establish and maintain an incomes policy; the problems of law and order; the long, complex negotiations over the Common Market and arms control, and the constant battle – ultimately in vain – to prevent the devaluation of sterling. Personalities loom large, with incisive portraits of friends and rivals, Harold Wilson, Henry Kissinger, Presidents Ford and Carter among them.

Time and Chance is a compelling account of life in high office, where international conflicts vie for attention with the bubbling cauldron of internal party politics.

'An accurately researched, engagingly and modestly presented account of one of the great political careers of the second half of this century.' Roy Jenkins – *Observer*.

FONTANA PAPERBACKS

Fontana Paperbacks: Non-fiction

Fontana is a leading paperback publisher of non-fiction, both popular and academic.

- [ ] Bedside Skiing *John Samuel* £3.95
- [ ] Bedside Rugby *Bill Beaumont* £3.50
- [ ] Bedside Tennis *John Newcombe* £2.50
- [ ] Bedside Jumping *Harvey Smith* £3.50
- [ ] Bedside Darts *Sid Waddell* £3.50
- [ ] Grid Iron *Tony Benyon & Robert Macey* £3.95
- [ ] Tarbuck on Golf *Jimmy Tarbuck* £3.50
- [ ] Squash Balls *Barry Waters* £3.50
- [ ] John Timpson's Early Morning Book *John Timpson* £3.95

You can buy Fontana paperbacks at your local bookshop or newsagent. Or you can order them from Fontana Paperbacks, Cash Sales Department, Box 29, Douglas, Isle of Man. Please send a cheque, postal or money order (not currency) worth the purchase price plus 22p per book for postage (maximum postage required is £3).

NAME (Block letters) _____

ADDRESS _____

_____

_____